MODERN INSURGENCIES AND COUNTER-INSURGENCIES

Modern Insurgencies and Counter-insurgencies explores how unconventional warfare tactics have opposed past and present governments all over the world, from eighteenth-century guerrilla warfare to the urban terrorism of today. Insurgency remains one of the most prevalent forms of conflict and presents a crucial challenge to the international community, governments and the military.

In addition to examining the tactics of guerrilla leaders such as Lawrence, Mao, Guevara and Marighela, *Modern Insurgencies and Counter-insurgencies* analyses the work of counter-insurgency theorists such as Gallieni, Callwell, Thompson and Kitson. It explores such conflicts as:

- The American War of Independence
- Napoleon's campaign in Spain
- The wars of decolonisation
- The superpowers in Vietnam and Afghanistan
- Conflicts in Northern Ireland, Sierra Leone and Colombia.

Encompassing both insurgency and counter-insurgency in an analytical and historical framework, this timely one-volume study is an invaluable aid for students of history, strategic studies and international relations, and for military professionals.

Ian F. W. Beckett is Professor of Modern History at the University of Luton and a Fellow of the Royal Historical Society. His many publications include *The Amateur Military Tradition* (1991) and *Encyclopedia of Guerrilla Warfare* (1999).

WARFARE AND HISTORY

General editor Jeremy Black
Professor of History, University of Exeter

AIR POWER IN THE AGE OF TOTAL WAR *John Buckley*

THE ARMIES OF THE CALIPHS: Military and Society in the Early Islamic State *Hugh Kennedy*

THE BALKAN WARS, 1912–1913: Prelude to the First World War *Richard C. Hall*

ENGLISH WARFARE, 1511–1642 *Mark Charles Fissel*

EUROPEAN AND NATIVE AMERICAN WARFARE, 1675–1815 *Armstrong Starkey*

EUROPEAN WARFARE, 1660–1815 *Jeremy Black*

THE FIRST PUNIC WAR *J.F. Lazenby*

FRONTIERSMEN: Warfare in Africa since 1950 *Anthony Clayton*

GERMAN ARMIES: War and German Politics, 1648–1806 *Peter H. Wilson*

THE GREAT WAR, 1914–1918 *Spencer C. Tucker*

ISRAEL'S WARS, 1947–1993 *Ahron Bregman*

THE KOREAN WAR: No Victors, No Vanquished *Stanley Sandler*

MODERN CHINESE WARFARE, 1795–1989 *Bruce A. Elleman*

MODERN INSURGENCIES AND COUNTER-INSURGENCIES: Guerrillas and their Opponents since 1750 *Ian F. W. Beckett*

NAVAL WARFARE, 1815–1914 *Lawrence Sondhaus*

OTTOMAN WARFARE, 1500–1700 *Rhoads Murphey*

SEAPOWER AND NAVAL WARFARE, 1650–1830 *Richard Harding*

THE SOVIET MILITARY EXPERIENCE *Roger R. Reese*

VIETNAM *Spencer C. Tucker*

THE WAR FOR INDEPENDENCE AND THE TRANSFORMATION OF AMERICAN SOCIETY *Harry M. Ward*

WARFARE AND SOCIETY IN EUROPE, 1792–1914 *Geoffrey Wawro*

WARFARE AT SEA, 1500–1650 *Jan Glete*

WARFARE IN ATLANTIC AFRICA, 1500–1800: Maritime Conflicts and the Transformation of Europe *John K. Thornton*

WARFARE, STATE AND SOCIETY IN THE BYZANTINE WORLD, 565–1204 *John Haldon*

WAR IN THE EARLY MODERN WORLD, 1450–1815 *Jeremy Black*

WARS OF IMPERIAL CONQUEST IN AFRICA, 1830–1914 *Bruce Vandervort*

WESTERN WARFARE IN THE AGE OF THE CRUSADES, 1000–1300 *John France*

MODERN INSURGENCIES AND COUNTER-INSURGENCIES

Guerrillas and their opponents since 1750

Ian F. W. Beckett

London and New York

First published 2001
by Routledge
2 Park Square, Milton Park, Abingdon, Oxon, OX14 4RN

Simultaneously published in the USA and Canada
by Routledge
270 Madison Ave, New York NY 10016

Routledge is an imprint of the Taylor & Francis Group

Transferred to Digital Printing 2005

© 2001 Ian F.W. Beckett

Typeset in Bembo by Taylor & Francis Books Ltd

British Library Cataloguing in Publication Data
A catalogue record for this book is available from the British Library

Library of Congress Cataloging in Publication Data
A catalogue record for this book has been requested.

ISBN 0–415–23933–8 (hbk)
ISBN 0–415–23934–6 (pbk)

CONTENTS

Introduction   vii

1 The roots of insurgency   1

2 The roots of counter-insurgency   24

3 Resistance and the partisan   55

4 Mao Tse-tung and revolutionary warfare   70

5 Formative experiences   86

6 'Wars of national liberation'?   121

7 The transition to urban insurgency   151

8 Insurgency and the superpowers   183

9 Forward to the past   217

Index   253

INTRODUCTION

Prior to the twentieth century, guerrilla warfare was generally understood as a purely military form of conflict. The classic tactics of 'hit and run' might be employed by indigenous groups in opposition to foreign or colonial occupation, where a conventional army either had been defeated or had never existed. It was thus a traditional tactical recourse of the weak faced by the strong. Alternatively, guerrilla warfare was also a term applied to the role of irregular troops acting as partisans in support of conventional military operations. Rarely did the primarily unsophisticated practitioners of guerrilla warfare in past centuries display any wider comprehension of the potential of irregular modes of conflict in the way that has become commonplace in the modern world and, especially, since 1945. Indeed, it was really only in the 1930s and 1940s that guerrilla warfare became revolutionary in both intent and practice, with social, economic, psychological and, especially, political elements grafted on to traditional irregular military tactics in order to radically alter the structure of a state by force. Thus, dissident groups that were initially in the minority, and weaker than the authorities, would seek power through a combination of subversion, propaganda and military action. More properly, therefore, modern revolutionary guerrilla warfare might be termed insurgency.

In the immediate post-1945 world, insurgency was most often motivated primarily by ideology, whether communism or nationalism, or a combination of both. Initially, it was also more likely to occur in the kind of rural environment in which guerrillas had traditionally best thrived and which offered the best opportunity to convert a guerrilla or insurgent force into a more conventional military force capable of taking on the authorities on their own terms. Indeed, insurgency was but a means to a particular end, guerrilla tactics being employed strategically to achieve a political goal.

By the late 1960s, however, insurgency was also becoming an urban phenomenon and shading into urban terrorism. However, while insurgents might routinely employ terror or intimidation in tactical terms, they have rarely done so at the strategic level. By contrast, purely terrorist groups, even if also motivated by a similar ideology to the insurgent group, have tended to employ terrorism indiscriminately and as political symbolism without the same intention of taking over the state apparatus themselves. Some terrorists, indeed, have merely been ideological mercenaries sponsored by rogue states in the international system.

Certainly, insurgency and terrorism have become the most prevalent forms of conflict since 1945. According to the figures of the US Defense Department, the number of insurgencies rose from 28 in 1958 to 43 by 1964. In 1983, a directory of the guerrilla and terrorist organisations in existence since 1945 catalogued 147 groups existing or having existed in Europe, 115 in Asia and Oceania, 114 in the Americas, 109 in the Middle East, and 84 in Africa. This provided a staggering total of 569 different groups, although, of course, many were small and obscure and of little account in either national or international politics. Yet the proliferation of organisations of this kind since the Second World War suggests that insurgency and terrorism are perceived widely as an effective means either of achieving power and influence or of bringing a cause to the notice of the national or international community. Moreover, while the end of European decolonisation and the collapse of the Soviet Union, which actively supported 'wars of national liberation', have together removed the motivational impulse that generated insurgency between the late 1940s and the late 1980s, insurgency has not disappeared. Indeed, it has taken on a new life through the emergence of such phenomena as 'spiritual insurgency' and 'economic' or 'commercial' insurgency.

In response to guerrilla warfare, insurgency and terrorism, armed forces have developed counter-measures to defeat such challenges and prevent their resurgence. In many respects, the development of counter-guerrilla warfare and counter-insurgency have mirrored the development of guerrilla warfare and insurgency. Thus, modern counter-insurgency encompasses those military, political, socio-economic and psychological activities employed by the authorities and their armed forces to defeat the threat in question. In more recent times, for reasons that will become apparent, counter-insurgency has been subsumed into wider definitions of the spectrum of conflict, being included both within 'low-intensity conflict' and, later, within 'operations other than war' alongside such other roles as peace-keeping and providing humanitarian aid. It is often assumed, from the obvious successes since 1945, that the insurgent is likely to win, but victory is not preordained. It has depended upon choice and circumstance, and counter-insurgency has also had its successes since 1945.

Surprisingly, insurgency and, especially, counter-insurgency have enjoyed relatively little attention from historians. To give an example, the original 1943 edition of a well-known text on military theory, *Makers of Modern Strategy*, had 547 pages of text, just 25 of which were devoted to French counter-insurgency in the nineteenth century. The new edition in 1986 had

871 pages, with that original chapter expanded to 31 pages. In addition, a new chapter of 47 pages on revolutionary warfare was included on the grounds that what had 'not existed' in 1943 had become a significant though conceivably short-lived factor in warfare, primarily through the decline of European colonial power. Most other standard histories of warfare are equally dismissive, with no references at all in such well-known work as J.F.C. Fuller's *The Conduct of War* (1972), Theodore Ropp's *War in the Modern World* (1973) or even Sir Michael Howard's *War in European History* (1976). Even if books specifically devoted to war since 1945 mentioned theorists of insurgency, they rarely mentioned those of counter-insurgency. Examples are Lawrence Martin's *Arms and Strategy* (1973), Lawrence Freedman's *Atlas of Global Strategy* (1985) and the 1975 and 1987 editions of *Contemporary Strategy*, edited by John Baylis, Ken Booth, John Garnett and P. Williams.

This volume, therefore, is intended to restore the balance and give some account of the evolution of both modern insurgency and modern counter-insurgency. As a form of conflict, it may not offer its practitioners any short cut to the triumphant ride through Persepolis, for it is distinctly unglamorous. Results are not necessarily obtained quickly or in conventional military terms of decisive battles won and lost. Yet, for those very reasons, insurgency confronts those who participate in it with political, societal and other pressures to a far greater extent than most other forms of conflict. Being too the classic 'poor man's war' at a time when warfare is ever more technologically innovative and expensive, insurgency is also likely to be with us for a long time to come.

1

THE ROOTS OF INSURGENCY

The word 'guerrilla' itself, meaning literally 'little war', derives from the activities of Spanish irregulars or *partidas* against occupying French forces between 1808 and 1814, but the first documented reference to guerrilla warfare appears to have been in the *Anastas*, a Hittite parchment dating from the fifteenth century BC. The actual minutiae of guerrilla tactics portrayed in the writings of Mao Tse-tung (Mao Zedong) in the 1930s are not recognisably different from those described by the ancient Chinese military theorist Sun Tzu in his *The Art of War*, a text now thought to date from between 400 and 320 BC, but with additions between the second and eleventh centuries AD. Similarly, the Bible, which dates in part from the first century BC, has many references to guerrilla warfare. One of the best illustrations is the account in the Old Testament's Book of Daniel and the two books of the Maccabees in the Apocrypha of the revolt against the Syrians led by Judas Maccabeus in 166 BC. Operating from desert mountain strongholds, the Maccabeans ambushed Syrian forces, seized weapons, visited villages by night to rally support and forced the Syrians back into fortified garrisons, ultimately compelling the Syrians to conclude a treaty in 158 BC.

Similarly, the works of classical ancient historians such as Polybius, Frontinus, Plutarch, Appian and Tacitus catalogue a succession of guerrilla campaigns fought against imperial Rome in North Africa, Spain, Britain, Germany and Gaul by leaders like Viriathus in Spain, Vercingetorix in Gaul and Tacfarinas in the Numidian desert. Nor were guerrilla tactics unknown in the mediaeval period. The Welsh scholar Giraldus Cambrensis left an account in the late twelfth century that provides a strikingly modern description of Welsh guerrilla tactics against the English:

> Though defeated and put to flight one day, they are ready to resume combat on the next, neither dejected by their loss, nor by their dishonour, and though, perhaps, they do not display great fortitude in open engagements and regular conflicts, yet they harass the enemy by ambuscade and nightly sallies.

The English also suffered from guerrilla raids conducted by the Constable of France, Bertrand du Guesculin, in the fourteenth century during the Hundred Years War, while Eastern Europe witnessed endemic guerrilla conflict between the Ottoman Turks and Balkan Christian groups like the *haiduks* and *klephts*, the latter effectively brigands.

All these campaigns were characterised by common features that have remained constant through the centuries. Invariably, guerrilla groups operated in difficult terrain such as mountains or deserts. They possessed local knowledge denied to their opponents and, conceivably, had a degree of support among what population inhabited such remote and inaccessible regions. They were generally more mobile than their opponents and would undertake the kind of hit-and-run raids that would enable them to evade larger forces and so prolong their struggle. On occasions, however, such conflict was merely brigandage, which might acquire the status of legend, as in the sagas of the *klephts* or, for that matter, Robin Hood. It is usually assumed that banditry is a 'pre-political' phenomenon and, therefore, unlikely to lead to any sustained or organised campaign of national resistance. In some situations, however, in conjunction with peasant or tribal social protest, banditry might assume a revolutionary aspect, albeit limited to a particular region.

By the eighteenth century, it was appreciated increasingly by military theorists that even conventional armies might benefit from the adoption of guerrilla tactics in certain circumstances, and from raising irregular troops in support of conventional operations. Irregular units were thus added to a number of European armies, notably that of the Habsburgs, for whom Croat and Magyar light infantry proved very successful in the Seven Years War (1756–63). In response, the Prussians raised so-called *Freibataillone* (volunteer battalions), while a particular proving ground for such irregulars was North America during the succession of so-called French and Indian Wars.

The destruction of a British force under Major-General Edward Braddock on the Monongahela in May 1755 by Indian allies of the French has frequently been regarded as an example of the failure of regulars to adapt to local conditions. In fact, Braddock had done his best to prepare ill-trained recruits for the campaign, and his force collided with his French and Indian opponents rather than being ambushed. Moreover, the disaster largely occurred from the British loss of offensive momentum at a crucial moment. One ranger unit had already been formed by Joseph Gorham as early as 1750, and more were raised in 1756, including that of Robert Rogers. Rangers, however, were not often as decisive in their skirmishing as has been supposed and were not capable of undertaking the assaults on fortified positions that effectively decided the struggle for North America in Britain's favour in the Seven Years War. In addition, since provincial units could prove difficult to discipline and lead, the first British regular light infantry battalion – the 80th Foot – was raised by Thomas Gage in 1758, followed by the mostly German-speaking Royal Americans. Other regular regiments also began to adapt uniform, equipment and tactics, and in February 1759 the commander-in-chief, Jeffrey Amherst, ordered part of each battalion to be detached for light infantry work.

Partisan units operated successfully on both sides during the American War of Independence (1775–83), especially in the southern states. Here, gifted British leaders of loyalist irregulars such as Patrick Ferguson, killed at King's Mountain in October 1780, and Barnaste 'Bloody' Tarleton were confronted by equally gifted American guerrilla leaders such as Andrew Pickens, Thomas Sumter ('The Carolina Gamecock') and Francis 'Swamp Fox' Marion in what was to become essentially a bitter civil war. So-named from his lairs amid the swamps of the Santee and Pedee rivers in South Carolina, which provided his men with a plentiful supply of birds, game and fish, Marion had learned his trade fighting against the Cherokees. Others enjoyed considerable success in what were effectively irregular operations rather than guerrilla warfare *per se*. These included Ethan Allen and George Rogers Clark, while the harassing operations of a former subordinate of Allen, Seth Warner, and a former member of Rogers' Rangers, John Stark, made a significant contribution to the defeat of John Burgoyne's army at Saratoga in October 1777.

In many respects, the outcome of the war in the South, to which the British switched their main effort in 1779–80, actually depended more on the irregular conflict at local level than on conventional battles between the British and Continental armies. Indeed, it was through the intimidatory presence of American guerrillas and militia – the former most often drawn from the latter – that so many areas where loyalism was potentially strong were successfully subdued and the Indian allies of the British such as the Cherokees suppressed. Neither side could deploy sufficient regulars to protect its own supporters, hence the spread of uncontrolled guerrilla war through Georgia and the Carolinas. From the point of view of the loyalists, attempts at conciliation of the population on the part of the British authorities were an irksome constraint and one often ignored in practice. The American militias proved very difficult to eliminate, representing, to quote John Shy, 'a great spongy mass that could be pushed aside or maimed temporarily but that had no vital centre and could not be destroyed'. From the point of view of the American rebels, the militia was a vital coercive element, since loyalism generally failed to flourish without a British regular presence.

Neither British nor American generals entirely understood this, with the exception of Charles Lee, a former British regular, who had experienced warfare in North America and had also seen service with the Polish and Russian armies. Offering his services to the American rebels, Lee was made the Continental army's third-ranking general but was eventually suspended in June 1778. He suggested an alternative guerrilla strategy to Washington's pursuit of conventional military victory, believing pitched battles played to the British strengths and that American regulars should be used to protect the militia while it won the local war that he felt was the key to victory.

Washington, however, recoiled from encouraging an internal conflict damaging to the social fabric and, in any case, believed that only winning a conventional war would demonstrate the legitimacy of the new nation. Though Daniel Morgan understood how to use irregulars in conjunction with his regulars, other Continental regulars like Horatio Gates and Nathanael Greene remained critical of militia and irregulars. Greene temporarily disbanded Sumter's command in August 1781 after the latter failed to stop the relief of the British post in South Carolina known as Ninety-Six. Circumstances, however, forced Greene to rely upon militia support, and it has been argued by John Dederer that the co-operation of irregular and regular forces under Greene's overall command was akin to the transitional phase between guerrilla and conventional war later described by Mao Tse-tung as 'mobile war'.

On the British side, there was also a belief that success in the conventional war guaranteed success in the local war, while a coercive strategy in the localities would prove politically counter-productive. Indeed, both Sir Henry Clinton and Sir William Cornwallis consciously shrank from unleashing the potential of the loyalists to conduct the full-scale counter-insurgent campaign advocated by those like Tarleton and Ferguson, even though the British had shifted their focus to the South precisely because this was where loyalism was strongest.

In fact, the final outcome of the war rested on French and Spanish intervention and what John Shy has characterised as 'a brilliant and lucky concentration of regular land and sea forces around the Yorktown peninsula'. American generals, however, ignored the real contribution of the guerrillas and militia to their eventual success. It left them poorly prepared to meet the post-war challenge of warfare against the Indians, who destroyed Arthur St Clair's army on the Wabash in November 1791 in what remained one of the worst defeats ever inflicted on an American army.

Nonetheless, whatever the American perception of irregular warfare, it was the experience of North American conditions that resulted in the first modern texts on irregular warfare in the late eighteenth century. *Treatise on the Small War* (1790) and *The Partisan in War or the Use of a Corps of Light Troops for an Army* (1789) were penned by two Hessian officers who had fought with the British army in America, Johann von Ewald and Andreas Emmerich, respectively. They were to be followed by others that derived lessons not from America but from Europe. Thus, the Prussians George Wilhelm von Valentini in *Treatise on Small Wars and the Use of Light Troops* (1799) and Carl von Decker in *The Small War in the Spirit of the New Conduct of Warfare* (1822), the Frenchman Le Mière de Corvey in 1823, and the Russian Denis Davidov in his *Essay on the Theory of Partisan Warfare* (1821) drew upon the experience of the French Revolutionary and Napoleonic Wars between 1792 and 1815.

In August 1793, in seeking to defend their newly won liberties, the French Committee of Public Safety instituted the *levée en masse*, by which all able-bodied Frenchmen were literally conscripted overnight as France was transformed into a 'nation in arms'. Driven by patriotic nationalism and revolutionary fervour, the new French citizen armies swept across Europe. However, defeat at the hands of the French Republic or, later, at the hands of Napoleon, and the imposition of republican ideals as well as such measures as new taxation and conscription ultimately engendered opposition among some of the defeated peoples. In Prussia after 1806, this took the form of emulating the concept of a 'nation in arms', but elsewhere it brought popular uprisings. It has to be stressed, however, to quote Charles Esdaile, that none of the revolts displayed 'any trace of modern political consciousness', the response being engendered largely by socio-economic factors and local and regional rather than national political loyalties.

One of the earliest revolts was that of Negro slaves on the French island of Haiti between 1791 and 1802 led by Toussaint L'Ouverture while, in western France, the province of La Vendée, loyal to the Catholic Church if not quite as attached to the monarchy, fought the republicans from 1793 to 1796. The outbreak of revolt in the Vendée came in response to the imposition of conscription in March 1793, although the agrarian and conservative region had already displayed opposition to the regime's anti-clerical ideology. There was also a longer tradition of opposition to militia service and the salt duty. In many respects, it was also a conflict between the peasantry, who formed the rank and file of the rebel 'Catholic Army' (later the 'Catholic and Royal Army'), and the urban-based supporters of the Republic.

Led by men like the nobles François Athanase Charette de la Contrie and Henri de la Rochejaquelein; but also by a former gendarme, Jean-Nicholas Stofflet; a former army lieutenant, Maurice d'Elbée; and a waggoner and church sexton, Jacques Cathelineau, the rebels had little sense of any wider aims beyond driving the Republican armies out of the Vendée. They lacked both organisation and co-ordination, not capitalising on the undoubted opportunity to march on Paris once they had captured Saumur in June 1793. A few weeks later, the elected nominal commander-in-chief, Cathelineau, was mortally wounded during an attack on Nantes. Maurice d'Elbée was mortally wounded at Cholet in October 1793 and, by December 1793, the rebel armies, once perhaps 120,000 strong, if poorly armed, had all but disintegrated. One by one, their remaining leaders were hunted down, Rochejaquelein being killed in January 1794, Stofflet executed in February 1796 and Charette suffering a similar fate a month later. Resistance to the Republic among the so-called *Chouans* (Owls) in Brittany, numbering perhaps 30,000 rebels at most, was also ruthlessly suppressed between 1794 and 1796. The British landed an *émigré* royalist army at Quiberon Bay in June 1795 in the hope of sustaining the revolts in both Brittany and the Vendée, but it was overwhelmed within a month.

In response to the extension of the subsequent Napoleonic empire, there were three principal uprisings: those in the Tyrol, Calabria and, of course,

Spain. All occurred in regions where there was already a tradition of banditry and, indeed, of local military organisation as well as existing socio-economic tensions. Moreover, all occurred where loyalty to the Catholic Church was strong. The Tyrolean revolt against Napoleon and his Bavarian allies in April 1809, led by Andreas Hofer, an innkeeper, and Josef Speckbacher, was inspired by Bavarian imposition of new taxes and of conscription. However, it was an area that had already resisted earlier Austrian attempts at reform, including a reduction of the influence of the Church and concessions to Jewish and Protestants groups in a staunchly Catholic region. There were serious economic problems, and the Tyrol also had a ready-made basis for resistance in the existence of the territorial militia known as *schützen* (sharpshooters). It was not enough, however, and while there was a success against the Bavarians at Berg in August 1809, Tyrolean resistance was soon crushed by the French. Hofer was betrayed and executed in February 1810.

Catholicism was again a factor in Calabria, part of the Kingdom of Naples, where the French lost 20,000 men in a brutal guerrilla war between March 1806 and November 1811, when the last real resistance was overcome. Earlier, Cardinal Fabrizio Ruffo had led a successful revolt against the French-inspired Parthenopean Republic in 1799, leading the *Sanfedisti* (Army of the Holy Faith) to restore the Bourbons. In 1806, clergymen, many displaying the kind of open hostility to the propertied later evident in twentieth-century 'liberation theology', frequently led guerrilla bands. Monasteries provided ready refuges for the guerrillas until the monastic orders were suppressed. The French introduced conscription and abolished feudalism, but since municipal and other taxes replaced feudal dues the peasantry detected little change and, indeed, traditional ways of life were severely disrupted. Significantly, the Calabrian Civic Guard allied to the French were often urban dwellers, and a distinct element of internal class conflict was involved in the war.

An equally significant factor, however, was endemic brigandage in a region of grinding poverty and near feudalism, the leading opponents of the French being brigand leaders such as Michele Pezza (aka Fra Diavolo), Guiseppe Rotella, Niccolo Gualteri (aka Pane di Grano) and Paolo Mancuso (aka Parafante). Although often riven by rivalries and vendettas, the brigands shared a common hostility to the centralising influence of the French, the imposition of conscription in 1809 stimulating a fresh upsurge in resistance. However, it was more religious fanaticism than nationalism that fuelled the resistance to the French.

In many ways, the struggle in Calabria was a precursor of the best-known insurrection, which was that in Spain between 1808 and 1814. Taking advantage of deep internal divisions in Spanish politics, Napoleon moved to take over the country in February 1808 and forced the abdication of the Spanish king in May 1808, declaring his own brother, Joseph, King of Spain. The Spanish army was soon routed and a British army sent to help driven into the sea at Corunna in January 1809, Napoleon mistakenly declaring the 'Spanish business' over.

Guerrillas began to appear first in Galicia and then in Aragon, mostly it would appear spontaneously among the lowest elements of society and led by men of humble origin such as the Castilian Juan Martín Diaz (aka 'El Empecinado'), Juan Palarea (aka 'El Medico') around Toledo, Juan Diaz Porlier (aka 'El Marquesito') in the Asturias, Jean de Mendietta (aka 'El Capuchino') in Zamora, and Francisco Espoz y Mina, a farmer's son from Navarre. However, a highly complex mix of personal, local, political, social and religious factors was involved in stimulating resistance. Those groups that emerged in Navarre arguably resulted more from a perception that the French threatened traditional autonomy, including a degree of tax exemption, than from any conscious identification with Spanish nationalism, although there was undoubtedly a considerable attachment to the Church, which came under particular attack from the French. Most resistance in Navarre came from the more prosperous Basque areas of the north, where the population was typically one of dispersed and independently minded small peasant land holders rather than the more urbanised Castilian areas of the south, which had experienced greater social tensions before the war and where there was less to lose through French occupation.

In the case of Valencia, existing peasant hostility to the Spanish government's attempt to widen conscription in 1801 and continuing resentment against seigniorial rights contributed to resistance when many prominent Spanish *afrancesados* (collaborators) were drawn from the ranks of the semi-feudal seigniors. This does not mean that guerrilla war in Valencia can be explained solely in terms of a social conflict. Nonetheless, Spain was in a state of considerable socio-economic unrest at the time of the French intervention, and in southern and eastern Spain in particular there was often an underlying opposition to noble and ecclesiastical authority, which was just as significant as the presence of the French in fuelling the guerrilla war. Previous regional traditions of banditry and smuggling also clearly contributed to resistance. So too did the existence of local home guards such as the Catalan *somatenes* and Basque *miqueletes*, while the link between Catholic fanaticism and violent counter-revolution was as pronounced as in the Vendée, Calabria or the Tyrol. Equally, local rivalries hampered co-operation against the French, as in Aragon, eastern Castile and Navarre, where Mina waged a ruthless campaign against his rivals in 1810.

Some groups expanded considerably, with Mina, for example, presiding over about 7,000 men by 1813, while the overall total of guerrillas may have been 30,000. Such expansion of guerrilla numbers coincided with a greater regularisation in some cases as several of the provincial juntas imposed regular-style organisation and discipline as a means of reasserting social control over the more unruly elements unleashed by the initial uprising against the French. Indeed, the Central Junta had effectively legalised banditry in December 1808 by authorising the retention of any property or goods seized from the French or their sympathisers. Whether the result of regularisation or not, however, growth came at the price of separating the guerrillas from the population to some extent and rendering them vulnerable to the French through the need to establish more permanent bases. That vulnerability, in turn, forced the guerrillas to live off rather among their own people.

Indeed, it might be argued that the guerrillas were as great a burden to the Spanish as to the French, since the often random and wanton plundering of their own people by the former was conceivably worse than the more systematic and regulated contributions imposed by the latter. In some areas, too, intimidation of an apathetic population by the guerrillas undoubtedly occurred. Consequently, there were cases in which the population appealed to the French for protection, and the French did successfully raise local anti-guerrilla units or *juramentado*. French reprisals, however, rather than the guerrillas' own depredations, appear to have had the greater impact on the loyalties of the population as a whole.

The French were forced to disperse large numbers of men through the countryside, so that one French marshal complained in 1811 that he could not concentrate even 10,000 men for fear of having his supply lines cut and too much territory overrun by guerrillas. Clearly, too, guerrilla activity did prevent the French securing easy access to Spanish economic resources, so war did not 'feed war' in the manner usually expected of Napoleonic campaigns. One French Hussar officer, Albert de Rocca, wrote in his memoirs of the French being attacked constantly, of being forced to construct hundreds of secure outposts in which they took refuge at night, only to hear the sound of celebrations as their enemies were feted in the surrounding villages; of the need for strong escorts for every convoy; and of how, unable to hunt down the guerrillas, the French resorted to terror against the population as a whole in an escalating cycle of atrocity and counter-atrocity.

Nonetheless, the guerrillas were largely ineffective in terms of turning the French out of their fortified posts. Indeed, the French were firmly in control of most of Spain from August 1809 until January 1812, while the British and Portuguese armies were largely bottled up in Portugal, and the performance of the Spanish army was seriously undermined by the constant desertion of its rank and file to the guerrillas, who were perceived to be less disciplined and to offer greater rewards. Strangely, too, in Navarre at least, a statistical survey has suggested that there was no significant correlation between terrain and guerrilla success, so that guerrilla success rested on factors other than a rugged physical environment.

Thus, while the guerrillas certainly helped to weaken French morale and provided the British army with invaluable intelligence, it must also be said that the guerrillas could not have survived without British logistic support and the pressure exerted on the French by the British. Ultimately, it was the British army, with its allied Portuguese and Spanish regular contingents, that liberated Spain, albeit only once Napoleon had committed himself to the invasion of Russia with all its implications for reinforcing his armies in Spain. Moreover, it should be noted that Spanish army officers had helped raise the revolt in some areas such as Galicia and sometimes led guerrilla bands, while perhaps the most celebrated supposed guerrilla success, the surrender of 20,000 French troops at Bailén in July 1808, was largely the achievement of Spanish regulars. One Spanish regular, José Moscoso, published a guerrilla warfare manual in Cadiz in 1809.

The real importance of the guerrillas was that, like the later European resistance movements of the Second World War, they enabled the Spaniards to claim a part in their own deliverance. This had a significant psychological effect on the people and one that was ultimately to contribute to a struggle between liberals and absolutists in Spain after 1814. Ironically, in that struggle a number of the prominent wartime guerrilla leaders were executed, including Diaz, Porlier and Mendietta. It was also the case that what Charles Esdaile has characterised as the 'exaggerated comfort' derived by the Spanish from the wartime activities of the guerrillas fuelled a resentment on the part of Spanish regulars, which contributed to increasing military intervention in Spanish politics through the remainder of the nineteenth century.

Thus, the guerrillas succeeded in Spain primarily because they were effectively supporting conventional operations, and they failed in the Tyrol and Calabria without such assistance, although there were some desultory British operations in the latter. Similarly, the Russian partisans who harried the French so successfully during the French retreat from Moscow in 1812 were regular troops conducting irregular operations. Consequently, those theorists mentioned earlier, who analysed guerrilla warfare between 1792 and 1815, as well as theorists of general war, all drew the conclusion that guerrilla warfare was synonymous with partisan warfare and most certainly could not succeed in any other context. Therefore, guerrilla operations were those in support of conventional troops undertaken by regulars, who were simply detached from the main army.

In later years, there were some further examples of guerrilla tactics, as in the Greek War of Independence (1821–27) and the American Civil War (1861–65). In the case of the Greek struggle for independence, the Greek land forces were primarily drawn from the *armatulai*, best described as indigenous local gendarmerie, and the *klephts*, whom they were supposed to keep in check. The only effective difference between them was that one had been licensed by the Ottoman authorities to attack the other, since the *armatulai* were generally recruited from among the *klephts*. Many of the best Greek military commanders, such as Odysseus Androutsos and George Karaïskakis, had served as *armatulai* under Ali Pasha, the increasingly independent Albanian-born Pasha of Yannina (Ioannina), against whom the Sultan sent his army in 1820. Indeed, it was primarily the Ottoman campaign against Ali Pasha that politicised the *armatulai* and *klephts* to the extent that it inspired popular resistance to the Turks independently of the activities of the middle-class secret societies known as *philiki etairia* (friendly societies), to whose influence the beginning of the Greek revolt is usually ascribed. In this instance, therefore, banditry took on a national significance.

In the case of the American Civil War, some very successful exponents of irregular tactics appeared, including the Confederates John Singleton Mosby and John Hunt Morgan. However, a distinction needs to be drawn between the contribution to both sides of raiding in support of conventional strategy and guerrilla warfare as such, waged, as it were, on an unorganised basis between rival groups in locally contested areas. It might have been expected that, given the disparity of resources between the Union and the southern Confederacy, the latter would resort to a guerrilla strategy. Like the Union military leadership, however, that of the Confederacy instinctively opposed guerrilla warfare. Indeed, the Partisan Ranger Act of 21 April 1862, which authorised Confederate partisan units, was repealed on 17 February 1864 after pressure from Robert E. Lee and other Confederate regulars, who feared the excesses that had already resulted from the lack of discipline among rival guerrilla groups on the Kansas and Missouri borders. Only Mosby's unit and that of John McNeill, also operating in northern Virginia, were exempted from the abolition of officially authorised Confederate partisan units by the repeal of the legislation.

In many cases, however, guerrillas identifying with the Confederacy operated well outside Confederate lines and Confederate control, leading to a certain ambiguity in official attitudes, since they did have their uses. Major-General Sterling Price, for example, attempted to co-ordinate with guerrillas during his unsuccessful large-scale cavalry raid into Missouri in the autumn of 1864. It can be noted, too, that the Partisan Ranger Act itself made little attempt at definition, other than prohibiting guerrilla action by other than authorised units.

On the Kansas and Missouri border, the pre-war struggle between pro- and anti-slavery factions spawned equally brutal groups on both sides, including George Hoyt's 'Red Legs' and Charles Jennison's 'Jayhawkers' for the Union, and those led by William Clarke Quantrill and 'Bloody Bill' Anderson for the Confederacy. Quantrill's raid on Lawrence in Kansas in August 1863, which resulted in at least 150 deaths and the burning of much of the town, epitomised this 'war within a war'. In all, perhaps 10,000 people died in Missouri and 300,000 fled their homes in an escalating cycle of violence, which destroyed any sense of security and left few refuges for neutrals. Indeed, mutilation, including scalping, was not unknown.

Guerrilla activity was also a feature of those up-country or back-country areas of states like North Carolina, Georgia, Alabama, Tennessee and Kentucky, in which there were significant internal divisions in terms of sympathy for Confederacy or Union. These areas, too, threw up notorious guerrillas, such as the Confederates Champ Ferguson, who killed over 100

Unionists in Tennessee, John Gatewood in Georgia and the Reverend Milus 'Bushwhacker' Johnston in Alabama. Notorious Unionists guerrillas included Thomas Clark, who led the 'Buggers' in Alabama, and George Kirk and Keith Blalock in North Carolina. Union-occupied Louisiana and Arkansas, too, saw conflict between Confederate guerrillas and Union sympathisers. Indeed, guerrilla conflict was the only direct face of war experienced by many in Tennessee and Kentucky, since the movements of the main armies remained distant from them throughout. Unionist guerrillas, for example, controlled many of the counties of eastern Tennessee, while Confederate guerrillas disputed Union control of western Kentucky and middle Tennessee. One of the ironies of the situation in the Appalachians, the Cumberlands and the Ozarks was that, while these areas of rugged terrain were favoured by Confederate guerrillas, they were also the very areas within the Confederacy which most Union sympathisers inhabited.

Yet it has been argued that those on both sides still shared a common racial, ethnic, linguistic, religious and cultural heritage as well as similar socio-economic interests and aspirations. In eastern Tennessee, for example, partisans on both sides coalesced around locally prominent figures and tended to be young, married and propertied, although Confederates tended to be wealthier than their Union counterparts. In Missouri, where the war had impacted upon a society already in transition from agricultural subsistence to a market-oriented economy, guerrillas were again predominantly young men drawn from a society of 'family-centred, property-owning farmers, evangelical Christians, and lovers of law and order'. Consequently, despite reciprocal atrocities, there were some generally observed limitations or perhaps inhibitions, particularly with respect to the treatment of women and children. Indeed, while their menfolk were routinely slaughtered, German and other immigrant women were invariably spared rape or murder. Of course, such limitations did not apply to black or Indian women. Even the guerrilla war between whites in Missouri remained within the accepted barriers, however perversely men defined them.

Elsewhere, guerrilla violence within the Confederacy was far from random and, whether directed against Confederate or Unionist sympathisers, often intended to maintain law and order as a means of safeguarding home, family and community. Equally, those facing such guerrilla violence also sought to protect home, family and community. However, what has been described as an epidemic of often violent crime in eastern Tennessee persisted from 1862 until at least 1867 and, here, women were victims on occasions. Yet, at the same time, Union and Confederate commanders attempted, albeit unsuccessfully, to reach a local agreement to end hostage taking on several occasions.

Whatever the realities of the guerrilla war in the southern states, it was not surprising that, while some Confederates contemplated a continued guerrilla struggle after the defeat of the Confederacy in April 1865, Lee refused to contemplate such a course. In any case, the Confederacy was too exhausted for many to wish to continue the struggle. The long-term impact of the bitter internal divisions in some areas was immense. Significantly, indeed, post-war outlaws such as Jesse and Frank James and the Younger brothers all rode with Quantrill during the war. Confederate defeat had seemingly further ennobled these outlaws within their own communities, their exploits being seen as an extension of the war. In the Appalachians, wartime vendettas and feuds persisted well into the 1870s.

The normal pattern of events in Europe, however, was either that of short conventional wars such as those waged by Prussia against Denmark (1864), Austria (1866) and France (1870–71), or short and generally unsuccessful urban insurrections such as those in several European cities in 1848 or the experience of the Commune in Paris in 1871. Urban insurrection attracted the interest of socialist thinkers such as Engels and Marx, and the latter stages of the Franco-Prussian War saw the Prussian and German armies increasingly irritated although not, in reality, seriously threatened by French *francs-tireurs* (literally, 'marksmen'), against whom the German reaction was especially violent. The *corps francs* was raised by the French Government of National Defence in September 1870, and 57,000 men served in it. Although poorly armed and badly led, the *francs-tireurs* tied down perhaps 120,000 German troops, inducing fears of a 'people's war', repugnant to regular soldiers, and hastening the German bombardment of Paris as a means of bringing the war to a swift conclusion.

Mainstream military thought was little affected by these non-conventional patterns of warfare, despite the fact that most European armies fought a whole succession of campaigns against irregular opponents throughout the world as colonial empires steadily expanded during the latter half of the nineteenth century. The British theorist of colonial warfare, Charles Callwell, divided potential opponents into six categories:

1 European-trained armies such as the Sikhs, against whom the British had fought in the 1840s, or the army's own native sepoys in the Indian Mutiny of 1857;
2 semi-organised troops such as the Afghan army encountered in the First and Second Afghan Wars of 1839–42 and 1878–80;
3 disciplined yet primitive armies such as the Zulus or the Matabele;
4 fanatics such as the dervishes of the Sudan;
5 true guerrillas such as the Maoris, the Kaffirs (principally Xhosa) of the Cape Frontier or *dacoits* (bandits) of Burma; and
6 in a category of their own, the Boers, who differed from other guerrillas in being both white and mounted.

Among those faced by the Europeans were a number of undoubtedly gifted guerrilla leaders, such as Abd el-Kader, whom the French encountered in Algeria between 1832 and 1847; Shamil (or Shamyl), who resisted the

Russians in the Caucasus between 1834 and 1859; Samouri Touré, who fought the French in the western Sudan; and Mohammed ben Abd el-Krim, who fought both the Spanish and the French from the Rif mountains in Spanish Morocco between 1921 and 1926. The latter stages of the British campaign against the Boers in South Africa between 1899 and 1902 and the US campaign in the Philippines between 1899 and 1902 were also examples of bitter guerrilla conflict. Only the political sophistication of Emilio Aguinaldo's organisation in the Philippines made any of these campaigns remotely a competition in government, Aguinaldo consciously trying to influence the American presidential election of 1900, in which the Republican incumbent, William McKinley, was opposed by the anti-imperialist Democrat William Jennings Bryan. Yet Aguinaldo was slow to initiate guerrilla warfare, since he and his leading followers wished to preserve social as well as political control over the Filipino population. In Batangas province at least, Miguel Malvar did eventually attempt to widen support for the insurgency among lower-class Filipinos. This, however, was only once support had declined among an elite, who increasingly found American occupation was not without its compensations in retaining their influence. Most lower-class Filipinos, therefore, saw little reason to support guerrillas who were perceived to be fighting in the interests of those 'who had consistently disregarded the aspirations of the common people'.

The Boers were obviously different from other colonial opponents and, of course, were well armed with modern weapons. They also began the war with a clear political aim of safeguarding their independence, a strong religious and nationalist ideology, albeit with a largely improvised strategy of invading Natal to secure strong defensive positions before large-scale British reinforcements could arrive. Conceivably better options would have been a hard drive to take the Natal ports or a greater concentration on Cape Colony. However, what should be noted is that the Boers adopted a semi-conventional strategy, which ultimately failed once the British had recovered from their early setbacks between October 1899 and January 1900.

With the capture of almost 10 per cent of the Boer field strength at Paardeburg in February 1900, and the fall of the Boer capitals of Bloemfontein and Pretoria in March and June respectively, many older Boer commanders, mostly drawn from the landed oligarchy and close to the president of the Transvaal, Paul Kruger, proposed bringing the war to an end. Supported by the president of the Orange Free State, Marthinus Steyn, younger men like Louis Botha, Christiaan De Wet, Koos de la Rey and Jan Smuts believed a prolonged resistance was possible. In some ways, the guerrilla struggle effectively began with a *krijgsraad* (war council) at Kroonstad on 17 March 1900, just after the fall of Bloemfontein, at which it was decided to concentrate on the British lines of communication rather than directly confronting the army advancing on Pretoria.

The commandos, originating from the military system established at the

Cape by the Dutch East India Company, had always been idiosyncratic, with commanders elected and decisions taken by vote. Moreover, no individual burgher was actually compelled to accept any orders, and at least 15,000 – the so-called *hensoppers* (hands-uppers) – surrendered voluntarily and took an oath of neutrality. About 5,400, indeed, became 'joiners', enlisted by the British in various burgher corps, including Piet De Wet, brother of Christiaan De Wet. The number of *bittereinders* (bitter-enders) dwindled to about 17,000 men by the end of the war in May 1902, supported, ironically, by black *agter-ryers* (after-riders). Ultimately, however, the steady attritional impact of British measures, increasing political and social fissures within Afrikaner society and increasing fears of escalating black participation in the war forced the remaining commandos to the negotiating table, Botha and Smuts in particular recognising that it was better to secure a negotiated rather than a dictated settlement.

For reasons that will become apparent in the next chapter, however, these guerrilla leaders and guerrilla campaigns did not contribute to any real recognition of guerrilla conflict as a distinct form of warfare. Moreover, the concept of 'people's war' so familiar to twentieth-century exponents of guerrilla warfare was hardly distinguishable in any of the earlier writing on the subject. Although Carl von Clausewitz was interested in guerrilla warfare as an operational strategy within the conventional military framework, his classic *On War*, published between 1832 and 1844, only briefly alluded to the political implications of national resistance to an invader. Clausewitz, who had studied the conflict in the Vendée, believed that guerrilla war could only be sustained over a long period if waged in the rugged interior of a large country. He also believed that national character was significant in shaping the suitability of a particular population for such a conflict. Moreover, while recognising that the growth of the nation-state suggested that European peoples would probably continue a struggle even if their armies were overthrown, Clausewitz did not interpret guerrilla warfare as a means of popular revolution.

Engels and Marx did make some effort to understand the role of guerrillas in the past in such conflicts as the Peninsular War and the Franco-Prussian War, but they did not produce any coherent theoretical position on guerrilla warfare and clearly believed that there was little scope for a people's war in industrialised Europe. Thus any revolution would depend upon a moral rather than a military collapse of capitalist authority at some appropriate moment in the future. Like Engels, Lenin was something of a student of military affairs, but it is difficult to find much of significance on guerrilla warfare in his writings, although he certainly distinguished between partisan warfare and terrorism. Indeed, on one occasion, Lenin dismissed guerrilla warfare as 'left adventurism' and regarded it as merely one of a number of tools that might be employed by the revolutionary as a substitute for adequate conventional military strength. His actual contribution to guerrilla warfare derived much more from the organisational weapon of a communist party capable of organising the proletariat as an instrument of revolution, his short book *Partisan Warfare* in 1906 laying particular emphasis on party control. Significantly, Leon Trotsky, who became the first People's Commissar for War and Chairman of the Supreme Military Soviet in March 1918, moved swiftly to eliminate what was termed *partisanshchina* (partisan spirit) in the newly established Red Army in the belief that it represented a weapon of the weak rather than the strong, and that it encouraged attitudes subversive of centralised party authority.

Only a handful of writers before the twentieth century seem to have made any real direct connection between guerrilla warfare and revolution, these being those primarily involved in the struggles for Italian and Polish independence. The Italian nationalist Giuseppe Mazzini certainly conceived of guerrilla conflict as a means of encouraging a wider insurrection against Habsburg rule of Italy. Another Italian, Carlo Bianco, Conte di Saint Jorioz, who fought in the Carlist Wars in Spain (1833–40), published a two-volume work in 1830 that offered 'people's war' as a means of freeing Italy from foreign domination. In the event it was not to be, although Giuseppe Garibaldi, who had earned his reputation leading guerrillas in Latin America, was successful in invading Sicily in 1859. Garibaldi's success, however, came only after the defeat of the Austrians in the Franco-Austrian War.

In turn, Mazzini and Bianco influenced Polish theorists such as Wojciech Chrzanowski, Karol Bogumil Stolzman, Henryk Kamienski, Ludwig Bystrzanowski, Józef Pawlikowski and Józef Bem. Writing between 1831 and 1863, they all identified 'people's war' as the means of both establishing a Polish national consciousness and liberating Poland from Russian domination. Stolzman, indeed, saw partisan warfare as the most suitable form of warfare for a people in revolt. The successive doomed Polish insurrections of 1830, 1846, 1848 and 1863, however, demonstrated that, without external aid, the Poles could not match the military power of the Russians. Consequently, most recognised the need to convert a guerrilla force into a conventional army, hence the frequent identification of people's war with partisan warfare in Polish works.

One other revolutionary who should be noted is Johannes Most. A German Social Democrat who eventually settled in the United States, Most can be regarded in some respects as a pioneer of both modern urban guerrilla warfare and international terrorism through his emphasis in a work of 1884, *Revolutionäre Kreigswissenschaft* (Revolutionary War Science) on the systematic use of terror by small groups of activists utilising the most modern technology available in pursuit of what he termed 'propaganda of the deed'.

In practice, however, guerrilla warfare continued to be waged along traditional lines even for much of the first half of the twentieth century, although some groups and individuals were beginning to harness guerrilla or terrorist tactics to the pursuit of overtly political ends. Two groups are particularly worth noting. Between the 1880s and 1890s, the Internal Macedonian

Revolutionary Organisation (IMRO) devoted considerable attention to building an integrated military and political organisation in its struggle against Ottoman Turkish dominance. However, it attempted a more general uprising against the Turks in August 1903, and its failure forced a return to low-level guerrilla activity, mostly from Bulgarian bases. Ultimately, the movement fragmented when the Bulgarians withdrew support in 1934.

Similarly, the original Irish Republican Army (IRA) was a true forerunner of modern revolutionary groups in terms of its politically inspired campaign against the British in Ireland between 1919 and 1921, although most theorists in the inter-war years failed to recognise it as such. In fact, many of the leaders of the IRA had been inspired by the example of the guerrilla phase of the South African War. During the Easter Rising in April 1916, Irish insurgents wore 'De Wet caps', and those executed included John MacBride, who had served alongside the Boers in the Irish-Transvaal Brigade. Michael Collins was sometimes referred to as the 'Irish De Wet', having long admired De Wet and modelling the IRA 'flying columns' on Boer commandos. Two flying column commanders, Dan Breen and Tom Barry, who served in the British army during the Great War, were also said to have been influenced by Boer tactics.

In reality, it must be said that many IRA units were far less effective than has sometimes been claimed and were by no means entirely in concert with the population they claimed to represent. Town dwellers in particular were often regarded with some contempt by the IRA, and, certainly in Cork, tramps and other itinerants were subjected to considerable intimidation. Thus, the attacks made upon the substantial but unfortified police house, euphemistically known as 'barracks', in 1920–21 were not so much a carefully calculated political campaign to destroy the Royal Irish Constabulary (RIC) but primarily because they were easy targets. Nor was the IRA's intelligence network as efficient as has been supposed, relying largely on its psychological domination of the population to deny intelligence to the British, although the RIC Special Branch and the Special Branch of the Dublin Metropolitan Police were clearly targeted for assassination. Thus, on 21 November 1920, twenty men were attacked in Dublin, thirteen being killed and six injured. Of the twenty, thirteen were involved in British intelligence work for army or police. IRA propaganda was much more effective than that of the British, however, and the political arm of the republican movement, Sinn Féin (Ourselves Alone), was steadily increasing its hold over local government through municipal and other elections. The republicans had also established Dáil Éireann as its own independent legislative assembly in January 1919 from those Sinn Féin MPs elected to the House of Commons in 1918 and not already in British custody. Consequently, it could pose as an alternative government, although most IRA units had only a tenuous connection to the Republic proclaimed by the Dáil and resisted taking the oath of loyalty that its 'minister of defence' instituted.

Dispersal of IRA units and their part-time nature assisted security. In rural areas, most appear to have been small farmers, farm labourers and shop assistants from a rural background. In urban areas, they were largely skilled or white-collar workers. Most were unmarried and young. But their scale of operations was always limited by the availability of weapons and ammunition. Indeed, in many respects, the conflict was characterised by attempts at arms raids by the IRA from landowners and the security forces, and arms seizures by army and police. In the summer of 1920, the IRA developed the concept of the 'active service' units or flying columns, relying largely on ambushes of army and police patrols such as that at Kilmichael in Cork in November 1920, in which seventeen 'cadets' of the RIC Auxiliary Division were killed. This was in itself largely a result of men being forced on the run by an increasing conviction rate of suspects seized under the Restoration of Order in Ireland Act, which brought a wide range of offences under the jurisdiction of the military courts. Moreover, while successful attacks by the flying columns would result in greater British casualties, they were not frequent, and larger groups were more vulnerable to British counter-attack, so that IRA casualties rose faster than those of the British. Certainly in Cork, most planned ambushes brought no contact with the British, and the columns were largely broken up into less vulnerable squads in early 1921.

The IRA's general headquarters often had little control over events in the provinces and was as ready as the British to seek a settlement by 1921. Both the IRA director of intelligence, Michael Collins, and the chief of staff, Richard Mulcahy, believed that the struggle could not be prolonged without the IRA being broken in view of the increasing success of British arms seizures and the recent massive reinforcement of the British security forces by seventeen infantry battalions in June and July 1921.

It might be argued that the IRA campaign succeeded largely through the lack of political direction on the British side. Nevertheless, Ireland did provide lessons for the future and had a considerable impact. The nationalist Ba Maw, who led the Japanese-sponsored administration in Burma during the Second World War, avidly read Sinn Féin literature during the 1930s, while a biography of Collins and the memoirs of Dan Breen were both translated into Burmese by the All Burma Youth League. Similarly, the future leader of the Japanese-sponsored Indian National Army, Subhas Chandra Bose, suggested that his followers in the New Violence Party, founded in 1927, study the IRA. Another keen student of the IRA's methods was the Russian-born Zionist Vladimir Jabotinsky, the founder of Irgun Zvai Leumi (National Military Organisation), and it has been suggested that Jabotinsky's successor, Menachem Begin, consciously followed the Irish model in shaping the Irgun's terrorist strategy against the British in Palestine between 1944 and 1947. It has likewise been suggested that there was an Irish influence on the group that broke from the Irgun in 1940, Lehame Herut Israel (Fighters for the Freedom of Israel) or LEHI, popularly known as the Stern Gang, and even

George Grivas, in the 1950s military leader of the Greek Cypriot terrorist group Ethniki Organosis Kyprion Agoniston (National Organisation of Cypriot Fighters, EOKA).

The IRA also inspired the establishment of the British Special Operations Executive (SOE) by Lawrence Grand and J.C.F. Holland during the Second World War. Holland had seen service with T.E. Lawrence in 1917–18, but he also served in Ireland in 1921. He was asked by the War Office to undertake a study of irregular warfare in 1938. While Holland worked in a new department of the General Staff, GS(R), Grand became first head of Section D of the Special Intelligence Service (SIS), the section being established after the German annexation of Austria. The first head of SOE's operations division, Colin Gubbins, had also served in Ireland with Holland as well as in North Russia in 1919. Seconded to assist Holland in 1938, Gubbins produced two pamphlets, *The Art of Guerrilla Warfare* and *Partisan Leader's Handbook*, which were eventually translated into sixteen languages for distribution during the Second World War. However, it should be noted that SOE, which was formally established in July 1940, was embraced enthusiastically by the British prime minister, Winston Churchill, who had been in South Africa as war correspondent and soldier. Moreover, Churchill revived the name 'commandos' in 1940 for special army and marine units intended to raid behind German lines.

Three individual guerrilla leaders are also worth mentioning as displaying a thoroughly modern understanding of the political and socio-economic potential of insurgency, namely Nestor Makhno, Augusto Sandino and Thomas Edward Lawrence. Makhno was a Ukrainian anarchist who fought against the Bolsheviks in the latter stages of the Russian Civil War (1917–21). At the peak of his power, Makhno had 25,000 men in his Insurgent Revolutionary Army. His forces showed far more discipline than might be implied by the anarchist ideology they expounded – at one stage, he operated four armoured trains – and he forced the Bolsheviks to make a number of temporary accommodations with him between 1919 and 1920 due to their pressing need to continue the struggle against the White Russian armies. Makhno's appeal was essentially agrarian, and the majority of his leading adherents came from the substantial village of Gulai Polye and its immediate vicinity. However, he also operated from across the Romanian frontier and eventually fled into Romania in August 1921 once the Bolsheviks were able to concentrate against him. An estimated 200,000 peasants died in the suppression of his revolt.

Perhaps even more significant was Augusto Sandino, a Nicaraguan radical, who waged a campaign against the Nicaraguan National Guard and its US marine allies between 1927 and 1933. American marines had frequently been landed in Nicaragua to restore order, as in 1910 and 1912–13, and a substantial legation guard was not withdrawn until 1925. American withdrawal only prompted further internecine political violence between competing conservative and liberal factions, however, and the marines returned to Nicaragua in December 1926. It was agreed that the Americans would disarm both conservatives and liberals. Sandino, then a relatively minor liberal leader in Nueva Segovia province in northern Nicaragua, refused to lay down his weapons and began to wage a guerrilla campaign in July 1927. While depicted initially by the Americans as a 'mule thief' and then as a communist, Sandino's ideology was vague and more religious mysticism than revolutionary. His motivation was solely to expel the American presence, as suggested by the title given to his movement, the Defending Army of the National Sovereignty of Nicaragua.

In ideological terms, therefore, Sandino was not a precursor of future revolutionary guerrillas, but aspects of his campaign certainly looked to the future. Weapons were improvised, such as dynamite bombs, but Sandino's men also had Thompson sub-machine guns. There was also a high degree of sophistication in targeting American-owned companies, especially the properties of the Standard Fruit Company in eastern Nicaragua, at a time of labour unrest on the banana plantations. Sandino also tried to disrupt the internal presidential elections in both 1928 and 1932 and enjoyed foreign recognition from the Communist International's Sixth World Congress in 1928, although he soon broke from his Salvadoran and Venezuelan communist advisers, Farabundo Martí and Gustavo Machardo. Indeed, he rejected any idea of land redistribution, believing that sufficient vacant land was already in public ownership. Curiously, there was also a Sandino division in the Chinese nationalist Kuomintang (Nationalist Party, KMT) army.

Within Nicaragua, Sandino enjoyed considerable support, particularly among the indigenous Indians, and he established his own administration in many areas. The intervention proved less and less popular in the United States and, in December 1930, it was announced that the marines would be withdrawn substantially by June 1931 and entirely after the 1932 election. An agreement was then reached between Sandino and the Nicaraguan government in February 1933, with Sandino laying down his arms in return for an amnesty and retiring to an agricultural co-operative. He was subsequently arrested and executed by the National Guard in February 1934.

The third individual and arguably one of the most influential theorists of the twentieth century in terms of revolutionary war was not a revolutionary at all, but T.E. Lawrence (1888–1935). Lawrence's precise role in the 'Arab Revolt' against the Turks during the First World War remains a matter of some controversy. There is little doubt that his military achievements were exaggerated, not only by his own hand but also by that of the British military writer Basil Liddell Hart, who saw Lawrence's theories and methods as ideally complementary to his own concept of the 'indirect approach'. In essence, the Arab revolt was a sideshow in a subsidiary theatre of war, although it has been calculated that 3,000 Arabs tied down up to 50,000 Turkish troops. Nevertheless, the significance of the campaign derived from Lawrence's account of it, in which it might be added he generally underestimated the impact of the British army's conventional operations against the Turks in Palestine. Arguably, Lawrence also appears to be an original theorist because he had no literary competitors among contemporary practitioners, but there have been few better descriptions of guerrilla conflict.

Lawrence's writings on guerrilla warfare began with an article in *Army Quarterly* in 1920. However, it was *Seven Pillars of Wisdom*, published privately in 1926 and made available in an abridged version for wider public consumption as *Revolt in the Desert* in the following year, and especially an article, 'The Science of Guerrilla Warfare' in the *Encyclopaedia Britannica* in 1927, which represented a classic and elegant exposition of the possibilities of guerrilla warfare, based on a sound assessment of the political implications for Arab nationalism. In common with other writers, Lawrence expounded on the military aspects of guerrilla warfare, believing victory would result from the key factors of mobility, security, time and doctrine. He stressed the importance of secure base areas and the exploitation of space by small and highly mobile forces furnished with good intelligence. As he expressed it,

> Armies were like plants, immobile as a whole, firm rooted through long stems to the head. We might be a vapour, blowing where we listed. Our kingdoms lay in each man's mind, and as we wanted nothing material to live on, so perhaps we offered nothing to the killing. It seemed a regular soldier might be helpless without a target, owning only what he sat on, and subjugating only what, by order, he could poke his rifle at.

Above all, Lawrence perceived the importance of popular support, claiming that a successful rebellion could be accomplished with only 2 per cent active support among the population, providing the remaining 98 per cent either sympathised with, or acquiesced in, guerrilla activity. As Lawrence again expressed it, 'We had won a province when we had taught the civilians in it to die for our ideal of freedom'. Indeed, Lawrence believed the printing press 'the greatest weapon in the armoury of the modern commander'. Among his three defined functions of command – algebraic, biological and psychological – the last embraced the motivation of both guerrilla and population and, also, the undermining of the morale of one's opponent. Allegedly, Mao Tse-tung read Lawrence, although this seems unlikely, but Lawrence did influence Orde Wingate, who would raise the Special Night Squads against Arab irregulars during the second Arab Revolt (1936–39) and later, the Chindits in the Second World War. Clearly, however, Lawrence's exposition of guerrilla warfare marked the transition that was taking place.

Although it is often thought that the Spanish Civil War (1936–39) was a significant guerrilla conflict, it was largely fought as a conventional war. The Spanish nationalist army did initially employ mobile columns as used against the Rifs in Spanish Morocco, where General Francisco Franco had first made his reputation. The nationalists, however, soon developed along conventional lines. Equally, the republicans failed to develop guerrilla units, since the conservative leadership doubted the military value of guerrilla tactics, and the political leadership distrusted the potential political independence of such units. The republicans had the so-called Fourth Guerrilla Corps, but it was trained by Soviet advisers for sabotage rather than guerrilla warfare. However, some participants in the war, such as the commander of the British battalion in the republican XV International Brigade, Tom Wintringham, did develop a good grasp of guerrilla tactics. Indeed, in May 1940 Wintringham established an unofficial training school in 'ungentlemanly warfare' at Osterley Park in Middlesex, intended to instruct the new Local Defence Volunteers (LDV), later the Home Guard, in ways of resisting the expected German invasion. Wintringham's wartime publications included *New Ways of Warfare* (1940), *Armies of Frogmen* (1940), *People's War* (1942) and *Weapons and Tactics* (1943). Other Spanish Civil War veterans of the International Brigades such as John Langdon-Davies and Hugh Slater also made their expertise available. However, the War Office was quick to take over Osterley Park, and the idea of a 'people's militia' found little favour among professional soldiers, who were deeply suspicious of both radicalism and unorthodox tactics. In June 1942, any guerrilla role for the Home Guard was officially ruled out.

By the beginning of the Second World War, guerrilla warfare was beginning to change and to develop into something that was more than simply a tactical method. Indeed, some theorists and practitioners had recognised the possibility of using guerrilla techniques in the pursuit of overtly political ends. These possibilities were to be investigated further during the Second World War by some European resistance movements, notably those influenced by communism as in Yugoslavia. Especially, however, the new emphasis was to be demonstrated by Asian revolutionaries, the most influential of all being Mao Tse-tung, whose own theories of revolutionary guerrilla warfare had steadily evolved through the 1930s.

Further reading

On banditry, see E.J. Hobsbawm, *Primitive Rebels* (New York, 1965) and *Bandits* (London, 1969). For the history of guerrilla warfare generally, see John Ellis, *A Short History of Guerrilla Warfare* (London, 1975); L.H. Gann, *Guerrillas in History* (Stanford, 1971); Walter Laqueur, *Guerrilla: A Historical and Critical Study* (London, 1977); John Pimlott (ed.), *Guerrilla Warfare* (London, 1985); Robert Asprey, *War in the Shadows* (London, 1976); Robin Corbett (ed.), *Guerrilla Warfare* (London, 1986). For the period between 1775 and 1865, see Anthony James Joes, *Guerrilla Conflict before the Cold War* (Westport, 1996). See also Anthony James Joes, *Guerrilla Warfare: A Historical, Biographical and Bibliographical Source Book* (Westport, 1996).

For more theoretical analyses, see Bard O'Neill, *Insurgency and Terrorism: Inside Modern Revolutionary Warfare* (Washington, 1990); Sam Sarkesian, *Revolutionary Guerrilla Warfare* (Chicago, 1975); Dougas Blaufarb and George Tanham, *Who Will Win?: A Key to the Puzzle of Revolutionary War* (New York, 1989); and J. Bowyer Bell, *The Dynamics of Armed Struggle* (London, 1998).

On the American experience in the eighteenth century, see Daniel Beattie, 'The Adaptation of the British Army to Wilderness Warfare, 1755–63' in Maarten Ultee (ed.), *Adapting to Conditions: War and Society in the Eighteenth Century* (Alabama, 1986), pp. 56–83; Michael Adams, 'Too Dumb to Take Cover: American Myths of the Redcoat Soldier', *Bulletin of the Military Historical Society* 51 (2000), pp. 25–32; John Shy, *A People Numerous and Armed: Reflections on the Military Struggle for American Independence* (2nd edn, Ann Arbor, 1990); John Dederer, *Making Bricks Without Straw: Nathanael Greene's Southern Campaign and Mao Tse-tung's Mobile War* (Manhattan, 1983); Paul Smith, *Loyalists and Redcoats: A Study in British Revolutionary Policy* (Chapel Hill, 1964); Clyde Ferguson, 'Functions of the Partisan-Militia in the South during the American Revolution: An Interpretation' in W. Robert Higgins (ed.), *The Revolutionary War in the South: Power, Conflict and Leadership* (Durham, 1979), pp. 238–58; Ronald Hoffman, Thad Tate and Peter Albert, *An Uncivil War: The Southern Backcountry during the American Revolution* (Charlottesville, 1985); Daniel Fitz-Simons, 'Francis Marion, the "Swamp Fox": An Anatomy of a Low-intensity Conflict', *Small Wars and Insurgencies* 6 (1995), pp. 1–16; John Waghelstein, 'Regulars, Irregulars and Militia: The American Revolution' in *ibid.*, pp. 133–58; and Mark Kwasny, *Washington's Partisan War, 1775–83* (Kent, 1996).

On the Spanish guerrillas, see John Tone, *The Fatal Knot: The Guerrilla War in Navarre and the Defeat of Napoleon* (Chapel Hill, 1994); Charles Esdaile, 'Heroes or Villains?: The Spanish Guerrillas in the Peninsular War' *History Today* 38, 4 (1988), pp. 29–35; Esdaile, 'Wellington and the Spanish Guerrillas: The Campaign of 1813' *Proceedings of the Consortium on Revolutionary Europe* (1991), pp. 298–306; Esdaile, 'Heroes or Villains Revisited: Fresh Thoughts on La Guerrilla' in Ian Fletcher (ed.), *The Peninsular War: Aspects of the Struggle for the Iberian Peninsula* (Staplehurst, 1998), pp. 93–114; Esdaile, *The Wars of Napoleon* (London, 1995); and Shell Kimble and Patrick O'Sullivan, 'Terrain and Guerrilla Warfare in Navarre', paper presented at Terrain in Military History Conference, University of Greenwich, January 2000.

For other guerrilla struggles during the French Revolutionary and Napoleonic Wars, see Anthony James Joes, 'Insurgency and Genocide: La Vendée' *Small Wars and Insurgencies* 9 (1998), pp. 17–45; Peter Paret, *Internal War and Pacification: La Vendée, 1789–96* (Princeton, 1961); Milton Finley, *The Most Monstrous of Wars: The Napoleonic Guerrilla War in Southern Italy, 1806–11* (Columbia, 1994); and F.G. Eyck, *Loyal Rebels: Andreas Hofer and the Tyrolean Uprising of 1809* (New York, 1986).

For the Greek War of Independence, see Dennis Skiotis, 'Mountain

Warriors and the Greek Revolution' in V.J. Parry and M.E. Yapp (eds), *War, Technology and Society in the Middle East* (London, 1975), pp. 308–29. For Poland, see Emanuel Halicz, *Partisan Warfare in Nineteenth Century Poland: The Development of a Concept* (Odense, 1975).

On the American Civil War, see Michael Fellman, *Inside War: The Guerrilla Conflict in Missouri during the American Civil War* (New York, 1989); Fellman, 'At the Nihilist Edge: Reflections on Guerrilla Warfare during the American Civil War' in Stig Förster and Jörg Nagler (eds), *On the Road to Total War: The American Civil War and the German Wars of Unification, 1861–71* (Cambridge, 1997), pp. 519–40; Daniel E. Sutherland (ed.), *Guerrillas, Unionists and Violence on the Confederate Home Front* (Fayetteville, 1999); Noel Fisher, *War at Every Door: Partisan Politics and Guerrilla Violence in East Tennessee, 1860–69* (Chapel Hill, 1995); Sean Michael O'Brien, *Mountain Partisans: Guerrilla Warfare in the Southern Appalachians, 1861–65* (Westport, 1999); Benjamin Cooling, *Fort Donelson's Legacy: War and Society in Kentucky and Tennessee, 1861–63* (Knoxville, 1997); William Trotter, *Bushwhackers: The Civil War in North Carolina. The Mountains* (Winston-Salem, 1988); Jeffry Wert, *Mosby's Rangers* (New York, 1990); and Anthony James Joes, 'After Appomattox: The Guerrilla War That Never Was' *Small Wars and Insurgencies* 8 (1997), pp. 52–70.

For Ireland, see Charles Townshend, 'The Irish Republican Army and the Development of Guerrilla Warfare, 1916–21' *English Historical Review* 94 (1979), pp. 318–45; M.R.D. Foot, 'The IRA and the Origins of SOE' in M.R.D. Foot (ed.), *War and Society* (London, 1973), pp. 57–69; Tom Bowden, *The Breakdown of Public Security: The Case of Ireland, 1916–21 and Palestine, 1936–39* (London, 1977); Andrew Selth, 'Ireland and Insurgency: The Lessons of History' *Small Wars and Insurgencies* 2 (1991), pp. 299–322; and Peter Hart, *The IRA and Its Enemies: Violence and Community in Cork, 1916–23* (Oxford, 1998). On the echoes of South African War for Ireland, see Donal Lowry, '"The Boers were the Beginning of the End"?: The Wider Impact of the South African War' in Donal Lowry (ed.), *The South African War Reappraised* (Manchester, 2000), pp. 203–46.

On South Africa itself, see Bill Nasson, *The South African War, 1899–1902* (London, 1999); André Wessels, 'Afrikaners at War' and Fransjohan Pretorius, 'The Experience of the Bitter-ender Boer in the Guerrilla Phase of the South African War' in John Gooch (ed.), *The Boer War: Image, Experience and Direction* (London, 2000), pp. 73–106, 166–86; Pretorius, *Life on Commando during the Anglo-Boer War, 1899–1902* (Cape Town, 1999); and Ian van der Waag, 'South Africa and the Boer Military System' in Peter Dennis and Jeffrey Grey (eds), *The Boer War: Army, Nation and Empire* (Canberra, 2000), pp. 45–69.

On Makhno, see P. Arshinov, *History of the Makhnovist Movement, 1918–21* (Detroit and Chicago, 1974); and M. Malet, *Nestor Makhno in the Russian Civil War* (London, 1982). On Sandino, see G. Selser, *Sandino* (New York, 1981); and N. Macaulay, *The Sandino Affair* (Durham, 1985).

2

THE ROOTS OF COUNTER-INSURGENCY

In discussing counter-insurgency generally, one factor needs to be borne in mind: regular soldiers believe that they exist primarily to fight large-scale conventional wars. In reality, this is usually not their actual experience of practical soldiering. To give one example, the US army fought over 1,000 separate engagements against hostile Indians between 1866 and 1890, yet there was a continuing tendency to regard its only fixed mission, which was one of policing a moving frontier, as a rather tiresome distraction from the study of what was termed 'real war' in Europe. Between 1960 and 1963, civilians in the administration of John F. Kennedy, and the president himself, identified communist-inspired insurgency as the predominant threat to the interests of the United States and, as Kennedy's National Security Action Memorandum No. 124 of 18 January 1962 put it, saw insurgency as a 'major form of politico-military conflict equal in importance to conventional warfare'. However, the army remained wedded to a doctrine suitable only for conventional warfare in Europe. As one American general memorably remarked of Vietnam to an interviewer from the Rand Corporation in 1970, 'I'll be damned if I permit the United States Army, its institutions, its doctrine and its traditions, to be destroyed just to win this lousy war.'

The obsession with 'real war' is equally strong in most armies, including the British and the French. In the case of the French army, it was the supposed undue influence of 'Africans' unfamiliar with European conditions that was blamed for the defeat against the Prussians in 1870–71. For all its wide colonial experience, the French army still clung to the vision, as Paddy Griffith has expressed it, of the 'golden days of Austerlitz and the Boulogne camp', that is of Napoleon's *Grande Armée*. Equally, modern British military doctrine is heavily based on the North-west Europe campaign of 1944–45. Yet, out of 94 separate operational commitments between 1945 and 1982, only fourteen were not in some form of low-intensity commitment. Indeed, the British army's only significant recent conventional experience has been the 35 months of the British participation in the Korean War (1950–53), when only five infantry battalions were deployed at any one time, followed by ten days at Suez in 1956, 24 days of the land campaign in the Falklands in 1982 and 100 hours of land operations in the Gulf War (1990–91).

To some extent, it is institutional conservatism that has guided armies, but the kind of low-intensity conflict that has actually provided the staple operational fare of most modern armies is regarded as distinctly unglamorous. Results will not be obtained quickly, and, in any case, success cannot be measured in conventional military terms of decisive battles won. Careers may not be enhanced even by such success as can be demonstrated. Above all, what one American general has described as 'uncomfortable wars' confront soldiers with political and social pressures to a far greater extent than most other forms of conflict. Small wonder then that there has been such distaste for low-intensity war over the centuries, expressed by one British writer as long ago as 1763, referring to the task facing a friend in North America:

> The War will be a tedious one, nor can it be glorious, even tho'
> attended with success. Instead of decisive battles, woodland skir-
> mishes; instead of colours and a cannon, our trophies will be stinking
> scalps. Heaven preserve you my friend, from a war conducted by a
> spirit of murder rather than of brave and generous offence.

Earlier, an American colonist during 'King Philip's War' in New England in 1675–76 had spoken of the need for the Europeans to respond to the Indian threat by learning the 'skulking way of war'. Similarly, reflecting on the war in Spain between 1808 and 1814, the Swiss military theorist Antoine-Henri Jomini wrote:

> I acknowledge that my prejudices are in favour of the good old times
> when the French and English Guards courteously invited each other
> to fire first – as at Fontenoy – preferring them to the frightful epoch
> when priests, women and children throughout Spain plotted the
> murder of isolated soldiers.

Such attitudes go far to explain why the British army has been accused of an absence of institutional memory by David Charters and of historical amnesia by Tom Mockaitis, and of invariably having to learn the same lessons over and over again when faced by the challenge of insurgency in different campaigns since 1945. Yet in the British case, and in the case of most other armies confronted by the new insurgency after 1945, there was a residue of experience to fall back on. Even if lessons were being transmitted wholly informally from one generation of soldiers to another, there was invariably a particular national tradition of how to go about counter-insurgency stemming from the nineteenth century, if not before.

Indeed, in many ways, the basic necessity of separating the population from the guerrilla became obvious as any such conflict progressed. The Spanish soldier Don Alvaro Navia Osoric, Marqués de Santa Cruz y Marcenado, for example, included sections on counter-guerrilla operations in the twelve volumes of his *Réflections militaires et politiques* (Military and Political Reflections), published between 1724 and 1730. Based on his experiences fighting irregulars in Spain and Sicily and the Moors in North Africa, Santa Cruz advocated the kind of 'hearts and minds' approach familiar to theorists of the twentieth century. He cautioned against trying to alter the traditions and customs of a people under occupation, and he also recommended that amnesties be utilised as soon as military resistance had ceased.

Nonetheless, one would not generally describe the usual practices of armies in the eighteenth and nineteenth centuries faced with insurgency as modern-style counter-insurgency. Indeed, it was little more than unsophisticated counter-terrorism. The French Republican response to the uprising of their fellow Frenchmen in the Vendée, for example, was to pass a law in March 1793 stipulating the death penalty for all rebels. Following the dispersion of the Catholic and Royal Army in December 1793, itself largely accomplished by the transfer of the Army of Mayence to the west following its parole by the Prussians, the war was carried to the population as a whole through the operations of General Turreau's twelve so-called *colonnes infernales* (infernal columns) killing, deporting, burning and confiscating as they marched. Those who took advantage of a proffered government amnesty in early 1794 were simply executed, and the troops were ordered to kill anyone found in areas already cleared. Atrocities against women were all too common, mothers and their 'wolf cubs' alike slaughtered, and priests drowned. Indeed, such was the lack of control that Republican supporters were frequently killed as well. All livestock and other supplies were removed by the *commission civile et administrative* (civil and administrative commission), ironically often depriving their own troops of sustenance. The campaign of suppression has been characterised as 'ideological genocide', costing perhaps 250,000 lives.

With the fall of the Jacobins, who had never grasped the intensity of religious beliefs in the Vendée, a more conciliatory approach was adopted from July 1794 onwards. General Louis-Lazare Hoche introduced a more sophisticated strategy in both the Vendée and Brittany, resistance in the former being assisted by the lack of adequate paved routes and the broken nature of the heavily wooded bocage. While the population was progressively disarmed, Hoche also tolerated the presence of priests, attempted to bring more discipline to his troops and, eventually, concluded truces in both regions by which religious toleration was promised, confiscated property returned and compensation offered for outrages committed by his troops. At the same time, Hoche introduced military measures first suggested by one of his predecessors, Jean Baptiste Kléber, who had been dismissed in December 1793 before he could put them into effect. Strong fortified posts were established around the region to isolate it. Mobile columns then pushed systematically to the west, estab-

lishing new lines of posts, which constantly reduced the freedom of movement of the remaining rebels. Hoche declared the campaigns in the west at an
end in July 1795. Sporadic resistance occurred, however, from time to time
during the ensuing years and, in June 1815, Brittany rose against Napoleon,
forcing him to despatch 30,000 men to the west.

In Calabria, where any peasant caught with weapons was summarily
hanged, Jean-Baptiste Verdier earned a particular reputation for brutality.
Generally, the French garrisoned the towns, constructed new roads and
bridges to speed movement, and employed flying columns to pursue guerrilla
bands. Jean Reynier began to use the locally raised Calabrian Civic Guards
and the mounted Calabrian Chasseurs to supplement his manpower in March
1806. Those recruited tended either to be urban dwellers or those pursuing
personal vendettas, with the result that they did not win the popular support
among the peasantry that French commanders had anticipated. However,
French pressure on the guerrillas increased from November 1810 onwards,
Charles-Antoine Mannès introducing a policy of strict food control to deny
the guerrillas supplies and taking hostages against the good behaviour of
communities. One by one, the bandit leaders were isolated and eliminated.

In Spain, the French were far less successful. It did prove possible to raise
civil guard and other local units in areas such as Andalusia, Aragon and
Catalonia, but not in Navarre. Here, therefore, the French increasingly
resorted to repressive measures. Local authorities were required to conduct a
census to ascertain those absent from home. Initially, fines were imposed if
captured guerrillas proved not to be on the lists. Subsequently, those absent
were assumed to be guerrillas and summarily executed if taken, while fines
were also imposed on heads of household who could not account for absen-
tees. An oath of allegiance was introduced, public meetings forbidden and
public holidays suspended, while troublesome clerics were deported. In
October 1810, General Honoré Reille decreed that four guerrillas would be
hanged for every Frenchman killed and civilians substituted if sufficient guerrillas were not in French hands. Ironically, while such measures reportedly
'cowed the spirit' of Navarre, Reille's concentration on terrorising the population gave some respite to Mina, enabling him to rebuild his force after
suffering a serious reverse in attempting a frontal assault on the garrison of
Tarrazona in October 1810.

The most successful French commander in the guerrilla war, however,
Louis-Gabriel Suchet, took a more conciliatory attitude towards the population, being given command of the III Corps, later designated the Army of
Aragon, in April 1809. Suchet sought 'peaceful co-existence' with the Spanish
population. This was a particular necessity when he never had sufficient
troops to pacify the whole of the province, especially after his jurisdiction was
extended over Catalonia and Valencia in 1810 and, briefly, over Navarre. In an
early proclamation, Suchet promised that his troops would neither impede the
harvest nor be billeted in such a way as to become an unequal burden on any

one location. Religious practices were to be respected and clergy only executed if captured under arms. Suchet also relied largely upon local Aragonese officials, who fixed district taxation quotas independently from the French, augmenting the administration with the few local nobles whose support he could attract. He also tried to supplement his strength with locally raised gendarmerie and civil guards, though their numbers remained no more than 400 from a population of 500,000. More efficient accounting also enabled Suchet to keep his own men better paid than most, reducing the temptation to plunder the local people, and Suchet also endeavoured to keep his men under control. In effect, therefore, Suchet enabled the people to maintain a kind of sullen neutrality.

However, even Suchet could never ensure total pacification, and his efforts were undermined by Napoleon's demands that his army become self-sufficient, so that exploitation rather than pacification became the main aim. In June 1810, for example, Suchet was forced to levy a new tax on Aragon as a fine to suppress brigandage, not in Aragon itself, but in Catalonia and Valencia. Moreover, resources could only be extracted from Aragon if Suchet had all his men available. This was an impossibility given the activities of the guerrillas in Catalonia and Valencia, from which guerrilla raids were then launched into Aragon, whose garrison Suchet had reduced in order to pacify the other two provinces. In many ways, Suchet's military policy, of maintaining strong garrisons to protect and sustain local administration by *afrancesados*, actually surrendered the initiative to the guerrillas. In the field, multi-column sweeps remained the pattern of French operations, hindered more often than not by poor relations between local French commanders as well as by the constant rotation of units, the poor quality of French conscripts, and the increasing lack of troops as Russia rather than Spain took precedence for reinforcements. At the time the French were forced to abandon Aragon in June 1813, it was still the most pacified of the Spanish provinces, but Suchet's success had been at best fleeting.

As a result of the French Revolutionary and Napoleonic Wars, one French soldier at least grasped the importance of subordinating military action to political action, as well as winning hearts and minds. General C.M. Roguet produced studies on urban insurrection, riots and street fighting in 1832, 1839, 1848 and 1850, his ideas being incorporated into the French army's standing orders for street fighting. Roguet's ideas on counter-insurgency, however, as expressed in a history of the campaign in the Vendée, published in 1833, appear to have been regarded as over-intellectual. In particular, Roguet suggested adapting the methods of Suchet to French practice in Algeria. Perhaps significantly, Thomas-Robert Bugeaud, who made his reputation fighting in Algeria against Abd el-Kader between 1840 and 1844, had served under Suchet in Spain. Bugeaud favoured mobile columns undertaking so-called *razzia* or punishment raids, seizing Arab livestock and destroying crops and buildings. Artillery was dispensed with, and those supplies that could not be obtained on the march were carried by mules. But Bugeaud had an under-standing of the relationship between military and political control, and his military operations provided a basis for the extension of French control over the countryside by the officers of the Bureau Arabe (Arab Bureau).

In many respects, however, it was the danger of urban insurrection in France that most interested French officers at this stage, and they were gener-ally successful in countering this, as well as engaging in limited conventional operations in Spain (1823–24), Greece (1827–29) and Belgium (1831–32). By contrast, as Paddy Griffith has remarked, in Algeria 'they were entering unknown territory' in more ways than one. Thus, it took over ten years to come to terms with the special difficulties of colonial campaigning, Bugeaud writing in 1843 that his army was well equipped to conquer Italy but not Algeria.

The US army found it equally difficult to come to terms with its guerrilla opponents in the 1830s and 1840s, the Seminoles of Florida proving particu-larly skilful opponents. Technically Lower Creek refugees from American territory who had moved into Spanish Florida, the Seminoles had also given refuge to runaway slaves. The First Seminole War (1816–18) was essentially American retaliatory action against raids, but Florida was then ceded to the United States by Spain in 1819. When the United States initiated a policy of Indian removal to west of the Mississippi, the Seminoles resisted. Following the ambush of Major Francis Dade's column in the Wahoo swamp of the Withlacoochie River in December 1835, successive American commanders failed to conclude the Second Seminole War (1835–42). Zachary Taylor, a future American president, was able to penetrate the Everglades, winning an action at Lake Okeechobee in December 1837 when the Seminoles opted for once for defence of a fixed position. Facing guerrilla war thereafter, Taylor subdivided the area and undertook constant patrols from his outposts. Crops were destroyed and livestock removed, but the war continued, and Taylor asked to be relieved of command in April 1840.

By the time the war ended, largely by the army announcing it was over, 3,800 Indians had been removed at a total war cost of $14 million, but at least 500 Seminoles remained at large. The Third Seminole War (1855–58) reduced them to 100 or so, who withdrew even further into the swamps. The Mexican War (1846–47) was mostly conventional, but Zachary Taylor, this time commanding in the northern theatre of operations, faced harassing raids on his lines of communication. Consequently, the local Mexican authorities were made responsible for the loss of supplies. Subsequently, one of Taylor's subordinates made the same authorities accountable for all attacks. In the southern theatre, Winfield Scott, who had been one of those who had conspicuously failed against the Seminoles, introduced similar methods, while also winning greater Mexican civilian co-operation by enforcing discipline among his own men.

However, few doctrinal lessons were learned from either the Seminole

Wars or the Mexican War. Consequently, commanders had to improvise when faced with guerrilla attack during the American Civil War. The Union response to guerrillas, therefore, varied widely. Following Quantrill's raid on Lawrence in Kansas in August 1863, four counties in what was ostensibly a state of the Union rather than the Confederacy were forcibly depopulated of 20,000 civilians and their homes burned under the provisions of Brigadier-General Thomas Ewing's General Orders Nos 10 and 11, no distinction being made between Union and Confederate sympathisers. Earlier, apart from prematurely announcing emancipation, John C Frémont's notorious proclamation of August 1861 had included summary execution for those taken in arms in southern Missouri. In the eastern theatre, Order No. 100 – the so-called Lieber Code – drawn up by a distinguished legal scholar, Francis Lieber and issued on 24 April 1863, subjected guerrillas to martial law, although making some attempt to counsel Union commanders to treat innocent civilians with justice. However, it is unlikely that many soldiers took the trouble to digest all of its 157 articles. In any case, the code excluded from protection combatants who did not wear uniform or identifiable insignia, Lieber using a historically based typology to distinguish between the 'regular' partisan and the 'irregular' guerrilla.

As indicated in Chapter 1, there were certain limitations to which both sides subscribed, but 'bushwhackers' could expect no mercy. Thus, although the Lieber Code indicated that even guerrillas were entitled to a military trial, Union commanders routinely discouraged the taking of prisoners. Indeed, it might be noted that, whereas Quantrill had previously executed only captured Jayhawkers, it was Major-General Henry Halleck's declared policy of shooting all captured 'outlaws' in December 1861 that prompted Quantrill to show no quarter himself. Similarly, in September 1864, following U.S. Grant's earlier order that Mosby's men should be hanged on capture, seven of Mosby's men were so executed by George Custer. Mosby promptly retaliated by executing seven of his prisoners.

No quarter, therefore, continued to be exercised, while the population under Union military control in occupied parts of the South was generally subjected to intimidation through application of comprehensive and restrictive oaths of loyalty, confiscation, retributive burning and other destruction of property, selective banishment, arbitrary imprisonment, and executions. In the Shenandoah, part of 'Mosby's Confederacy', all houses within five miles of the railroads were burned and, generally, Philip Sheridan's policy of destroying all resources in the valley reduced the ability of Confederate guerrillas to operate. General Order No. 60, issued in the western theatre in July 1863, imposed collective responsibility for guerrilla activity on local communities, with individuals presumed to have failed to stop guerrilla activity being liable to loss of their property. Increasingly, too, in Missouri, there was little prior attempt to apply distinctions between the loyal and the disaffected before action was taken by Union troops. Hostage taking became prevalent on both sides in eastern Tennessee.

In military terms, occupied towns became the centres for pacification, with former Confederate forts often reconstructed to control the supply routes, including rivers, down which Union gunboats constantly patrolled. However, the number of static guards required was equivalent to at least a third of the Union army's strength in the east and nearer two-thirds in the west. In Arkansas, where the flight of civilians had resulted in a shortage of food supplies, Union forces even resorted to establishing 'fortified colonies', in which small garrisons protected new farming communities, often comprising Unionist refugees from elsewhere. Similarly, after the Union occupation of Tennessee, a loyalist National Guard was established in September 1863 as an additional constabulary.

In facing Unionist partisans and guerrillas, Confederates adopted similar methods, leaving subordinate commanders to judge between conflicting imperatives to end guerrilla activity at all costs yet respect civilians. At Shelton Laurel in North Carolina in January 1863, thirteen suspected guerrillas, including two boys, were summarily executed while supposedly being taken to Knoxville for trial. In eastern Tennessee, martial law was employed to detain loyalists, seize their property and banish their dependants. Conscription was also employed as a weapon against loyalists, forcing several thousand Unionists to flee into Kentucky and thus reducing the threat to their control. Home Guards were raised for local defence against guerrillas, although they were frequently ill disciplined and inclined to pursue their own vendettas.

In Europe, the German army generally observed the conventions of war with regard to civilians in the Franco-Prussian War of 1870–71 but, for all intents and purposes, *francs-tireurs* were regarded as murderers to be disposed of accordingly. Heeding the advice of Sheridan, attached to German head-quarters as an observer, Otto von Bismarck urged that villages be burned down to terrorise the French into rapid submission. The German chief of staff, the elder Helmuth von Moltke, declined to do so. However, it was still the case that, in practice, harsh measures were frequently used. Some German commanders demanded large financial contributions from towns believed to support guerrilla activities, and, on occasions, took hostages and permitted plundering. As the British military theorist Edward Hamley expressed it, the Germans failed to recognise that 'while ascribing influence to fear, they ignore the counter influence of desperation'.

Increasingly, however, most European armies encountered irregular opponents as European colonial empires expanded. The British army, for example, fought 35 major campaigns and many more minor ones between 1872 and 1899. Between 1849 and 1914, there were 52 large-scale expeditions on the North West Frontier of India alone. Similarly, the French campaigned in North and West Africa, Madagascar and Indo-China; the Russians in the Caucasus and Central Asia; the Germans in German South West and German

31

East Africa; the Dutch in the East Indies; the Italians in Libya and Abyssinia; the Spanish in Cuba and the Philippines; and the Portuguese in Portuguese Guinea, Angola and Mozambique. It took the Dutch from 1873 to 1912 to pacify the sultanate of Atjeh (Aceh) in northern Sumatra, while southern Sumatra was not pacified until 1907. In the case of the Portuguese, there were fifteen major campaigns in the Dembos region of northern Angola between 1631 and 1919, and 27 separate revolts in Mozambique between 1878 and 1904. Portuguese Guinea was not pacified until 1936. There were over 60 reported expeditions in German East Africa between 1891 and 1897, an average of four a year between 1897 and 1899, one in 1900, a major campaign in 1903 and then the so-called Maji-Maji rising in 1905–07. Although not essentially an imperial power as such until 1898, as already indicated, the United States faced a series of Indian wars prior to 1890. But American power was also projected overseas. Between 1867 and 1900, for example, US marines went ashore eight times on Haiti and had intervened in Nicaragua nine times by 1912.

The problem was that the kind of enemies encountered and usually, but not always, defeated by European armies were widely divergent in character-istics and methods. Accordingly, the British had no standard manual until the publication by the War Office in 1896 of Charles Callwell's celebrated *Small Wars: Their Principles and Practice*. Based on the wealth of colonial experience over the past century, Callwell's book divided colonial campaigns into three broad categories: campaigns of conquest and annexation; campaigns of pacifi-cation to suppress insurrection or restore order; and punitive campaigns intended as retaliation for particular outrages, although they might also inci-dentally extend European control.

Most expeditions were as much against terrain and climate as against human opponents. Often the Europeans fought against topographical igno-rance, whereas their opponents had local knowledge. Communications were frequently tenuous and at risk, and time was often against expeditions in terms of disease or climatic change. In 1870, for example, during Sir Garnet (later Field Marshal Lord) Wolseley's Red River campaign in the Canadian North-West, there was a need to get to Fort Garry and back before the lakes and rivers froze. In his Ashanti campaign in 1873–74, Wolseley could not risk European troops for long before they succumbed to disease. Certainly, exten-sive preparations were needed, as in the Abyssinian expedition of 1867–68 and Ashanti. Even as late as the South African War, the 7,792 British battle dead were outnumbered by the 13,250 who died from disease. Between 1868 and 1878, the Spanish army in Cuba lost an estimated 30,000 troops to yellow fever alone in the so-called 'Long War' against Cuban insurgents, while the subsequent campaign between 1895 and 1898 cost another 44,000 dead, nearly all from disease. Each kind of terrain also posed its own problems, with the need to take the high ground in mountain warfare, the need to move along single tracks in jungle, the need to fire clearing volleys in bush, as in

West Africa, and the need to build *zaribas* of thorn or *laagers* of waggons in open country like the Sudan or Zululand.

Numbers were often small in action, even if large numbers could be put into a campaign, as in the South African War where, of the eventual 450,000 British and imperial troops deployed, probably only 10 per cent were actually in the field, with the remainder on lines of communication. Indeed, on campaign there was a tendency to split columns, which could lead to disaster, as for George Custer at the Little Big Horn in June 1876. Generally, indeed, the Europeans often courted disaster. The British were defeated by the Zulus at Isandlwana in January 1879, and by the Boers at Majuba in February 1881. The French were defeated at Lang Son in French Indo-China in March 1885 and had a number of columns overwhelmed in West Africa. The Italians were defeated by the Abyssinians at Adowa (Adua) in March 1896, the latter costing General Oreste Baratieri 11,700 casualties in dead, wounded and captured out of his army of 17,000 men. As late as July 1921, a Spanish army fighting Abd el-Krim of the Rifs in Spanish Morocco lost 12,000 dead at Anual, including its commander, Fernández Silvestre.

Indeed, it might be argued that the indigenous populations held the strategic advantage. It was often difficult for the Europeans to identify a suitable strategic centre, the emphasis often being on capitals, which might not hold that much significance for their opponents. In such cases, as Wolseley once wrote, the objective should be 'the capture of whatever they prize most, and the destruction or deprivation of which will probably bring the war most rapidly to a conclusion'. Clearly, however, the Europeans usually had the tactical advantages deriving from better discipline and organisation, more advanced technology, and a monopoly of firepower over most indigenous opponents. As suggested by Hilaire Belloc's ditty – 'Whatever happens we have got, the Maxim Gun which they have not' – Gatling, Nordenfelt, Gardner and Maxim machine guns increasingly appeared in British campaigns, as at Ulundi in Zululand in 1879, Abu Klea in the Sudan in 1885, and, especially, at Omdurman during the reconquest of the Sudan in 1898. There, for the loss of just 48 dead, the British and Egyptian forces destroyed an army of 52,000 Dervishes, killing an estimated 11,000 of them: 500,000 rounds of ammunition were discharged. Similarly, it has been calculated that the Imperial Russian army suffered only 2,000 battle casualties in all its many Central Asian campaigns between 1847 and 1873. The United States, likewise, suffered only 151 combat deaths in Central America and the Caribbean in the whole of the nineteenth century and first half of the twentieth century.

However, early machine guns were not always reliable, and artillery might also be of limited utility in rugged terrain. Moreover, although some indigenous armies had great difficulties acquiring modern firearms, and, even when they did, as in West Africa, often stood up to fire breechloaders as if they were muskets, this was not universally so. The Abyssinian army that defeated the Italians at Adowa, for example, had acquired 100,000 rifles and two million tons of ammunition from French Somaliland. Similarly, George Custer's troopers were outgunned at the Little Big Horn by Indians armed with repeating rifles. However, the only known use of machine guns against Europeans was by mutinous Sudanese troops in Uganda in 1897.

If technology generally supported the Europeans, an additional help was that their indigenous opponents often continued to fight each other, and it was rare for the Europeans to face alliances. Indeed, divide and rule worked to the favour of the Europeans. Of course, an important aspect of divide and rule was the use made by the colonial powers of native troops. Perhaps the best example is Britain's Indian army, maintained at the expense of the Indian taxpayer and used by the British in Abyssinia in 1867, Perak (Malaya) in 1875, and in Egypt and the Sudan at varying times between 1882 and 1898. An Indian expeditionary force was even despatched to Malta in 1878 in case of war between Britain and Russia and was used subsequently to occupy Cyprus. France had a colourful array of native troops, including Zouaves, Turcos and Spahis in North Africa and the Tirailleurs Sénégalais, who policed French West and Central Africa. Belgium, the Netherlands, Italy, Spain, Imperial Germany and Portugal also depended largely upon locally raised military and police forces. In the United States, Indian scouts were employed, especially by George Crook, who was particularly successful in using Apache scouts to track down other Apaches. However, there was resistance to recruiting larger units, and it was only in 1893 that Captain Arthur Wagner's *The Service of Security and Information* described the tactics of Apache scout companies in the field.

Such locally raised troops were less liable to disease than Europeans, while, in the case of the Indian army, it fitted well into the structure of traditional society providing a framework in which family and caste links could play their part. The British tended to indulge in the theory of 'martial races' after the Mutiny not only in India but Africa as well, identifying some racial groups or tribes as more suitable for soldiering than others. Thus, in India, Gurkhas, Sikhs and Dogras from the north were preferred to any groups from Bengal, Madras or Bombay. In East Africa, Angoni and Yao were preferred to Masai and Swahili. The Royal Dutch Indies army maintained a similar policy, preferring Ambonese soldiers, although this was expressed more in terms of their loyalty and Christianity rather than inherited military attributes. Ironically, the Javanese, who were considered inferior, tended to come forward in larger numbers. In the Philippines, the American-raised constabulary known as the Philippine Scouts was mainly recruited in February 1901 from Ilocanos, Visayans and, especially, Macabebes, although there was no conscious martial races policy. Service in the well-paid constabulary was a clear indication of the rewards available to the loyal, and it should be noted that military service generally was often a deliberate choice of the ruled for reasons of reward of varying kinds, both material and spiritual.

Apart from weapons, other technology that counted in the favour of the

Europeans included the field railway, the heliograph (first used in the Second Afghan War), the field telegraph and steam power, which generally took European forces up navigable waterways, as in the First Burma War of 1824–26 or in the Dutch East Indies. Also, if slowly, there was the development of medicine and, although the mosquito was not identified as a bearer of malaria until 1898, quinine was used regularly from the 1840s onwards as a preventive.

In trying to synthesise the varied nature of colonial warfare, Callwell, who had first rehearsed his theories in contributions to the *Proceedings of the Royal Artillery Institution* in 1884 and 1885 and then in a prize-winning essay at the Royal United Services Institution in 1887, 'Lessons to be Learned from the Campaigns in which British forces have been employed since the year 1865', did not confine himself to British experience. His work represented a real willingness on the part of at least some soldiers to assimilate collective lessons. Indeed, it can be argued that Callwell made the only distinctive contribution by any British soldier to the development of military thought in the nineteenth century. However, it should be noted that Wolseley had issued a pamphlet on jungle warfare tactics in Ashanti in 1873–74 and that some specialist essays or articles on hill warfare had been published by British officers of the Indian army following the Umbeyla campaign of 1863, although their impact was limited. Similarly, the Black Mountain expedition of 1888 and the large-scale revolt on the North West Frontier in 1897–98 led to further publications such as Francis Younghusband's *Indian Frontier Warfare* in 1898 and C. Miller Maguire's *Strategy and Tactics in Mountain Ranges* in 1904.

Callwell added a chapter on hill warfare to his second edition in 1899, but there was no official manual devoted to hill warfare until the appearance of *Frontier Warfare*, produced by the Adjutant-General's Department in India in 1900. To cover the Burmese theatre of operations, an appendix, *Bush Fighting*, was added to the manual in 1903. The two sections were then combined in *Frontier Warfare and Bush Fighting* in 1906. The opening of an Indian Staff College at Quetta then prompted the publication of W.D. Bird's *Some Principles of Frontier Mountain Warfare* in 1909. Like Callwell and others before him, Bird stressed the importance of offensive action, noting that 'savages' were only formidable when you were running away from them. The British army, however, as opposed to the Indian army, took little notice, adding just six paragraphs on hill warfare to a new chapter on 'warfare in uncivilised countries' in *Field Service Regulations* in 1912. One unofficial contribution by a British officer to bush warfare theory was W.C.G. Heneker's *Bush Warfare*, published in 1904 and drawing mostly on West African campaigns.

Callwell, who remained the principal guide for British officers, cautioned against becoming involved in guerrilla warfare if at all possible, recognising that:

> the crushing of a populace in arms, the stamping out of widespread disaffection by military methods, is a harassing form of warfare even

in a civilised country with a settled social system. In remote regions peopled by half civilised races or wholly savage tribes such campaigns are most difficult to bring to a satisfactory conclusion.

Thus, there was a need to bring guerrillas to battle before they could disperse and a great emphasis upon offensive action. Many of Callwell's operational principles were outdated in contemporary European warfare, such as the use of rallying squares, which would have been suicidal against Europeans with modern weapons. Callwell himself believed machine guns not proven sufficiently to be used in Europe, where Europeans would not be so foolish as to walk into their fire. He also believed cavalry retained its usefulness in colonial campaigning. Other principles, however, such as the stress Callwell placed on the importance of intelligence, and the need to seize the initiative with boldness and vigour, remain relevant to the present.

Certainly, too, Callwell identified some common approaches that were emerging entirely independently in different armies faced with the same kind of difficulties. Thus, in the British campaign against the Boers in the latter stages of the South African War, the Spanish campaign on Cuba between 1895 and 1898 and the US campaign in the Philippines between 1899 and 1902, all three armies adopted what became known as reconcentration. The gathering of a civilian population in guarded locations to deny guerrillas in the field ready access to food or other material support from civilians was not a new idea. The Russians, for example, had introduced 'slow strangulation' against the Murids, the fanatical Islamic monastic order led by Shamil in the Caucasus in the 1840s, cutting the guerrillas off from the population by a *cordon sanitaire* of military outposts allied to a political offensive to restore proprietary and social rights to tribal leaders usurped by the Murids.

In the case of the Spanish on Cuba, Valeriano 'Butcher' Weyler, who assumed command in November 1896, revived a system already briefly used on the island in the 1870s by constructing successive fortified lines across the island from west to east. It was based on blockhouses and wired fieldworks in clearings in the jungle known as *trocha*. At the same time, small mobile columns combed the areas behind these fortified lines but also reconcentrated the population and imposed a range of emergency laws, including the death penalty. In fact, it was largely a defensive strategy forced on Weyler due to the high rates of sickness among his men and the general incompetence of many of his subordinates.

Weyler was removed due to American pressure in October 1897, the continuing Spanish campaign being an important factor in the subsequent outbreak of the Spanish–American War. Ironically, when faced with Filipino insurgency after occupying the former Spanish colony, the Americans themselves were forced to adopt reconcentration. Commanded by Douglas MacArthur's father, Arthur MacArthur, the American forces began to move the rural population into towns in December 1900, reissuing the Civil War vintage Order No. 100. In the province of Batangas, Brigadier-General Franklin Bell reconcentrated 10,000 people into protective zones and destroyed all crops, livestock and buildings outside these zones. Bell's methods, and those of Brigadier-General Jacob Smith on the island of Samar, were widely criticised. Following the massacre of an American infantry company at Balangiga in September 1901, Smith had directed that no prisoners be taken and all males over the age of ten be executed.

Smith was court-martialled and admonished, while the situation in Batangas was subject to a Senate hearing. However, it has emerged that, although the population of Batangas declined by 90,000 between 1896 and 1902, the key factors in what has been characterised as a 'demographic disaster' were 'mosquitoes, micro parasites and *carabos* (cattle)'. In other words, it was not resettlement, to which perhaps 11,000 of the deaths can be directly attributed, but a malarial epidemic, the epidemiological origins of which long pre-dated even the beginning of the struggle against Spain in 1896, which depopulated the province. Reconcentration continued to be used in the case of serious local disturbances in the Philippines after 1902, while American outposts generally were intended to become a focus for the local population, who would thus be exposed to the full benefit of colonial rule.

In many ways, reconcentration was also an extension of the reservation policy, which had contributed to the suppression of the Indians on the Great Plains. An offensive against Indian food supplies and Indian pony herds, particularly by campaigning through the winter when food was scarce and the ponies weakened, had driven the tribes into the reservations. There was a problem, however, in that Indians could leave their women and children on the reservations while off raiding and then hide back among the reservation population. Reservations might also be considered symptomatic of another aspect of the American approach to pacification, namely 'civic action', by which was meant extending the benefits of civilisation through such means as vigorous sanitation campaigns and public works projects. Some army officers had undertaken some aspects of civic action when the army controlled reservation policy and, together with Captain Richard Pratt, General Nelson Miles had established an Indian School at Carlisle in Pennsylvania in 1879.

Within the newly expanding American empire after 1898, an example of the civic action tradition was the 'attraction' programme in the Philippines, which went hand in hand with military measures, General Elwell Otis beginning the building of schools and a variety of public works projects to improve communications and health. It was a policy continued by Arthur MacArthur, and it is significant that the controversial campaigns on Samar and in Batangas occurred after MacArthur had been succeeded in overall command by the less committed Adna Chaffee. Another example was the work of Brigadier-General John Pershing among the Moros on Jolo and Mindanao between 1909 and 1913, with the establishment of a general store, industrial training stations and a homestead for squatters. However, the imposition of American cultural values could itself be problematic. The abolition of slavery had prompted the Moros to revolt in 1903, and they did so again when Pershing tried to disarm them in 1911. Similarly, the *cacos* revolt on Haiti in 1919 resulted from Major Smedley Butler's attempt to enforce a little-used law compelling Haitians to undertake regular road maintenance. American insistence on proper sanitation was not always appreciated, while the insistence on fiscal and political integrity implicit in the American approach equally proved too great a shock for many communities in the Caribbean and Central America.

Problems were also posed by the paradoxical attitudes of Americans, which made it difficult to comprehend the nature of their irregular opponents. On the one hand, there could be a certain sympathy for those who, like Americans themselves in the past, were fighting for 'freedom'. Yet Americans also displayed considerable contempt for other races, to the extent that even black American troops in the Philippines described their opponents as 'goo-goos'. Although contemporary accounts, and those of many later historians, were greatly exaggerated, there were still 117 verifiable atrocities against Filipinos between 1898 and 1902.

Nonetheless, at least a theoretical base for what might be termed 'benevolent pacification' was established, through the study by the head of the military information department, Captain J.R.M. Taylor, of the campaign in the Philippines. Taylor's study was suppressed, however, due to the political controversies surrounding the conduct of the campaign and his criticism of the American civil administration. In any case, it has been argued that Taylor was more interested in collecting documents than analysing them, with the result that the study had the appearance of a somewhat fragmented compendium. Consequently, the lessons were not widely disseminated. Thus, the 1905 field service regulations and the 1911 infantry regulations gave little attention to guerrilla warfare. Nor had there been any official texts as a result of the Indian wars, although Edward G. Farrow's *Mountain Scouting* (1881) was a popular unofficial guide to tactics.

In the third characteristic campaign at the turn of the century in South Africa, the mobility of the Boer commandos was progressively restricted by lavish use of blockhouses and wire on the *veld*, mobile columns driving the Boers back on to these defences, and by the systematic removal of Boer civilians to what were called 'concentration camps' while farms and crops were destroyed and livestock removed. Initially, following the capture of Bloemfontein in March 1900, Field Marshal Lord Roberts had issued proclamations safeguarding Boer property and allowing Boers who took an oath of loyalty to return to their homes. In June 1900, however, in the face of the emerging guerrilla activity, Roberts ordered that houses in the vicinity of any railway lines, bridges and telegraph lines that had been attacked should be burned down or blown up. Collective fines were also instituted and, briefly, Boer civilians were compelled to ride on trains as a deterrent against attack.

Military administration had been imposed on both the Boer republics, with martial law declared in the Orange Free State in March 1900 and in the Transvaal in September 1900. More controversially, martial law was also imposed in Cape Colony for fear of a rising among the Cape Afrikaners, resulting in considerable friction between the army and local politicians.

However, a problem was posed by the civilians evicted from those homes destroyed as well as by the number of refugees gathering, first in Bloemfontein and then in Pretoria, as the scorched earth policy became increasingly indiscriminate. In July 1900, Roberts tried shipping Boer families back towards the Boer forces as they retreated before him. In September, burghers who had surrendered were accommodated in camps in Bloemfontein and Pretoria. Realising that the Boer civilians were being left by the commandos to fend for themselves on the *veld* and were conceivably at the mercy of the black population, the British began establishing what were deemed refugee camps. Roberts had modified his earlier policy in November 1900 by suggesting that only homes from which troops were fired upon or which were being actively used for Boer bases should be destroyed. Lord Kitchener, however, who succeeded Roberts in December 1900, extended the internment system throughout the Boer republics and began to remove the population entirely. By May 1902, an estimated 30,000 farmhouses had been destroyed.

The intention of Kitchener's policy was to confine women, who were thought to be instrumental in encouraging Boer resistance, and, in some measure, holding them hostage. The policy was branded 'methods of barbarism' by the Liberal leader, Henry Campbell-Bannerman, on one occasion. Indeed, through mismanagement rather than deliberate intent, perhaps 28,000 of the 116,000 Boer civilians held in the 40 or so camps had died by May 1902, largely from disease. In addition, between 16,000 and 20,000 out of 115,000 blacks held in a further 66 camps also died. In September 1901, Kitchener proclaimed that Boers still in the field risked permanent banishment from South Africa and that the cost of keeping their families in the camps would be recouped by selling their land and property. By the end of the war, 7,000 Boers were held as prisoners of war in South Africa, while a further 24,000 were held in camps on Bermuda and St Helena or in India and Ceylon (Sri Lanka).

How far the camps increased or decreased resistance among the *bittereinders* remains a matter of debate. Clearly, however, reconcentration was effective when linked to the purely military measures. Initially, stone blockhouses were constructed along railway lines, but the system was revolutionised by the development of a cheap prefabricated galvanised iron circular design by Major S.R. Rice in February 1901, which could be erected in only three or four days. Eventually, over 8,000 blockhouses were erected, with intervals between some on key rail lines being as little as 185 metres. Some 50,000 troops and 16,000 black auxiliaries garrisoned these posts. In addition, 6,400 km of barbed wire entanglements linked to the blockhouses crossed the *veld*. The drives across sectors by mounted columns, described by Callwell in his third edition in 1906 as 'the last word in strategy directed against guerrilla antagonists', put immense attritional pressure on the commandos, although the British columns often moved somewhat ponderously, and over 347,000 horses were 'expended' by the British during the course of the war, largely due to poor 'horse-mastership'. As indicated previously, use was also made of over 5,000 burghers willing to fight for the British against erstwhile colleagues, the National Scouts being formed in the Transvaal and the similar Orange River Colony Volunteers in the former Orange Free State.

The French also recognised the need for a concerted military and political response to insurgency, although, in practice, they tended to continue to stress the primacy of military action. The same combination of military and political methods used by Bugeaud in Algeria was applied by the French to West and Central Africa in the 1850s and 1860s by Louis Faidherbe. Faidherbe, though, put more emphasis than Bugeaud upon political and economic pressure and was prepared to contemplate French co-operation with local rulers to establish protectorates rather than colonies. He was also instrumental in raising the Tirailleurs Sénégalais. The Bugeaud method was also used during the abortive expedition to Mexico between 1862 and 1866.

The Bugeaud method was then refined further by the two great French exponents in the nineteenth and early twentieth centuries of what became known as *tache d'huile* (oil slick), Joseph-Simon Galliéni and Louis-Hubert-Gonsalve Lyautey. Galliéni made his name in French Indo-China and Madagascar in the 1890s, and Lyautey, who served under him in Indo-China and Madagascar, in Morocco between 1912 and 1925. Indeed, the classic statement of the doctrine was by Lyautey in an article in the prestigious journal *Revue des Deux Mondes* in January 1900 entitled 'Du Rôle Coloniale de l'armée' ('On the army's colonial role').

Tache d'huile rested on the idea that a dual military–political strategy would extend French control more effectively. Thus, as the French military advanced so French administrators were introduced immediately. Often, in fact, they were soldier-administrators with a dual role, systematically spreading French influence over the countryside. As described in a letter to Galliéni by Lyautey in November 1903, conquest would be achieved 'not by mighty blows, but as a patch of oil spreads, through a step by step progression, playing alternately on all the local elements, utilising the divisions between tribes and between their chiefs'. Thus, the military would establish control but then attempt to win over the population, not only by offering protection but also by such methods as extending free medical help or establishing subsidised markets and reassuring local political leaders that France would uphold their traditional authority. Soldiers would act not only as administrators and police but also as 'overseers, workshop managers, teachers, gardeners, farmers'. In short, as Lyautey put it, military occupation would 'consist less in military operations than in an organisation on the march'. On another occasion, he wrote that the 'magnificence and beauty' of colonial warfare was that it immediately became 'the creator of life'.

It should be noted, however, that French culture was actually being imposed upon indigenous culture in much the same way that American civic action in the Caribbean and Central America automatically imposed American values on indigenous values. Moreover, by establishing markets for native products at which good prices could be obtained, the French often disrupted normal trade patterns and alienated vested economic interests in the locality. The ultimate aim of French imperialism was that natives should become totally assimilated in due course as black or yellow Frenchmen. Indeed, Algeria was to be regarded not as a colony at all but as part of metropolitan France. Yet there was something of an exaggeration of the extent to which persuasion and winning hearts and minds prevailed over sheer military force. The French were quite prepared to use maximum force if necessary, as in the case of their reaction to the rebellion in the Rif mountains of Morocco by Abd el-Krim between 1924 and 1926, eventually crushed by joint French and Spanish action. The final subjugation of the extreme south of Morocco between 1933 and 1934 saw the deployment of 40,000 men and both aircraft and tanks. Similarly, in Syria between 1920 and 1925, the French adopted a draconian approach to opposition, bombarding insurgent positions in Damascus with artillery and aircraft. One other aspect of *tache d'huile* worth mentioning is that it involved a potential politicisation of the French army itself, Lyautey emphasising that the army might be required to move beyond colonial administration to regenerate French society and politics as well in the interests of maintaining the empire.

In surveying the contribution of European colonial soldiers to the beginnings of counter-insurgency theory, it should be noted that Dutch soldiers often displayed considerable tactical initiative in their campaigns in the East Indies. Between 1825 and 1830, for example, General M.H. de Kock developed techniques very similar to those of Galliéni while campaigning on Java. De Kock established a network of *benteng* (small outposts), from which small mobile columns moved into the interior. However, the outposts also became a focus for population, enabling the Dutch to attempt to win hearts and minds by extending facilities to the islanders. Study of colonial warfare was not generally regarded as likely to enhance a military career in the Royal Dutch army, but it was studied more seriously in the Royal Dutch Indies army. Apart from frequent articles in military periodicals, works on colonial campaigning were produced by P.F. Vermeulen Krieger in 1829, Major W.A. Van Rees in 1862 and Major P.M. La Gort Dillie in 1863.

In 1896, Captain Klaas van der Maaten published the three-volume *De Indische Oorlogen* (The Indonesian Wars), which has been compared to Callwell's work. Influenced by a celebrated specialist on Islam, Dr C. Snouck, Maarten had considerable understanding of the military characteristics of the indigenous cultures whom the Dutch encountered. Unfortunately, however, its lessons were ignored by the official manual on colonial tactics issued in 1927, *Voorschrift voor de Politinek-politionele Taak van het Leger* (Precepts for the Politico-policing task of the Army) or VPTL, with an additional appendix of case studies known as the *Aanhangsel*. This drew its lessons largely from the last phase of Dutch operations against Aceh between 1903 and 1910, in which intensive patrolling had been used to hunt down the last remnants of Acehanese resistance. Significantly, a third of the content was on patrolling, and it was too limited to be relevant to the kind of politicised insurgency already developing in the first half of the twentieth century.

Generally speaking, as the twentieth century dawned, the European approach still involved considerable brutality, which was not conducive to the success of any pacification strategy, and the death toll among opponents was always likely to be heavy. British expeditions on the North West Frontier were cheerfully labelled 'butcher and bolt' by the troops involved. It has become fashionable to suggest that colonial warfare was a precursor of 'total warfare' in the twentieth century, the context being the degree of violence rather than the extent of economic, social and political mobilisation. Yet the methods used, for example, by the British in South Africa, while a violation of the accepted conventions of war as recently codified at the Hague in July 1899 but not signed by the Boer republics, fell well short of the total destruction of the enemy implied by total war. However, there was a continuing assumption on the part of all European armies that the extreme use of force was an appropriate psychological response to insurgency. Crude racial theories had much to do with this, but then it was also applied to insurgents who were white.

As already indicated, the Germans simply shot French *francs-tireurs* out of hand in 1870–71. Once the South African War became a prolonged guerrilla conflict, the Boers were increasingly cast in the role of 'the other', with a new intensity given to the already prevailing image of Afrikaner society as backward and uncivilised. Moreover, controversies over alleged Boer abuses of white flags and uses of dum-dum bullets, which the British government refused to allow to be used by British forces, accentuated the process of dehumanisation. Indeed, the Boers came to be viewed as just another uncivilised native opponent. British forces and, notably, colonial contingents raised in Australia, Canada and South Africa itself, became involved in a bitter circular spiral of reprisals against the Boers. In a now celebrated case, four officers of the mainly Australian Bushveld Carbineers were court-martialled for the murder of Boer prisoners and two, Harry Morant, known as 'The Breaker', and Peter Handcock, were executed in February 1902. The dum-dum bullet was regularly used in other colonial campaigns prior to the First World War. The Germans extinguished perhaps well in excess of the official figure of 75,000 natives in suppression of the Maji-Maji rising in German East Africa between 1905 and 1907, while the Herero population of German South West Africa declined by over 60,000 during the Herero revolt of 1904–07.

German treatment of irregular opponents continued to be within this tradition. Nazi *abschreckung* (loosely translated as 'terror tactics'), indeed, was no different from the *schrecklichkeit* (frightfulness) of General Lothar von Trotha in German South West Africa and was effectively the same policy. Denied a spectacular military victory, von Trotha had Herero fighting men shot out of hand and women, children and the elderly driven into the desert to die of starvation. Compelled by Berlin to modify his policy, Trotha had those Herero males who surrendered branded with the letters GH (for *genfangene* or captive Hereros) and given over to forced labour. German brutality against the Herero then contributed to the rising of the Nama, who proved much more elusive opponents so that a peace treaty had to be negotiated by von Trotha's successor in March 1907. Against the Maji-Maji rising in German East Africa there was no official extermination policy, but it evolved nonetheless. In 1914, the Germans were also fearful of a repetition of their experience with *francs-tireurs*, and their advance into Belgium and northern France was also marked by atrocities.

As greater technology became available, so this, too, was applied to the suppression of insurrection and of colonial opposition. Italian air power, for example, was much in evidence against the Senussi tribes in Libya in the 1920s and in Ethiopia in 1935, where mustard gas was dropped. The Italians had also been the first to bomb any opponents from the air, during the Italo-Turkish war in Libya in 1911–12.

The Americans experimented with aircraft against Sandino in Nicaragua in 1927 and even tried out the first fixed-wing rotary aircraft – the autogiro – as a means of lifting supplies into the jungle. Air power drove Sandino from his bases at first El Chipote and, then, Ocotal, the twelve aircraft available carrying out 84 attacks in twelve months, dropping 300 bombs and expending 30,000 rounds of ammunition. Aircraft were also used to resupply American units on patrol, 68,614 pounds of supplies being lifted in one week alone in August 1928. The Soviets used air power against their internal opponents, while Britain, too, used air power in what was termed aerial policing or air control in Iraq, the Aden Protectorate, the Sudan, Somaliland and on the North West Frontier in the 1920s and 1930s. Partly this was an expedient to save money on garrisons, the first sustained experiment against the elusive 'Mad Mullah', Seyid Mohammad, in January and February 1920 breaking up his forces in Somaliland at a cost of only £83,000.

However, many British soldiers had genuine moral reservations about the use of 'frightfulness' against women and children. They also considered troops on the ground a much more effective method of policing the recalcitrant, since aircraft could not occupy disputed ground. In many respects they were right, since it was actually very costly to maintain aircraft and airfields in inhospitable terrain, and troops were still needed on the ground to hunt down rebel bands. Thus, in the communal violence in Palestine in 1929, when bombing Jerusalem and Jaffa would have been unacceptable, aircraft were used instead to transport more troops rapidly from Egypt. Ironically, in the suppression of the revolt in Iraq in 1920, while air power and armoured cars were both employed with only modest success, horsed cavalry, albeit using light automatics as well as swords, proved remarkably successful.

British manuals on colonial policing increasingly incorporated the introduction of more modern technology, but they also began to become more politically perceptive towards the changes in insurgency generally. Curiously, however, the politically motivated insurgency that occurred in Ireland between 1919 and 1921 was largely ignored by British texts such as Sir Charles Gwynn's *Imperial Policing* in 1934 and Hugh Simson's *British Rule, and Rebellion* in 1937, although both did have some understanding of the dangers of politicisation of an insurgent cause. The product of Gwynn's tenure as commandant of the Staff College between 1926 and 1930, *Imperial Policing* was based on a number of cases studies such as Amritsar, the Moplah Rebellion in India's Malabar region in 1921 and the revolt on Cyprus in 1931. Gwynn laid down four principles of imperial policing that were sufficiently sound to be fundamental to the post-1945 British approach to more politically motivated insurgency. These four principles were:

1   the primacy of the civil power;
2   the use of minimum force;
3   the need for firm and timely action; and
4   the need for co-operation between the civil and military authorities.

Gwynn's principles responded to the realities of the experience since 1919. While Gwynn recognised that propaganda was a weapon in the hands of the insurgent, however, he favoured collective punishments and saw little need to address the grievances of an insurgent population. Nor did he choose to describe the campaign in Ireland, although, paradoxically, he did recommend reading memoirs by IRA members such as Charles Dalton's *With the Dublin Brigade, 1917–21*, published in London in 1929, as throwing 'an instructive light on the psychology of irregular forces'.

The influence of Gwynn is manifest in the official manual issued in January 1934, *Notes on Imperial Policing*, later supplemented by *Duties in Aid of the Civil Power* in 1937. Indeed, Gwynn may have written the manual, which identified six principles of military action: provision of adequate forces; the necessity for offensive action; co-ordinated intelligence under military control; efficient 'inter-communication'; mobility; and security measures, by which was meant care to preserve secrecy as to military movements. Primarily, however, the manual dealt with the military minutiae of cordons, searches and drives as well as spelling out the nature of martial law at length. As might be expected, the manual did not address wider political issues beyond differentiating between general unrest and 'a more highly organised opposition'.

Generally, the British had failed to appreciate the serious nature of the IRA's challenge, partly due to the relatively slow emergence of sustained insurgency between 1919 and 1921, the consequent belief that only a small number of 'murder gangs' were involved, and a reluctance to alienate supposed 'moderate' opinion. Initially, the response was to reinforce and to militarise the RIC through recruiting ex-servicemen into the 'Black and Tans' and ex-officers into the Auxiliary Division, RIC, the former deployed from March 1920 and the latter from August 1920. However, inconsistency marked government policy. Thus, control was effectively handed to the army in January 1920, only for military powers to be reduced in May, before being extended once more in July. In any case, there was a manpower shortage following post-war demobilisation and amid other escalating imperial commitments. Consequently, the strategy became one of establishing army and police strong-points from which motorised patrols could be mounted. However, reliance upon motorised transport tied the British to the roads and made them more liable to ambush. As it happened, the improved conviction rate under the Restoration of Order in Ireland Act, which forced more IRA members to go on the run, enabled the IRA to concentrate into larger 'active service' flying columns capable of undertaking such ambushes. The result was an escalating cycle of ambushes and reprisals in rural areas like Cork and Sligo.

A propaganda department had been created in August 1920 under a former journalist and war correspondent, Basil Clarke, to counter IRA propaganda and improve British morale. It was never as effective as the IRA's equivalent organisation, however, and British rather than IRA atrocities were those that were reported. It was unhelpful, indeed, that alongside unofficial reprisals, such as the burning of part of Cork city by Auxiliaries in December 1920, there were 'official' reprisals such as collective fines and house burning. Ultimately, martial law was introduced in four counties, including Cork, on 11 December 1920 and extended to a further four counties later in the month, but raids and searches proved less than effective. By early 1921, some units were experimenting with small patrols on foot in rural areas and the initially poor operational intelligence also began to improve. In many respects, however, the situation had reached stalemate by the time negotiations opened in London in June 1921.

Simson, whose military career had included service at Tsingtao in 1914, in Russia in 1919, elsewhere in China in 1927 and as British military attaché in Tokyo between 1930 and 1932, made some limited reference to Ireland. Simson, however, primarily based his book on his experiences during the first phase of the Arab revolt in Palestine between 1936 and 1939. He correctly identified the growing politicisation of what he characterised as 'sub-war', with terror tactics and propaganda utilised to undermine the police and to wage a political-psychological campaign against government. He suggested, therefore, that an equally sophisticated political response was required with co-ordination of civil, military and police agencies, especially in the matter of intelligence. However, he still regarded martial law as both a viable and a desirable option. Much more clearly related to the experience in Ireland was Major B.C. Denning's article in *Army Quarterly* in 1927, 'Modern Problems of Guerrilla Warfare'. Like both Gwynn and Simson, Denning recognised that propaganda had become a weapon 'which draws blood upon the home front of the great power'. Consequently, security forces must display restraint despite the advantages thus conceded to their opponents. However, Denning did not countenance making political concessions to insurgents.

Generally, British soldiers much preferred the application of martial law and, when given the chance, applied it as under the Moplah Outrages Act enacted in Malabar in 1921 and, as already related, in parts of Ireland that same year. It removed them from the confusing and restrictive legal frame-work of the common law, which required them to judge the precise amount of force justified in any given situation. In 1831, for example, Colonel Brererton had been cashiered for using what was deemed insufficient force to disperse rioters in Bristol – he committed suicide – whereas, in 1919, Brigadier-General Reginald Dyer was equally condemned for using excessive force in dispersing an unarmed Indian crowd at Amritsar – 380 Indians were killed – although soldiers believed Dyer's action had saved the Punjab from wider insurrection.

Nonetheless, entrusting primacy to the civil authorities and the primary role in meeting internal violence to the police rather than to the military did assist in preventing escalation and in retaining an air of normalcy, especially if there was a good understanding between the civil and military authorities, as in the Moplah revolt and the Tharrawaddy revolt in Burma in 1930–32, unlike the situation in Ireland between 1919 and 1921. It is possible that there was a joint army and police headquarters in each operational area during the Moplah revolt and this was certainly the case in Burma, where a special commissioner was appointed in June 1930 to co-ordinate the overall civil, police and military response, and joint command arrangements were made at area level. The use of minimum force, as much by necessity as from preference in terms of the limited resources usually available to the British, and the encouragement of full co-operation between the civil and military authorities were obviously closely linked to this concept of ensuring normalcy. Military resources could then be targeted efficiently in a firm or timely way to forestall or contain actual violence.

As in Ireland, the failure of the initial large-scale sweeps in both Moplah and Burma pointed to the importance of small unit operations. Emphasis on the civil authorities in its way also suggested a willingness to recognise that most rebellions or insurgencies had political causes, which might be best addressed by a political response. Thus, in Cyprus in 1931 it was recognised by the British authorities that political initiatives were required to counter the demands of the Greek Cypriots for *enosis* (union with Greece), and the initial outbreak of the Arab revolt in Palestine in 1936 was at least temporarily defused by the promise of a royal commission on Jewish immigration.

On occasions, however, the British either did not recognise the depth of feeling, as in the Peshawar riots in 1931, or, as in Ireland, were unable to satisfy nationalism for political reasons. Moreover, most of the inter-war opponents faced by the British were not as politically developed as the IRA. Thus, the Palestinian Arabs have been characterised by Tom Bowden as 'ideological innocents', the revolt of 1936–39 rooted in tribal brigandage. Nonetheless, it was a significant military challenge, since intelligence was poor through the weakness of the Palestine Police's CID and the unreliability of its Arab members. Special emergency regulations in June 1936 enabled the army to take stronger action, since martial law was resisted lest it suggest that Palestine, held as a mandate of the League of Nations territory rather than as a colony, was out of control. Nevertheless, it would have been declared in September 1936 had the Arabs not accepted the proposed royal commission.

Dissatisfied with the results of the commission, the Arabs began guerrilla attacks once more. Now, however, there was a clear political aim on the part of the authorities of preparing the way for a conference, and the police came under military control in September 1938. Police posts were set up as a permanent presence in insurgent villages and patrols undertaken from them. This 'village occupation' policy, intended to isolate Arab guerrillas from the population, was supplemented by the erection of physical barriers, including 'Tegart' blockhouses, named after their designer, Sir Charles Tegart, and wiring of the border with Trans-Jordan. A young British officer sympathetic to Zionism, Orde Wingate, helped to train the military arm of the Jewish Agency, the Haganah, and enlisted Jews in three clandestine so-called Special Night Squads in May 1938 to raid Arab guerrilla camps and to protect the oil pipeline from Iraq to the port of Haifa. Again, Wingate's operations proved the value of small units and, following the failure of larger-scale sweeps, the British became used to applying constant military pressure in what Tom Mockaitis has characterised as 'a tedious process involving thousands of hours of patrolling, often with minimum results'. By such means, however, military control was re-established by November 1938, albeit through the commitment of large numbers of troops, and the promised conference convened in London in February 1939.

Immediately after the Second World War, some who had served in Palestine between 1936 and 1939 tended to expect Jewish terrorists to operate much as had the Arabs. This was not the case, but it did prove possible to adapt the methods used in some inter-war campaigns to the new post-war conditions. In this regard, the Tharrawaddy revolt was particularly significant. The development of techniques in Burma was echoed in a more purely military context by some continuing work on hill warfare, which had arisen from the seemingly perennial operations in Waziristan for much of the 1920s and 1930s. Hill warfare was even included on the syllabus of the Royal Military

College at Sandhurst after the First World War, *Notes on Frontier Warfare* being compiled for use at the college in 1922. A popular guide for British officers was Sir Andrew Skene's *Passing it on: Short Talks on Tribal Fighting on the North West Frontier*, published in 1932 and going through four editions in seven years. Meanwhile, changes wrought by technology such as the introduction of air power and light tanks were recognised in the *Manual of Operations on the North-West Frontier of India*, produced in India in 1925 and revised as *Frontier Warfare (Army and Royal Air Force)* in 1939. During the Second World War, moreover, a Frontier Warfare School was opened at Kakul in 1941, and certainly frontier lessons were to prove of some value to British officers after 1945, especially those serving in South Arabia and the Radfan in the early 1960s.

Recognition of the increasing need for a political response to insurgency was also a feature of American doctrine as it emerged in the 1930s. Indeed, the *Small Wars Manual* of 1935, which was revised five years later and largely compiled by Harold Utley, was based very much on the experience in Nicaragua. Viewing the problem of insurgency largely from the perspective of American intervention in other states, it was initially entitled 'The Tactics and Techniques of Small Wars' and built on an early study of the lessons of small wars written by Major Samuel Harrington in the *Marine Corps Gazette* in 1921–22. Utley himself had also contributed three articles to the same journal in 1931 and 1933 addressing general issues, intelligence and staff functions. By 1924–25, seven hours worth of instruction in small wars techniques was being imparted at the marine base at Quantico in Virginia and, by the time Utley wrote his articles, he was contributing to a nineteen-hour course. The course eventually reached a duration of 45 hours in 1938.

The *Small Wars Manual* itself outlined five phases of operations: initial landing; reinforcement and initial military operations, increasingly based on small patrols and self-sustaining detachments; assumption of administration; policing leading to elections; and withdrawal. There were a number of contradictions, however. Thus, in terms of military technique, despite an implicit rejection of maximum force, there was already something of an obsession with firepower as a substitute for manpower, with 'reconnaissance by fire' a feature of American tactics in Nicaragua. Captain (later Lieutenant-General) Lewis 'Chesty' Puller, for example, dispensed with flank guards altogether when operating with a company of the Nicaraguan National Guard, relying on the firepower of a light machine gun, automatic weapons and grenade launchers in the event of being ambushed. The same preference appeared in a study of tactics in Nicaragua contributed to *Infantry Journal* by Major Roger Peard in 1931.

Similarly, in civil terms, there was an acceptance that indigenous peoples would be potentially hostile but, beyond cautioning against adopting a superiority complex, the manual offered no really coherent answer to winning hearts and minds. Indeed, the marines would be permitted methods likely to alienate the population such as bombing and reconcentration, although the latter was to be avoided if at all possible. Moreover, while not assuming superiority over the indigenous culture, the marines would be imposing American values. To give another example of the contradictions, it was intended to address the reasons for the outbreak of disorder, yet the United States' intervention might well imply co-operating with indigenous governments whose policies had led to the disorder. Equally, it was intended to be non-partisan, yet the emphasis placed on securing American property and interests might lead to a decidedly partisan approach.

Since an intervention was not intended to lead to permanent occupation, there was stress on establishing a local gendarmerie or constabulary in the interest of greater political stability. Gendarmerie such as those established on Haiti and in the Dominican Republic were intended to instil a sense of national identity but, in the event, dictators often emerged from the gendarmerie once the Americans had withdrawn, such as Rafael Trujillo in the Dominican Republic in 1930 and Anastasio Somoza in Nicaragua in 1936. In Nicaragua, the marines had also experimented with small mixed groups of Nicaraguans and indigenous Indians known as Voluntarios as a kind of pseudo-gang, but they proved too undisciplined. The manual also developed the idea of Americans supervising free and honest elections as something of a panacea for instability in those regions to which American forces were committed.

By contrast to the beginning of what might be termed a 'hearts and minds' approach in British and American practice as it emerged in the inter-war period, the Soviets extended political concessions to their opponents only as temporary expedients until they could bring maximum force to bear. The political cynicism was evident in most of the campaigns the Bolsheviks waged to maintain their control of the Soviet Union such as the suppression of the 'Green' revolt in the Tambov province of the Volga region between 1920 and 1921, and the Basmachi revolt in Central Asia between 1918 and 1931. The Soviet version of resettlement was forced deportation allied to confiscation and redistribution of property, vigorous purging conducted by the secret police, then known as the Cheka, and the general application of collective guilt. By way of temporary concessions in the Tambov, a region lying across the important grain route from the Volga to Moscow, food requisitioning was suspended, some goods such as textiles, salt and kerosene made available, some capitalist incentives extended to farmers, and an amnesty declared. Propaganda was also stepped up with, for example, 215,000 copies of various leaflets distributed between February and April 1921 and 326,000 between May and July.

At the same time, however, Orders No. 130 and 171 allowed counter-terror to be employed with an automatic death penalty for offences such as concealing weapons and harbouring insurgents. A list of over 10,000 suspects was compiled based on the identification of wealthier peasant or *kulak* families in 'bandit' villages from the 1917 census. Over 5,000 hostages were taken under Order No. 130, and families were detained and deported. Indeed, between 80,000 and 100,00 so-called 'bandit families' were deported from the Tambov and the Ukraine as a whole by July 1921.

In Central Asia, where the Basmachi (from the Turkish word meaning 'to plunder') revolt was centred on the Fergana valley, forced labour and land confiscation was suspended, *sharia* courts and Islamic schools reopened and private trading authorised. Again, there were periodic amnesties. In the final phase of the insurgency, however, the three major towns of Namangan, Margilan and Dushanbe were totally destroyed, as were 1,200 villages. An estimated 270,000 ethnic Turks were deported. The Soviets were also adept at the old Tsarist policy of divide and rule, exploiting traditional tribal rivalries in Central Asia. Equally, against Makhno, they employed Chinese and Lettish units and, in the Tambov, Tatars, whom other Muslims regarded as heretics.

The Soviet marshal later executed by Stalin, Mikhail Tukhachevsky, contributed an article, 'Borba s Kontrrevoliutsionnim Vosstanian' (Struggle with Counter-revolutionary Uprisings) to *Voina i Revoliustsiia* (War and Revolution) in 1926 and is sometimes erroneously regarded as a father of modern counter-insurgency. Tukhachevsky had commanded the Soviet forces in the Tambov province in 1921. Within the limits of an ideology that compelled him to attribute 'banditry' to the inspiration of *kulaks*, Tukhachevsky did show some understanding of political necessities. Thus, he stressed the need to take account of the local culture and religion and the value of appointing a single individual with full authority over all aspects of the response. He suggested raising local forces and employing those insurgents who had surrendered against erstwhile colleagues. In typical Bolshevik fashion, however, he regarded concessions to the population as temporary and thus happily advocated the eviction of bandit families, the confiscation and redistribution of their property, the assumption of collective guilt and widespread use of detention and deportation. Not only, therefore, did he display the limitations of Bolshevik ideology, but it is also highly unlikely that the article had any wider currency outside the Soviet Union.

Not unexpectedly, whatever the traditions of colonial campaigning, the Second World War concentrated military minds primarily on 'real war' and, with the exception of the German army, which greatly improved its own techniques of counter-insurgency on the Eastern Front, those other armies that had previously engaged in counter-insurgency more often than not found themselves promoting guerrilla warfare rather than combating it. SOE and Force 136 were the instruments in the case of the British, while the Americans formed the Office of Strategic Services (OSS). The Soviets, in turn, reverted to the traditions of partisan warfare. For most armies, the need to embrace the lessons of conventional war made it all too easy to forget the lessons of the irregular campaigns of the past. Nor was there that true grasp of the changes taking place in guerrilla warfare during the inter-war period.

There was thus a slowness to adapt to the new challenges posed by politically inspired insurgency after 1945. Yet, in formulating a response, most Western armies had either a recognisable doctrine or, at the very least, established principles for such situations. These could be readily adapted, albeit often slowly, as the basis of new doctrine. In every case, therefore, post-1945 counter-insurgency doctrines reflected the particular army's past experiences.

Further reading

For early counter-insurgency generally, see the essays in Ian Beckett (ed.), *The Roots of Counter-insurgency: Armies and Guerrilla Warfare, 1900–45* (London, 1988).

On the eighteenth century, see Christopher Duffy, *The Military Experience in the Age of Reason* (London, 1987). On the Revolutionary and Napoleonic Wars, see Peter Paret, *Internal War and Pacification* (Princeton, 1961); Don W. Alexander, *Rod of Iron: French Occupation Policy in Aragon during the Peninsular War* (Wilmington, 1985).

For the Seminole, Mexican and American Civil Wars, see Mark Grimsley, *The Hard Hand of War: Union Military Policy towards Southern Civilians, 1861–65* (Cambridge, 1995); Kenneth Noe, 'Exterminating Savages: The Union Army and Mountain Guerrillas in Southern West Virginia, 1861–62' in Kenneth Noe and Shannon Wilson (eds), *The Civil War in Appalachia: Collected Essays* (Knoxville, 1997), pp. 104–30; Philip Paludan, *Victims: A True Story of the Civil War* (Knoxville, 1981); John D. Waghelstein, 'The Mexican War and the Civil War: The American Army's Experience in Irregular Warfare as a Sub-set of a Major Conventional Conflict' *Small Wars and Insurgencies* 7 (1996), pp. 139–64; and John K. Mahon, *History of the Second Seminole War, 1835–42* (Gainesville, 1967). On American campaigns against the Indians, see James Tate (ed.), *The American Military on the Frontier* (Washington 1978); John D. Waghelstein, 'Preparing the US Army for the Wrong War: Educational and Doctrinal Failure, 1865–91' *Small Wars and Insurgencies* 10 (1999), pp. 1–33; and Thomas Dunlay, *Wolves for the Blue Soldier: Indian Scouts and Auxiliaries with the US Army, 1860–90* (Lincoln, 1982).

On colonial campaigning in general, see Brian Bond (ed.), *Victorian Military Campaigns* (London, 1967); Jaap A. de Moor and H.L. Wesseling (eds), *Imperialism and War: Essays on Colonial War in Asia and Africa* (Leiden, 1989); and Bruce Vandervort, *Wars of Imperial Conquest in Africa, 1830–1914* (London, 1998). For colonial armed forces and police forces, see David Killingray and David Omissi (eds), *Guardians of Empire: The Armed Forces of the Colonial Powers, 1700–1964* (Manchester, 2000); and David Anderson and David Killingray (eds), *Policing and Decolonisation: Nationalism, Politics and the Police, 1917–65* (Manchester, 1992).

For the British in India, see T.R. Moreman, *The Army in India and the*

Development of Frontier Warfare, 1849–1947 (London, 1998); and David Omissi, *The Sepoy and the Raj: The Indian Army, 1860–1940* (London, 1994). For the South African War, see S.B. Spies, *Methods of Barbarism?: Roberts and Kitchener and Civilians in the Boer Republics, January 1900 to May 1902* (Cape Town, 1977); Keith Surridge, *Managing the South African War, 1899–1902: Politicians versus Generals* (Woodbridge, 1998); and Surridge, 'Rebellion, Martial Law and British Civil–Military Relations: The War in Cape Colony, 1899–1902' *Small Wars and Insurgencies* 8 (1997), pp. 35–60.

For the French, see Douglas Porch, *The Conquest of Morocco* (New York, 1983); Porch, *The Conquest of the Sahara* (New York, 1984); A.S. Kanya-Forstner, *The Conquest of the Western Sudan: A Study in French Military Imperialism* (Cambridge, 1969); Porch, 'The French Marines and the Conquest of the Western Sudan, 1880–99' in de Moor and Wesseling, *Imperialism and War*, pp. 121–45; C. Fourniau, 'Colonial War before 1914: The Case of France in Indochina' in *ibid.*, pp. 72–86; A.T. Sullivan, *Thomas-Robert Bugeaud* (Hamden, 1983); D. Woolman, *Rebels in the Rif: Abd el-Krim and the Rif Rebellion* (Oxford, 1969); Anthony Clayton, *France, Soldiers and Africa* (London, 1988); Paddy Griffith, *Military Thought in the French Army, 1815–51* (Manchester, 1989); W.A. Hossington, *Lyautey and the French Conquest of Morocco* (London, 1996); and R.E. Dunn, *Resistance in the Desert: Moroccan Responses to French Imperialism, 1881–1912* (London, 1977).

For the Germans, see J. Bridgman, *The Revolt of the Hereros* (Berkeley, 1981); and Kirsten Zirkel, 'Military Power in German Colonial Policy: The Schutztruppen and Their Leaders in East and South-West Africa, 1888–1918' in Killingray and Omissi, *Guardians of Empire*, pp. 91–113.

For the Dutch, see Jaap A de Moor, 'Colonial Warfare: Theory and Practice: The Dutch Experience in Indonesia, 1816–1949', paper at Dutch–Japanese Symposium on the History of Dutch and Japanese Expansion, Tokyo and Kyoto, October 1989; de Moor, 'The Recruitment of Indonesian Soldiers for the Dutch Colonial Army, 1700–1950' in Killingray and Omissi, *Guardians of Empire*, pp. 53–69; and de Moor, 'War Makers in the Archipelago: Dutch Expeditions in Nineteenth Century Indonesia' in de Moor and Wesseling, *Imperialism and War*, pp. 50–71.

For the later American experience in the Philippines, Central America and the Caribbean, see Glenn May, *Battle for Batangas* (New Haven, 1991); May, 'Was the Philippine–American War a "Total War"?' in Manfred Boemeke, Roger Chickering and Stig Förster (eds), *Anticipating Total War: The German and American Experiences, 1871–1914* (Cambridge, 1999), pp. 437–57; B.M. Linn, *Guardians of Empire: The US Army and the Pacific, 1902–40* (Chapel Hill, 1997); Linn, *The US Army and Counterinsurgency in the Philippine War, 1899–1902* (Chapel Hill, 1989); R.E. Dupuy and W.H. Baumer, *The Little Wars of the United States* (New York, 1968); J.M. Gates, *Schoolbooks and Krags: The United States Army in the Philippines, 1898–1902* (Westport, 1973); Gates, 'Indians and Insurrectos' *Parameters* 13 (1983), pp. 59–68; Gates, 'Two

American Wars in Asia: Successful Colonial Warfare in the Philippines and Cold War Failure in Vietnam' *War in History* 8 (2001), pp. 47–71; Gates, 'The Official Historian and the Well-placed Critic: James LeRoy's Assessment of John R M Taylor's *The Philippine Insurrection against the United States*' *The Public Historian* 7 (1985), pp. 57–67; Lester D. Langley, *The Banana Wars* (Lexington, 1985); S.C. Miller, *Benevolent Assimilation* (New Haven, 1982); Sam Sarkesian, *America's Forgotten Wars* (Westport, 1984); Ronald Schaffer, 'The 1940 Small Wars Manual and the "Lessons of History"' *Military Affairs* 36 (1972), pp. 46–51; B.J. Calder, 'Caudillos and Gaudilleros versus the US Marines' *Hispanic American Historical Review* 58 (1978), pp. 649–75; L.A. Perez, 'The Pursuit of Pacification: Banditry and the US Occupation of Cuba, 1899–1902' *Journal of Latin American Studies* 18 (1986), pp. 313–82; and R.E. Welch, 'American Atrocities in the Philippines: The Indictment and the Response' *Pacific Historical Review* 43 (1974), pp. 233–55.

On the Russian and Bolshevik experience, see W.E. Allen and P. Muratoff, *Caucasian Battlefields* (Cambridge, 1953); P.B. Henze, 'Fire and Sword in the Caucasus' *Central Asian Survey* 2 (1983), pp. 5–44; Rod Paschall, 'Marxist Counterinsurgencies' *Parameters* 16 (1986), pp. 2–15; D. DuGarm, 'Peasant Wars in Tambov Province' in V.N. Brovkin (ed.), *The Bolsheviks in Russian Society: The Revolution and the Civil Wars* (New Haven, 1997), pp. 177–98; O.H. Radkey, *The Unknown Civil War in Russia: A Study of the Green Movement in the Tambov Region, 1920–21* (Stanford, 1976); M. Saray, 'The Russian Conquest of Central Asia' *Central Asian Survey* 1 (1982), pp. 1–30; A. Bennigsen, 'The Soviet Union and Muslim Guerrilla Wars, 1920–81: Lessons for Afghanistan' *Conflict* 4 (1983), pp. 301–24; M.B. Broxup, 'The Basmachi' *Central Asian Survey* 2 (1983), pp. 57–81; G. Fraser, 'Basmachi' *Central Asian Survey* 6 (1987), pp. 7–42; H.A. de Lageard, 'The Revolt of the Basmachi according to Red Army Journals, 1920–22' *Central Asian Survey* 6 (1987), pp. 1–35; Martha Olcott, 'The Basmachi or Freemen's Revolt in Turkestan, 1918–24' *Soviet Studies* 33 (1981), pp. 352–69; and W.S. Ritter, 'The Final Phase in the Liquidation of Anti-Soviet Resistance in Tadzhikistan: Ibrahim Bek and the Basmachi, 1924–31' *Soviet Studies* 37 (1985), pp. 484–93.

On the British inter-war experience, see Tom Mockaitis, *British Counterinsurgency, 1919–60* (London, 1990); Mockaitis, 'The Origins of British Counterinsurgency' *Small Wars and Insurgencies* 1 (1990), pp. 209–25; Charles Townshend, *Britain's Civil Wars: Counterinsurgency in the Twentieth Century* (London, 1986); Townshend, *The British Campaign in Ireland, 1919–21: The Development of Political and Military Policies* (Oxford, 1975); Townshend, 'The Irish Insurgency, 1918–21: The Military Problem' in Ronald Haycock (ed.), *Regular Armies and Insurgency* (London, 1979), pp. 32–52; Townshend, 'Civilisation and Frightfulness: Air Control in the Middle East between the Wars' in Chris Wrigley (ed.), *Warfare, Diplomacy and Politics* (London, 1986), pp. 142–62; Townshend, 'Martial Law: Legal and Administrative Problems of Civil Emergency in Britain and the Empire, 1800–1940' *Historical Journal* 25

(1982), pp. 167–95; Townshend, 'The Defence of Palestine: Insurrection and Public Security, 1936–39' *English Historical Review* 103 (1988), pp. 917–49; Townshend, 'Policing Insurgency in Ireland, 1914–23' in Anderson and Killingray, *Policing and Decolonisation*, pp. 22–41; Mark Jacobsen, 'Only by the Sword: British Counter-insurgency in Iraq, 1920' *Small Wars and Insurgencies* 2 (1991), pp. 323–63; J. Bowyer Bell, 'Revolts against the Crown: The British Response to Imperial Insurgency' *Parameters* 4 (1974), pp. 31–46 [Reproduced in R. Weigley, *New Dimensions in Military History* (San Rafel, 1975), pp. 359–84]; Keith Jeffery, 'Colonial Warfare, 1900–39' in Colin McInnes and Gary Sheffield (eds), *Warfare in the Twentieth Century: Theory and Practice* (London, 1988), pp. 24–50; Randal Gray, 'Bombing the Mad Mullah' *Journal of the Royal United Services Institute for Defence Studies* 125 (1980), pp. 41–7; J.L. Cox, 'A Splendid Training Ground: the Importance to the RAF of Iraq, 1913–32' *Journal of Imperial and Commonwealth History* 13 (1985), pp. 157–84; and David Killingray, 'A Swift Agent of Government: Air Power in British Colonial Africa, 1916–39' *Journal of African History* 25 (1984), pp. 429–44.

On technology generally, see Edward Spiers, 'The Use of the Dum Dum Bullet in Colonial Warfare' *Journal of Imperial and Commonwealth History* 4 (1975), pp. 3–14; Philip Towle, *Pilots and Rebels* (London, 1989); and David Omissi, *Air Power and Colonial Control* (Manchester 1990).

3

RESISTANCE AND
THE PARTISAN

Events in Europe and in South-east Asia and the Pacific during the Second World War contributed to the development of guerrilla and counter-guerrilla warfare in a number of ways. On the one hand, resistance to the German occupation of much of Europe after the summer of 1940, and to the Japanese occupation of much of South-east Asia after December 1941, stimulated the revival of partisan and guerrilla warfare in some areas. Such resistance was not always successful in military terms, but it was highly significant in political terms, often shaping the character of post-war political development. In particular, it offered the example of the fusion of two potent ideologies in nationalism and communism. On the other hand, armies found new uses for irregular operations and developed a variety of specialist forces, many of which were to survive the war and prove readily adaptable in face of the new challenges posed by politically motivated insurgency.

Wartime British special forces included both army and Royal Marine commandos; a plethora of seaborne raiding forces such as the Royal Marine Boom Patrol Detachment and the Royal Navy's Combined Assault Pilotage Parties, the Long Range Desert Group of Major Ralph Bagnold and the Special Air Service (SAS), originally created by Major David Stirling and Jock Lewes in mid-1941 as 'L' Detachment of a non-existent 'Special Air Service Brigade' to raid behind enemy lines in North Africa. Rather similarly, the first of the US army's Ranger battalions was formed by Colonel William Darby in June 1942 and the 1st Special Service Force by Lieutenant-Colonel Robert Frederick in the same year.

In Burma, Orde Wingate formulated the concept of 'long-range penetration', the 77th Indian Infantry Brigade being established as a formation that could be supplied by air to operate in the jungle behind Japanese lines. In the event, this first 'Chindit' operation (the name being taken from the Burmese word for the stone lions characteristically found at the entrances of Buddhist temples) had only limited success in striking at the railway between Mandalay and Myitkyina. Wingate, however, caught the imagination of Churchill, and approval was given for a still more ambitious operation, using five brigades to assist the KMT advance on Myitkyina in March 1944. Immense difficulties were encountered flying the men into the jungle by glider, and Wingate's expectation that his men could hold jungle air strips and operate almost as conventional forces for long periods proved erroneous. It can be argued that the operation caused considerable confusion in the Japanese rear but at heavy cost to the Chindits, Wingate himself being killed in an air crash at an early stage. The Chinese advance was also supported by an American raiding unit, the 5307th Composite Unit (Provisional), known as Merrill's Marauders.

Before arriving in Burma in March 1942 to run a jungle warfare school at Maymyo, Wingate had raised Gideon Force in Ethiopia (as Abyssinia was to become during the Second World War) in November 1940. Recruited from Ethiopians and Sudanese and led by British officers and NCOs, Gideon Force was intended, in Wingate's words, to create a 'patriot revolt' against the Italians in favour of the exiled emperor, Haile Selassie. While intended to support British conventional operations against the Italians, Gideon Force, the concept of which had originated in pre-war plans in 1938 to raise the tribes, was something of a precursor of other liberation armies of the future. Together with independent irregular 'patriot' forces, Gideon Force captured over 15,600 Italian troops and accompanied Haile Selassie's triumphal return to Addis Ababa in May 1941. It also serves to illustrate the existence of other clandestine forces, which operated directly in support of resistance groups, in addition to various agents employed by organisations such as SOE, which sent 7,500 agents into Western Europe and 400 into Southern Europe during the war, and the American OSS, formed in June 1942 under 'Wild Bill' Donovan, who had taken charge of American overseas intelligence in July 1941.

In the Far East, for example, SOE's Force 136 fought alongside the Malayan People's Anti-Japanese Army (MPAJA) and the Karens in Burma, while the United States Armed Forces in the Far East (USAFFE) incorporated guerrilla groups fighting the Japanese in the Philippines, and the OSS ran Detachment 101 among the Kachins in Burma. Some 700 US personnel served with the Kachins at one time or another, and there were 10,000 tribesmen under arms by February 1945. In the Philippines, Lieutenant-Colonel W. Fertig had 37,000 men under command on Mindanao and held 90 per cent of the island by the end of the war, while Lieutenant-Colonel R. Volckmann's guerrillas assisted the US landing at Lingayen in January 1945. SOE's Operation Nation in early 1945 was estimated to have caused over 3,500 Japanese casualties in Burma, while the 2,000 Karens deployed in Operation Character in July 1945 were said to have inflicted more losses on the Japanese than the British XXXIII Corps. Subsequently, some former SOE operatives such as Cromarty 'Pop' Tulloch helped the Karens in their struggle against oppression by the post-independence Burmese government. It might be noted that, throughout the Second World War, it was 'business as usual' on India's North West Frontier. Indeed, in 1944, there were no less than 48 British or Indian battalions on the frontier, representing 38 per cent of the Indian army's peacetime establishment and, to quote the report of the post-war Frontier Commission, 'the cheapest concentration camp for allied servicemen the Axis ever possessed'.

Resistance itself took many forms and developed at different times in different countries. Neither resistance nor, indeed, collaboration necessarily occurred immediately after German or Japanese occupation. In France, for example, it has been argued that there were three distinct phases of reaction, in coming to terms with defeat, in coming to terms with the German presence, and in coming to terms with the ideological domination manifest in German occupation policies. Individuals, however, moved through these phases at different speeds, if at all, since it was possible not to make any transition from one phase to another. Much would also depend upon location. Again, to use France as an example, whereas Alsace and Lorraine were effectively reannexed into the Reich, much of central and southern France remained under the nominal control of the Vichy authorities until November 1942. Even in occupied France outside of Vichy control, the German presence would be felt more in towns than in the countryside.

Indeed, German occupation policies varied quite considerably. Like Alsace and Lorraine, Luxembourg and Austria were integrated into the Reich, while Moravia and Bohemia were regarded as part of a 'greater Germany'. Denmark and the Netherlands were regarded as potential allies, while Serbia and Greece were occupied under military rather than civil administration. In the remainder of Yugoslavia, the Italians occupied the Dalmatian coast and Montenegro, Croatia was made nominally independent, and other areas incorporated within Austria, Hungary and Bulgaria. Still other territories such as Poland and the occupied parts of the Soviet Union were regarded as fit only for the most ruthless exploitation. At one extreme, therefore, there was a certain reluctance to offend, as in Denmark and the Channel Islands, and, at the other, total repression. If necessary, however, the Germans were quite prepared to use maximum force, even in states regarded as having some affinity with Germany.

Thus, in the Netherlands, economic exploitation and coercion steadily increased. Dutch citizens were compelled to undertake guard duties on German and public property, and over 10,000 Dutch civilians were taken as hostages in 1942 alone. Five were executed after an attempted attack on a German troop train in Rotterdam in August 1942 and ten more after the death of a German medical orderly in Haarlem in January 1943. The rate of reprisal shootings increased dramatically after September 1944, and perhaps 8,000 lives were lost through German military or police action. At one point, indeed, the Germans organised a counter-terror group known as 'Silver Fire Action' responsible for at least 45 deaths in the course of 1943–44.

Elsewhere, the Germans were far more ruthless, as suggested by the vengeance visited on the Czech village of Lidice in June 1942, where 172 men were executed after the assassination of Himmler's deputy, Reinhard Heydrich. In Poland, 2,000 opponents of the new regime were executed in

May and June 1940, and a further 15,000 Poles were executed between October 1943 and March 1944, in addition to the workings of the death camps. Greece suffered such a level of food requisitioning that an estimated 250,000 people died directly or indirectly through the resulting famine between 1941 and 1943.

It is not surprising that, faced with such overwhelming coercive potential, many chose a form of resistance falling well short of overt military action against the Germans. Indeed, resistance could begin in any case with unspoken thoughts or unseen gestures, such as defacing posters, reading clandestine newspapers or listening to the BBC, before graduating to more active resistance such as intelligence gathering, hiding allied airmen and, ultimately, sabotage or guerrilla warfare. With regard to the latter, terrain was especially significant.

It was clearly nearly impossible to organise full-time guerrilla resistance in, say, Denmark, but it could be done in the Massif Central of France, the mountains of Greece, Albania and Yugoslavia, and the forests and marshes of occupied Russia. However, much depended upon the availability of former members of the defeated armed forces or, in the case of Russia and Yugoslavia, troops cut off by the German advance who evaded capture.

Nevertheless, taking on the Germans in the open was a high-risk strategy if guerrillas or partisans were isolated from conventional support. Wisely, many groups, such as the Norwegian *Milorg* (Military Organisation), resolved to delay any major armed action until liberation was imminent. Governments in exile in London tended to favour this conservative approach, since the emergence of powerful resistance movements might pose a political threat in the future, especially if leftward-leaning. By and large, SOE similarly supported a less active military role, since it also served allied strategic interests. Moreover, the difficulties of overt military opposition to the Germans were well illustrated by the fate of the French *maquis* (deriving from the Corsican for scrubland).

Generally, those *maquis* affiliated to the Armée Secrète (Secret Army, AS), an arm of the Gaullist Mouvements Unis de la Résistance (United Resistance Movements) or MUR, followed the allied strategy of awaiting liberation. By contrast, the communist-dominated Francs-tireurs et Partisans Français (French *francs-tireurs* and partisans, FTPF) sought a more active role. In 1944, however, de Gaulle's principal liaison officer with the resistance, Jean Moulin, and the head of the AS, General Delestraint, believed it would be possible to concentrate the *maquis* for a major conventional role in support of the forthcoming allied invasion of France. The result was disaster. In the Savoy region of the Massif Central between February and March 1944, 500 *maquis* were killed at Glières. At Vercors near Grenoble in July 1944, another 3,500 *maquis* were dispersed with at least 800 dead when attempting to hold the 'Republic of Vercors' after the allies had already landed in Normandy. Another large *maquis* group concentrated around Mont Mouchet escaped a similar fate only by dispersing rapidly in May 1944. The rising in Paris in August 1944 would have been equally disastrous had not the German commander, General von Choltitz, declined to employ armour and totally destroy the city. In fact, the rising was largely the work of the communists. Their action, instigating the rising on the back of a call for a general strike, forced the Gaullists to support it and, indeed, to push a Free French armoured division into the city to restore control.

Partisans who emerged in Italy after the Italian surrender to the allies in September 1943 were similarly unsuccessful, the allied commander-in-chief, General Sir Harold Alexander, broadcasting an appeal in November 1944 for them to cease large-scale operations after the German success in crushing one supposed 'liberated zone'. The most conspicuous success, indeed, of the estimated 300,000 Italian partisans was the capture and execution of Mussolini and his mistress in April 1945. Again, while awaiting the arrival of the Red Army in Prague in May 1945, 2,000 died in the abortive Slovak rising, while there were an estimated 20,000 dead as a result of the rising by the Polish Home Army in Warsaw in August 1944. The Red Army was close to the city but was held back deliberately by Stalin to ensure the destruction the non-communist resistance.

In many respects, resistance was more successful in the less overt roles: by enabling the allies to build up detailed intelligence; by enabling over 33,000 allied servicemen to escape from occupied Western Europe; by spreading anti-German propaganda; and by some individually significant acts of sabotage. The latter included the attack on the heavy water plant at Vemork in Norway in February 1943, the destruction of Germany's remaining stocks of heavy water through the sinking of the Tinnsjö ferry in Norway in February 1944, and the disruption of German communications in France prior to D-Day in June 1944. Arguably, one of the most effective of all acts of resistance was actually a passive one – the strike action of Norwegian school teachers against the imposition of a new fascist-oriented syllabus by the collaborationist regime of Vidkun Quisling in February 1942.

Where resistance fell short of overt military action, it was normally combated by the Germans through routine policing methods, although with the addition of new techniques such as radio direction finding and code breaking. In the Netherlands, for example, identity cards were issued at an early stage, restrictions imposed on movement and, later, rationing cards linked to identity cards to force out those in hiding. The Germans fully exploited the black market, manipulating criminals and employing *agents provocateurs* to unmask opposition groups. In France, 150,000 assorted police and local defence units were available, including so-called *Ost* units recruited from anti-communist Russians. In the Vichy zone, the 10,000-strong Groupes Mobiles de Réserve was employed against the resistance, and there were between 25,000 and 30,000 men in the Milice Française (French Militia), a paramilitary organisation raised by Joseph Darnand. Consequently, German troops were not usually required. However, it was also the case that, even where facing a significant partisan threat, as in Russia and Yugoslavia, the Germans often enjoyed considerable military success.

Turning to Russia, it will be recalled that *partisanshchina* was deemed incompatible with the need to create a regular army since it encouraged independent attitudes subversive of centralised authority. Indeed, in the debate on the future of the Red Army in the 1920s, Trotsky had argued correctly that partisan war was as much the recourse of the White Russian and other anti-Bolshevik forces as of the Bolsheviks themselves. In 1928, therefore, a Soviet guide to insurrection had only one chapter on guerrilla warfare, and that written by the young Vietnamese nationalist Nguyen That Thanh, who had originally adopted the name Nguyen Ai Quoc (Nguyen the patriot) and then that of Ho Chi Minh (He who enlightens). Nonetheless, the Red Army itself had included a chapter on partisan operations in its field manual in 1918, and its high command had published *Instruction for Organising Local Partisan Detachments* in 1919. A few studies of partisans in the Russian Civil War were also published in the 1920s.

Consequently, when partisan groups re-emerged in the Second World War, they were regarded by the Soviet political leadership as valuable rather more for the political presence implied in German rear areas than for the military presence. Indeed, there were no pre-war plans to use partisans, and it was the unexpected German invasion that led Stalin to broadcast on 3 July 1941, calling upon the Soviet people to resist the invaders. Initially, the partisans were largely Red Army troops cut off by the speed of the German advance, although Communist Party functionaries were also given the task of organising resistance. Subsequently, more regulars were sent into German rear areas to bolster the partisan organisation up to brigade level, and Red Army soldiers constituted conceivably between 40 and 60 per cent of the total partisan forces over the war as a whole.

Throughout, the partisans were firmly under army and party control, a *Tsentral'nyi shtab partizanskoi dvizheniie* (Central Headquarters of the Partisan Movement) being established in Moscow in May 1942 under P.K. Ponomarenko, a former secretary of the Communist Party in Belorussia subsequently given lieutenant-general's rank. It was disbanded in March 1943 but then revived two months later, and it continued to exist until January 1944. Moreover, the successor to the Cheka, the NKVD, dominated the partisan command structure, and, as the Red Army advanced subsequently, so partisans were reabsorbed into it.

Large areas of the Soviet Union were not suited to partisan warfare through the absence of cover, and activity was confined to the forests and marshes of Central European Russia. Nonetheless, it was in these areas that German military movement was confined, in any case, to relatively narrow corridors, making it easier for partisans to attack before melting back into the forests. Moreover, in winter, military movement was often confined even further to a small number of road and rail links. Initially, the partisans numbered about 30,000 in early 1942, increasing to possibly 250,000 by 1943, although some suggest the figure was closer to 500,000 once turnover in personnel is considered. But actual fighting was surprisingly limited in view of the numbers involved. Chiefly, they disrupted communications and had some impact in slowing troop movements, curtailing supplies reaching the front and destroying rolling stock. Indeed, they were directed to attack German units only when they had superiority.

Partisans did play a major role in postponing the German Operation Zitadelle (Citadel) at Kursk in the summer of 1943 by attacks on main railway lines in Operation Rel'sovaia voina (Rail War). They also co-operated successfully with Red Army units during Operation Bagration, which forced the German Army Group Centre out of Belorussia in the summer of 1944, again concentrating on German communications. However, the major partisan offensive mounted in August and September 1943 following the German failure in July failed to paralyse German communications sufficiently to prevent an orderly German withdrawal. Intelligence derived from the partisans was also important. They also appear to have had some limited success in disrupting German economic exploitation of agricultural resources in occupied areas such as the Ukraine, although less success in preventing exploitation of industrial resources, albeit that the re-establishment of industry was only realised by the Germans to a limited extent.

Much more significantly, however, partisans represented an arm of Soviet government behind German lines in collecting taxes, enforcing discipline and obedience, and disseminating Soviet propaganda. It should be noted that, apart from targeting collaborators, the partisans also aimed to provoke the Germans into reprisals against the civilian population, which, to quote Alexander Dallin, was thus 'caught between the hammer and the anvil'.

In fact, only limited German resources were devoted to fighting partisans, since few troops were available for rear area operations. In 1943, for example, while 250,000 men were available for rear area security, a single Sicherungsdivision (security division) of 4,000 men might be responsible for 25,000 square kilometres of territory. In the case of Army Group Centre, one division was responsible for 35,000 square kilometres. Large areas of occupied territory were not garrisoned at all, and the German front line was never continuous. German commanders were used to operating in an independent role with highly mobile forces. They were not overly disturbed by partisans to their rear or the establishment of the so-called partisanskie kraya (partisan regions). Indeed, many German commanders were quite content to hold roads and railways with second-rate, often elderly, troops from the Sicherungsdivisionen of Rear Area Commands, allied contingents such as Hungarians and Rumanians, or locally raised units recruited from subject peoples such as Ukrainians, Belorussians, Latvians and Estonians.

Such locally raised troops served as auxiliary Hiwi (Hiswillige or willing helpers) units, *Landeseigne Sicherungsverbände* (security units), *Schutzmanschaften* (local guard units) or *Ordnungsdienst* (local auxiliary police). In fact, despite their general brutality towards civilians, which invested even the Stalinist regime with a degree of legitimacy that it would not otherwise have enjoyed, the Germans still recruited enough Soviet citizens to have possibly between 3,000 and 4,000 of them in each German division on the Eastern Front by 1943. As many as 250,000 Soviet citizens may have served in the Waffen SS alone. To give some examples, Special Unit Bergmann was raised in the Caucasus, and the 162nd Infantry Division and Infantry Battalion No. 450 from among ethnic Turks and Azeris. Elsewhere, the 13th SS Waffengrenadier (*Handschar Kroatische*) Division was raised from Croatian Muslims. Hitler disliked the use of locally raised anti-partisan units and forbade the creation of new ones after February 1942. The prohibition did not apply to police units controlled by the SS, however, and in practice many German commanders ignored it. In the Ukraine, the nationalist Ukrainska Povstancha Armia (Ukrainian Insurgent Army) or UPA, established in October 1942, fought both the Germans and the Soviets, continuing its resistance against the Soviets into the post-war period.

When compelled to respond actively to partisan activity, the Germans did so almost entirely in terms of military measures, based heavily on reprisals. The jurisdiction order issued in May 1941 for the forthcoming invasion of Russia by the supreme headquarters of the armed forces, Oberkommando der Wehrmacht (OKW), was uncompromising in authorising summary execution and reprisals in the event of guerrilla opposition. Since it appeared to contradict the Hague Convention, which the Soviets themselves had never signed, it was theoretically withdrawn. In September, however, another OKW directive suggested executing between 50 and 100 'communists' for every German soldier killed by partisans. An order issued in General Walther von Reichenau's Sixth Army in October 1941 was scarcely less draconian in authorising death as a penalty for any sign of hostility. Moreover, various directives in July 1941 ruled that those found with arms who were not wearing uniform or recognisable insignia were not to be afforded the status of prisoners of war. Famously, the so-called *Kommissarbefehl* (commissar order) had also been issued in June allowing for the summary execution of Communist Party commissars serving with the Red Army.

In August 1941, Army Group Centre's Rear Area Command directed that even those in uniform west of the Berezina River should be regarded as guerrillas. The notorious *Nacht und Neberlas* (Night and Fog) decree of December 1941 laid down that those suspected of sabotage should be despatched to concentration camps unless there was an absolute certainty that a court martial would sentence them to death. In the same month, OKW also authorised the shooting of ten civilians in retaliation for any member of the Wehrmacht killed by the resistance. Orders issued by many lower formations in Russia suggest that the definition of 'partisan' was wide and that the euphemism of 'anti-partisan operations' served to cover the army's deep involvement in the implementation of Nazi racial policies.

Generally, under a policy of *Kollective Gewaltmassnahmen* (collective reprisal measures), local officials were made accountable for attacks in their districts, with hostages taken and executed in retaliation. Censuses were often compiled and travel restrictions applied. Subsequently, there was a certain recognition of the counter-productivity of reprisals and, in 1942, the army's high command, Oberkommando des Heeres (OKH), directed that troops should undertake retaliatory measures in a more judicious fashion. The general intolerance towards indigenous administrations, however, coupled with the introduction of forced labour, undermined German control. Many men fled to the partisans rather than be subjected to labour conscription, in much the same way that the introduction of such labour conscription in France in July 1943 swelled the numbers of *maquis* in the Massif Central.

The first directive on anti-partisan operation was issued by OKH in October 1941, outlining five different kinds of operation. *Befriedungsunternehmungen* (pacification) by troop detachments and task forces envisaged such a lengthy occupation of specific areas that it could rarely be contemplated. *Grossunternehmungen* (large-scale operations) up to division strength again required too great a diversion of resources from the front line to be considered effective. *Kleinunternehmungen* (small-scale operations) up to company strength was regarded as the best method. *Säuberungsunternehmen* (mopping up) was to follow other operations. Establishing defensive *Stutzpünkte* (strong-points) along main supply routes was the last of the five suggested methods. The directive stressed the need for swift and vigorous reaction to partisan attacks and the benefits of encirclement in ensuring annihilation.

A memorandum by Major Stephanus, serving with Erich von Manstein's Eleventh Army, in December 1941 also stressed careful planning and accurate intelligence as a basis for anti-partisan operations. By mid-1942, most of the German armies in Russia had evolved their own response, Army Group North utilising partisan hunter groups of about 100 men and Army Group South, small mobile groups of so-called *Jagdkommandos* (hunter commandos). The latter were well armed and moved by foot and at night with an emphasis upon reconnaissance, ambush and pursuit.

In August 1942, Hitler issued a new directive, vesting responsibility for anti-partisan warfare, or anti-bandit warfare as it was now officially described, in the hands of Heinrich Himmler. In common with the sentiments of the directive, Himmler paid some lip service to the need to avoid reprisals against civilians unless absolutely necessary. A further OKW directive in November 1942 reiterated the new approach, although those taken with arms and those who harboured partisans were still to be executed. Such restraint as was recommended, however, did not apply to German agencies other than those directly employed in combating partisans. Thus, labour conscription and other exploitative policies remained unchanged. In military terms, Himmler stressed the need for timely intelligence and adequate defensive measures as a basis for the necessary offensive action to be taken against partisan bands. Even decoy partisan bands – what would now be called pseudo forces – were to be established.

In October 1942, Eric von dem Bach-Zelewski was appointed plenipotentiary for combating partisans and, in 1943, *chef der bandenkampfverbände* (chief of anti-bandit warfare). A former soldier who had joined the Nazis in 1930 and risen in the ranks of the SS, Bach-Zelewski had been Higher SS and Police Leader for the Rear Area of Army Group Centre and was later to command the German forces committed to the destruction of the Polish Home Army during the Warsaw rising in August 1944. Operational control, however, remained in the hands of field commanders.

The OKW directive of November 1942 had been informed by reports on anti-partisan experience called for from units by a supplementary addendum to the directive in August. However, it was only belatedly in May 1944 that OKW published an actual manual, *Warfare Against Bands*, by which time the Soviets were on the brink of the major conventional offensive that swept the Germans out of Russia altogether. The manual drew on the best practice, recommending the use of *Jagdkommandos* and counselling encirclement as the best means of annihilating partisans. This might be achieved by 'partridge drives' or a 'spider's web' approach with a partisan 'cauldron' being split into sub-areas and each encircled group being destroyed in turn. Sections were included on the use of air support and armoured trains, while emphasis was also given to the need for a proper delineation of authority between military and SS units, with close co-operation between all relevant authorities.

Figures vary considerably, but it is clear that the Germans inflicted heavy losses on Soviet partisans at little cost to themselves, German losses appearing to average about 6 per cent of those attributed to partisans. So few actual German resources were devoted to the anti-partisan role, indeed, that the considerable effort devoted to partisan warfare by the Soviets appears questionable. It was certainly more effective after 1943, however, when the Germans were generally on the defensive and commanders often faced with demands to hold every yard. This rendered German commanders less free to make tactical withdrawals and more concerned to keep open their lines of communication.

The other most obvious example of partisan warfare was in Yugoslavia, which was invaded by German and Italian forces in April 1941. Although they rapidly overcame the Yugoslav army, the Axis forces then faced an uprising in Croatia in July and in Bosnia and Serbia in August. As indicated earlier, Croatia was given nominal independence, a puppet regime being established by the *Ustase* movement of Ante Pavelic. Pavelic, however, abandoned the Dalmatian Croats to Italian rule and, in many respects, his followers were those who had been marginalised in Croat society before the war: the main pre-war Croatian political leader, Anton Macek, refused to co-operate with the Germans. Indeed, by 1943, for all that Pavelic eliminated hundreds of thousands of Serbs, two-thirds of the partisans fighting the *Ustase* and the Germans were ethnic Croats and not Serbs as is usually supposed. The communists, led by Josip Broz, who took the name Tito (the hammer), were also largely Croats and Slovenes, numbering possibly 150,000 by November 1942.

By contrast, many Serbs collaborated with the Germans. In theory, the main Serbian opponents of the Germans were Draza Mihailovic's *Cetniks*, principally Montenegrin and Serbian royalists. In the event, Mihailovic, as an anti-communist also intent on creating an ethnically pure greater Serbia, drifted into the German camp possibly as early as the autumn of 1941. He was still in receipt of allied aid, however, until November 1943, Tito having begun to receive allied recognition only in June of that year. Confusingly, the Serbian puppet government under General Milan Nedic, established by the Germans in Belgrade, also called its forces *Cetniks*. By the end of 1941, Nedic deployed 25,000 Serbs in various collaborationist units, largely drawn by the expectation that the Germans would enable them to realise the dream of a greater Serbia.

The Germans afforded relatively little military priority to Yugoslavia once they were at war with Russia, but it had considerable economic significance in being the route for Balkan mineral resources diverted to Germany, as well as covering the German flank in Russia and shielding it from allied interference across the Mediterranean. It is usually claimed that Tito tied down fifteen divisions, but the German troops deployed in Yugoslavia after 1941 were distinctly second-rate and over-aged. Indeed, the German strategy was really only a holding action, interspersed with occasional forays as represented by seven different offensives between November 1941 and May 1944, most of which inflicted considerable damage on the partisans even if not eliminating them. Initially, the Germans had relied upon well-armed mobile pursuit detachments of 30 to 50 men, which each battalion was ordered to designate in August 1941. In September, however, it was concluded that this was insufficient and that larger-scale operations would be required, a proposal by General Foertsch, the chief of staff to the Commander South-east, for holding only a 'corridor' through Serbia being rejected by his superior, Field Marshal von List.

In the first German offensive in November 1941, the partisans suffered over 14,600 casualties (60 per cent) but evaded encirclement around Uzice and Cacak in Serbia. In the second German offensive of January 1942, they were driven from the mountains between Sarajevo and Visegrad. In the third, in June 1942, they were ejected from the mountains south of Foca. In both the second and third offensives, however, poor co-ordination between the Germans and their Italian and Croatian allies enabled the partisans to escape, Tito retreating on a 'Long March' of 350 kilometres from south-east Bosnia to Bihac in Croatia between June and September 1942. The fourth German offensive, towards Bihac in January 1943, reduced Tito to 20,000 men and, although he escaped across the Neretva River, it took him into the path of the planned German fifth offensive between May and August 1943, aimed primarily at Cetniks in the Durmitor mountains. Once more, Tito survived. The sixth German offensive, in September 1943, was in effect an occupation of the zones previously occupied by the Italians after their surrender to the allies. Tito's own offensive into Serbia was defeated between December 1943 and January 1944. The seventh, and last, German offensive then came close to capturing Tito, an SS punishment battalion being dropped by parachute on his headquarters at Drvar in May 1944. Tito was forced to relocate his headquarters to the island of Vis in the Adriatic.

What undermined the German effort was a shambolic administration of competing agencies and problems of co-ordination with the Italians, despite the creation of a unified command by the Abbazia agreement of March 1942. Again, too, as elsewhere, the Germans won few friends by their reprisal-led response to opposition, 20,000 hostages alone being shot in the six months following the commencement of the first German offensive in September 1941, 5,000 in a single day at Kragujevac. German mortality rates remained low, however, and the conflict was more of a vicious civil war between Yugoslav factions, at least 600,000 perishing in the internecine wartime ethnic conflict. German efforts ceased in the summer of 1944 as troops were recalled to the collapsing Eastern Front. Nonetheless, the Germans did succeed in their main aim of keeping the partisans out of Serbia and the capital, Belgrade, until October 1944, when it was lost through the combined action of the partisans and the Red Army.

While it could be argued that Tito could not have succeeded in liberating Yugoslavia if the Germans had not been involved in a wider war, the partisans did survive without substantial external assistance. In the process, the communists also built a network of people's liberation committees as a proto-administration. Effectively, political revolution was spread by military means, particularly as the partisans were so frequently forced by German action to move from region to region. Even before the war, the communists had been strengthening their organisation in the countryside and in October 1940 had encouraged members to enlist in the Yugoslav armed forces to receive military training. Following the German invasion, small cells were formed, weapons collected and communication and intelligence networks established. Subsequently, an Anti-Fascist Council of People's Liberation of Yugoslavia was established at Bihac in November 1942 and Tito formally announced the creation of a People's Liberation Army. However, a provisional government was not proclaimed until November 1943, in deference to Stalin. Stalin did not wish to cause himself undue difficulties with his Western allies, who recognised the Yugoslav government in exile in London, of which Mihailovic was nominally minister of war. Whether nominally a council rather than a government, however, the communist administration still exercised control over partisan-controlled areas through a national liberation executive council. In effect, Tito was creating the fabric of a post-war socialist state at the same time that he was fighting the Germans and his rivals.

The politicisation of the partisan conflict in Yugoslavia in itself points to the most significant factor regarding resistance generally. In many cases, the choice of resistance or collaboration was determined by pre-war political events, although the choices made were not always those that might have been expected. Resistance and collaboration equally offered a kind of upward social mobility for groups that had not often enjoyed access to political power before the war. Few of the pre-war elites remained prominent after 1945, although, ironically, the qualities required of resistance leaders did not necessarily equip them for peacetime administration, and pre-war and wartime officials often remained in post.

At least on the surface, resistance was reformist in character. Communism in particular gained prominence through resistance in states like France and Italy, although the communist role was distinctly ambiguous prior to the German invasion of Russia. In Yugoslavia and also in Albania, where Enver Hoxha's National Liberation Movement emerged victorious in another simultaneous struggle against Germans and royalists, communism obviously triumphed. Its influence was blunted in Greece, however, where Colonel Napoleon Zervas's Ethnikos Dimokratikos Ellinikos Syndesmos (National Democratic Greek League, EDES), was opposed by the *andartes* (guerrillas) of the communist Ethniko Apeleftherostiko Metopo (National Liberation Front, EAM), and its military wing, Ellinikos Laikos Apeleftherotikos Stratos (National Liberation Army, ELAS), in a civil war that broke out even before the German evacuation of Greece in October 1944.

Both EAM and EDES had emerged in September 1941 and, initially, co-operated in destroying the viaduct over the Gorgopotamos gorge with the assistance of SOE in November 1941. However, EAM was already trying to establish a proto-administration in rural areas, establishing village committees and dispensing 'people's justice', at the same time targeting and intimidating EDES supporters. Similarly, ELAS moved to eliminate another monarchist group, Ethniki Kai Koinoniki Apeleftherosi (National and Social Liberation, EKKA), killing its leader, Colonel Dimitrios Psarros, in April 1944. By taking advantage of the Italian surrender and seizing most of the Italians' weapons, EAM launched an attack on EDES in October 1943. The so-called Plaka agreement terminated this first round of the civil war in February 1944, but EAM then declared a provisional government in March 1944.

A further complication was that, as elsewhere, the Germans raised local units, while the Greek puppet administration under Ioannis Rallis, who became prime minister in March 1943, raised its own 'security battalions' to fight ELAS, which together with German-organised ethnic Vlach, Pontic and Macedonian militias mustered 18,000 men. By 1944, the Germans had also begun to sponsor what were effectively local death squads, such as Ethnikos Agrotikos Syndesmos Antikommounistikis Draseos (National Agricultural Federation of Anti-Communist Action, EASAD), to counter ELAS. The general German reaction to the *andartes* was familiar, reprisals being substituted for a more coherent strategy. Similar directives to those issued in both Russia and Yugoslavia were applied in Greece, possibly 25,000 Greeks dying as a result.

There was some division of opinion among the British on the policy to adopt with regard to EAM, and there was a decided ambiguity towards the security battalions. Ultimately, British troops engaged ELAS forces in Athens in December 1944 on behalf of the Greek government in exile. EAM was forced for the time being to accept a cease-fire in January 1945. In theory, under the Varkiza agreement in the following month, ELAS disbanded in return for an amnesty, a plebiscite on Greece's future and a general election.

If the German occupation of Europe had brought the spectre of communist-inspired insurgency in those states that had not fallen under Soviet control in 1945, the impact of the Second World War was arguably even more significant in the Far East. Those indigenous nationalists who had fought the Japanese, and also those who had co-operated with Japanese administration, were equally determined to prevent the return of the colonial authorities defeated by the Japanese in 1941–42. In seeking a model for national liberation, groups such as MPAJA in Malaya and two other communist-dominated anti-Japanese coalitions, the Viet Nam Doc Lap Dong Minh (Vietnam Independence League, or Viet Minh), in French Indo-China and the Hakbo ng Bayan laban sa Hapon (People's Anti-Japanese Army), popularly known as the Hukbalahap or Huks, in the Philippines did not need to look to Europe. A much more relevant model was already available to them in the theories of the leader of the Chinese Communist Party, Mao Tse-tung.

Further reading

On resistance, see M.R.D. Foot, *Resistance* (London, 1976); David Stafford, *Britain and European Resistance, 1940–45* (London, 1980); Tony Judt (ed.), *Resistance and Revolution in Mediterranean Europe, 1939–48* (London, 1989); Stephen Hawes and Ralph White (eds), *Resistance in Europe, 1939–45* (London, 1975); H.R. Kedward, *Occupied France: Collaboration and Resistance, 1940–44* (Oxford, 1985); Kedward, *In Search of the Maquis: Rural Resistance in Southern France, 1942–44* (Oxford, 1993); and Henri Michel, *The Shadow War* (London, 1972).

On SOE and OSS, see M.R.D. Foot, *SOE in France* (London, 1966); R. Harris-Smith, *OSS* (Los Angeles, 1972); and B.F. Smith, *The Shadow Warriors* (New York, 1983). On Wingate, see Derek Tulloch, *Wingate in Peace and War* (London, 1972); and Dawn Miller, 'Raising the Tribes: British Policy in Italian East Africa, 1938–41' *Journal of Strategic Studies* 22 (1999), pp. 96–123. On other special forces, see Tony Geraghty, *Who Dares Wins: The Story of the Special Air Service* (London, 1980).

On Soviet partisans, see E. Howell, *The Soviet Partisan Movement, 1941–44* (Washington, 1956); John A. Armstrong (ed.), *Soviet Partisans in World War Two* (Madison, 1964); C.A. Dixon and Otto Heilbrunn, *Communist Guerrilla Warfare* (London, 1954); Otto Heilbrunn, *Partisan Warfare* (New York, 1967); Heilbrunn, *War in the Enemy's Rear* (London, 1963); F. Osanka (ed.), *Modern Guerrilla Warfare: Fighting Communist Guerrilla Movements, 1941–61* (New York, 1962); and Leonid Grenkevich, *The Soviet Partisan Movement, 1941–44* (London, 1999).

On Yugoslavia, see Phyllis Auty, *Tito* (London, 1970); Philip J. Cohen, *Serbia's Secret War: Propaganda and the Deceit of History* (Houston, 1996); P.H. Hehn, 'Serbia, Croatia and Germany, 1941–45: Civil War and Revolution in the Balkans' *Canadian Slavonic Papers* (1969), pp. 344–73; M.J. Milazzo, *The Chetnik Movement and the Yugoslav Resistance* (Baltimore, 1975); and Tim Judah, *The Serbs: History, Myth and the Destruction of Yugoslavia* (New Haven, 1997).

On German counter-insurgency, see Alexander Dallin, *German Rule in Russia, 1941–45* (2nd edn, Boulder, 1981); H.H. Gardner, *Guerrilla and Counterguerrilla Warfare in Greece, 1941–45* (Washington, 1962); Paul H. Hehn, *The German Struggle against Yugoslav Partisans in World War Two: German Counter-insurgency in Yugoslavia, 1941–43* (Boulder, 1979); R.M. Kennedy, *German Anti-guerrilla Operations in the Balkans, 1941–45* (Washington, 1954); C.P. von Luttichau, *Guerrilla and Counter-guerrilla Warfare in Russia during World War Two* (Washington, 1963); Keith Simpson, 'The German Experience of Rear Area Security on the Eastern Front, 1941–45' *Journal of the Royal United Services Institute for Defence Studies* 121 (1976), pp. 39–46; Timothy Mulligan, 'Reckoning the Cost of the People's War: The German Experience in the Central USSR' *Russian History* 9 (1982), pp. 27–48; Malcolm Cooper, *The Phantom War: The German Struggle against Soviet Partisans, 1941–44* (London, 1979); Omar Bartov, *The Eastern Front, 1941–45: German Troops and the Barbarisation of Warfare* (London, 1986); Bartov, *Hitler's Army: Soldiers, Nazis, and War in the Third Reich* (Oxford, 1992); Mark Mazower, *Inside Hitler's Greece: The Experience of Occupation, 1941–44* (New Haven, 1993); and Theo Schulte, *The German Army and Nazi Policies in Occupied Russia* (Oxford, 1989).

4

MAO TSE-TUNG AND REVOLUTIONARY WARFARE

Theories of guerrilla warfare invariably reflect the experience of their author and are specific to a particular point in time and to particular circumstances. Consequently, while widely emulated, a theory may not easily be translated into success in an entirely different context from that in which the original was perceived to have succeeded. There is no better example of this than the theory of revolutionary warfare associated with Mao Tse-tung, one of the most influential theorists of insurgency in the twentieth century. Mao's example was consciously emulated by many of those who waged insurgent conflict against Western states and Western interests after 1945. They were not always successful, however, for the context of China in the 1920s and 1930s could not be easily reproduced elsewhere.

Mao himself repeatedly described China in his writings as being both semi-colonial and semi-feudal in the 1920s and 1930s, since 80 per cent of the population were rural peasants, often existing in conditions of extreme hardship and privation. In 1911, the Manchu Ching (Qing) Dynasty had finally collapsed and China had broken up into a number of near-autonomous warlordships. In the eastern and south-eastern cities, however, there was a growing nationalist movement, drawing support primarily from the industrialised urban population and known as the KMT. Founded in 1911 by Sun Yat-sen, the KMT claimed to represent the legitimate government of the republic proclaimed in February 1912 and sought to reunite China by force. After Sun's death in March 1925, leadership of the KMT was assumed by Chiang Kai-shek, best described as a revolutionary militarist. Chiang was determined to instigate a national renaissance based on disciplined unity.

Sun Yat-sen had admired Bolshevik organisation and had accepted support from the Soviet Union after 1917, although he never believed that Marxist-Leninism would become popular in China. Consequently, when a Chinese Communist Party was founded in Shanghai in 1921, its members were encouraged to participate in the KMT. When Chiang moved decisively against the warlords in 1926, however, the communists began to try to establish peasant associations and trade unions in those rural and urban areas cleared of warlord troops. They also supported that faction within the KMT critical of Chiang's authoritarianism. Regarding any dissent or deviation within the KMT as dangerous, Chiang halted his northern advance in 1927 in order to purge the communists from the KMT. Guided by advice from Moscow, the Communist Party leadership attempted the so-called 'Autumn Harvest' urban uprising in the cities of the south-east such as Canton (Guangzhou), Nanchang and Shanghai. The result was utter disaster for the communists, with those who survived fleeing southwards and westwards. Assuming victory, Chiang established a national government in Nanking (Nanjing) in October 1927.

Among those forced to flee was Mao Tse-tung, who took refuge in the Chingkang (Jinggang) mountains. Born in 1893 and the son of a prosperous farmer in Hunan province – Mao never lost his pronounced accent – he completed his secondary education and took employment in 1917 as a library assistant at Peking (Beijing) University. There he came into contact with Marxism for the first time. Indeed, he was one of the founders of the Communist Party in 1921, but he frequently clashed with the party leadership and was not to establish his own primacy until the mid-1930s. Mao recognised the scale of the defeat in 1927, and the subsequent failures between 1927 and 1934 of conventional positional warfare. The latter was favoured by the party leadership, under the influence of the German communist and representative of the Comintern, Otto Braun, and by conventionally trained communist military leaders such as Chu Teh (Zhu De), who had studied at the Yunnan Military Academy and in Germany; Hsu Hsiang-ch'ien, a graduate of China's elite Whampoa Military Academy; and Liu Po-ch'eng, who had graduated from the Frunze Military Academy in Moscow.

Chu Teh, however, changed his mind following the disasters of 1927. Indeed, he is credited with the guerrilla mantra first articulated in May 1928: 'The enemy advances, we retreat; the enemy camps, we harass; the enemy tires, we attack; the enemy retreats, we pursue'. He Long and Fang Chih-min (Fang Zhimin) have also been credited with significant contributions to the evolving alternative of guerrilla warfare. Mao in particular, however, began to recognise that the Marxist-Leninist model of urban revolution was inappropriate for an overwhelmingly rural population, which was both conservative and parochial in outlook and attitudes.

In fact, Chinese rural society was not entirely dominated by the large landlords, whom Mao so readily identified as the real villains within the social system, since it was actually a society of many smallholders. The KMT, however, certainly had the support of many local landowners, who were more than capable of organising village militias through the traditional *bao jia* system of societal control. Indeed, in many respects, while Mao was to exploit issues such as land reform, the outcome of his revolution would depend largely on the respective strengths and weaknesses of communist and KMT organisation in the countryside.

However, it should be emphasised that Mao's theories did not evolve overnight. Nor did they find ready acceptance within the party until further failures had forced the communists to retreat even further into the interior. In fact, the KMT was increasingly successful in its operations against the communists once Chiang, having completed the defeat of the warlords of the north, turned his mind in 1930 to the eradication of the remaining communist groups in the 'soviets' established in the southern areas of Kiangsi (Jiangxi) and Oyuwan, which straddled the borders of the provinces of Hunan, Hupei (Hubei) and Anwhei (Anhui).

Chiang's first two 'encirclement and annihilation' campaigns in 1930 and 1931 were largely conventional sweeping operations entrusted to former warlord troops, but they were ill co-ordinated and failed to crush the communist soviets. However, some damage was done to communist organisation by infiltration on the part of Chiang's Anti-Bolshevik Corps. The third and fourth 'encirclement and annihilation' campaigns in 1931 and 1933 did rather greater damage but were still not sufficient to eliminate the soviets. Accordingly, Chiang himself took personal command of a fifth campaign in the summer of 1933 and, with advice from the German army's former chief of staff, Hans von Seeckt, assembled 700,000 troops under officers newly instructed in counter-guerrilla techniques.

The communist soviets were sealed off and progressively divided with networks of over 3,000 well-defended and fortified blockhouses, and new roads patrolled by armoured cars and aircraft. Four categories of area were identified – safety zones, adjacent to bandit areas, semi-bandit areas and full-bandit areas – and co-ordinated mobile columns were used progressively to drive the communists against the blockhouse lines. It was not unlike the methods used by the British against Boer commandos. Robbed of mobility, by October 1934, the communists were forced to abandon their base areas and try to break out of the encirclement, initiating that great epic of Chinese communist history, the 'Long March'. Of the 120,000 communists who began the 6,000-mile journey, only 20,000 finally reached the relative security of Yenan (Yanan) in Shensi (Shaanxi) province in the far north in the autumn of 1935, although they had picked up about 40,000 recruits along the way.

Mao and the principal communist military commander, Chu Teh, had rejected the party leadership's call for further urban campaigns in September 1930 and now became more influential as a result of the disasters of 1933–34. In many respects, though, the process of change had begun in 1927–28 immediately prior to the party's sixth congress, convened in Moscow in June 1928. It was a matter, in the short term, of finding a means of survival and, in the long term, of finding a strategy appropriate to the situation in which the communists found themselves and to the reality of China in the 1930s. As it evolved, the key to survival and to ultimate success would be the intimate connection between the concepts of time, space, will and substitution.

Time was required in order to rebuild the party's organisational strength, for it was clearly much weaker than its opponent and the army itself was little more than a ragtag of workers, peasants, mercenaries, bandits and those who had either deserted the KMT or been taken prisoner by the communists and persuaded to join them. Time would also allow the inherent weaknesses of the KMT to be exposed. Time could be won for the revolution by trading space for time, Mao writing:

> To gain territory is no cause for joy and to lose territory is no cause for sorrow. To lose territory or cities is of no importance. The important thing is to think up ways of destroying the enemy.

Given the weakness of the communists in 1934, the one resource on which they could draw was the geographical remoteness of the mountains into which they had now retreated, and which offered ample space. The time won could then be translated into building will, which meant forging a common cause and a determination to win among both communists and the population, upon whose support they were entirely dependent for ultimate victory. At the same time, it also implied the parallel destruction of the opponent's will, since the winner of a revolutionary war would be the side with the greater will to outlast its opponent. Substitution implied finding means of drawing upon what strengths were possessed in order to offset weaknesses. Thus, propaganda might substitute for weapons, subversion might substitute for air power, manpower for mechanisation, political mobilisation for industrial mobilisation, and so on.

In the short term, guerrilla warfare offered the most suitable means of survival, but it must be emphasised that Mao always regarded the ultimate aim as the creation of a regular army capable of meeting and defeating opponents on the conventional battlefield. Guerrilla warfare was but one step on the revolutionary road, and the strategic role of the guerrilla was to transform himself in due course into a regular soldier. In isolation, guerrilla warfare could achieve no more than tactical gains, and it was thus fully integrated into a wider revolutionary strategy. Indeed, to succeed guerrilla war also needed a clear political aim, and here Mao appears to have been influenced by the work of Clausewitz, whose works had long been available in Chinese translation and used at the Chinese military academies. Clausewitz regarded guerrilla tactics as an adjunct of conventional war and also saw war as an extension of political action. In fact, Mao quoted Clausewitz directly in one of his essays, and there is more than an echo in another Maoist phrase, 'Politics is war without bloodshed; war is politics with bloodshed'. The marked feature of the Maoist approach throughout was its political nature, the decisive elements not being purely military factors but the political and the psychological.

Mao believed the whole process would be protracted and would take place in the context of three phases of revolution. Different authors have given these phases differing names, but the essential meaning remains the same. It should also be noted that, in practice, the phases were likely to be less distinct than in theory and could merge one into another. Temporary setbacks, for example, might compel the revolutionary forces to revert to a less developed phase and, in any case, there was no set timetable for the application of each phase.

The first phase, essentially a pre-revolutionary one, has been variously described as 'strategic defensive', 'organisation and consolidation', and even 'conspiracy'. 'Strategic defensive' is probably the best translation, since it was a phase in which the communists would be much weaker than their opponents and, while not passive, must remain largely on the defensive. The aim was to expand party organisation and to establish the essential infrastructure for the future development of the revolution. Cadres would be infiltrated into key positions in localities through organisation of peasant associations, and party workers recruited and trained to generate support for the movement. Preparation would be both lengthy and covert in order to prepare the way for guerrilla action. Limited force might be applied to intimidate and coerce the population before being directed more precisely at the organisation of the opposing authority in order to foster a climate of dissent, civil disobedience and economic unrest. Popular support would be increased by identification with popular causes such as land reform and grievances such as the high rents paid to absentee landlords, the communist message conveyed to a largely illiterate peasantry through familiar traditional forms such as plays, poems and songs. Opponents would be neutralised or eliminated, and the authorities discredited. In fact, the initial recruits for the party were nearly always drawn from marginal members of society rather than the 'masses' as such, and it was the presence of party cadres that was crucial to growth.

The careful political preparation of this first phase was designed to convince the peasantry that their lives could be improved only by supporting the communists, and it was essential if the guerrillas were to survive, for 'the guerrilla must be in the population as little fishes in the ocean'. Thus, although there might well be an element of coercion and intimidation, for no neutrals could be tolerated, stress was laid on the need to cultivate the good opinion of the peasant. This is illustrated by the tone of the 'Three Rules', articulated by Mao immediately before the Long March and the 'Eight Remarks', articulated earlier by Mao and Lin Piao (Lin Biao) in January 1928. The Rules stated:

> All actions are subject to command; Do not steal from the people; Be neither selfish nor unjust.

Equally, the Remarks directed:

> Replace the door when you leave the house; Roll up the bedding on which you have slept; Be courteous; Be honest in your transactions;

Return what you borrow; Replace what you break; Do not bathe in the presence of women; Do not without authority search the pocket-books of those you arrest.

The remark concerning doors reflects the custom of lifting them off and using them as beds in the summer months.

At an appropriate time, the first phase would lead to the second phase of what has again been variously called 'strategic stalemate', 'preparation for counter-offensive', 'progressive expansion' or, perhaps best, 'equilibrium'. In this phase, there was deemed to be sufficient popular support, sympathy or acquiescence to allow the expansion of political action into guerrilla warfare in a situation of rough equivalence in strength between the communists and their opponents. Bases would be established, the tempo of recruitment increased and regular units trained for future employment. Minor guerrilla actions would become widespread, and a pattern would emerge in which revolutionary domination of a particular locality would result in the establishment of a revolutionary administration. This competition in government would demonstrate that the communists were capable of providing an alternative and better administration than that of the existing authorities, who would be further weakened and disheartened. Above all, this was a phase of attritional struggle between the opposing sides.

The guerrilla aspects of this second phase itself were not original in conception but drew clearly on the Chinese classics, such as *Outlaws of the Marshes* (*The Water Margin*) and especially Sun Tzu's *The Art of War*. Indeed, Mao's 'Ten Principles' were at best banal:

Attack dispersed and isolated enemy first. Concentrate forces later; Win control of rural areas first; Wipe out the enemy's effective strength; Use local superiority; Do not fight unless you are sure to win; Fear no sacrifice; Seize weak areas first; Use captured men and weapons; Rest, regroup and train between battles.

Finally, there would come the third phase, variously described as one of 'decision and destruction', or, most succinctly, 'strategic offensive', in which the communists would now be stronger than their opponents and could achieve victory. In what would be seen as a far shorter phase than the other two, mobile warfare would now commence with the regular units introduced in a near conventional conflict, although retaining some characteristics of guerrilla warfare where appropriate. In some circumstances, such careful preparation might have been undertaken that such a final phase might not even be required.

While this may appear a well-integrated approach to revolution, it is necessary once more to reiterate that it was not formulated overnight. Indeed, the three phases corresponded to three distinct phases in the actual development of the Chinese Civil War. Thus, Mao's articles between 1928 and 1936 reflected the early struggle against the KMT, his articles between 1936 and 1945 the next phase, which covered the period of Japanese intervention in mainland China, and those from 1946 to 1949 related to the last and largely conventional phase of the conflict between 1945 and 1949, which led to the defeat of the KMT and the proclamation of the People's Republic of China on 1 October 1949. However, the theory was essentially developed between 1936 and 1938, in three separate articles: 'Problems of Strategy in China's Revolutionary War', written in December 1936; 'Problems of Strategy in the Guerrilla War against Japan', dating from May 1938; and, in its most developed form, 'On Protracted War', also in May 1938. Elements of the second article also appeared earlier in a pamphlet of 1937, *On Guerrilla War*, which was translated by an American marine observer in China, Samuel Griffith. This was the first English version of Maoist thought, although, curiously, no actual copy of the original pamphlet has ever been found.

Not unnaturally, given the ultimate success of Mao in coming to power in China, his theories were to have wide currency thereafter. But, at this point, it is important to stress one further significant factor in the Chinese equation, namely the intervention of the Japanese. Japan had seized Manchuria in September 1931, and one reason why Chiang chose to take command of the fifth campaign against the communists himself in 1933 was the growing menace of Japanese aggression, which suggested a need to settle internal matters swiftly. Moreover, one reason why the communists were able to escape to Shensi in 1934–35 was the reluctance of some nationalist commanders to annihilate them through their greater fear of Japanese ambitions. His subordinates having failed to extinguish the communists by an all-out offensive on the Shensi base area as intended in September 1935, Chiang again prepared to take the field himself.

On arriving to conduct the new campaign in December 1936, however, Chiang was arrested by his generals in the so-called Sian (Xi'an) incident and not released until he had agreed to form an anti-Japanese united front with the communists, which effectively ended the KMT's anti-communist drive. Indeed, the communist army became the Eighth Route Army under the nominal control of the national government. Ultimately, however, the united front ended with a pitched battle between the KMT and the communist Fourth Red Army in January 1941. Probably influenced by the 'new democracy' theories of the Bulgarian communist and general secretary of the Comintern, Georgi Dimitrov, who advocated the formation of anti-fascist 'popular fronts', Mao recognised the usefulness of the concept of the 'united front' as a means of mobilising opinion of all classes as an integral step towards the goal of societal transition. Henceforth, a 'people's republic' could embrace all but 'enemy classes'.

In July 1937, the Japanese launched a full-scale war of conquest against the remainder of China, which saw the KMT effectively defeated by 1939 and pushed back sufficiently to be contained relatively easily. Certainly, the KMT no longer posed any threat to the communists. Previously, the communists had taken the path of least resistance and operated only in areas where KMT organisation was weak and where there were no KMT rural co-operatives, which could readily call upon KMT forces for assistance. Now, it could be argued, the communists got all the time they required for political preparation, since they were largely separated from the KMT by the Japanese presence.

The Japanese did not regard the communists as a serious threat and, in any case, could not spare the manpower to occupy and control much of the territory they had overrun. Provided vital urban centres and strategic lines of communication were under their control, they were not overly concerned by what they saw as merely banditry. After the communists' only major offensive against them, the so-called 'Campaign of a Hundred Regiments' from August to October 1940, the Japanese did adopt a more pro-active, anti-guerrilla stance sufficient to deter the communists from any repetition, but, by 1941, their involvement in the Second World War had diverted their attention elsewhere. Much was left, therefore, to the forces of the puppet administration of the China National Government, established in March 1940 to succeed an earlier China Restoration Government.

In 1940, indeed, this government had 41,000 troops, a gendarmerie of 72,000 men and 63,000 police. They were neither well armed nor well trained, however, and were regarded as easy targets by the KMT and the communists.

As it happened, the Japanese had evolved relatively effective anti-bandit methods in Manchuria after 1931, characterised as a combination of 'peace preservation operations' to deprive bandits of any popular support, 'submission operations' to induce bandits to surrender, and 'subjugation operations' to destroy bandit groups, which mustered about 3,000 activists, drawn mostly from former warlord armies. It involved a surprising amount of attention to what could be called 'winning hearts and minds', with attempts to improve the quality of local officials. The Japanese constructed more roads, which provided some employment for the local population, but also concentrated the people within protected villages. Amnesties were also instituted to draw out the bandits.

Those who declined to surrender would then be targeted by the subjugation operations, which would take place in the winter months and be conducted by small groups of hand-picked and well-armed but lightly equipped volunteers. The subjugation units would remain in the field all winter, relying on pre-located supply dumps in 'cave shelters' and specially constructed 'guard stations'. By the late 1930s, most of the bandits had been eliminated or had fled into the Soviet Union. One of the latter was Kim Il Sung, later communist leader of North Korea.

In China proper, the task of combating any communist threat devolved to the North China Army, which also attempted to restore local administration and economic life as well as re-establishing the ancient *pao chia* mutual surveillance system of collective responsibility. A local militia was also established. There were occasional sweep operations, such as the 25 mounted in Shantung (Shandong) province between March 1939 and December 1940, but most effort was devoted to guarding the railways, with villages adjacent to the lines – now called 'cherishing villages' – being made partly responsible for security in their areas. Roads were constructed parallel to the railway lines, and pillboxes and blockhouses erected at regular intervals.

The targeting of the railways by the communists in their campaign of summer 1940 stirred General Yasuji Okamura, who took command of the North China Army in July 1941, into the rather more active coercion of the 'three-all campaign', standing for 'take all, burn all, kill all'. In many respects, it was aimed as much at those likely to support the guerrillas as at the guerrillas themselves. The pattern was set in the experimental 'security strengthening campaign' ordered by Okamura, by which four areas were flooded with 18,000 troops for 'pacification by prolonged occupation'. The Japanese began to do serious damage to the communists, reducing the population of communist-controlled areas by 15 million and communist forces by 100,000. It was intended to continue the campaign for three years. However, this effort could not be sustained after December 1941, and the extreme measures to which the Japanese resorted, including indiscriminate use of artillery, merely further strengthened peasant support for the communists. The latter were to benefit further by being available to accept the Japanese surrender in northern China in 1945 and to take the Japanese weapons and equipment.

The communists were considerably stronger than the KMT by 1945, the People's Liberation Army (PLA) being formally established in May 1946. Indeed, Chiang had lost many of his best troops during the war against the Japanese. Conventional communist operations began in earnest in 1947, with KMT forces largely isolated in the cities by September 1948. The PLA then went on to the offensive, defeating the KMT in a two-month battle at Hsuchow (Xuzhou) between December 1948 and January 1949. Mao entered Peking on 21 January 1949, launching his forces across the Yangtze River (Changjiang) in April to take Nanking and Shanghai.

Having been largely prepared simply to contain rather than neutralise the communists at a crucial time between 1937 and 1940, therefore, the Japanese effectively conspired with the KMT to give Mao all the time he required to prepare for the future. That was a factor not necessarily likely to recur for those who slavishly emulated Maoist revolutionary strategy without regard for the circumstances in which it had succeeded in China. Yet, clearly, Maoism was to have significant currency because it suggested that even the weakest movement or the most primitive of societies could adopt a militant political stance, and a form of military and political resistance, that could prevail against a vastly superior opponent. Subsequently, too, Mao argued that the assumption by the United States of an imperialist role in Asia and elsewhere after 1945 provided revolutionaries with the opportunity to cloak revolution in the kind of nationalist and quasi-democratic rhetoric that had supported the notion of the united front against the Japanese. Maoist principles were therefore applied by communist or other insurgent groups in such states as Malaya between 1948 and 1960, Burma between 1949 and 1955, the Philippines between 1946 and 1954, Algeria between 1954 and 1962, Portuguese Africa between 1961 and 1974, Rhodesia between 1972 and 1980, and the Dhofar region of Oman between 1966 and 1975. The persistence of Maoism is also illustrated by its revival in the Philippines between 1968 and 1993, the insurgency in Thailand between 1965 and 1983, that in Peru since 1980 and the initial Maoist influence over the insurgency in Sri Lanka since 1971.

In Africa in particular, the Maoist influence was clear in the case of Amilcar Cabral, the leader of Partido Africano da Independência de Guiné e Cabo Verde (African Party for the Independence of Guinea and Cape Verde, PAIGC), against Portuguese rule in Portuguese Guinea between 1956 and his assassination in 1973. It is also apparent in the case of Robert Mugabe, who emerged as leader of the Zimbabwe African National Union (ZANU) in Rhodesia in 1974, and who wrote of the Rhodesian war ending in the second phase of the revolutionary struggle. Kwame Nkrumah's work on guerrilla warfare, *Handbook of Revolutionary Warfare*, published in 1968, two years after his own overthrow in Ghana in a military coup, has elements of Maoism. Similarly, although they produced no actual theorist as such, members of Jonas Savimbi's group, União Nacional para a Independência Total de Angola (National Union for the Total Independence of Angola, UNITA), which fought the Portuguese in Angola between 1964 and 1974 and has continued to fight the post-1975 Marxist government, were known as the 'Black Chinese' for their adherence to Maoist principles. In the case of Sri Lanka, it was Rohanna Wijeweera's Janatha Vimukthi Peramuna (People's Liberation Front, JVP), founded in 1969, that showed most Maoist influence. The JVP was largely broken in 1971, however, and a revival of its activities in 1987 had been ended by 1990. By contrast, most of the Tamil groups, whose insurgency gathered pace after 1978 and still continues, were originally more avowedly influenced by Ernesto Che Guevara's *foco* (focus) theories.

The Indonesian nationalist Abdul Harris Nasution, whose *Fundamentals of Guerrilla Warfare* was originally published in 1953, worked independently of Mao. His theories are strikingly similar, however, not least in the belief that the ultimate aim of guerrillas should be the transition to a conventional army.

However, the most obvious followers of Mao were the two Vietnamese theorists of revolutionary war: Truong Chinh, the pen name of Dang Xuan Khu, who was secretary-general of the Indochinese Communist Party; and Vo Nguyen Giap, commander-in-chief of the Viet Minh and minister of the interior in the Democratic Republic of Vietnam proclaimed by Ho Chi Minh in September 1945. Generally, the Viet Minh's debt to Mao is obvious from its emphasis upon creating a broad united front, attaching equal importance to political and military considerations, relying upon a protracted guerrilla war, ultimately building a conventional army, and establishing a secure rural base. However, both Truong Chinh and Giap laid great stress on the mobilisation of international opinion in support of the revolution, reflecting a changing world from that of China in the 1930s.

Like Mao, Truong Chinh's *Primer for Revolt: The August Revolution*, published in 1945 before the French reasserted control in Indo-China, and his *The Resistance Will Win*, published in 1947, stressed the total mobilisation of the population in a prolonged struggle. He envisaged the struggle as one of opposing strengths with, for example, Vietnamese political and motivational strength prevailing over French military and technological strength in the First Indo-Chinese War of 1946–54. Both Truong Chinh and Giap also restyled Mao's three phases, Truong Chinh referring to them as *phong ngu* (contention or defence), *cam cu* (equilibrium) and *phan khoi nghia* (general counter-offensive). Giap's *People's War, People's Army*, published in 1962, placed less emphasis on mass support and even more on the role of conventional military operations, notably expounding the 'bloody blow' to break an opponent's will, the concept of 'mobile warfare' marking the transition from defensive guerrilla tactics to offensive conventional operations.

However, it has been argued that the impetus towards adopting and adapting Maoist theory probably emanated from Ho Chi Minh. Ho had written the article on guerrilla warfare in 1927 previously mentioned and, on his return to Vietnam in 1941, translated a number of Chinese and Russian works on guerrilla warfare as well as an account of the evolving campaign in China. In particular, he emphasised the need to operate in both rural and urban areas. Indeed, there was a tendency on the part of the Vietnamese to view the 'August Revolution', by which the Viet Minh moved in August 1945 to supplant the Japanese after they had surrendered to the allies and before the French could return, as a combination of the political aspects of armed insurrection and the military aspects of protracted war. Truong Chinh also suggested that the third stage of the revolution could be launched without the decisive military superiority demanded by Mao.

In practice, too, Giap sought to achieve a short cut in the protracted struggle by moving too early into the third phase in his Red River delta campaign against the French in 1950–51. The development was heralded in his pamphlet, 'The Military Task in Preparation for the General Counter-offensive', which emphasised the idea that mobile war could lead to the liberation of territory and annihilation of the enemy that would truly mark victory in a revolutionary war. Indeed, as reiterated in *People's War, People's Army*, Giap believed the escalation from guerrilla to mobile war a necessary 'general law' of revolution. Consequently, Giap followed much the same course in both the Tet offensive against South Vietnam in 1968, which appears to have been modelled on the 'Campaign of a Hundred Regiments', and the Easter offensive of 1972. On each occasion, Giap suffered heavy military defeat, although this did not prevent ultimate victory in 1975. Moreover, as in China in 1949, victory did indeed result from conventional rather than guerrilla warfare.

It should be noted that the Vietnamese version of Maoist methods involved more obvious intimidation of the population in the early stages of the revolution. In practice, however, the use of terror was actually highly selective, so that its victims could be explained away by communist propagandists as collaborators, exploiters or criminals.

Obviously, the Vietnamese version of Mao was successful, but application of Maoist theory did not automatically produce victories, and none of the other Maoist insurgencies in South-east Asia succeeded. Partly, as will be seen in a later chapter, this was through the evolution of suitable methods of counter-insurgency in the case of Malaya and the Philippines, but in any case, the world was rapidly changing by the late 1940s and 1950s. Thus, Truong Chinh and Giap internationalised Maoist thought by projecting the revolutionary cause beyond the confines of Indo-China and, in effect, carrying the struggle to the domestic populations of France and the United States. In this regard, the emergence of the superpowers after 1945 was also crucial, since it introduced the possibility of sponsored proxy struggles. As previously mentioned, the Soviet leader, Nikita Khrushchev, promoted 'wars of national liberation' in 1961, and the Kennedy administration responded with a global counter-insurgency doctrine.

Contributing to the globalisation of insurgency after 1945 was the development of mass communications and the ability of the insurgent to use the media in ways undreamed of by Mao, especially in urban areas. The development of technology implicit in communications was also reflected in the technological evolution of weaponry so that guerrilla groups were increasingly far better armed than in the past, even if the monopoly of firepower was likely to remain with the security forces. The development of urban insurgency in itself suggested that a theory intended for an undeveloped rural environment might not be relevant to an increasingly industrialised urban world. Yet, even where Maoist revolutionary warfare theory did continue to appear in predominantly rural environments such as Thailand in the 1960s and 1970s, and Peru in the 1980s, it was increasingly less effective, primarily because lessons had been learned by the opponents of Maoist insurgency. Moreover, where states genuinely embraced or moved towards democracy the Maoist model had little to offer, since much depended upon convincing the population that the limited consultation process envisaged in the relationship between the party and the 'masses' was sufficient democracy.

The Thai Communist Party (CPT) was originally a creation of ethnic Chinese and Vietnamese prior to the Second World War. Increasingly dominated by Maoists, the CPT resolved on launching a 'people's war' at its 1961 congress and opened its campaign in August 1965. Some limited support was derived from the communist Pathet Lao (Land of the Laos) in neighbouring Laos. Support for insurgency was strongest in the north-east of Thailand, where there was a strong sense of regional identity and also tension between Thais and the H'mong hill tribes, from whom most insurgents were drawn. As elsewhere in Maoist-style insurgencies, the CPT built an elaborate infrastructure of committees down to village level to generate sources of manpower, intelligence, money, food and shelter. Faced with the insurgency, the Thai government contributed troops to the war against communism in South Vietnam and covert assistance to the government of Laos. It also established a Communist Suppression Operations Command (CSOC) in December 1965 under the direction of Saiyud Kerdphol.

Unfortunately, Saiyud's attempts to co-ordinate the government response encountered considerable opposition within the Royal Thai Army, which remained addicted to counter-productive large-scale search-and-destroy operations. US economic assistance, directed through an Accelerated Rural Development (ARD) scheme, also failed to reduce the level of insurgency, because, as a one-dimensional economic approach, it did not address the need for simultaneous political development of the north-east. The general political instability in Thailand, which resulted in coups in both 1973 and 1976, also hampered progress in combating insurgency.

However, Maoist methods were equally inappropriate to a society that, while technically 'rural', was actually largely concentrated in regional urban centres. Moreover, the only centre of power that mattered was Bangkok, with a population in excess of four million. An internal debate within the CPT on whether or not to change strategy caused divisions, which were exacerbated by those over how to react to the Sino-Vietnamese War in 1979. Meanwhile, a new response to insurgency was evolved after 1973 by the deputy commander of the Thai Second Army, Prem Tinsulanonda, building on that by Saiyud. In 1976, Prem assumed command of the Second Army and then became army commander-in-chief in September 1978 and prime minister in March 1980. Prem made CSOC, now the Internal Security Operations Command (ISOC), an integral part of the chain of command rather than merely an advisory body. The emphasis was also placed on political as well as military measures, building new mass organisations in support of the three traditional pillars of Thai society, namely Buddhism, the concept of a Thai nation and the monarchy. Indeed, the CPT's error in denouncing the monarchy, which remained immensely popular, assisted in establishing a 13,000-strong militia known as 'Rangers'. The CPT's headquarters was captured in early 1982 and, by mid-1983, it had ceased to be a significant threat.

As will become apparent later, rural insurgency in Latin America had been dealt a further blow by the failure of Guevara's *foco* theory in the 1960s. Significantly, however, Peru remained the least populated Latin American state after the urban growth of the 1960s. Like other states in Latin America, it had experienced periods of military government but was relatively untouched by insurgency until the 1980s. A new and serious challenge then emerged in 1980 in the form of Sendero Luminoso (Shining Path).

Unusually, Peru experienced a radical rather than a conservative military coup in 1968, led by General Juan Velasco Alvarado. Velasco began a programme of land reform and nationalisation, which was intended to benefit disadvantaged groups such as Andean Indians. The cause of the Indians had previously been championed by the Alianza Popular Revolucionaria Americana (American Popular Revolutionary Alliance, APRA), which had briefly formed the government in 1962 before being overthrown by the military. However, Velasco was overthrown by more conservative officers in 1975, and the reform process was halted. APRA remained the largest opposition party but had itself become more moderate. Therefore, as the Peruvian economy deteriorated, new revolutionary movements appeared despite the fact that the military surrendered power in 1980 to a civilian government.

The most prominent of the new revolutionary movements was Sendero Luminoso, which emerged in the isolated mountainous Ayacucho province of the south-west under the leadership of Abimael Guzmán Reynoso in 1980. Sendero Luminoso largely followed Mao's rural revolutionary guerrilla warfare principles, albeit in the context of almost a provincial urban insurrection since it was increasingly drawn into attacking targets in the Peruvian capital, Lima, from 1983 onwards. While *Senderistas* frequently employed the language of Mao's three phases of revolutionary warfare, Guzmán himself outlined five stages, namely agitation and propaganda, economic sabotage, guerrilla warfare, expanding political bases and an army, and general civil war and the fall of the cities. However, there was an implicit rejection of any notion of a united front, other Marxists being dismissed as 'cretins' and the Soviet Union, Cuba and sometimes even China classed with the United States as equally 'fascist' states. The movement's appeal was based largely on state corruption and arbitrary authority, since there had been land reform. Support was sought mainly from the Quechua Indians. Yet most of its estimated 23,000 victims between 1982 and 1992 were also Indians. Guzmán and his colleagues were university-educated and largely spoke Spanish rather than Quechua. Indeed, Guzmán was professor of philosophy at the National University of San Cristóbal de Huamanga at Ayacucho. Established at the university, Guzmán and his colleagues used the classroom as an *entrée* to the local peasant community, but at least half the activists remained middle-class youths.

The reality of the alienation of much of the illiterate Indian peasant population from the middle-class elite dominating Sendero Luminoso explained the conscious use of violence and terrorism against the population. This clearly violated the spirit of pure Maoism and was closer to the Vietnamese model. It was apparently reasoned that calculated intimidation would convince the people that the movement would ultimately triumph, especially as there was little government presence in Ayacucho. Given the effective power vacuum that existed in the province, it proved possible for Sendero Luminoso to establish regional dominance with perhaps not much more than 180 activists in 1980 amid a population of over half a million. Those organs of the government that did exist were also liable to terror attack, including those advocating the kind of political reform that might weaken support for insurgency. Thus, Peruvian and foreign aid workers were killed, such as Maria Elena Moyano, whose 'Glass of Milk a Day' programme helped the youth of Lima's shanty towns. Peasant militias, known as *rondas campesinas*, were also attacked, while Sendero Luminoso also waged a campaign against economic targets. This was intended both to reduce the state's ability to alleviate poverty and to impose an anti-technology, subsistence-model economy.

The government failed to bring inflation under control, and the scale of insurgency escalated steadily. National elections went ahead, however, in 1985, and APRA returned to power for the first time since 1962. Its leader, Alan García, promised new reforms and secured a cease-fire with one revolutionary group, but Sendero Luminoso continued its campaign. At the same time as grappling with Peru's economic problems, not least the crippling levels of foreign debt, García attempted to eradicate excesses by soldiers and police. Inflation continued to rise, however, and with criticism of his policies rising within APRA, García actually resigned as party leader, while remaining president, in December 1988.

The 1990 elections were unexpectedly won by Alberto Fujimori, a Peruvian of Japanese extraction, and his Cambio 90 (Change 90) movement. Fujimori's response to continued violence was a 'self-coup' in April 1992, in which he dismissed Congress and took dictatorial powers. At the same time, the Peruvian army improved its tactics by introducing small-unit operations, and its reputation by instituting civic action projects. Fujimori's hard-line stance had its reward when Guzmán was captured in September 1992 by distinctly old-fashioned police detection. In January 1994, Sendero Luminoso fragmented when Guzmán offered peace terms from his prison cell.

Despite the temporary setback when an entirely separate urban guerrilla group, Movimiento Revolucionario Tupac Amar (Tupac Amaru Revolutionary Movement, MRTA), a Marxist group formed in 1983 and named after an Indian leader executed by the Spanish in 1780, seized the Japanese ambassador's residence in Lima in December 1996, Peru remains on course to defeat the remaining insurgent groups. However, the internal conflict has cost an estimated 27,000 lives and $3 billion since 1982.

If Maoist precepts proved less than universally applicable in the long term, however, armed forces faced with the challenge of Maoist insurgency in South-east Asia immediately after the Second World War were still required to adapt quickly to the new circumstances that faced them.

Further reading

On Mao and the Chinese Civil War, see Mao Tse-tung, *Selected Military Writings* (Peking, 1967); Samuel Griffith (ed.), *Mao Tse-tung on Guerrilla Warfare* (New York, 1978); William Wei, 'Insurgency by the Numbers I: A Reconsideration of the Ecology of Communist Success in Jiangxi Province, China' *Small Wars and Insurgencies* 5 (1994), pp. 201–17; Marcia Ristaino, *China's Art of Revolution: The Mobilisation of Discontent, 1927 and 1928* (Durham, 1987); Dick Wilson, *China's Revolutionary War* (New York, 1991); S.I. Levine, *Anvil of Victory: The Communist Revolution in Manchuria, 1945–48* (New York, 1987); and Yung-fa Chuen, *Making Revolution: The Communist Movement in Eastern and Central China, 1937–45* (Berkeley, 1986).

On the roles of the Japanese and KMT, see C.S. Lee, *Counterinsurgency in Manchuria: The Japanese Experience* (Santa Monica, 1967); L. Li, *The Japanese Army in North China, 1937–41* (Tokyo, 1975); G.Z. Hanrahan, *Japanese Operations against Guerrilla Forces* (Chevy Chase, 1954); Hsi-sheng Ch'i, *Nationalist China at War* (Ann Arbor, 1982); Lloyd Eastman, *Seeds of Destruction: Nationalist China in War and Revolution, 1937–49* (Stanford, 1984); and William Wei, *Counter-revolution in China: The Nationalists in Jiangxi during the Soviet Period* (Ann Arbor, 1985).

On Vietnamese theorists, see William J. Duiker, *The Communist Road to Power in Vietnam* (Boulder, 1981); Robert O'Neill, *General Giap: Politician and Strategist* (New York, 1969); C.B. Currey, *Victory at Any Cost* (New York, 1997); Douglas Pike, *A History of Vietnamese Communism* (Stanford, 1978); George Tanham, *Communist Revolutionary Warfare* (New York, 1967); and Greg Lockhart, *Nation in Arms: The Origins of the People's Army of Vietnam* (Sydney, 1989).

On other Maoists, see Tom Marks, *Maoist Insurgency since Vietnam* (London, 1996); Marks, 'Maoist Miscue: The Demise of the Communist Party of Thailand, 1965–83' *Small Wars and Insurgencies* 3 (1992), pp. 112–69; Saiyud Kerdphol, *The Struggle for Thailand: Counterinsurgency, 1965–85* (Bangkok, 1986); Robert Mugabe, *Our War of Liberation* (Gweru, 1983); Elaine Windrich, *The Cold War Guerrilla* (Westport, 1992); and J. McCulloch, *In The Twilight of the Revolution: The Political Thought of Amilcar Cabral* (London, 1983).

On Shining Path, see David Scott Palmer (ed.), *The Shining Path of Peru* (London, 1992); Tom Marks, 'Making Revolution: Sendero Luminoso in Peru' *Small Wars and Insurgencies* 3 (1992), pp. 22–46; and Christopher Harmon, 'The Purposes of Terrorism within Insurgency: Shining Path in Peru' in *ibid.*, pp. 170–90.

5

FORMATIVE EXPERIENCES

As indicated earlier, the Japanese occupation of much of South-east Asia in 1941–42 proved the catalyst for growing nationalism on the part of the indigenous populations. In Malaya, the Philippines, the Dutch East Indies and French Indo-China, therefore, the returning colonial powers faced significant challenges to restoring their authority, particularly when communists began to exploit the appeal of nationalism. In the Philippines between 1946 and 1954, Indo-China between the same years and in Malaya between 1948 and 1960, the United States, France and Britain, respectively, encountered Maoist-style insurgency campaigns. The Dutch faced a similar, but non-communist, insurgency in the East Indies between 1947 and 1949. In each case, the armed forces had to find solutions to politically motivated insurgency quite unlike the colonial campaigning of the past. While the British and the Americans succeeded, the French and the Dutch did not.

Partly, the success of the British in Malaya and of American advisers in the Philippines can be attributed to lessons learned during the Second World War, but also to the lessons already being assimilated from two other on-going politically motivated insurgencies in Palestine and Greece. The campaign waged against the British authorities in Palestine by Jewish insurgent and terrorist groups between 1944 and 1948, and the more limited British participation in the Greek Civil War between 1944 and 1947, were highly formative experiences for the British army. Similarly, some Americans also derived lessons from their role in Greece.

In the case of Palestine, the roots of insurgency lay in the belief on the part of the Jews that the British had breached past pledges to keep open Palestine by attempting to restrict Jewish immigration. In reality, the British faced an intractable problem in trying to juggle Jewish and Arab interests in Palestine, which had been established as a British mandated territory by the League of Nations in 1922. The Jewish population had been about 85,000 in 1914 but, with increasing, and often illegal, immigration, it had reached 700,000 by the end of the Second World War, compared with an Arab population of about 1.3 million.

During the Second World War, the British received assistance from the military arm of the Jewish Agency in Palestine, the Haganah (Defence Force), which had originally been formed as a militia to protect Jewish settlements during communal riots, and from the Palmach (Shock Companies), which had been formed to defend Palestine against possible Italian invasion and was a successor to Wingate's Special Night Squads. Rather less welcome military assistance was offered by the Irgun, formed in 1937 as the military arm of the New Zionist Organisation with the aim of undertaking retaliatory action against the Arabs. The British were not able to tolerate Jewish counter-terror during the Arab Revolt, and the Irgun killed its first policeman in May 1939. Nevertheless, at the outbreak of the war, the Irgun had been prepared to declare a truce, although some elements regarded Britain as a greater enemy than Hitler and broke away from the Irgun in 1940 to form LEHI, known more commonly as the Stern Gang after its leader, Avraham Stern.

A true revolutionary, Stern was ready to enlist the support of both Arabs and Axis powers in an anti-imperialist front against the British. He was killed in a police raid in February 1942 and, by December 1943, leadership had been assumed by Menachem Begin, who declared war against the British authorities on 1 February 1944. This was not regarded as beneficial to Jewish interests by the Jewish Agency and, after the Stern Gang assassinated the British Minister Resident in Cairo, Lord Moyne, on 6 November 1944, the Haganah and Palmach were directed to neutralise both the Irgun and LEHI. However, this campaign ceased at the end of the war in Europe. Moreover, as the new Labour government in Britain held out against demands to raise the quota of Jewish immigration, so the Agency lost patience and patched up its differences with the Irgun and LEHI in the Tenuat Hameri (United Front). A joint military campaign was then launched against the British on the night of 31 October 1945, with attacks on the railway system by the Haganah and the sinking of two police launches by the Palmach.

As indicated in a previous chapter, ELAS was effectively the instrument of the Kommounisitikon Komma Ellados (Greek Communist Party, KKE). Under the Varkiza agreement in February 1945, ELAS had been formally disbanded in return for an amnesty, a plebiscite on the future of Greece and a general election. In the event, the election in March 1946 was boycotted by the KKE, which claimed that government promises had not been upheld. In any case, there had been many within ELAS who had never accepted disbandment, and violence had continued unabated. Increasingly, communist guerrilla groups began to operate in northern Greece adjacent to the Yugoslav and Albanian frontiers and, under the overall command of Markos Vaphiadis, adopted the title of Dimokratikos Stratos Ellados (Democratic Army of Greece, DSE) in December 1946. There were few social, economic, religious or ethnic divisions of significance in Greece, the conflict being essentially a political and ideological competition. Indeed, neither side was wholly successful in mobilising mass support, with the DSE increasingly conscripting mountain villagers and relying largely upon one group particularly alienated from the remainder of Greek society, the Slavophones of Macedonia. The Greek National Army (GNA) also relied upon conscription, and many pre-war reservists particularly resented being called up when others who had not previously served evaded it. In October 1946, the British estimated that at least 15 per cent of the GNA sympathised with ELAS.

In terms of insurgent methods, the Jewish organisations were somewhat more sophisticated than those of DSE, which waged a more traditional guer-rilla campaign. In Palestine, those operations mounted by the Haganah and Palmach were restricted by the Jewish Agency to those that might loosely be defined as facilitating further immigration. By contrast, the nature of Irgun and LEHI participation was shown on 27 December 1945 by their joint raid on the Jerusalem and Jaffa CID buildings and a REME workshop in Tel Aviv, which left ten British dead and twelve wounded. In fact, the Haganah and Palmach were to mount only eight operations during the joint campaign as the Agency agonised over the extremism of its partners, which Begin had carefully calculated as an exertion of terrorist pressure on a power he was convinced could never seriously contemplate outright suppression. Arguably, indeed, the Jewish groups were the most effective post-war opponents the British ever faced.

The last straw for the Agency appears to have been the Irgun's bomb attack on the British mandate secretariat in the King David Hotel in Jerusalem on 22 July 1946, which killed 91 people and injured 45 others. The Agency dissolved its partnership with the Irgun and LEHI on 23 August and withdrew its 45,000 members, leaving operations in the hands of the Irgun's estimated 1,500 activists and the 300 activists of LEHI. Over 58 per cent of all terrorist attacks were now to be directed at British military and police personnel. LEHI favoured taxi or truck bombs, while the Irgun favoured road mines. In all, just under two-thirds of terrorist attacks were with mines and just under a quarter with bombs. Some were particularly spectacular, such as the Irgun's 600-pound barrel bomb, of high explosives packed into steel drums, driven on a lorry and launched down a ramp into the Haifa police headquarters in September 1947. Subsidiary operations were mounted against economic targets, with the railways attracting 18 per cent of all attacks. The campaign was also briefly exported, with the bombing of the British embassy in Rome in October 1946 and attacks on British servicemen in Germany and Austria.

In addition, any British measures against the terrorists were invariably followed by specific reprisals. After two Irgun members were punished with eighteen strokes of the cane in December 1946, a British major and three NCOs were abducted and flogged. The execution of four terrorists was followed by a successful raid on Acre prison on 4 May 1947, which freed 41 Jewish prisoners and large numbers of Arabs. In the most notorious incident, Sergeants Clifford Martin and Mervyn Paice of the British Field Security Police were kidnapped by the Irgun on 12 July 1947 in retaliation for death sentences passed on three terrorists. Following the executions, the booby-trapped bodies of the two sergeants were found hanging from a tree near Nathanya on 31 July.

The campaign was also supplemented by a highly effective propaganda machine, which was now shown to be particularly significant in the success or otherwise of insurgency. The protracted nature of modern insurgencies made it important for both sides to maintain the determination and will to prevail. While some insurgents might have felt the righteousness of the cause sufficient, there was still the need to reinforce the ideological appeal for others and, indeed, for the population. Propaganda could strengthen solidarity and also undermine the authority of the security forces in the eyes of the population and, increasingly in contemporary conflicts, the international community. Propaganda might also make the insurgents appear far stronger than they were in reality and, therefore, represent a force multiplier. Violence could also be legitimised through propaganda.

The Jewish propaganda machine was especially effective in the United States, where, for example, the Irgun-backed American League for a Free Palestine (ALFP) raised large funds at performances of Ben Hecht's virulent anti-British play, 'A Flag is Born', which cultivated the image that Palestine was under illegal British occupation and made an explicit analogy with the American 'patriots' of 1776. Another message conveyed by the many front organisations in the United States, such as LEHI's Political Action Committee for Palestine, was that Jewish and Arab differences were merely a product of British imperialism, anti-imperialism generally having a strong appeal in the United States. One American newspaper even reported in November 1945 that British troops singing the Nazi 'Horst Wessel' song had shot down twenty Jewish children in Tel Aviv. In Palestine itself, both the Irgun and LEHI operated their own radio stations, although the British captured LEHI's transmitter. One successful device used by both the Irgun and LEHI was the pamphlet bombs, exploding and showering streets with propaganda leaflets. Overall, insurgent propaganda maintained internal solidarity, neutralised Arab opinion, brought considerable support in the United States and certainly contributed to undermining British resolve.

Effectively, the terrorist campaign, which cost 338 British lives, confronted Britain with a direct choice between total repression and total withdrawal. While the Labour government tried to make up its mind, the security forces had to maintain law and order as best they could amid often considerable provocation. Ultimately, the government could not bring itself to grasp the nettle, and on 18 September 1947, it was announced that Britain would turn over the Palestine problem to the United Nations as successor to the League of Nations. On 26 September 1947, it was further announced that the mandate would be surrendered, withdrawal being set for 15 May 1948. As the British prepared for withdrawal, so the focus of activity in Palestine became escalating violence between the Jewish and Arab communities.

In Greece, the guerrilla conflict was of a different nature, since the DSE had pretensions to be a regular army and operated largely in the mountains of north and central Greece. It drew supplies from across the Yugoslav, Albanian and Bulgarian frontiers, but it also had its own underground support organisation, known as Yiafka within Greece. This may have attained as many as 50,000 adherents. Moreover, apart from the advantages of terrain, DSE enjoyed, at least initially, a certain residue of support that had existed for ELAS as a nominally broadly based wartime nationalist movement. However, it never numbered more than 26,000 men. Moreover, DSE's field leadership was variable in quality; its military resources limited, despite receiving at least 47,000 weapons from the Yugoslavs; its training rudimentary; its mobility highly restricted; and its higher commanders undecided on precisely what strategy to follow. This was particularly so after the political leadership of the KKE under Nikos Zachariadis was forced to abandon Athens in October 1947 and made its way to join the DSE command. Zachariadis insisted on establishing control over a sufficiently sizeable area of northern Greece in order to claim an effective administration. Consequently, in December 1947, DSE was committed to a major offensive to seize Konitsa as the seat of a newly proclaimed Provisional Democratic Government.

Such a conventional and positional strategy was well beyond the DSE's capabilities, and while it settled into an attempted siege of Konitsa after the initial assault failed, it was soon dislodged by the GNA's relief columns. Subsequently, the guerrillas were driven from many of their mountain strongholds during the summer of 1948, Operation Dawn clearing the Roumeli mountains in April and May and Operation Crown advancing into the Grammos in June, although a limited follow-up advance into the Vitsi mountains was less successful. Notwithstanding the lessons that should have been learned, Zachariadis again insisted on conventional positional warfare and ousted Vaphiadis, who wished to concentrate on guerrilla tactics, in January 1949. The political leadership was also too wedded to the idea that revolution stemmed from mobilising the urban proletariat, with the result that it sought only to control the rural population in the mountains rather than winning its support for a coherent political programme. Indeed, the KKE had actually dismantled its rural organisation in October 1945. With communist neighbours increasingly wary of supporting the failing efforts in Greece, and Tito in particular withdrawing support in July 1949 as his quarrel with Stalin came to a head, such a conventional strategy was far too risky. DSE was destroyed in its last mountain strongholds in the Grammos, where Zachariadis had concentrated his remaining 1,200 men behind fixed defences, in August and September 1949. On 16 October 1949, DSE declared a cease-fire 'to prevent the complete annihilation of Greece'.

Turning to the British response, in both Palestine and Greece there was a tendency to think largely in terms of pre-war imperial policing and internal security. As indicated previously, however, there were a number of officers who had seen irregular service during the Second World War. Moreover, the War Office had undertaken studies of counter-guerrilla warfare in November and December 1944 based on what could be learned from these kinds of operation in case the British should meet guerrilla opposition to its subsequent occupation of Germany. However, the studies stressed purely military responses. When confronted with insurgency in Palestine and Greece, soldiers tended to turn to familiar methods. Although the services of some wartime members of SOE were retained by both the Secret Intelligence Service (SIS) and the War Office, the problem was exacerbated by the post-war prominence of some soldiers who had seen service in the Arab Revolt, not least the CIGS from 1946 to 1948, Field Marshal Montgomery, who insisted on an even greater use in Palestine of large mobile columns, the creation of army-controlled areas and mass hangings. In the case of Greece, he had in mind traditional mountain warfare tactics, as practised in India. The draft version of a new updated manual to replace those of 1934 and 1937, which appeared in 1947, suggested that traditional methods were 'usually successful'. Its final version in June 1949 as *Notes on Duties in Aid of the Civil Power* only incorporated a few of the lessons from Palestine and Greece and retained most of the traditional official wisdom.

Not surprisingly, therefore, the army's offensive operations in Palestine usually consisted of cordon and search, involving the isolation and systematic combing of given locations for arms, documents and suspects. Over 170 such operations were mounted, usually at battalion or brigade level in response to particular incidents. Over 25 per cent brought no results at all and only exposed the troops to false accusations of brutality or looting. This resulted in inhabitants being required to sign clearance certificates after searches in order to prevent such claims at a later date. Two especially large-scale series of operations were mounted, from June to September 1946 and from March to August 1947. Operation Agatha between 29 June and 1 July 1946 involved 10,000 troops in a search of three cities and over 30 settlements. Operation Shark from 30 July to 2 August 1946 employed 21,000 troops in imposing a 36-hour curfew on Tel Aviv's population of 170,000 and netted 787 suspects, although Begin escaped by hiding in a secret compartment in his house for four days. But the army was never able to find large numbers of men for offensive operations, despite the fact that the British had 90,000 men eventually deployed, simply because of the need to maintain so many static guards over important installations such as railways and oil pipelines. In fact, the commitment of the 6th Airborne Division, the bulk of the Palestine garrison and supposedly Britain's strategic reserve for emergencies in Europe, to internal security duties seriously interrupted its parachute training. Worse still, the uncertain state of government intentions was not conducive to the success of traditional suppression.

The Labour Party had traditionally been a friend of Zionism, and there had been some expectation that it would revive some partition of Palestine as once recommended before the war, especially as the United States favoured the creation of a Jewish state. However, the Foreign Secretary, Ernest Bevin, endorsed the growing Foreign Office belief that longer-term British interests might be better served by concessions to Arabs. Oil supplies were beginning to be a consideration, and there was the idea that Palestine could become the main Middle Eastern base for Britain should Britain be forced to quit Egypt, and at least a continued staging post to India. Thus, Bevin announced in November 1945 that Britain favoured only a Jewish home and not a Jewish state in Palestine and that the pre-war Macdonald White Paper would be implemented, leading to an independent state with an Arab majority. The involvement of the United States in a joint commission to report on immigration levels in 1946 offered no real solution, and the decision to quit India, and signs that the Canal Zone could be retained after all, robbed Palestine of any strategic importance.

In addition to uncertainty in overall policy, the frequent capitulation to terrorist intimidation − twelve Jews were executed, but 22 had death sentences commuted under duress of hostage taking − merely suggested weakness. Indeed, it was only after the abduction and flogging of British servicemen in December 1946 that the government considered stronger methods. Yet, when martial law was finally imposed at Montgomery's insistence in Tel Aviv and parts of Jerusalem in March 1947, it had already been decided to turn over the problem to the UN. Moreover, martial law lasted less than three weeks, although it was briefly reimposed after the Martin and Paice murders. Amid such self-imposed restraints, it has been suggested that the British response in Palestine was that of a 'police state with a conscience'.

Nor was the response to Jewish propaganda well handled. The security forces equally needed to employ propaganda to get over the government's message to the population and to the international community. Propaganda could also be used by the security forces to exploit the fact that the rank and file of the insurgent movement would often be less committed than the leadership, and could be 'turned' by offers of safe conduct, money or other rewards for surrender. However, there was a requirement to state the government position clearly. All involved in counter-insurgency had to understand the need for counter-propaganda, to be aware of the propaganda risks of all actions, and to combat specific themes in insurgent propaganda. Yet there was an absence of any coherent political programme on the part of government. There was a Public Information Office, which distributed information through publications, and organised mobile cinema vans and press conferences. The wartime Ministry of Information in Britain had disappeared in 1946, however, to be replaced by the less powerful and less impressive Central Office of Information (COI). Indeed, COI had no role overseas, for this was now left to the Foreign Office and the BBC's External Services. The British case was projected only defensively and in a low-key manner. Indeed, it is sometimes said that the one successful public relations campaign undertaken by the British authorities was that in Britain itself, to encourage more recruits for the Palestine Police, although at least British newsreel companies provided reasonably positive images of the army in Palestine. In Palestine itself, where heavy local censorship was imposed, the army had to improvise the protection of its image by avoiding provocation, trying to manage the press, and by jamming insurgent broadcasts. Crucially, British propaganda lacked any definite programme to project that might have provided an alternative to the appeal of the insurgents.

Yet lessons were learned in both Greece and Palestine. Officially, Britain was not involved in the conflict in Greece. In reality, there was a continuing covert involvement in the direction of the GNA campaign through the agency of the British Military Mission to Greece (BMM(G)). Initially, BMM(G) had assisted in rebuilding the GNA, which with the addition of the gendarmerie eventually reached a total of 250,000 men. BMM(G) had also stressed normal mountain warfare tactics. However, doubts began to grow as to the appropriateness of the GNA's tendency towards 'scorched earth' methods such as massed artillery barrages. In October 1946, former members of the SAS were involved in establishing GNA mobile commando units, capable of what was termed 'deep patrolling' and of acting as a vanguard force for large-scale operations. At the same time, and based on analysis of the past, BMM(G) sponsored a 'counter-organisation' plan to attack the political infrastructure supporting DSE by relocating population away from those areas vulnerable to guerrilla infiltration into 'security camps'. In effect, this simply revived the concept of reconcentration familiar in the South African War. Resettlement was allied to civic action to win over the relocated population. Depopulation of the mountain villages – possibly 700,000 people were removed – and suspicions among many Greeks of the support that DSE derived from states like Yugoslavia and Bulgaria with designs on Greek territory, deprived the guerrillas of food and recruits.

Clandestine British support was halted abruptly in March 1947 when Bevin announced the withdrawal of British aid to Greece and Turkey, but it was revived in the autumn at the request of the United States, which had taken over the British commitment under the auspices of the Truman Doctrine. By April 1948, at least 175 British advisers were again working with the GNA and now urging a move towards smaller-unit operations and independent patrolling by the GNA commandos of up to several weeks duration. The nature of the war was changing at this time, however, with the DSE itself switching more to conventional operations and the GNA more obviously influenced by American advisers in the Joint US Military Advisory and Planning Group (JUSMAPG), as well as learning lessons from its earlier setbacks and taking on board the need for continuous pursuit of DSE groups. Moreover, in January 1949, the well-respected veteran Greek general, Alexander Papagos, was invested with full control over all military affairs, free to conduct military operations without political interference. The final assault on the last guerrilla strongholds in the Grammos and Vitsi mountains was spearheaded by Curtiss Helldiver dive-bombers as flying artillery. Generally, the GNA embraced the American preference for maximum use of firepower, particularly valuing the 105 mm howitzers made available to them. JUSMAPG, however, had somewhat reluctantly concluded that the British-inspired commando units could continue to make a significant contribution in raiding and deep-penetration patrolling. Figures for the cost of the civil war in Greece vary, but deaths may have exceeded 60,000 between 1943 and 1949, while possibly over 136,000 people were forced into involuntary long-term exile by either communist or government action.

In Palestine, too, lessons were being learned. As in the Burma revolt of 1930–32, a committee structure was put in place to enhance co-operation between civil and military authorities, although, in the vital area of intelligence, there was no overall co-ordinating organisation to make sense of the data being collected from various sources. Curiously, too, the GOC in Palestine was not officially a member of the directing Central Security Committee, although he was invariably present at its meetings. Lessons, too, were certainly learned during cordon and search, which led to continuing refinements in technique, although this was hindered by rotation of troops and pressures on time, which often meant only limited attention to retraining exercises. Some attention was even paid to the propaganda battle, with troops carefully impressed with the need to avoid taking unnecessarily provocative action that might yield a propaganda success for the insurgents. An example of the latter was the notorious non-fraternisation order issued on 26 July 1946 by the GOC, Lieutenant-General Sir Evelyn Barker, after the bombing of the King David Hotel, suggesting that troops should boycott Jewish businesses.

The perceived intelligence gap led to a significant experiment in policing, which, ironically, offered a propaganda victory to the terrorists. The Palestine Police was chronically short of personnel and did not enjoy good relations with the population. Less than 4 per cent of its British members spoke Hebrew, and the small Jewish component was unreliable, with the great majority of ordinary constables actually Arabs. Modelled like so many other colonial police forces on the Royal Irish Constabulary, the force therefore had little hope of winning the confidence of the Jewish population. It was certainly temperamentally ill suited to the recommendations made in December 1946 by Sir Charles Wickham, the head of the British Police and Prisons Mission to Greece, that it should forsake a mobile paramilitary role and get back to foot patrols on the streets. Both the lack of affinity with the Jewish population and the paramilitary role made accurate intelligence hard to come by, and in January 1947, the Inspector-General of the Palestine Police and a former Royal Marine commando, Nicol Gray, asked the former Chindit on secondment to the police, Bernard Fergusson, to examine new methods of combating terrorism. Encouraged by the Directorate of Military Operations, who seconded more former SAS and SOE personnel, Fergusson established special undercover police squads in April. Unfortunately, however, the operation's cover was blown and a highly decorated former SAS man, Roy Farran, was accused of the murder of a LEHI member who had disappeared in May 1947. Farran briefly sought refuge in Syria before returning for trial in October, when he was acquitted for lack of evidence. Inevitably, the Farran case was made good use of by the terrorists: Farran's brother was later killed in Britain by a parcel bomb meant for him.

At least Gray's experiment, even if ill fated, showed a willingness to adopt a new approach, and others in Palestine were also less traditional in their outlook. As High Commissioner in Palestine, Lieutenant-General Sir Alan Cunningham was far more aware than Montgomery of the politicisation involved in the campaign. Cunningham urged a more novel approach, such as more small-unit operations, although, ultimately, Montgomery prevailed in the application of martial law.

Lessons from both Greece and Palestine were soon to be applied in Malaya. The so-called Ferret Force established in July 1948, for example, under the command of Lieutenant-Colonel Walter Walker and designed to take war to the MCP in the jungle, was modelled on the undercover police squads in Palestine. The first GOC in Malaya, Major-General Charles Boucher, and the C-in-C, Far East Land Forces, General Sir Neil Ritchie, were both familiar with Greece, Boucher having been there himself and Ritchie's chief of staff having also served there immediately prior to his posting to the Far East. Two British battalions recently in Greece also transferred to Malaya in mid-1948. Sir Henry Gurney, who was to become High Commissioner in Malaya in 1948, had previously been Chief Secretary to the administration in Palestine, and Gray also resurfaced as police commissioner in Malaya. At one point, Farran was offered command of a squadron in the newly formed Malayan Scouts, which were to be subsequently renamed the SAS in 1951, but the War Office thought better of it and blocked the appointment in October 1950. Walker was also tasked with establishing a Far East Land Forces Training Centre in Singapore to tutor army and police officers in small-unit patrolling. Indeed, Ferret Force was disbanded by Ritchie in December 1948 because he assumed that the new training centre would have already immeasurably improved jungle tactics.

This did not mean that the British response to the Malayan emergency was instantly effective, and there were to be many setbacks initially and many who continued to favour older methods. Indeed, when Boucher fell ill in February 1950, his successor, Major-General Robert Urquhart, with no experience of irregular warfare, favoured traditional sweeps and drives. However, Greece and Palestine did begin to show that lessons could be learned that could be added to some of the basic principles of inter-war imperial policing in such a way as to provide a successful response to the challenge of the Maoist insurgency. This was to be beaten in both Malaya and the Philippines, although 'winning' did not necessarily mean the total elimination of the insurgent presence.

In both Malaya and the Philippines, insurgency was able to begin as a result of political and related socio-economic grievances, which could be exploited by the communists. Post-war administrations did not redress these grievances, partly as a result of the need for extensive reconstruction after the Japanese occupation, which, in any case, had weakened authority. In Malaya, this derived partly from the psychological blow dealt to colonial officials by the Japanese victory, and, in the Philippines, by the taint of wartime collaboration that hung around the administration. It was also the case that the Hukbalahap and MPAJA had the prestige of having resisted the Japanese, although, in the case of the Huks, there had also been something of a civil war, in which many of their pre-war opponents were attacked under the guise of being collaborators with the Japanese.

The Malayan Communist Party (MCP), which had been founded in 1930, enjoyed its greatest support among the ethnic Chinese minority. Comprising about 38 per cent of the population, the Chinese had come to Malaya in the nineteenth century as labourers and traders. During the Japanese occupation of Malaya, the MCP had dominated MPAJA, which had received support from SOE. Indeed, the man who was to become the MCP's general secretary in 1947, Chin Peng, had received the OBE for his wartime role. MPAJA, which claimed to have carried out over 340 attacks on the Japanese during the war, was supposedly disbanded in December 1945 in return for the legal recognition of the MCP by the returning British authorities. The MCP developed a strong influence among the trade unions, but its appeal remained largely ethnic. Indeed, the Malay majority leaned more towards the emerging United Malayan National Organisation (UMNO), which successfully challenged Britain's post-war plans for a Malay union, in which the Chinese would have had some representation.

With the failure of the union plan, the British proposed a Malay federation, in which the various states and provinces would enjoy some autonomy. This was more acceptable to the Malays, but the Chinese would have fewer rights. The MCP therefore moved to exploit the particular grievances of the half-million-strong Chinese 'squatter' population, which had fled to illegally occupy government land in subsistence-oriented communities along the fringes of the jungle during the Japanese occupation. The problem was compounded by the British failure to re-establish the pre-war 'Chinese Protectorate', which had dealt with all Chinese affairs. Generally, as Britain sought to revive its own post-war economy, prices in Malaya were high, wages low and goods in short supply, adding to the overall sense of malaise.

MPAJA weapons, which had never been surrendered, were passed to a new Malayan Races Liberation Army (MRLA), the escalating violence resulting in the declaration of a state of emergency by the British authorities on 17 June 1948. The Malayan Security Services had concentrated on radical Malay politics to such an extent that, just two days before the declaration, it produced a forecast that there was 'no immediate threat to internal security'. In fact, the evidence of an actual communist plot to overthrow the British authorities in Malaya, emanating from the deliberations of the communist-inspired Southeast Asia Youth Conference in Calcutta in February 1948, at which it was made known that the Cominform favoured violence as a means of fighting imperialism, is inconclusive and unsubstantiated. At the same time, however, evidence of some 'colonial conspiracy' on the part of the authorities to eliminate the 'only party committed to the liberation of the Malayan people' is equally unconvincing. Indeed, in many respects, the declaration of the emergency may have been primarily a response to the need to restore confidence in the colonial authorities amid increasing lawlessness. Nonetheless, even if the MCP had lost control of some of its members and was unprepared for a major insurrection, the party leadership was at the very least opportunist in exploiting tensions. Ironically, the declaration of the state of emergency endowed the MCP in some measure with a *casus belli* and helped to precipitate the wider insurrection.

The Hukbalahap drew on traditional peasant grievances in the central Luzon plain, being essentially an alliance between an urban communist leadership in Manila and pre-war rural peasant unions in the four provinces of Pampanga, Bulacan, Tarlac and Nueva Ecija, which were to become collectively known as 'Huklandia'. Indeed, while the communist leadership of the Partido Komunista ng Pilapinas (Philippine Communist Party, PKP), espoused the notion of land redistribution, with slogans such as 'Land for the Landless' and 'Equal Justice for All', their *tao* (peasant) supporters appear to have had the more limited aim of achieving a larger share of the crop. *Datus* (landlords) traditionally took up to 50 per cent of this, as well as demanding *corvee* (unpaid labour). Moreover, population growth and progressive subdivision of land had put even greater pressure on tenants, who found that landlords also increasingly ceased to fulfil responsibilities such as providing the loans and support in hard times once regarded as part of the *datuk* (relationship between landlord and peasant). Significantly, many peasant supporters of the Huks continued to refer to them as the pre-war Kalipunang Pambansa ng mga Magsasaka sa Pilipinas (National Society of Peasants in the Philippines). The Democratic Alliance forged between the Pambansang kaisahan ng mga Magbubukid (National Peasant's Union, PKM) and the Huks won all the central Luzon seats in the April 1946 elections. President Manuel Roxas, himself tainted by wartime co-operation with the Japanese, for whom he had organised rice procurement, debarred the DA on the grounds of alleged electoral fraud. Negotiations broke down and the Huks, renamed the Hukbong Mapagpalaya ng Batan (People's Liberation Army) in 1950, took to the hills.

Faced with an unfamiliar challenge from groups posing as alternative administrations, there was a tendency in both Malaya and the Philippines to regard insurgency simply as criminal activity and to adopt an initial strategy of coercion and enforcement. In Malaya, force was used indiscriminately by both army and police. The police commissioner, Nicol Gray, fresh from Palestine, believed in a paramilitary role, while another 400 or so former members of the Palestine Police who joined Gray's new command had little knowledge of Malaya, not least of the Malay, Chinese or Tamil languages.

Meanwhile, notwithstanding the efforts of those who had been in Greece or Palestine, the army largely engaged in what have been characterised as 'nostalgic' large-scale sweeps, although the small teams of Ferret Force had considerable initial success in carrying the war against the MCP into the jungle. There were some regrettable incidents where discipline lapsed, as at Batang Kali in December 1948, when 24 suspects were killed, but there was remarkably little brutality given the difficult circumstances pertaining in guer-rilla warfare. At the same time, the escalating costs of the emergency could not be met. As a result, the scale of the insurgency expanded alarmingly, with the MRLA deploying about 7,000 men by 1950 with the passive support of the squatter population as a whole.

Fortunately, the Malay population remained largely indifferent to the MCP, and Malaya was geographically isolated from external assistance. Since Malaya was a colony, the British also enjoyed wide powers, and, ultimately, they were able to gift independence to Malaya in 1957 in a way that the MCP could not match. An economic boom, generated by the rapidly rising prices of rubber and tin as a consequence of Western rearmament during the Korean War (1950–53), made increasing resources available with which to fight the insurgency. Thus, government revenue increased from M$443.4 million in 1950 to M$735.4 million in 1951, enabling government expenditure to be increased from M$350 million to M$550 million. Moreover, the population as a whole shared in the resulting prosperity. Another advantage was the inexpe-rience of the MCP's leadership, Chin Peng becoming general secretary when his predecessor, Lai Tek, was revealed as a British agent in March 1947. Before fleeing, Lai Tek had enabled the British, and the Japanese earlier, to neutralise many of the more able communist leaders. Indeed, the MCP made the mistake of withdrawing into the deep jungle in 1949 to reorganise for a longer military campaign at the very moment when the British most needed a respite. At an equally critical moment in October 1951, the MCP chose to lay greater emphasis upon political mobilisation than military action in belated recognition that the struggle had been launched prematurely without the long period of preparatory politicisation of the population advocated by Mao. An element of luck for the authorities was that the declaration of the state of emergency took the MCP by surprise and enabled the British to pick up some key individuals in June 1948. Moreover, the Chinese community itself was split in its loyalties, and many wealthier Chinese saw no advantage in a communist victory.

Faced with an insurgency inspired by the principles of Mao Tse-tung, Roxas resorted to a strategy of 'mailed fist' military coercion. Every *barrio* (village) in the affected area was assumed to be a Huk haunt, and so-called 'screening' in *zona* operations, not least those of the notorious *Nenita* (skull) squadrons, brought many instances of brutality. Ample use was made of artillery with little regard for civilian safety, while curfews, passes and the collection of 'tolls' at road blocks were greatly resented. Headed by another former collaborator, Alberto Ramos, the Police Constabulary, previously known as the Military Police Command, largely protected the property and economic interests of the political elite, at the same time resorting to extortion and intimidation of Roxas's political opponents. After Roxas's death from a heart attack in 1948, his successor, President Elpido Quirino, attempted negotiations, but these also broke down and Huk success continued. By 1950, there were perhaps 11,000 to 15,000 Huks, perhaps 150,000 active supporters and, conceivably, up to a million passive sympathisers. As in Malaya, however, there were some government advantages.

Just as the MCP was effectively isolated from external assistance, 'Huklandia' itself – about 15,000 square kilometres – was clearly defined in geographical, socio-economic and political terms. Moreover, the basis of the Huks' popular support rested effectively on the single issue of land reform. There was also the increasing disparity between the aims of the urban-based communist leadership and peasant leaders such as Luis Taruc, who was to resign as Huk commander-in-chief in March 1951 only to find that he had already been dismissed by the politburo. Ordered to the distant Cagayan valley in October 1951, Taruc called for new negotiations in September 1952 and was dismissed from the politburo in August 1953. By contrast to Malaya, the residual authority within the more autonomous and nominally democratic government system in the Philippines would ultimately enable the interests of the political establishment to be by-passed. If Malaya had the revenue from tin and rubber, the Philippines was to receive American economic assistance totalling $820 million between 1946 and 1952, most of it after 1949 since neither Roxas nor Quirino had gone out of their way to call for American assistance. Just as the Korean War brought prosperity to Malaya, so it raised the United States' concerns for the region as a whole, but leverage over the government in Manila was limited when Washington wished to avoid any appearance of neo-colonialism in its influence. As in Malaya, too, there had been a similar miscalculation on the part of the communist leadership, which believed that a revolutionary situation already existed and that there was no need for mass organisation or lengthy political preparation. Yet again, as in Malaya, there was a lucky break for the authorities when most members of the politburo in Manila were captured in October 1950.

Whatever their inherent advantages, however, both the British and the Filipino government, with its American advisers, still had to adopt a more appropriate response to Maoist-style insurgency. While the build-up of the security forces by 1950 was sufficient to ensure that they did not lose, there was little expectation of insurgency being suppressed. The long road to success began in Malaya with the appointment of Lieutenant-General Sir Harold Briggs as director of operations in March 1950. A former Indian army officer, Briggs had considerable experience of Burma, where he had served during the Tharrawaddy Revolt, during the Second World War as a divisional commander, and during immediate post-war internal security duties. Evolved initially from his appreciation of 10 April 1950, what became known as the 'Briggs Plan' identified the first priority as the elimination of the MCP's mass political support organisation, the Min Yuen, rather than the elimination of insurgent groups operating from jungle bases. Thus, there was a recognition that political action designed to separate the insurgents from their supporters should take priority over purely military action, and an atmosphere should be created in which insurgency did not disrupt the process of legitimate government.

Another crucial element was the creation of an elaborate committee structure from a Federal War Council down through state, district and even village committees. On each sat representatives of army, police, civil agencies and, from January 1955, representatives of the ethnic communities. This ensured a co-ordinated response at every stage. A third part of the Briggs Plan was the introduction of large-scale resettlement to ensure the separation of the squatter population from the insurgents. The process had begun somewhat slowly before Briggs's arrival but now gathered pace. Eventually, 509 'new villages' were created to house the squatters: 410 with 423,000 inhabitants were already in place by the end of 1952. Resettlement was not immediately successful and, initially, security issues rather than the identification of good agricultural land determined the chosen locations. Initial security was often poor, and there was a decline in food production as the acreage under cultivation fell and a concomitant increase in food prices at a time when employment opportunities were also curtailed. In the longer term, and at a cost of M$41 million, resettlement worked and, since over a third of the new villages were close to urban areas, there were new employment opportunities for many of the squatters as the economy expanded amid the Korean War boom.

Labour forces on the estates and mines were also grouped. However, the application of the same solution to the *Sakai* or jungle aboriginals later in the campaign was abandoned when it became evident that nomadic aboriginals were not socially or economically suited to resettlement, whereas the Chinese squatters had no traditional attachment to the land they illegally occupied and were also used to living in close communities. The jungle aboriginals, therefore, were won over by establishing jungle forts, which became a focus for voluntary settlement by offering inducements such as clothing, agricultural tools, seeds, transistors and shotguns, as well as medical and other facilities.

The inevitable logic of the effort to ensure an integrated political and military strategy was that a single individual should control all aspects of the response to the insurgency. Therefore, following the death of the High

Commissioner, Sir Henry Gurney, in an ambush in October 1951 and the departure of Briggs on health grounds in December 1951, Lieutenant-General Sir Gerald Templer was made both High Commissioner and director of operations in February 1952. Gray's resignation had been accepted in December 1951 and the existing director of intelligence, Sir William Jenkin, had resigned just before Gurney's death. Such were the advantages enjoyed by the British, not least in terms of the ethnic nature of the conflict, that it has been argued that the MCP was effectively broken before any of the new villages had any but the most rudimentary of facilities and before Templer's 'hearts and minds' strategy became evident. At the time, however, the situation at the end of 1951 seemed at a low ebb. Undoubtedly, therefore, by sheer force of personality, Templer rejuvenated the campaign and, in combining the two posts, he had the authority that Briggs had crucially lacked.

Briggs had already established a police Special Branch freed from criminal work in May 1950 and had appointed a director to co-ordinate intelligence at all levels in August 1950. Templer went further in establishing a combined intelligence staff and an intelligence training school, while adding the director of intelligence to the Federal War Council. Similarly, while Briggs had created an emergency information service under Hugh Carleton Greene in June 1950 to improve the delivery of propaganda, Templer appointed a director general of information services in October 1952 independent from the director of operations. In fact, Templer's own relationship with the press was strained, but he well understood the significance of propaganda. Thus, he also established a new psychological warfare section in March 1954, whose Surrendered Enemy Personnel (SEP) programme had some success in encouraging defections from the guerrillas, many subsequently serving in the Special Operations Volunteer Force (SOVF) against their erstwhile colleagues. Substantial rewards were on offer for information, varying in 1951 from M$2,000 for information leading to the arrest of a rank-and-file member of the MCP to M$60,000 for Chin Peng.

Over 100 million leaflets were air dropped over the jungle in 1956, while there were over 2,200 broadcast flights that same year and 90 mobile information vans in operation by 1958, film being an especially popular entertainment medium in Malaya with all communities. Indeed, the 'Tarzanesque' anti-bandit film hero, Yaacob, was created by the Malayan Film Unit to appeal to the Chinese penchant for Tarzan films. The authorities also co-operated with the commercial film industry in Rank's 1952 production, The Planter's Wife, aimed partly at American audiences, and in the 1953 semi-documentary, Operation Malaya. Significantly, too, British propaganda changed in May 1952 from characterising the insurgents merely as bandits to describing them as communist terrorists to underline to audiences outside Malaya the gravity of the threat posed.

Templer also moved to give the squatter population in the new villages tangible proof of genuine concern for their welfare by 'winning hearts and minds'. Indeed, Templer appears to have coined the phrase itself, remarking on one occasion that 'the shooting side of the business is only 25 per cent of the trouble and the other 75 per cent lies in getting the people of this country behind us'. However, Templer made it clear that a choice was to be made and, as at Tanjong Malim in April 1952, showed that he was quite ready to impose curfews, collective fines, food control and other restrictions if necessary. At Tanjong Malim, the murder of twelve government officials resulted in the imposition of a 22-hour curfew, a halving of the rice ration and the closing of the school when the villagers refused to co-operate in giving information on the incident. On another occasion, Templer had a village dismantled and moved elsewhere. Alongside the stick, however, came the carrot. Amenities such as clean water, electric light, clinics and schools were increasingly made available, education in particular being highly valued by the Chinese. In addition, permanent legal title was granted the squatters for the land they now occupied in December 1951. Templer introduced village councils in May 1952, and a new federal citizenship law came into force in September 1952. Chinese affairs officers were also recruited from former missionaries in China and others with knowledge of Chinese to consolidate the link between government and the Chinese community. A Rural Industrial Development Authority was also established to assist in small-scale development projects.

The nature of policing was also transformed. Building on the recommendations of an earlier police advisory mission to Malaya in 1949, Operation Service, was launched by Gray's successor, Arthur Young, the former Commissioner for Police for the City of London, in December 1952. Young emphasised a more traditional British role rather than a paramilitary one. While increasing pay, training and equipment, Young reduced the police from 71,000 men to 54,000, so weeding out the undesirables. In the event, Chinese recruits did not appear in the numbers hoped, and the police found it difficult to shake off their over-militarised approach.

A compulsory home guard had been established in the new villages in July 1951, extending the *kampong* (village) guard established for Malay settlements in 1949. A similar home guard was also established for the tin mines in May 1952. By 1953, Templer felt confident enough to make the home guard solely responsible for village defence, although field labourers, who might encounter guerrillas during the day, were subsequently banned from the home guard after May 1956. The first 'white area', freed of all emergency restrictions, was announced in Malacca in September 1953, the original idea of Briggs to work systematically from south to north having been abandoned in favour of clearing the easiest areas where the MCP was weakest first. Recognising the need to keep the Malay population on side amid all the apparent efforts being made on behalf of the Chinese population, Templer also encouraged the merger of UMNO with the Malayan Chinese Association and the Malayan Indian Congress to form the multi-racial Alliance Party, led by Tunku Abdul Rahman, which became the government upon independence in August 1957.

By the time Templer left Malaya in May 1954 the MCP was on the defensive, the successful separation of the insurgents from their core support making it possible to free the armed forces for a primary role of striking at the insurgent groups in the jungle. Increasingly, it had been recognised that the most successful military operations against the insurgents were those linked to rigorous food denial, by which all those moving out of villages were thoroughly searched from June 1951 onwards, the time and effort involved paying dividends in the longer term. Aircraft could then be used to spot any cultivated areas in the jungle, which were subsequently destroyed more effectively by troops uprooting crops by hand than by air-dropped defoliants. The most effective military operations were by small units of platoons, sections and even sub-sections undertaking deep-penetration patrols into the jungle. The process was assisted by the 'framework deployment' of battalions on a long-term basis in particular areas.

The lessons were enshrined in a new manual overseen by Templer but written largely by Walter Walker, *The Conduct of Anti-Terrorist Operations in Malaya* (known as ATOM). Published in July 1952, it was partly based on the syllabus of Walker's training centre as well as two wartime pamphlets, MTP Nos 51 and 52, issued to the British 14th Army in Burma in 1944. Some 6,000 copies had been distributed on publication, and regular courses were begun for all units from August 1952. In turn, ATOM was to form the basis for *A Handbook of Anti-Mau Mau Operations*, issued in Kenya in 1954, as well as being published in two more Malayan editions in 1954 and 1958. The tactical lessons were also informed by Templer's creation of an operational research team, which analysed patrol reports for data.

The availability of helicopters from 1953 onwards was especially valuable for dropping patrols into the jungle, and, assisted by the aboriginal trackers of the Senoi Pra'aq (Fighting People) and others recruited from the Iban tribe in Borneo, the reformed SAS pushed the surviving insurgents back towards the frontier with Thailand. During the emergency, over 5,000 casualties were evacuated by helicopter, over 19,000 passengers carried, over 110,000 troops transported and over 2.5 million pounds of freight carried. Moreover, ten minutes flying time was the equivalent of ten hours marching through the jungle. 'Feet on the ground', however, was a painstaking process, with an individual member of the security forces expected to spend perhaps 100 hours on patrol or 300 hours lying in ambush in order to encounter one insurgent. It worked, however, and the emergency was declared at an end on 31 July 1960, although insurgent groups continued to exist along the frontier. Indeed, Chin Peng only emerged to surrender to the Malaysian authorities in December 1989. The British success was not achieved either cheaply or quickly. Insurgent casualties amounted to 13,191, including 2,980 surrendered, while the security forces suffered 4,436 casualties, and there were 4,668 civilian casualties. The protracted nature of the conflict also cost an estimated M$487 million.

In the Philippines, both the Roxas and Quirino administrations were venal with little interest in enhanced government responsiveness, since they consistently sought to control the peasantry and deny increased participation in government. Nevertheless, Roxas did pass a new crop-sharing law in 1947 and, after succeeding Roxas, Quirino did recognise that the existing strategy was not working. Thus, as well as instituting financial reforms to make the collection of taxes more efficient, in September 1950 Quirino appointed a former USAFFE guerrilla leader, Ramón Magsaysay, as secretary for national defence, although doubtless without fully grasping how different Magsaysay's agenda might prove. Magsaysay recognised that a new strategy required a change in existing attitudes, which might require a redistribution of political and economic power to those seen as supporting insurgency.

The control of the counter-insurgency effort Magsaysay now instituted did not mirror that in Malaya, since he subordinated the police to the army in December 1950. Ramos was removed as head of the police, and the army's commander-in-chief, Mariano Castaneda, was another of many officers whom Magsaysay eased out. Nonetheless, if not entirely similar to the structure in Malaya, Magsaysay's Department of National Defense became a multi-faceted general-purpose agency in such a way that there was only one strategy being pursued. He did take a similar view of the importance of intelligence to the British, making the compilation of a Huk order of battle a priority. Magsaysay's principal American adviser, Edward Lansdale, revitalised the Philippine Intelligence Service and the Intelligence School, while creating a new Military Intelligence Corps. Another significant creation was the Civil Affairs Office within Magsaysay's department, which was responsible for an enhanced psychological warfare effort. In one two-year period, no less than thirteen million leaflets were distributed, while extensive use was made of mobile projection units and mobile shows to bring the government message to the population in the guise of entertainment. Newspapers ostensibly meant for soldiers also played a part, while Taruc's mother was persuaded to record a radio appeal for his surrender. Energetic attempts were also made to purchase the large number of surplus weapons, many originally taken from the Japanese, that were available on the black market.

Psychological warfare was but one part of the effort Magsaysay launched to win the hearts and minds of the population. The despised police force was integrated into the army, with better pay to discourage looting, and it was barred from using excessive force. Troops carried extra food so that they could distribute it to civilians if a need was perceived, and sweets and chewing gum were regularly passed out to children. Civic action programmes were begun, including a well-publicised resettlement project for former Huks and their families at three sites: Kapatagan and Buldon on Mindanao and one in northern Luzon. Known as the Economic Development Corps (EDCOR), it actually relocated only 100 families. Of the 5,200 people eventually resettled, perhaps only 20 per cent were former Huks. What mattered, however, was the symbolism of establishing land-hungry peasants on new and relatively spacious farms. Thus, Huk efforts to portray EDCOR's settlements as concentration camps failed dismally.

Magsaysay well knew that propaganda and physical control would not deliver the message that the *status quo* was worth supporting and that there must be more tangible proof of genuine government concern, thus giving the population a vested interest in the existing administration. Consequently, alongside EDCOR, Magsaysay made it possible for people to send a reduced-rate telegram of complaint to him and to receive a reply within 24 hours. He also toured extensively to listen personally to peasant fears and expectations. The Judge Advocate General's Department provided free assistance to peasants to defend themselves against landlords, and the ethnic Chinese community was persuaded to improve rural credit facilities and reduce interest rates. New agencies such as the Agricultural Credit and Co-operative Financing Association and the Social Welfare Administration also emerged. A minimum wage was theoretically introduced in August 1951 and free compulsory primary education in 1953. Above all, Magsaysay was seen to use the security forces to ensure relatively honest mid-term congressional and regional elections in 1951. Magsaysay's efforts were supplemented by the appearance of two new organisations, the National Association for Free Elections (Namfrel) and the Philippine News Service, which appear to have been orchestrated by Lansdale.

With the assistance of American advisers like Lansdale from the Joint United States Military Assistance Group (JUSMAG), which had been established in December 1947, Magsaysay also reorganised the army into self-sufficient all-arms battalion combat teams (BCTs). Like British battalions in Malaya, the BCTs increasingly deployed on a long-term basis in particular areas, with which they could become thoroughly familiar. Similarly, lacking heavy equipment or helicopters, the BCTs and the associated specialist units known as Scout Rangers – usually three- to ten-man squads with dog teams – undertook sustained small-unit action based on food denial, mobility and intensive patrolling, often guided by reconnaissance aircraft such as Piper Cubs. Pseudo Huk units were also formed, and members of the security forces also manned decoy buses to lure the insurgents into attempted robberies. Civil affairs officers were also attached to each BCT to carry Magsaysay's message as it were into the front line of the conflict. The Huks were forced on to the defensive, and 9,695 had been killed, 1,635 wounded and 4,269 captured by 1954. In addition, 15,866 had surrendered, including Taruc, who did so in May 1954. The security forces had suffered 1,578 casualties. Magsaysay went on to become president of the Philippines in April 1953, and by the time of his death in an air crash in March 1957, the Huk uprising had been broken.

Malaya, which became part of the federation of Malaysia in September 1963, remained relatively stable and democratic, illustrating the importance of putting in place reforms sufficient to prevent the recurrence of significant insurgency. Thus, although surviving guerrillas continued to operate along the Thai–Malaysian frontier, necessitating joint Thai and Malaysian operations as in 1977 and 1985, the threat was not serious. Similarly, there was a brief Huk revival in the Philippines between 1965 and 1970, but it had little impact. However, growing opposition to the rule of Ferdinand Marcos, who became president in 1965, resulted in Marcos declaring martial law in September 1972, although there was little evidence that there was any danger of the communist insurrection that Marcos claimed. His principal opponents were the Moro National Liberation Front (MNLA) on Jolo and Mindanao, and the communist New People's Army (NPA). Moro opposition to Marcos, which stemmed from continuing resentment at the Catholic domination of government in Manila and the influx of non-Muslims into Mindanao, fragmented in the late 1970s. The NPA was a more serious threat, since land reform had long since stalled and the reappearance of widespread corruption had eroded confidence in the government and its security forces. Continued US economic aid had been channelled into preserving Marcos's personal rule rather than addressing social problems. Indeed, by declaring martial law Marcos was able to extend indefinitely his tenure as president, which had been due to end in 1973 after completion of the maximum two terms.

The NPA had emerged in 1969 as the military wing of the Communist Party of the Philippines (CPP). In classic Maoist style, the NPA gradually built an elaborate and sophisticated web of political support, capitalising on the notion of a broad anti-Marcos united front, which enabled it to fill the vacuum left by the split in the Moros. By 1980, the NPA had an estimated 24,000 activists in its various organising groups, organising committees, party branches, sections, districts, fighting fronts, party and regional commissions answerable to the politburo and the central committee. It had also spread from Luzon to other islands affected by poverty and deprivation such as Samar, Panay, Negros and Mindanao, and from rural to urban centres. NPA intimidation, especially by *yunit partisano* (partisan units) known as 'sparrows', however, brought about a popular backlash, which led to the growth of a government-sponsored militia. The NPA then suffered from the fall of Marcos through the remarkable display of 'people power' in February 1986 and the new government's subsequent adoption of a more considered political response to communist insurgency.

This was largely masterminded by a former army officer, Victor Corpus, who had defected to the NPA in 1970, returned to the government side in 1976 and promptly been imprisoned but released from detention after the fall of Marcos. Codenamed Lambat Betag (Net Trap) and introduced in 1989, the new strategy was one of 'gradual constriction' of communist areas by a combination of military pressure and social reform. Neutralisation of the NPA infrastructure was accorded the first priority. The scale of insurgency has decreased significantly, despite the failure of all post-Marcos governments to introduce genuine land reform.

Essentially, the experience of Maoist insurgency in both Malaya and the Philippines demonstrated the importance of six factors in formulating the response of government and security forces:

1   The recognition of the need for political action designed to prevent the insurgents gaining popular support should take priority over purely military action;
2   the requirement for complete civil–military co-operation;
3   the need for co-ordination of intelligence;
4   the separation of the insurgent from the population through the winning of hearts and minds;
5   the appropriate use of military force to support pacification; and
6   lasting political reform to prevent the recurrence of insurgency.

In the case of Malaya, these lessons were enshrined by Robert Thompson, a former RAF liaison officer with the Chindits, who was assistant commissioner for labour and Chinese affairs in Perak when the emergency was declared. Thompson had helped to establish Ferret Force and became the civil staff officer to Briggs, going on to be co-ordinating officer (security) in 1955, deputy secretary of defence in 1957 and, in 1959, permanent secretary for defence. In what became known as the 'five principles', Thompson outlined the requirements for successful counter-insurgency as the need for government to have a clear political aim; to function within the law; to establish an overall plan, whereby all political, socio-economic and military responses were co-ordinated; to give priority to the elimination of political subversion; and to secure the government's base area before conducting a military campaign. Implicit within the five principles was Thompson's belief in the primacy of the police over the military, while, in terms of military operations, Thompson stressed the need for small-unit operations to meet and defeat the insurgents in their own element. Subsequently, Thompson headed the British Advisory Mission to South Vietnam (BRIAM) between September 1961 and March 1965. Ironically, although encapsulating the British experience and method, Thompson's five principles were only widely made known outside the British army with the publication of *Defeating Communist Insurgency* in 1966.

Generally, the United States had not entirely drawn the right conclusions from the activities of JUSMAPG in Greece and JUSMAG in the Philippines. It has been argued that, in each case, three requirements for success were identified as ensuring security, good government and socio-economic and political progress. In the event, as already indicated, the Americans did not have as much leverage as might be expected, and insurgency was defeated without the requirements of American policy necessarily being met, if at all, in the way intended.

In the case of Greece, American economic aid was intended to be conditional upon political and economic reform. In reality, the only solution to Greece's problems appeared to be encouraging the emergence of Papagos as head of government and generally condoning the strengthening of the political right. In the event, as already indicated, Papagos became Greek commander-in-chief, which had the effect of reducing venal political influence over the GNA's military decisions. The process was undoubtedly assisted by the establishment of JUSMAPG in December 1947 and the arrival of General James Van Fleet to head it in February 1948. JUSMAPG, however, had not fully understood the psychological aspects of the impact of civil war upon Greeks and the GNA in particular. Nor had JUSMAPG come to terms with DSE's guerrilla tactics, and in any case, in identifying the DSE as partisans and as little more than adjuncts of the Soviet army, it channelled much of the American aid into purely military responses. It was concluded that the DSE could not have functioned without recourse to sanctuaries across international frontiers and that a combination of interdiction and clearing operations backed by substantial firepower was sufficient to defeat it. In effect, it was the increasing willingness of DSE to fight a positional war, almost on American terms, that had contributed most to its defeat.

While the GNA was reorganised by JUSMAPG into larger standardised divisions, it was not possible to train the GNA sufficiently quickly in American methods, and the Americans could not sufficiently influence operations much below battalion level. Nonetheless, as Larry Cable has commented, the Greek experience suggested that 'big battalions seemed to work in any type of conflict'. Moreover, despite its frequent failure in Greece, Americans believed that encirclement was the best technique in combating partisans since it had seemed to work against North Korean guerrillas in the Taebaek mountains during the Korean War.

By contrast, since it was clearly an insurrection rather than a partisan war, the experience in the Philippines potentially offered significant lessons concerning the importance of civil rather than military response. Lessons concerning psychological warfare and special operations were taken on board, but, to American military observers, the Philippines suggested no more than Greece that US military doctrine need be changed. Indeed, Magsaysay instructed his officers to ignore the tactics they had been taught in the United States and by JUSMAG and, in many respects, his solutions generally were rooted in the existing Philippine political system. Nor did the Philippines alter the belief that 'self-supporting, spontaneously created guerrilla groups are a rarity'. Moreover, the clear importance of Magsaysay's role suggested the identification of a local strong man as the real key to success. But the Americans failed to take into account the political context in which Magsaysay was able to operate, not least the familiarity of the Philippine people with basic democratic principles.

In this regard, in promoting Magsaysay's reputation, Lansdale arguably served a similar role to Thompson in formulating the overriding lesson that the Americans derived from the Philippines. A former advertising executive, Lansdale had received a wartime commission with the USAAF and then served with OSS-backed guerrillas fighting the Japanese in the Philippines. He was lecturing at the USAF Strategic Intelligence School when he met Magsaysay in September 1950, Magsaysay subsequently requesting his services. Although only a second-grade staff officer with JUSMAG, Lansdale became a close and influential adviser, playing a particular part in EDCOR. Subsequently, Lansdale went to the new South Vietnam in June 1954 to head the CIA's Saigon Military Mission even before the French had fully withdrawn. He became a close adviser to the president of South Vietnam, Ngo Dinh Diem, but his influence over United States policy declined as he continued to support Diem's cause when others had concluded that Diem was not a Magsaysay-type strong man but a political liability.

If insurgency had been defeated in Malaya and the Philippines, this was not the case in either the Dutch East Indies or French Indo-China, where colonial authorities and security forces alike failed to make the necessary adaptation to the new circumstances. In both cases, the nationalist opposition had again been effectively created by the Japanese intervention in the Second World War.

With the Netherlands itself occupied by the Germans in May 1940, the Japanese overran the Dutch East Indies, which surrendered on 9 March 1942. Just as puppet administrations were established in Burma and the Philippines, so the Japanese allowed the nationalists, Mohammad Hatta and Kusno Sosro Sukarno, to establish the Putera (Centre of Power) organisation in March 1943, although they subsequently disbanded it. Full independence had been promised to Indonesia, but the Japanese surrendered on 15 August 1945 before granting it. With the allies unable to organise an immediate return to occupied countries, the Indonesian nationalists seized the opportunity to declare their own independence on 17 August 1945. The first allied troops to land on Java on 29 September 1945 were British. The British intention was to evacuate former internees and prisoners of war of the Japanese. The nationalists, however, believed the British intended to facilitate the return of the Dutch, and fighting occurred at Surabaya in October. The British, whose last forces left Indonesia in November 1946, urged the Dutch to negotiate, and talks were opened. The Dutch, however, would not concede total independence, presenting the nationalists with an ultimatum in May 1947 demanding that Dutch sovereignty be recognised until February 1949. There was no response. On 20 June 1947, therefore, the Dutch, who had built up their forces to about 100,000 men, launched what they termed a 'police action' in Java, Sumatra and Madura. The Dutch Labour Party within the coalition government had also limited the campaign to regaining control of the most economically significant areas in the expectation of encouraging concessions by the moderates among the nationalist leadership.

The Dutch achieved some success, but pressure from the United States and the UN led to further negotiations on a form of federalism. The Indonesians did not believe this acceptable and fighting continued, the Indonesian Republican Army (TNI) having about 175,000 men. Backed by the army and by the right-wing Catholic Party within the coalition, a second Dutch 'police action' opened on 18 December 1948, with the Dutch seizing the nationalist capital, Djakarta, in eastern Java and capturing Sukarno and much of the nationalist leadership. The United States threatened the Dutch with economic sanctions on 7 December 1948, and this led to a final round of negotiations and independence for Indonesia on 27 December 1949.

The Dutch, who deployed 140,000 men by the end of 1948, relied too much on methods that had served against old-style guerrillas in Aceh at the turn of the nineteenth century. Initially, the aim was one of occupation of nationalist territory, followed by pacification and counter-guerrilla operations. An assumption was made that seizing perceived command centres and taking out 'extremist' leaders would paralyse the nationalist forces. The strategy remained essentially unchanged through both 'police actions' and, in many respects, initial occupation was successful. The difficulty was that counter-guerrilla operations were all but impossible to bring to a successful conclusion given the lack of intelligence concerning the guerrillas, who were generally supported by the population. Economic inducements were held out to encourage co-operation, but the carrot went hand in hand with the stick of restrictive emergency measures such as curfews and detention, as well as intimidation and brutality, such as that on south Sulawesi associated with a Dutch captain, Raymond 'Turk' Westerling. In addition, the dispersed nature of the Dutch deployment did not assist rapid reaction to guerrilla activity, and in any case, the resupply of Dutch posts depended upon vulnerable road communications. As international pressure on the Dutch increased, the likelihood of securing popular support in the East Indies further declined and, as guerrilla activity increased in turn, the Dutch forces were further stretched and resorted to greater reliance upon artillery and air power.

Rather as previous methods of colonial warfare worked against Dutch understanding of the nature of their enemy, French *tache d'huile* was to prove no match for the disciplined organisation of the Viet Minh, who could also appeal to Vietnamese nationalism. The Viet Minh had come into existence as an anti-Japanese coalition in May 1941 at a time when the fall of France to Germany had seriously weakened the ability of the French colonial authorities to resist Japanese pressure. France had first extended its control over Laos, Cambodia and the territories of Annam, Tonkin and Cochin-China, making up modern Vietnam, between 1859 and 1899, and in common with other colonial powers in south-east Asia, colonial policies were based upon the exploitation of resources, which tended to destroy traditional economic structures and threaten indigenous cultures. As elsewhere, it was those closest to the French who emerged to lead nationalist movements, since a by-product of the educational opportunities offered to subject peoples was the realisation that principles of freedom and self-determination stressed by Western education did not apply to themselves. In fact, Laos and Cambodia were generally receptive to French rule as it was seen as a safeguard against Vietnam, and it was in Vietnam that nationalism developed as opposition both to the French and to the Chinese middle classes, whose influence remained substantial in the economy.

With the fall of France, the Vichy French authorities in Indo-China came under increasing pressure from the Japanese. Initially, the French agreed to stop supplying fuel to the KMT in China, then to allow the Japanese to occupy airfields and other bases throughout the country. With the liberation of France in 1944, however, de Gaulle's provisional government planned to begin military operations against the Japanese in Indo-China. Unfortunately, the Japanese discovered the intentions and in March 1945 seized total control of French Indo-China, executing the majority of the French military and political administration, including the French Governor-General, and massacring French garrisons. The Japanese then proclaimed Vietnam independent under the titular emperor of Annam, Bao Dai.

The plans of the Western allies for Indo-China had been heavily influenced by President Roosevelt, who had a general dislike of the European colonial empires and a particular dislike of de Gaulle. The latter at most was prepared to concede limited autonomy to Indo-China within the French community in line with the Brazzaville declaration of January 1944, which rejected any real measure of self-government as being a remote possibility for the French empire. The OSS had given the Viet Minh equipment and weapons during the war as well as their goodwill in return for intelligence and rescue of aircrew. Although Roosevelt's successor, Harry Truman, was to have second thoughts on the desirability of openly supporting a communist organisation, it was agreed at the Potsdam conference in July 1945, without reference to the French, that the Japanese forces in Indo-China would be disarmed by the nationalist Chinese north of the 16th parallel and by the British south of the parallel. Indeed, in any case, the French were entirely dependent upon the British and Americans for transport of any French troops sent to Indo-China.

That transport was in such short supply that it was virtually impossible to deal simultaneously with the disarming and repatriation of Japanese troops and the urgent recovery of Allied prisoners of war. However, that did present the problem of how quickly Allied forces of any description could be put back into those areas occupied by the Japanese and, in virtually every case, a power vacuum opened as the Japanese were thrown into confusion by the dropping of the two atomic bombs at Hiroshima and Nagasaki on 6 and 9 August, respectively, by the Soviet invasion of Manchuria on 8 August, and by the announcement of Japan's surrender on 15 August 1945.

On 8 August, Bao Dai's government resigned and Ho Chi Minh, who had been making detailed preparations for an uprising ever since the Japanese takeover in March, seized the opportunity to take control of Hanoi on 19 August and to proclaim the independence of a Democratic Republic of Indochina on 2 September. Ho meant the three Vietnamese areas of Annam, Tonkin and Cochin-China, and his version of Indo-China did not include Laos and Cambodia. Bao Dai, who had abdicated as emperor on 30 August, was given the honorary role of 'supreme adviser'. With the French still in no position to react, the first allied troops to arrive were British Indian army forces, who, in accordance with the Potsdam agreement, occupied Saigon on 11 September. Major-General Douglas Gracey found a chaotic situation in which French civilian and those French troops who had survived the Japanese massacres were engaging in open conflict with the Viet Minh. In order to restore order he even rearmed the Japanese, and British and Japanese forces therefore waged what has been called Britain's Vietnam War to clear the Viet Minh from the area south of the 16th parallel. In fact, while steadily replaced by French troops, the last British forces did not leave Vietnam until 15 May 1946. In the north, the KMT had moved in to disarm the Japanese, but it did not interfere with the Viet Minh, and while elements within the KMT wished to remain in the north, the increasing need to deploy more men against Mao led to their withdrawal in March 1946.

In fact, both the French and Ho Chi Minh were prepared to negotiate and, in March 1946, Ho accepted political recognition of a Vietnamese state within the French Union, which allowed French forces back into Hanoi on the understanding that further talks would follow. While such an agreement was acceptable to Cambodia and Laos, limited self-government under the nominal leadership of Bao Dai was not sufficient in Vietnam and the negotiations broke down. Moreover, many of the principal French participants in the negotiating process had never regarded the agreement in March 1946 as more than a means of hastening the KMT's withdrawal from the north, particularly after de Gaulle had resigned from the French government. On 21 December 1947, therefore, Ho Chi Minh proclaimed war on the French. By the end of this first Indo-China or Vietnam War on 20 July 1954, 375,000 French and associated troops had been deployed. In all, almost 77,000 French and associated troops were killed or recorded as missing and almost 40,000 taken prisoner, over 29,000 of whom were never repatriated and are presumed to have died in captivity. Viet Minh casualties are unknown but may have totalled at least 200,000.

Ostensibly, the French were not fighting to retain colonial control but to establish supposedly autonomous states within the French Union, and their constant aim was to find indigenous groups that would find such a situation acceptable. Indeed, they continued to negotiate with Bao Dai and reached a formal agreement with him in March 1949, which led to a state of Vietnam being proclaimed in July 1949 as a preliminary to the achievement of the associated status granted to Laos at this time and extended to Cambodia in

November 1949. Subsequently, under the pressure of the declining military position in Indo-China, the French gave full independence to Laos and Cambodia in October and November 1953, respectively. The French also hoped to find support from the surviving pre-war nationalists and among the 1.7 million Vietnamese Catholics and other minority religious sects such as the Cao Dai and Hoa Hoa. Seeking support from those like Bao Dai, however, gave the French little credibility in Indo-China, and the Viet Minh was able to establish a monopoly in terms of the appeal to patriotism and nationalism, to which the French had no ideological reply. Indeed, a decision by the French to devalue the currency in May 1953 without consulting the indigenous administrations further undermined their political credibility.

Moreover, whatever the nominal interest in granting autonomy, France remained very much a captive of the centralist concept of state authority whereby France and French possessions must form an indivisible whole, with any form of secession akin to heresy. The idea of empire remained extremely important to national status. Similarly, while France was far from dependent upon its colonies in economic terms, there was a settler population in Indo-China. In a sense, this made French imperialism stronger at the peripheries than at the centre, and this was accentuated in the case of the French army, which was divided into distinctly metropolitan and colonial institutions. The metropolitan army was composed primarily of conscripts, whose liability was restricted to home service, while the Armée d'Afrique in North Africa and La Coloniale outside North Africa included substantial contingents of indigenous troops.

With such an essentially peripherally driven imperial policy, successive French governments were all but held hostage by colonial interests highly resistant to the notion of making political concessions to indigenous groups. With no less than seven different political parties operating in the unstable Fourth Republic on a system of proportional representation, the influence of the colonial lobby was increased, not least that of the Catholic right of centre Mouvement Republicain Populaire (Popular Republican Movement, MRP), whose adherents invariably secured the Foreign, Overseas Territories and Indo-China ministries in successive coalitions. Moreover, the support for Ho Chi Minh by the French Communist Party tended to make it difficult for other parties to entertain negotiations with the Viet Minh and drove the Socialists into coalitions with the imperially minded parties if they were to share the fruits of office. Yet because French conscripts did not serve in Indo-China, there was little real commitment to the war by ordinary French men and women, and the French colonial forces felt increasingly isolated by the perceived lack of domestic support in France for the war, as well as by the corruption in Bao Dai's administration and the squalid nature of political argument in France. The war certainly became increasingly unpopular in France, with the percentage supporting its prosecution falling from 37 per cent of those asked in July 1947 to 19 per cent by July 1949. Communist opposition also became openly hostile, with strikes and sometimes sabotage in ports where stores were being loaded for Indo-China. Eventually, returning wounded were kept away from Paris for fear of demonstrations, and it was felt better to treat them with blood plasma drawn elsewhere than from the national blood donor organisation.

Another factor to be taken into account was the role of external states. In 1949, the balance tipped decisively against France with the victory of Mao in China. This provided the Viet Minh with a safe haven, and it was at this time that the Viet Minh began the transition from purely guerrilla forces to the establishment of the regular units of the Chu Luc. By 1954, the Viet Minh had about 125,000 regulars, with another 350,000 in a rudimentary militia. These received Chinese military equipment, especially artillery and anti-aircraft guns, and, in January 1950, Peking officially recognised the Viet Minh. Chinese training missions appeared, while Chinese recognition in itself also compelled the Soviet Union to follow suit.

Even more significant in some respects was the role of the United States, of which the French were deeply suspicious. In fact, the outbreak of the Korean War in June 1950 persuaded the Truman administration to give material support to the French in their struggle against what looked like just another branch of a monolithic communist bloc. The Americans were also persuaded that a French defeat in Indo-China would undermine the confidence of the French army, which was vital to the defence of Western Europe and not just Indo-China. Thus, by October 1952 the Americans were contributing 75 per cent of the cost of the war. However, the price of American support was real-istic concession to indigenous autonomy and the notion of Vietnamisation, hence the French agreement with Bao Dai in 1949 and the subsequent attempt to create a Vietnamese army, which had still failed to reach its target strength of 115,000 men by the time the war ended. The Americans also demanded greater French commitment, which was translated into the achievement of a substantial military success. It was partly in search of that success that the French undertook the ultimately disastrous operation to seize Dien Bien Phu in November 1953. When that operation went wrong, the French requested American intervention. This was threatened at one point but would only have occurred if a number of preconditions were met, including support from the UN and total independence for the associated states. In the event, Eisenhower's administration chose not to take any action before a proposed international conference to be convened in Geneva, by which time Dien Bien Phu had fallen to the Viet Minh.

Mention of Dien Bien Phu raises the military aspects of the French response. *Tache d'huile*, which remained the basis of French doctrine, had been successful where opponents had been largely tribal with little sense of nation-alism and had lacked the vigorous appeal and moral certainty of a revolutionary communist organisation such as the Viet Minh. Another diffi-culty was that French pacification also rested on tactical mobility based on positional defence – that is to say mobile columns operating from large numbers of strongpoints. Thus, neither aspect of French military strategy worked well against the Viet Minh.

In the case of strongpoints, whether large like Cao Bang or Dien Bien Phu or small like the hundreds of *postes* established in the so-called de Lattre line in the Red River delta, they proved vulnerable to defeat in detail. Thus, the Cao Bang position was overrun by the Viet Minh in October 1950. Often, too, the French reacted too slowly to threats to their defensive positions and their relieving forces were ambushed, as occurred again at Cao Bang. In any case, holding large numbers of strongpoints was not relevant to winning the war when it was necessary to try to defeat the Viet Minh in the field. Manning such positions also reduced the available manpower for mobile operations. As a result, the French tended to sit in their positions, not least at night, and allow the Viet Minh to dominate countryside and population. There were successes if the Viet Minh committed itself to large-scale frontal assaults on defended positions, as they did around Na San in late 1952, but this was the exception. Yet mobile operations also brought problems for the French, since their mobility was limited. Helicopters were in their infancy, and never more than ten were available during the war. That left the French dependent upon the roads and thus vulnerable once more to ambush. In October and November 1952, for example, Operation Lorraine was intended as an advance deep into Viet Minh territory along the Red River, but was so ponderous that nothing tangible was achieved and no substantial Viet Minh forces were encountered until the French began to withdraw.

Some French officers did grasp that traditional pacification was no answer to modern revolutionary insurgency, and pilot schemes in the Cambodian frontier province of Svay Rieng in 1946 and in Kompong Chau, also in Cambodia, in 1951 saw the resettlement of the indigenous population within a defended zone. This deprived the Viet Minh of support and left these previously infiltrated areas in the control of the French. Commando groups were also formed among indigenous tribesmen. Originally known as Groupement de Commandos Mixtes Aéroportés (Composite Airborne Commando Groups, GCMA), and, after December 1953, as Groupement Mixte d'Intervention (Composite Intervention Groups, GMI), they numbered about 15,000 men by the end of the war, although opinions as to their usefulness varied. Nonetheless, these new methods contributed to the evolution of the new counter-insurgency doctrine of *guerre révolutionnaire*, which the French were subsequently to apply in Algeria.

In terms of their actual strategy, the French first aimed at what has been termed 'decapitation' of the insurgent leadership between 1946 and 1949, but the difficulty was to prevent the Viet Minh dispersing. Following the so-called battle of the frontiers in 1950–51, which started badly for the French around Dong Khe and Cao Bang, Jean-Marie-Gabriel de Lattre de Tassigny was sent out as both High Commissioner and commander-in-chief. On the one hand, de Lattre sought to close off the delta and the approaches to Hanoi and Haiphong with outposts and to use mobile combat groups to strike out from it. On the other, he tried to push ahead a Vietnamisation of the war. He had some success and benefited from the Viet Minh becoming overcommitted to large-scale conventional assaults in the Red River delta when Giap wrongly concluded that the French were weak. Giap's forces were badly mauled, suffering an estimated 12,000 casualties between January and June 1951. Dying from cancer, de Lattre handed over command to Raoul Salan in December 1951. Salan attempted to maintain the initiative through Operation Lorraine, the failure of which should have suggested the dangers of committing French forces deep inside Viet Minh territory. However, under Salan's successor, Henri-Eugène Navarre, the French then tried to strike at the main Viet Minh forces in an attritional battle.

The main threat from the Viet Minh appeared to be in Laos, which had now been given independence but where the communist Neo Lao Issara (Laso Freedom Front), the forerunner of the Pathet Lao (Land of the Laos), threatened stability. Accordingly, Navarre conceived that he could dominate the Laotian frontier and the routes to China by seizing the area around Dien Bien Phu. Not only would this pose a significant threat to any Viet Minh force attempting to invade Laos but it would also support those local indigenous montagnard units – primarily T'ai and Meo tribesmen – that supported the French. Both former intelligence officers, Salan and Navarre were emotionally committed to what they regarded as a new *maquis* capable of redressing the deteriorating military situation. However, a factor of even greater importance was that possession of Dien Bien Phu meant control of the opium crop. Traditionally, the French had held the monopoly of the refinement and sale of opium and had encouraged its planting by the Meos. However, the Viet Minh had seized this valuable crop and were using it to buy weapons from the Chinese. Thus, although the French administration had bowed to international pressure since 1946 to end the opium trade, the French military and intelligence services recognised its value as a source of revenue and as an opportunity to cultivate new support among the Meos.

It was not appreciated that the distance from Hanoi of 300 kilometres or so was significant, as was the fact that Dien Bien Phu lay in a valley. The assumption was that the single road into Dien Bien Phu would prevent the Viet Minh deploying more than 20,000 troops and that the logistic support available to the Vietnamese as well as the nature of the terrain would prevent them bringing in any heavy weapons. The Viet Minh would thus have to attack prepared French positions and suffer the consequences. In fact, there was some logic in this and the Vietnamese were to take staggering casualties, even given the fact that they were attacking a garrison placed into a poorly conceived position that lacked air support, was dominated by Viet Minh artillery and in which only a quarter of the defenders put up serious resistance. It has been said that there was some confusion within the French command as to whether Dien Bien Phu represented a 'hedgehog' or an anchor point for mobile operations. In reality, there was no incompatibility between the two concepts, and it was partly the initial conduct of mobile operations by those French forces parachuted into Dien Bien Phu on 20 November that led to the establishment of strong defensive positions being neglected. Moreover, despite what has sometimes been said about the failure of the French intelligence services to anticipate Vietnamese reaction, the radio security of the Viet Minh was extremely poor and the French had more than accurate intelligence. The real failure was that Navarre did not make logical decisions on the basis of that intelligence and, as the Viet Minh closed in, elected to make a stand rather than cut his losses and pull his forces back to the delta.

In the event, the Viet Minh were able to concentrate 60,000 men against the garrison and heavy guns, beginning a major offensive on 13 March 1954 in which French outposts were overwhelmed in human wave assaults. Two of the major outposts fell in the first two days and rendered the airstrip vulnerable to artillery bombardment. The last outpost fell on 7 May 1954. Of an estimated 15,000 men, the French lost about 3,000 dead and about 2,000 indigenous desertions, with the rest captured. The Viet Minh lost 23,000 casualties, including 8,000 dead.

Part of the reason for the willingness of Giap to commit his troops to such human wave assaults was the need to secure victory before the opening of the Geneva conference. The origins of this lay in the death of Stalin and the termination of the Korean War, which altered the international climate to a marked degree and prompted the French government to hint that it might be prepared to negotiate. In many respects, the assumption was that there would be a decisive military victory at Dien Bien Phu to force a suitably chastened Viet Minh to the table. The formal sessions began on the day after the surrender of the last French forces and, while the French wished to retain an influence in Indo-China, the new balance of military power dictated otherwise. The independence of both Laos and Cambodia was recognised, while the agreement, signed on 20 July 1954, also proposed that free elections be held throughout Vietnam in July 1956. As is well known, both North Vietnam, as it now became, and the new government of South Vietnam headed by Diem, a former minister of Bao Dai, subsequently declined to proceed with such an election. Thus, the partition of Vietnam along the 17th parallel brokered by the Chinese set the scene for a still greater conflict in Indo-China.

The Dutch army was not faced with any subsequent insurgency after withdrawal from the East Indies. For the French army, however, defeat in Indo-China was a bitter one, leading to particular distrust of French politicians. As a result, the new counter-insurgency doctrine, *guerre révolutionnaire*, which emerged as a result of the army's study of the lessons of Indo-China, was to lead to increasing politicisation of the army when confronted by a new insurgency in Algeria between 1954 and 1962.

Further reading

On Palestine, see David Charters, *The British Army and Jewish Insurgency in Palestine, 1945–47* (London, 1989); Charters, 'Special Operations in Counter-insurgency' *Journal of the Royal United Services Institute for Defence Studies* 124 (1979), pp. 56–61; Charters, 'British Intelligence in the Palestine Campaign' *Intelligence and National Security* 6 (1991), pp. 115–40; Bruce Hoffman, *The Failure of Britain's Military Strategy in Palestine, 1939–47* (Ramat Gan, 1983); Saul Zadka, *Blood in Zion: How the Jewish Guerrillas drove the British out of Palestine* (London, 1985); Tom Clarke, *By Blood and Fire* (New York, 1981); J. Bowyer Bell, *Terror out of Zion* (New York, 1977); and Joseph Heller, *The Stern Gang: Ideology, Politics and Terror, 1940–49* (London, 1995).

On Greece, see Tim Jones, 'The British Army and Counter-guerrilla Warfare in Transition, 1944–52' *Small Wars and Insurgencies* 7 (1996), pp. 265–307; Jones, 'The British Army and Counter-guerrilla Warfare in Greece, 1945–49' in *ibid.*, 8 (1997), pp. 88–106; David H. Close (ed.), *The Greek Civil War, 1943–50: Studies of Polarisation* (London, 1993); and C.M. Woodhouse, *The Struggle for Greece, 1941–49* (London, 1976).

On Malaya, see Richard Stubbs, *Hearts and Minds in Guerrilla Warfare: The Malayan Emergency, 1948–60* (Singapore, 1989); John Coates, *Suppressing Insurgency: An Analysis of the Malayan Emergency, 1948–60* (Boulder, 1992); Richard Clutterbuck, *The Long Long War: The Emergency in Malaya, 1948–60* (London, 1966); Raffi Gregorian, 'Jungle Bashing in Malaya: Towards a Formal Tactical Doctrine' *Small Wars and Insurgencies* 5 (1994), pp. 338–59; Karl Hack, 'Screwing Down the People: The Malayan Emergency, Decolonisation and Ethnicity' in Hans Antlöv and Stein Tønnesson (eds), *Imperial Policy and Southeast Asian Nationalism, 1930–57* (Richmond, 1994), pp. 83–109; Anthony Short, *The Communist Insurrection in Malaya, 1948–60* (London, 1975); Short, 'The Malayan Emergency' in Haycock, *Regular Armies and Insurgency*, pp. 53–68; John Cloake, *Templer: Tiger of Malaya* (London, 1985); Anthony Stockwell, 'Insurgency and Decolonisation during the Malayan Emergency' *Journal of Commonwealth and Comparative Politics* 25 (1987), pp. 71–81; Stockwell, 'A Widespread and Long-concocted Plot to Overthrow the Government in Malaya?: The Origins of the Malayan Emergency' in Robert Holland (ed.), *Emergencies and Disorder in the European Empires after 1945* (London, 1994), pp. 66–88; Holland, 'Policing during the Malayan Emergency, 1948–60: Communism, Communalism and Decolonisation' in Anderson and Killingray, *Policing and Decolonisation*, pp. 105–26; and Malcolm Postage, *Operation Firedog: Air Support in the Malayan Emergency, 1948–60* (London, 1992). Thompson's analysis of the Malayan experience can be found in his theoretical work, *Defeating Communist Insurgency: Experiences from Malaya and Vietnam* (London, 1966), and his auto-biography, *Make for the Hills: Memories of Far Eastern Wars* (London, 1989).

On British practice generally, see Mockaitis, *British Counterinsurgency, op cit.*, which covers Palestine and Malaya; John Pimlott, 'The British Army: The

Dhofar Campaign, 1970–75' in Ian Beckett and John Pimlott (eds), *Armed Forces and Modern Counter-insurgency* (London, 1985), pp. 16–45; David Charters, 'From Palestine to Northern Ireland: British Adaptation to Low-intensity Operations' in David Charters and Maurice Tugwell (eds), *Armies in Low-intensity Conflict: A Comparative Analysis* (London, 1989), pp. 169–250; Colin McInnes, *Hot War, Cold War: The British Army's Way in Warfare, 1945–95* (London, 1996), pp. 114–48; Susan Carruthers, *Winning Hearts and Minds: British Governments, the Media and Colonial Counter-insurgency, 1944–60* (Leicester, 1995); Carruthers, 'Two Faces of 1950s Terrorism: The Film Presentation of Mau Mau and the Malayan Emergency' *Small Wars and Insurgencies* 6 (1995), pp. 17–43; Keith Jeffery, 'Intelligence and Counter-insurgency Operations: Some Reflections on the British Experience' *Intelligence and National Security* 2 (1987), pp. 118–49; Richard Popplewell, 'Lacking Intelligence: Some Reflections on Recent Approaches to British Counter-insurgency, 1900–60' in *ibid.*, 10 (1995), pp. 336–52; and Christopher Harmon, 'Illustrations of "Learning" in Counterinsurgency', *Comparative Strategy* 11 (1992), pp. 29–48, which also covers the French and American experience.

On the Philippines, see Laurence Greenberg, *The Hukbalahap Insurrection* (Washington, 1987); Wray Johnson and Paul Dimech, 'Foreign Internal Defense and the Hukbalahap' *Small Wars and Insurgencies* 4 (1993), pp. 29–52; Peter M. Sales, 'Back to the Future?: Gradual Constriction as a New Phase of Counter-insurgency in the Philippines' in *ibid.*, pp. 73–88; Tom Marks, 'Maoist Miscue II: The Demise of the Communist Party of the Philippines, 1968–93' in *ibid.*, pp. 99–157; Dana Dillon, 'Comparative Counter-insurgency in the Philippines' in *ibid.*, 6 (1995), pp. 281–303; B.J. Kerkvliet, *The Huk Rebellion: A Study of Peasant Revolt in the Philippines* (Berkeley, 1982); and Napoleon Valeriano and Charles Bohannan, *Counterguerrilla Operations: The Philippine Experience* (New York, 1966). Lansdale's account of his contribution to the defeat of the Huks can be found in Edward Lansdale, *In the Midst of Wars: An American's Mission to Southeast Asia* (New York, 1972), while an overall assessment is in Cecil B. Currey, *Edward Lansdale: The Unquiet American* (Boston, 1988).

On the lessons Americans derived from Greece, the Philippines and other immediate post-war conflicts, see Larry Cable, *Conflict of Myths: The Development of American Counter-insurgency Doctrine and the Vietnam War* (New York, 1986); D. Michael Shafer, *Deadly Paradigms: The Failure of US Counterinsurgency Policy* (Leicester, 1988); and D.S. Blaufarb, *The Counterinsurgency Era: US Doctrine and Performance* (New York, 1977).

On Indo-China, see Anthony Clayton, *The Wars of French Decolonisation* (London, 1994); Jacques Dalloz, *The War in Indochina* (New York, 1990); Bernard Fall, *Hell in a Very Small Place* (London, 1966); Jules Roy, *The Battle of Dien Bien Phu* (London, 1965); T. Smith, 'The French Colonial Consensus and People's War, 1946–58' *Contemporary History* (1973), pp. 217–47; and Martin

Shipway, 'Creating an Emergency: Metropolitan Constraints on French Colonial Policy and its Breakdown in Indo-China, 1945–47' in Holland, *Emergencies and Disorder*, pp. 1–16. For Britain's brief involvement, see Peter M. Dunn, *The First Vietnam War* (London, 1985).

On the Dutch East Indies, see Petra M.H. Groen, 'Militant Response: The Dutch Use of Military Force and the Decolonisation of the Dutch East Indies, 1945–50' in Holland, *Emergencies and Disorder*, pp. 30–44; and Peter Dennis, *Troubled Days of Peace: Mountbatten and South-east Asia Command, 1945–46* (Manchester, 1987).

6

'WARS OF NATIONAL LIBERATION'?

While the challenge of communist ideology had been overcome in Malaya and the Philippines, it remained a potent threat to Western interests amid the escalation of the Cold War. Indeed, as suggested by the announcement in January 1961 by Khrushchev of the Soviet Union's support for 'wars of national liberation', the link between communism, anti-colonial nationalism and insurgency was more than coincidental. In facing this challenge, the lessons learned in Malaya were crucial to the evolving pattern of British counter-insurgency, being applied both during the Mau Mau emergency in Kenya between 1952 and 1960 and in the Confrontation between Malaysia and Indonesia between 1962 and 1966. Moreover, the Malayan influence was also clear in the European response to other African insurgencies, such as that confronted by white Rhodesia between 1966 and 1979 and those in Portugal's African colonies between 1961 and 1974. To a certain extent, it was also evident in the South African campaigns in South West Africa (Namibia) between 1966 and 1984.

It should be noted, however, that while the British were successful in both Kenya and Borneo, some of the lessons of Malaya were misused, while others required adaptation to different circumstances. The same was true of Rhodesia and Portuguese Africa, at least in terms of the failure to reproduce those elements in Malaya that had made resettlement work. The Rhodesian and Portuguese experiences also proved that even comparative success in counter-insurgency meant little when events were determined by external political pressures.

The prime cause of Mau Mau was pressure of population and, indeed, Mau Mau frequently called itself *ithaka na wiathi* (Freedom through Land), usually characterised as the Kenya Land Freedom Army. The greatest pressure was in the so-called White Highlands, where 3,000 white settler farmers controlled 16,196 square miles, or an average of 3,460 acres each, while over 1.3 million Africans on native land units of 52,141 square miles possessed an average of only 23.6 acres each. Most African agriculture was barely at the subsistence level. Those who were employed as labour by the white farms and variously known as resident labourers or squatters worked in a kind of quasi-feudal system in which an average of 200 days labour per annum brought a sub-economic wage and the limited use of land increasingly subject to strict stock control and acreage regulations. Further restrictions on land use were represented by the existence of Crown land and forest reserves, so that, as the African population increased, the land available became more and more inadequate to support it. There was some limited African political representation in the legislature, but the monopoly of political, agricultural and industrial power lay in the hands of the white settlers. Much of the wholesale and redistribution sector of the economy was controlled by a second settler community, the Asians. The situation was exacerbated by the arrival of new white settlers after 1945.

Black ex-servicemen sometimes took the lead in forging the Mau Mau organisation within the framework of the legal Kenya African Union (KAU), the membership of Mau Mau being distinguished by the administration of secret oaths among the deeply superstitious tribesmen of Kenya's largest tribe, the Kikuyu, and two closely related ethnic groups, the Embu and Meru. It is important to stress, however, that it was not a national uprising, since the other African peoples of Kenya were either indifferent or firmly opposed to Mau Mau. Many among the Kikuyu also opposed Mau Mau's methods, even if they sympathised with its political aims, particularly tribal elders and Christian or propertied Kikuyu. Indeed, the more militant Mau Mau were largely drawn from the more marginal members of the tribe, such as squatters and the unemployed. There remains considerable uncertainty as to the origins and precise meaning of the name 'Mau Mau' itself, while the precise connection of the leading Kikuyu nationalist, Jomo Kenyatta, with Mau Mau is also unproven.

With increasing violence, a state of emergency was declared on 20 October 1952 following the murder of a Kikuyu chief loyal to the government. It has been argued that, as in Malaya, the declaration of the state of emergency was intended to be pre-emptive and to neutralise an emerging nationalist movement, defining the problem as one of law and order rather than anti-colonialism. In fact, an internal security scheme pre-dated the first Special Branch reports on Mau Mau in 1950, and measures were undertaken in accordance with it before the declaration, which it was hoped would bring a swift return to normality. In the event, the measures introduced, which included widespread detention, compulsory registration of the Kikuyu population, seizure of livestock and a new punitive tax to pay for the additional costs of the emergency, had the effect of actually stimulating the wider insurgency the declaration was intended to avert by inducing many younger Kikuyu to take to the forests. Although the heart of the insurgency was defeated by October 1956 with the capture of the last leading insurgent leader, Dedan Kimathi, the emergency remained in force until January 1960.

The Confrontation arose from the attempt by President Sukarno of Indonesia to expand and establish a 'greater Indonesia'. In particular, Sukarno strongly opposed the creation of a Malaysian federation embracing the territories of Sarawak, Brunei and north Borneo (also known as Sabah) as well as Malaya and Singapore. Moves for this had been under way since 1961, and there was general support, or at least no particular opposition to it, among the majority of the inhabitants of northern Borneo. A minority, however, did oppose federation: in Sarawak, the largely Chinese Sarawak United People's Party and, in Brunei, the Brunei People's Party. In December 1962, the latter attempted an armed revolt in Brunei. This was quickly suppressed, although many of the rebels escaped into the jungle. Sukarno meanwhile announced that Indonesian 'volunteers' would liberate northern Borneo, or Kalimantan Utara as it was called by the Indonesians. These 'volunteers' comprised elements from the Sarawak United People's Party, surviving rebels from Brunei, Indonesian communists from the so-called Clandestine Communist Organisation in Sarawak and, from September 1963, Indonesian regular troops.

The first such group of volunteers crossed into Sarawak on 12 April 1963 to initiate the undeclared war of the Confrontation or *Konfrontasi*. Ultimately, Sukarno having fallen ill in August 1965, his army moved to destroy communist influence in Indonesia after an attempted communist coup in the following month. The army then stripped Sukarno himself of political power in March 1966, with General T.N.J. Suharto reaching an agreement with Malaysia on 11 August 1966, ending the Confrontation by accepting the *status quo*. Malaysia itself came into existence during the emergency in September 1963, although without the participation of Brunei, which did not become fully independent from Britain until 1984, while Singapore withdrew from the federation in August 1965.

Although lacking any real ideology or an adherence to any recognised theory of guerrilla warfare, Mau Mau had both a military and a passive wing, the latter being tasked with supporting the military wing in the field with money, supplies, recruits and intelligence. Supposedly, it was directed by the 'Kenya Parliament' and a central committee based in Nairobi, but its only real organisation was in Nairobi itself. The military wing was based largely in the Aberdare forests at the foot of Mount Kenya and may have numbered about 12,000 at its peak strength in 1952–53. However, it is clear that organisation was fairly rudimentary with little contact between individual groups or gangs, so that, for example, when the Mau Mau leader on Mount Kenya, Waruhiu Itote (known as 'General China'), was captured he knew nothing of the organisation in the Aberdares. Indeed, the lack of obvious leaders made it difficult for the authorities to dismantle the organisation without large-scale detention.

Nor were arms and ammunition abundant: possibly less than 12 per cent of the Mau Mau possessed firearms, and those they did possess were often home-made. Their actual methods, involving mutilation of both humans and animals by gangs armed with *pangas* or axes, were characterised by the authorities as atavistic savagery. Terrorism was directed primarily at Kikuyu in government service or who owned property or land. Indeed, most Mau Mau victims were other Africans. Typical incidents included the attack on the Naivasha police station on 26 March 1953, in which two police constables were killed, 173 suspects released and 47 weapons seized; and that on the settlement of Lari on the same day. In this, 97 people, mostly women and children, were killed, 29 wounded and a further 50 or so went missing, presumed dismembered. It has been suggested that the Lari attack was essentially the result of a long-standing local land feud rather than a Mau Mau attack *per se*, but, as David Percox has remarked, since it was still directly related to Kikuyu land grievances, 'the distinction is largely irrelevant'. Other tactics included arson and cattle rustling, virtually all such activity being at night.

By comparison, the attacks on northern Borneo during the Confrontation were much more traditional guerrilla tactics, the greatest difficulty for the security forces being the defence of 970 miles of open and often unmapped frontier of thick jungle. There were few tracks, let alone roads, while fast-flowing rivers running north to the sea were navigable by insurgent groups trying to infiltrate. Consequently, the insurgents invariably held the initiative in choosing where and when to strike from bases close to the international frontier, although their logistic and other support organisation was extremely primitive. Once Indonesian regulars became involved in September 1963, the rate of incursion rose dramatically, forcing the British to go over to the offensive to stop them. Indeed, concerned with a possible threat to Papua New Guinea, Australia also dispatched troops to northern Borneo in 1964, while Britain undertook planning to forestall any full-scale invasion by destroying the Indonesian navy and air force. As it happened, there was a landing by a combined force of Indonesian regulars and guerrillas on the Johore coast of Malaya in August 1964 and an airborne landing in September 1964 as well as other later attempted landings, but all were easily contained.

Initially, accurate intelligence on Mau Mau was limited given the low level at which it had originally operated immediately prior to the declaration of the state of emergency. The Kenya Police had little representation in the Kikuyu Reserve, while Special Branch had confined itself to matters in Nairobi. Special Branch moved to arrest identifiable political leaders such as Kenyatta immediately, but it was effectively blind to the growth of Mau Mau outside Nairobi, and the authorities were slow to recognise the scale of the insurgency. It was only in January 1953 that Major-General Robert Hinde was appointed chief staff officer to the Governor and not until June 1953 that Kenya was belatedly made an independent military command under the direction of General Sir George Erskine as both commander-in-chief and director of operations. Erskine did not enjoy the proconsular powers given Templer in Malaya, since the insurgency was much more geographically restricted, but he did have authorisation to take over the civil administration if he deemed it necessary.

As in Malaya, a committee structure was also instituted by Erskine, with a Colony Emergency Committee and province and district committees on which sat military, police and civil agency representatives. However, there were more problems in Kenya than in Malaya through the demands of settler groups to be represented on the committees, and in March 1954, the settlers got additional representation on a new War Council, although Erskine tended to ignore settler opinion generally. Further co-ordination was also acquired from March 1953 onwards through posting Special Branch personnel to provincial and district headquarters, and army officers were also seconded to Special Branch as field intelligence officers. Erskine took control of the police in May 1953, but his successor, Lieutenant-General Sir Gerald Lathbury, was able to relinquish it in May 1956.

From the beginning of the emergency, special regulations were introduced, with both the Aberdares and Mount Kenya being declared prohibited areas, in which anyone was liable to be shot on sight. Similarly, the Kikuyu Reserve was designated a special area, in which anyone failing to respond to a challenge could also be shot. The death penalty was steadily extended, with 1,086 executions carried out by April 1956, while 78,000 individuals were detained in prisons or special camps during the emergency, compared with a maximum of 1,200 detained in Malaya and only 500 in Palestine. Detainees were put through a programme of psychological purification, which included the administration of anti-Mau Mau oaths by government witch doctors and various moral education lessons. Re-education bore some similarity to de-Nazification in occupied Germany, and it is significant that several key individuals in the security apparatus had previously served there, including Hinde; the first director of information, Brigadier William Gibson; and the commissioner of police, M.S. O'Rorke.

However, Erskine was especially conscious of the grievances that had led to the emergency and instituted rural public works, agricultural development and resettlement or 'villagisation' schemes, which affected possibly a million Kikuyu, who were moved from Mount Kenya and the fringes of the Aberdares. Unlike the Chinese in Malaya, however, the Kikuyu preferred to live in more scattered groups, and this was resented, although it offered the authorities the same advantages in Malaya of establishing effective food control. There were other reforms. Frank Carpenter, for example, reported on conditions among urban blacks and set new minimum pay rates, while David Lidbury's report on the civil service led to greater opportunities for Africans. Richard Swynnerton's agrarian reform programme freed Africans from many of the restraints on growing cash crops, while assisting in the introduction of new breeds of cattle, co-operatives and tea plantations, although only £5 million – less than 10 per cent of emergency expenditure – was devoted to agricultural improvement.

As in Malaya, a Kikuyu Home Guard – eventually 25,000 strong – was also established in March 1953. As in Malaya, cinema was also regarded as a significant weapon in Kenya itself, while the government's case was also presented for British and other audiences in the Rank Organisation's feature film *Simba*, in 1955, which like the American film *Something of Value* in 1957, tended to suggest that most Mau Mau victims were white. The American film, indeed, was based on a novel by the *Life* correspondent Robert Ruark, who was convinced of Mau Mau's link to communism. There was some initial disagreement within the authorities in Kenya on the desirability of appointing a specialist in psychological warfare, and reluctance at least in public to titillate through emphasis on the salacious features of Mau Mau oathing while simultaneously exploiting images of the atavistic savagery of the insurgents. However, winning hearts and minds was not as successful as in Malaya, perhaps largely because neither independence nor significant political concessions were on offer. Indeed, development had been undertaken in order to avoid a prolonged conflict rather than because there was any particular conviction that the lot of the Africans should be improved. It would appear that the majority of Kikuyu simply gave up the fight once it became clear that the authorities would prevail rather than changing their attitudes towards the government, or abandoning sympathy for Mau Mau's political aims altogether.

In terms of purely military response, five British battalions and six battalions of the King's African Rifles were eventually deployed alongside a much expanded police force. Erskine's first priority was to neutralise the insurgent organisation in Nairobi. Operation Anvil in April 1954, which was modelled on cordon and search operations in Palestine, threw 25,000 troops and police in a cordon around the city, which progressively screened the population and resulted in the detention of over 16,000 suspects. Having worked outwards from the city, Erskine then mounted operations in early 1955 to force the insurgents back into the forests, often by large-scale sweeping operations such as Hammer and First Flute. Troops were moved along specially bulldozed tracks or 'rides' with cleared fire zones created and deep ditches dug to prevent insurgents breaking out. The efforts were coupled with amnesty offers (Operation Chui), which brought about 1,000 surrenders in 1955. However, bombing of the forests by the RAF did not prove successful, and Erskine suspended these operations. The ambush techniques used in Malaya were also not as successful since Mau Mau had few firearms and would flee rather than press an attack as the Malayan communists had done when making contact with a patrol. Operation Hammer, for example, deployed nine battalions yet resulted in only 161 dead Mau Mau, the overall cost of producing one dead Mau Mau in that year being an estimated £10,000. Subsequently, Lathbury emphasised small-unit operations within an area framework, deployment similar to that used in Malaya.

Ironically, however, the old-style sweeps and especially Anvil had actually broken the back of the insurgency, and it was only then that more modern counter-insurgency techniques began to work, with operations concentrated on the use of army tracker combat teams and Special Branch pseudo forces known as counter gangs. This kind of technique had been used briefly by the police counter-terror squads in Palestine and with SEPs in Malaya, but it became much more sophisticated in Kenya under the guidance of Ian Henderson of Special Branch, Eric Holyoak and a seconded field intelligence officer, Frank Kitson. In fact, it was a pseudo operation that resulted in the capture of Kimathi.

In the case of the Confrontation, the director of operations was Major-General Walter Walker, who had experience with Ferret Force in Malaya and had written ATOM. Walker could not prevent infiltration. However, he sought to hit those infiltrated groups that could be detected as hard as possible through concentrating units at strategic points in defended bases and relying heavily for mobility upon 70 helicopters, which had not been available in Malaya in any numbers. In addition, drawing on his Malayan experience, Walker issued a five-point directive requiring unity of operations achieved through a joint headquarters for all the armed forces involved; timely and accurate information; speed, mobility and flexibility; security of bases; and domination of the jungle. Walker sat on the State Emergency Executive Committees established for Sarawak and Sabah as well as on the Sultan of Brunei's Advisory Council. He was also a member of the Malaysian National Defence Council and had complete authority in the theatre of actual operations.

Walker also wished to win hearts and minds. Already many of the indigenous tribes were well-disposed towards the British, and soldiers and police were sent into villages and settlements to protect and advise. Medical and agricultural help was offered, and some troops, notably SAS teams, lived and worked alongside villagers. Walker, indeed, maintained that 70 SAS men were as valuable as 700 ordinary infantrymen in winning hearts and minds, undertaking surveillance of the border and providing an early warning system. Assistance given the Iban during a cholera outbreak in 1964 was much welcomed, and other activities included children's parties aboard the aircraft carrier *HMS Hermes*.

In addition, Malaysia was able to present such a good international case regarding Indonesian aggression that Sukarno withdrew from the UN in January 1965. It made it increasingly difficult for the insurgents to secure food, shelter or intelligence, while the flow of intelligence to the security forces was steadily improved. A permanent presence was established in contested areas with patrols replenished by helicopters or light aircraft in such a way that the jungle was dominated. Helicopters could also airlift howitzers to pre-cut firing positions close to likely escape routes to cut off fleeing insurgents. While the Indonesians were not finding much support among the population, however, it was not possible to do more unless authority was given to cross the international frontier.

When this was granted as a result of Malaysian pressure on the British government in March 1964, such counter raids or 'Claret' operations into Indonesian territory from August 1964 had to be personally authorised by Walker, although there is some evidence that SAS and Gurkhas were operating inside Indonesia from May or June 1964 onwards. They were also restricted under the so-called 'Golden Rules' to no more than 5,000 yards, although this was later raised to 10,000 yards and very occasionally to 20,000 yards. No air support was possible, and each operation had to be self-contained, since such operations were to be entirely covert, a necessity also requiring the evacuation of all personnel alive or dead. Often the raids were led by Iban trackers of the 1,500-strong Border Scouts, such as those earlier used by the British in Malaya, assisted by personnel from the SAS. Such methods, which were continued and expanded by Walker's successor in March 1965, Major-General George Lea, pushed the Indonesians back from the border and convinced the Indonesian army that confrontation could not succeed. Since the illusion that there had been no war had been maintained by both sides, it was easier for the Indonesians to withdraw without losing too much face.

As the British Defence Secretary, Denis Healey, wrote, the campaign was 'a textbook demonstration of how to apply economy of force, under political guidance for political ends'. In this respect, the lack of media coverage of the Confrontation was invaluable, and generally it was a low-key war, in which the British and their Commonwealth allies suffered only 59 dead, compared with about 2,000 Indonesian dead. The security force casualties in Kenya were also relatively light, with about 600 dead, 63 of whom were white. Another 32 white civilians were killed and perhaps 2,000 Africans loyal to the government. However, at least 11,500 Mau Mau were killed in action and, besides those executed, 402 prisoners died in captivity – largely from disease. It has been argued that the suppression of Mau Mau hardly represented the use of minimum force, which invariably characterised other British counter-insurgency campaigns, and this aspect of the security forces' response drew increasingly unfavourable publicity in Britain and elsewhere. In particular, conditions at the Hola detention camp in March 1959, where there was an attempted cover-up of eleven deaths, caused a major political scandal in Britain and the establishment of the Fairn committee to enquire into conditions at all camps. The majority of the problems arose, however, not from the action of the army but from that of the expanded police or the Kikuyu Home Guard, the latter actually being responsible for 42 per cent of all casualties inflicted on Mau Mau and clearly guilty of many excesses in the process.

In the case of the police, 700 men were recruited on short-term contracts from England, and the 4,800-strong Kenya Police Reserve (KPR), drawn from white settlers, was fully mobilised. The former were not always scrupulous about how they achieved results, while the latter in particular declined to give up a paramilitary role and even formed their own unofficial groups like Dobie Force to hunt down Mau Mau. Arthur Young, who had reformed the police in Malaya, was sent out to Kenya in 1954. He again recommended the adoption of more traditional approaches towards use of weapons, treatment of suspects and prosecution of members of the security forces for excess. In addition, he called for the police to be freed from the direct control of the district administration. Young, however, failed to break the prejudice and, as commissioner of police, was not included on the War Council as he had been in the case of the top operational committee in Malaya. Consequently, he resigned after a series of disputes with the Governor in December 1954. The Deputy Governor had complained that Young's objectives 'were as unrealisable as trying to turn the Royal Irish Constabulary into the Winchester Police in the middle of the Irish rebellion'.

Branded 'undisciplined sadists' by one Swahili-language newspaper, the KPR was clearly guilty of many excesses, although it has to be noted that the rigorous investigations undertaken into complaints were manipulated by Mau Mau to place good policemen under suspicion. Problems also arose from the expansion of the African members of the police and especially the recruitment of 14,000 prison guards. By February 1954, a total of 130 cases of police brutality had been prosecuted, 73 of which had resulted in conviction, and there were an additional 40 cases still pending. After the arrival of Richard Catling from Malaya, however, first as deputy commissioner of police in April 1954 and then as commissioner from December 1954 onwards, police training improved dramatically.

In terms of lessons learned, the British army's *Handbook on Anti-Mau Mau Operations*, issued in 1954, was based on ATOM and, in many respects, Kenya only added to the sum of knowledge in terms of the additional experience gained by individuals in counter-insurgency. Intelligence operatives in Kenya such as A.M. Macdonald, Trevor Jenkins and John Prendergast passed on to other campaigns, Prendergast serving subsequently in both Cyprus and Aden, while Ian Henderson was to advise Ian Smith in Rhodesia. Kenya became a regional training centre for Special Branch throughout East Africa, while soldiers like Kitson also went on to other campaigns in Cyprus and Northern Ireland, and there was much cross-posting of battalions. The Kenyan campaign, though, was not glamorous and the opponent hardly rated, with the result that the campaign's impact was not as great as that of Malaya. Moreover, colonial administrators did not tend to transfer, and the attempt made by the Colonial Office to appraise the lessons of this and other campaigns in 1955 bore little fruit. In many respects, Borneo, where thirteen battalions and 20,000 men had been deployed by 1965, was more significant in displaying the steady refinement of British techniques in rural environments. Certainly, there were not the same delays in implementing those elements of co-ordination required for success as there had been in Kenya.

In terms of the six requirements for successful counter-insurgency apparent from the Malayan experience, all were eventually put in place in both campaigns with recognition of the need for a political response, co-ordination of effort, co-ordination of intelligence, and a strategy for winning hearts and minds implemented in both Kenya and Borneo, although, as indicated above, winning hearts and minds was not necessarily effective in Kenya. Military force was certainly used appropriately in Borneo but, again, it might be argued that it was used excessively in Kenya. Long-term reform was not appropriate to the Borneo situation, but it was effected in Kenya with the White Highlands being opened to Africans in 1960, segregated schools being discontinued and progress to independence accelerated by a Conservative government for which Mau Mau had rung alarm bells.

It might also be said that the Kenyan experience impacted upon southern Africa generally. It precipitated the break-up of the Central African Federation of Northern and Southern Rhodesia and Nyasaland and encouraged South Africa's road to apartheid as the remaining white colonial states faced the increasing twin ideological challenge of nationalism and communism. Northern Rhodesia and Nyasaland were to proceed to independence as Zambia and Malawi, respectively, but Southern Rhodesia was to defy Harold Wilson's Labour government by announcing its own unilateral declaration of independence (UDI) on 11 November 1965, ushering in a conflict with the nationalists that escalated into a large-scale guerrilla war between 1972 and 1979. South Africa, too, faced insurgency in South West Africa (Namibia) between 1966 and 1984, while the Portuguese fought a long war to hold on to their African colonies of Angola, Guinea and Mozambique from 1961 to 1974.

Portugal was the first European colonial power to arrive in Africa, and, with its Iberian neighbour, the last to withdraw. Portuguese navigators reached each of the three principal colonies of Portuguese Guinea, Angola and Mozambique by the end of the fifteenth century, although control was only asserted gradually over the interior, with pacification continuing in Guinea as late as the 1930s. The durability of the Portuguese presence in Africa can be attributed in some measure to Portugal's neutrality during the Second World War, which enabled it to avoid the defeats in Europe and the Far East that undermined the resolve of other powers to retain their colonies. It can also be explained by a genuine belief in a 'civilising mission', the economic benefits derived from the colonies and a realisation that the continued possession of empire alone conferred international status on an otherwise underdeveloped and impoverished state. Indeed, as the Portuguese prime minister Marcello Caetano once expressed it: 'Without it [Africa] we would be a small nation; with it, we are a great country'.

The Portuguese always claimed that their version of imperialism was unique, since it was not based upon racial discrimination and aimed at total assimilation of the African. From 1951 onwards, the colonies were regarded as overseas provinces of Portugal itself. In reality, Portuguese policy was economically and socially exploitative, with slavery replaced in 1878 by an equally restrictive low-wage contract labour system and compulsory cultivation of cash crops. Moreover, assimilation fell far short of realisation. The 1933 constitution had divided the colonial population into *indigenas* (natives) and *nôa indigenas*, the latter being regarded as Portuguese and including whites, *mestizos* (mulattos) and assimilated Africans or *assimilados*. However, barely 1 per cent of the native population of the colonies had achieved *assimilado* status by 1961, which would entitle them to vote, travel without permission or pass cards and be exempt from contract labour. Initially, nationalist groups, invariably dominated by *mestizos* or *assimilados*, were content to pursue political objectives, but there was growing militancy by the end of the 1950s bred of disenchantment but also encouraged by the collapse of Belgian authority in the Congo in 1960.

The catalyst came in Angola, where cotton crops and property came under attack in 1961. This coincided with the hijack of a Portuguese liner to Luanda by an opponent of Portugal's dictator António Salazar, which brought the world's press to the colony. On 4 February 1961, Luanda prison and two police barracks were attacked, conceivably for the benefit of the assembled press. A widespread revolt then erupted in the northern cotton plantations on 15 March 1961, taking the Portuguese by surprise. Some 600 whites were killed with extreme brutality on the first day alone. Concessions were made by abolishing compulsory cash crop cultivation and replacing assimilation with a declaration that all Africans were now equal with Europeans as Portuguese citizens, but insurgency spread to Portuguese Guinea in January 1963 and to Mozambique on 25 September 1964. It continued until a military coup in Portugal itself on 25 April 1974 resulted in the installation of a radical military government determined to quit Africa. Portuguese Guinea was given independence as Guinea Bissau in September 1974, Mozambique in June 1975 and Angola in November 1975.

By contrast to the Portuguese colonies, Southern Rhodesia had originated as the creation of the British South Africa Company of Cecil Rhodes, which annexed Mashonaland and Matabeleland in 1890 and 1893, respectively, and continued to run the administration until 1923. More prosperous than either Northern Rhodesia or Nyasaland, Southern Rhodesia dominated the short-lived Central African Federation between 1953 and 1963. As the other two proceeded to independence, however, the larger white settler population in Southern Rhodesia rejected the concept of majority rule amid the spectre of the chaos in the Belgian Congo and the evolution of a nationalist movement increasingly moving towards violence as a means of achieving its political aims. Ian Smith's Rhodesian Front Party swept to electoral victory in December 1962, the advent of Harold Wilson's Labour government in Britain in 1964 dedicated to majority rule catapulting all sides closer to confrontation. Ian Smith declared UDI on 11 November 1965 and, in March 1970, declared Rhodesia a republic. There were talks between Wilson and Smith in both December 1966 and September 1968, while the new Conservative government sent the abortive Pearce Commission to Rhodesia in 1972 to test the acceptability of new constitutional proposals. All, however, failed to bring about a settlement.

Following the collapse of the Portuguese position in Mozambique, Rhodesia became more exposed to infiltration and also suffered from increasing pressure from the South African government to reach an accommodation with the nationalists. Talks between 1975 and 1977 resulted in Smith's concession of the principle of majority rule, but no overall settlement. Subsequently, therefore, Smith reached an internal agreement with some of the nationalist groups in March 1978, leading to the emergence of a black government after elections in April 1979, and of what was known as Zimbabwe-Rhodesia in June 1979. Ultimately, following further international pressure, the Lancaster House Conference in London brought a British-supervised cease-fire in December 1979, with new elections in February 1980 won by the nationalists and legal independence for Zimbabwe in April 1980.

The ability of Ian Smith to reach an internal agreement indicated the fragmentation of the nationalist movement. Joshua Nkomo's African National Congress (ANC) emerged in 1957, eventually becoming after a number of changes in nomenclature, the Zimbabwe African People's Union (ZAPU) in 1962. As early as 1963, however, the Reverend Ndabaningi Sithole split with Nkomo and founded ZANU, previously mentioned in an earlier chapter. Essentially, it was a split along tribal lines, ZAPU appealing largely to the minority Ndebele of western Rhodesia and ZANU to the majority Shona of eastern Rhodesia. As previously indicated, ZANU also differed from ZAPU in favouring Maoist principles of guerrilla warfare, although it was also assisted by East German military advisers. With largely Soviet advisers, Nkomo preferred to mass most of his guerrillas outside Rhodesia for some large-scale conventional assault at an appropriate moment. James Chickerema also split from Nkomo in 1972 to found the Front for the Liberation of Zimbabwe (Frolizi), while Sithole found himself increasingly outmanoeuvred by more radical elements within ZANU such as Mugabe, who became its effective leader in 1974. Chickerema's defection forced Nkomo to forge a short-lived joint military command with ZANU, and subsequently, the so-called Patriotic Front (PF) with Mugabe in 1976. Sithole then entered Smith's transitional government in March 1978, together with Chief Jeremiah Chirau and Bishop Abel Muzorewa, who had emerged as a nationalist of some authority at the time of the Pearce Commission. Leader of the United African National Congress (UANC) party, Muzorewa became the first black prime minister of Rhodesia as a result of the internal settlement.

An equally complex situation existed in each of the Portuguese colonies through the existence of rival nationalist groups, such divisions resting again primarily on tribalism. In Portuguese Guinea, for example, the main group, already mentioned in a previous chapter, was PAIGC. Founded in 1956, it was dominated by Cape Verdean *mestizos* such as the Portuguese-trained agronomist Amilcar Cabral but was drawn mainly from urban *assimilados* and the Balante tribe, comprising only 29 per cent of the population. The Muslim Fula and Mandinka people, representing 22 per cent of the population, remained loyal to the Portuguese, while a rival nationalist group known as Frente para a Libertação e Independência de Guine (Front for the Liberation and Independence of Guinea, FLING), with a particular hatred of Cape Verdeans, also existed briefly. In Mozambique, Frente de Libertação de Mocambique (Front for the Liberation of Mozambique, Frelimo), emerged from the merger of three earlier groups in 1962. Led initially by the *assimilado* Dr Eduardo Mondlane, and subsequently by another *assimilado*, Samora Machel, Frelimo was predominantly Makonde, a tribe representing less than 3 per cent of the population, with opposition to the Portuguese also prevalent among the Ajaua and Nianja. Again the Muslim Macua, accounting for 40 per cent of the population, supported the Portuguese, while there was also a dissident nationalist group known as Comité Revolucionaire de Mocambique (Revolutionary Committee of Mozambique, Coremo), which emerged in 1965.

The most complicated division, however, was in Angola. Movimento Popular de Libertação de Angola (Popular Movement for the Liberation of Angola, MPLA), which had been formed in 1956, was led by the *mestizo* Viriato da Cruz and subsequently by the *assimilado* Dr Angostinho Neto. It drew its rank and file mostly from the Mbundu tribe. There were differences within the MPLA and, indeed, its eastern commander, Daniel Chipenda, was ousted by Neto in the early 1970s, and several of Chipenda's followers were murdered. What eventually became known, also in 1962, as Frente Nacional de Libertação de Angola (Angolan National Liberation Front, FNLA), was drawn from the Bakongo tribe of northern Angola and led by the nephew of one of the tribe's traditional king-makers, Holden Roberto. Indeed, it was the FNLA's forerunner, União das Populações de Angola (Union of Angolan Peoples, UPA), originally founded in the mid-1950s, which launched the revolt in 1961. FNLA also drew some support from the Ovimbundu of the south and the Chokwe of the east, but these latter groups became adherents of the breakaway movement UNITA, also mentioned in an earlier chapter, which was founded in 1966 by Roberto's former 'foreign minister', Jonas Savimbi. There were also ideological differences with MPLA, PAIGC and Frelimo receiving assistance from the Soviet bloc, while the Chinese supported FNLA and, especially, UNITA. Indeed, the latter were known as the 'Black Chinese' for their Maoist methods, although, as it happened, both Cabral of PAIGC and Machel of Frelimo also espoused Maoist theories of guerrilla warfare.

It is difficult to ascertain the exact numbers of guerrillas involved in the war against the Portuguese. Roberto claimed 10,000 men fighting on three 'fronts' in 1971/72. While FNLA may have had 6,200 men, it is unlikely that more than 1,000 were actually inside Angola at any one time, and two of the three 'fronts' were largely illusory. In fact, operating out of Zaire, FNLA was only sporadically active after 1970. Similarly, while MPLA had about 4,700 men by 1974, there were probably no more than 1,500 inside Angola. MPLA was increasingly able to operate only from the Congo Republic and Zambia, while the Portuguese estimated that UNITA had no more than 500 activists. Frelimo may have had perhaps 8,000 men by 1971 but found it difficult to penetrate from Tanzania much beyond the frontier provinces, its infiltration from Zambia into the Tete region after 1968 also failing seriously to interrupt work on the important Cabora Bassa dam project. The most effective of the insurgents was PAIGC, operating out of Senegal and the Congo Republic and numbering perhaps 6,000 or 7,000 men by 1973.

The campaigns were entirely rural in character, often conducted in difficult terrain such as the 1,300-mile frontier of mountain, swamp, jungle and elephant grass separating Angola from FNLA's bases in Zaire. MPLA operations in the Moxico region, which they reached from Zambia, ranged over a plateau of savannah and forest. By contrast, Guinea was 40 per cent water, with tidal inlets, rivers and extensive swamps denying both sides easy movement. The terrain and tropical and subtropical climate did not necessarily confer advantages on either side, while demographic factors were of considerable importance. Thus, while Frelimo benefited from the fact that the Makonde lived on both sides of the Mozambique/Tanzania frontier, it was unable to penetrate further south through the concentration of the hostile Macua across northern and central Mozambique. Similarly, FNLA's effectiveness was diminished by the movement of large numbers of Bakongo into Zaire, which reduced the degree of assistance forthcoming inside Angola. MPLA was unable to operate from Zaire due to the influence of Roberto, who was the brother-in-law of Zaire's president, Mobutu Sese Seko, and was compelled to attempt long-distance infiltration from Zambia and operations in the virtually uninhabited regions of eastern Angola. Nonetheless, international frontiers provided readily accessible havens, only UNITA being denied such an external refuge after being expelled from Zambia at an early stage following attacks on the Benquela railway judged vital to Zambia's export trade.

All the insurgent groups attempted to establish 'liberated areas', the most successful being PAIGC, which undoubtedly dominated much of the interior until a more vigorous Portuguese commander, Antonio de Spinola, arrived in May 1968. In Angola, MPLA attempted to set up woodland *kimbos* (protected villages) of their own. However, these not only proved too vulnerable to air attack, but MPLA operations were generally too far from population centres to be really effective. FNLA was especially inept at the political role, preferring outright military operations, this being one reason for Savimbi's break with Roberto in 1966. The variety of military action can perhaps be illustrated by PAIGC's claim in 1967 to have undertaken that year 142 attacks on camps and barracks, 22 raids on airfields and ports and 476 ambushes in which, supposedly, they captured 26 mortars, 86 sub-machine guns and 397 rifles while killing 1,905 Portuguese for the loss of only 86 insurgents. Claim and counter-claim are particularly difficult to reconcile, but the PAIGC figures do indicate a typical pattern of ambush of road traffic and of bombardment of targets at the maximum possible range. Frelimo's attacks on the Cabora Bassa dam, for example, were mostly by 122 mm rockets fired at a maximum 17 kilometres. In Angola, the war has been characterised as 'mines versus helicopters' with often minimum contact. Overall, most insurgent activities were undertaken by small groups in short-range incursions across international frontiers with a minimum presence permanently inside Portuguese territory. There was growing sophistication of weaponry, such as the introduction of SAM-7 Strella ground to air missiles by PAIGC, which claimed to have shot down 21 Portuguese aircraft in 1973, but vital economic concerns such as Gulf Oil's installations in Angola's Cabinda Enclave, the same colony's Cassinga iron ore mines and Mozambique's Cabora Bassa dam remained secure.

Just as in the case of the Portuguese colonies, ZANU and ZAPU operations were constrained by geography and the location of their natural constituencies in terms of tribal following. Thus, ZAPU and its military wing, the Zimbabwe People's Revolutionary Army (ZIPRA), operated out of Zambia and Botswana. Originally forced to try to infiltrate into eastern Rhodesia from Zambia, ZANU and its military wing, the Zimbabwe National Liberation Army (ZANLA), were able to operate from Mozambique once the Portuguese had withdrawn. In fact, the initial attempts of the guerrillas to cross into Rhodesia through the Zambezi valley, which began in April 1966, were comfortably contained to the extent that the Rhodesian army was rarely used and operations remained in the hands of Rhodesia's British South Africa Police (BSAP). The local Africans were not sympathetic to the guerrillas, and the valley was inhospitable terrain. Indeed, the war did not escalate until ZANU opened a new front in the north-east in December 1972 by infiltrating through that part of Mozambique which the Portuguese were increasingly failing to control. Ultimately, the Rhodesians' own calculations suggested that the number of guerrillas able to operate inside Rhodesia grew from 400 or so in July 1974 to 700 by March 1976, 2,350 by April 1977, 5,598 by November 1977, 6,456 by March 1978, 11,183 by January 1979 and possibly 12,500 by the end of 1979, the majority from ZANLA. At that time, an estimated 22,000 ZIPRA and 16,000 ZANLA guerrillas remained uncommitted outside the country.

Turning to the response of the security forces, when revolt broke out in Angola in 1961, the Portuguese army had not fought in a major conflict since the First World War, and within months it had suffered a humiliating defeat at the hands of the Indian army when the small Goa garrison was overwhelmed in a few hours in December 1961. However, while caught by surprise in Angola, there was little difficulty suppressing the original uprising since the rebels were poorly armed. Early use was made of air power in a ferocious response said to have cost the lives of 50,000 Africans between August and September 1961. In preparing for the real war to come, the Portuguese could also draw on recent experience of other European armies, not least the British. The 1957 version of the British manual *Keeping the Peace (Duties in Support of the Civil Power)*, last updated in 1949 and incorporating some of the lessons of Malaya, was translated into Portuguese in 1959, and the Portuguese also sent observers to Algeria that same year.

It was once claimed that Portuguese soldiers had also been trained in counter-insurgency in the United States, but, in reality, American doctrine made little contribution to Portuguese theories compared with the influence of British and French techniques in the study *Apontamentos para o Emprego das Forças Militares em Guerra Subversiva* (Notes on the Employment of Military Forces in Subversive War), prepared under the direction of Colonel Artur Nunes da Silva and published in 1960. Subsequently, Nunes da Silva was also responsible for the official five-volume manual, *O Exército na Guerra Subversiva* (The Army in Subversive War) in 1963. Drawing on Malaya and Kenya, the Portuguese doctrine emphasised traditional British concepts such as minimum force, civil–military co-operation, co-ordination of intelligence, separation of insurgent from civilian, and small-unit operations. From French *guerre révolutionnaire*, the Portuguese absorbed the need for psychological warfare, which translated into a co-ordinated civic action programme based on education, sanitation, agricultural and cattle husbandry development, improvements to local infrastructure and communications, and self-defence villages.

Nonetheless, initial reaction to insurgency was hesitant largely due to a lack of military resources, and it must be noted that the Portuguese were attempting to sustain three separate but simultaneous campaigns at a considerable distance from each other and from Portugal itself. Moreover, both Angola and Mozambique were vast territories, respectively fourteen and nine times the size of metropolitan Portugal. Thus, until troop levels could be built up, the Portuguese withdrew into defended outposts and relied upon air attack to contain the guerrillas. What were termed 'Westmoreland-like' sweeps in Portuguese Guinea, named after the American commander in South Vietnam, had little impact and, as indicated earlier, the initiative was effectively surrendered to PAIGC. The situation was much the same in Angola and even in Mozambique, despite the fact that the Portuguese had had longer to prepare.

Troop strength was steadily built up, rising in Guinea from 4,736 men in 1961 to 32,000 by 1974; from 18,852 in Mozambique in 1964 to 51,463 by 1974; and in Angola from 33,477 men in 1961 to 65,592 by 1974. Eventually, therefore, the Portuguese had 149,090 men deployed in Africa by 1974, which, in proportion to the Portuguese population, represented a troop level five times greater than the American presence in South Vietnam. However, an increasing proportion of these troops were actually black Africans, amounting to perhaps 40 per cent by 1971. Indeed, the number of Africans prepared to fight for Portugal far exceeded those fighting them as guerrillas. There were also black and white settler militias, including the Katangan *Fiéis* (Faithful), while rifles were freely distributed to the Fula in Guinea. In Angola, there were also *flechas* (arrows), originally raised from the Bushmen of the east, who continued to use bows and arrows with poisoned tips as well as light weapons in their reconnaissance role.

Such an increase in troops enabled the Portuguese to undertake a much more active role after 1968. First, they tended to be better at establishing effective command co-ordination once a stroke had removed Salazar from influence in 1968, although the intelligence system tended to remain dependent upon civilian agencies such as the *Polícia Internacional de Defesa do Estado* (International Police for the Defence of the State, PIDE), which controlled the *flechas* and did not always enjoy a good relationship with the army. Generally, the adoption of a French-style *quadrillage* structure at local level in the form of *zona de acção* (zones of operation) also assisted in the development of a British-style framework deployment of units.

The second feature of the enhanced counter-insurgency effort was the concentration of population in defended villages variously known as *senzalas do paz* or *dendandas* in Angola and as *aldeamentos* in Mozambique. The process began in Angola in 1961, being extended to Guinea in 1964, where eventually 150,000 people were resettled under the *reordenamento* (reordering) programme, the emphasis being on the Balante tribal areas. In Angola, too, many of the early villages were rarely given adequate facilities or even sufficient rifles to enable the inhabitants to form a self-defence militia. In any case, population was distributed irregularly amid varying degrees of economic subsistence. Subsequently, there was some discussion in Angola on the merits of extending resettlement even in areas unaffected by the war, which suggested that some Portuguese regarded resettlement as a means of control rather than as a basis for winning hearts and minds. In all, perhaps a million Angolans, or approximately 20 per cent of the native population, were resettled in about 3,000 villages. This included the semi-nomadic Herero and Ovambo peoples of southern Angola, who were not suited to resettlement.

When Spinola arrived in Guinea in 1968, he initiated a fully co-ordinated hearts and minds strategy under the slogan *Um Guiné Melhor* (A Better Guinea) based on the villages and using the army to build 15,000 houses, 164 schools, 40 hospitals, 163 fire stations and 86 water points. In addition, he established *cadmils* (co-operatives) and waged campaigns against disease in both humans and animals. Another significant project was to build new irrigation dams. Although his counterpart in Mozambique, Kaulza de Arriaga, is usually credited with favouring military rather than political solutions, here, too, there was an energetic programme of civic action with new farms, medical centres, cattle dips and a road-building programme greater than that of the United States in South Vietnam, the significance of this being that tarred roads made it less easy for the insurgents to use mines. Just under a million people, representing 15 per cent of the native population, were reset-tled in 953 villages, and Arriaga planned a 'human border' of settlements linked by all-weather roads that widened every few kilometres into airstrips.

In Angola, 70 per cent of the Portuguese forces were devoted to psycho-social or social promotion programmes. Educational opportunities were certainly enhanced in all three colonies, and the standard of health care made available certainly increased the flow of information to the Portuguese in Angola and Mozambique. There was also an extensive propaganda campaign in both Angola and Mozambique, with pseudo forces variously known as Grupos Especiais (Special Groups, GE), and Grupos Especiais Pára-quedistas (Special Group Parachutists, GEP), raised partly from insurgents who had been captured or who had deserted. The overall problem for the Portuguese, however, was that they lacked sufficient resources for a comprehensive winning hearts and minds programme. Thus, while the lot of the African probably did improve, this did not match the extent to which matters improved for white settlers and, since independence was not on offer, the Portuguese could not satisfy wider aspirations.

The third feature of the enhanced strategy was the more effective employ-ment of the military forces available. Air power was now used to seal off infiltration and supply routes across the frontiers and as an immediate reaction force after insurgent attacks. Napalm was used from an early stage and, from 1970, herbicides and defoliants. The mainstay of the air operations were trainers converted to an anti-guerrilla role such as the British Auster, the American Harvard T-6 and the German Dornier DO-27, but with support from the Fiat G-91 fighter-bomber. Even more important, however, was the use of the helicopter from 1966 onwards, largely French Alouette IIIs, as *heli-canhões* (helicopter gunships) and also to land elite units of *força de intervenção* (forces of intervention) such as commandos, paratroops and marines behind identified guerrilla concentrations and across supply routes. These forces were not always available in sufficient numbers, and helicopters were expensive to operate and maintain, but, at its best, the co-ordination of light bombers, heli-copters and reinforced ground patrols saw particularly successful dry season operations in eastern Angola, to which Francisco da Costa Gomes devoted special attention after his appointment to the Angolan command in May 1970.

In Mozambique, Arriaga's Operation Nó Gordio (Gordian Knot), spread over seven months in 1970 and using similar techniques. deployed 10,000 troops and netted 651 insurgent dead and 1,840 captured despite the lack of surprise resulting from the build-up for what was more a large-scale sweep than proper counter-insurgency. However, modern technology was not always the remedy, and cavalry was used extensively in central and eastern Angola, where the terrain was too difficult for vehicles. Similarly, empty beer bottles slung on wires around Portuguese posts were just as successful as an early warning device as sophisticated sensors, which the Portuguese did not possess.

Moreover, small-unit operations also became increasingly substituted for the large-scale sweeps of the past, with 30-man four- to five-day patrols the norm in both Guinea and Angola. Indeed, in Guinea, Spinola consciously modelled his own combat groups on the *bi-grupo* (bi-groups) of PAIGC.

Hot pursuit was threatened by the Portuguese on occasions but was not part of their strategy, although there were occasional accusations by neighbouring states that Portuguese forces had violated the frontiers. However, the Portuguese were clearly reluctant to incur additional international criticism, although they were implicated in the abortive landing of armed exiles in the Republic of Guinea, from which PAIGC drew support, in November 1970. Operation Mar Verde (Green Sea) was originally intended to destroy PAIGC and Guinean naval and air assets, and to release some Portuguese captives, but it became inflated into an attempted coup. In the event, while a tactical success, the Guinean president, Sékou Touré, escaped capture, and the raid encouraged the Soviet Union to increase arms supplies to PAIGC. The Portuguese may also have been implicated in the assassinations of both Mondlane in February 1969 and Cabral in January 1973. Mondlane died by a parcel bomb, but Cabral by the hand of his naval commander, Inocêncio Kani, again indicating the internal divisions within PAIGC. Some leverage could also be obtained from the dependence of both Zambia and Malawi on the Portuguese rail system.

The initial ease with which the Rhodesians had dealt with infiltration into the Zambezi valley in 1966–67, had resulted in any military intervention in support of the BSAP being handled through temporary brigade areas and a Joint Operations Centre (JOC) involving military, police and civil representatives. The system was simply extended in 1972, with the new 'front' in the north-east being met by the creation of a permanent JOC known as Operation Hurricane, with six other operational areas – Thrasher, Repulse, Tangent, Grapple, Salops and Splinter following in due course between 1976 and 1978. A War Council was established in September 1976 and a Combined Operations Headquarters (COMOPS) in March 1977. In theory, COMOPS should have led to the development of a well-co-ordinated strategy. In reality, the command system failed at a number of levels as a result of friction between army and BSAP, as the police were displaced in positions of responsibility on the JOCs by the military. Moreover, COMOPS lacked effective control over civil affairs and had above it both the National Joint Operations Command (NATJOC) and the War Council, chaired by Smith. COMOPS also became so entangled in the day-to-day conduct of the war that it neglected long-term planning. Its commander, Lieutenant-General Peter Walls, who had served with the Rhodesian Squadron of the SAS in Malaya, assumed direct control of all offensive and special forces, relegating the army commander, Lieutenant-General John Hickman, another veteran of Malaya, to control over only black troops and white territorials. There was tension between Walls and Hickman, and between COMOPS and NATJOC.

Rivalry between police and army was also apparent in the attempted co-ordination of intelligence. Prior to 1972, it was firmly the responsibility of Special Branch, but the escalation of conflict persuaded the army to establish its own Military Intelligence Department in 1973 and an Intelligence Corps two years later. However, army agencies were treated with suspicion by the BSAP, just as rivalry also emerged between Special Branch and the intelligence-gathering unit formed by another Malaya veteran, Ron Reid-Daly, in November 1973 and known as the Selous Scouts after the celebrated white hunter, Frederick Selous, who had guided the original pioneer column into Southern Rhodesia in 1890. Primarily intended as a pseudo force, the Selous Scouts increasingly became effective in the hunter-killer role. However, there was tension between the Scouts and the army, resulting in Reid-Daly being court-martialled in January 1979 after he had confronted Hickman with evidence of having his telephone bugged as a result of allegations that the Scouts were involved in ivory poaching. Certainly, there were occasions when the Scouts attacked protected villages in order to preserve their bona fides while trying to sow distrust among the guerrillas. Their generally unkempt appearance had also led to them being nicknamed 'armpits with eyeballs', while some military and police officers doubted the merit of releasing into the Scouts captured guerrillas, who would otherwise have faced the full force of the law. Hickman himself was also dismissed in March 1979, possibly as a result of his uneasy relationship with Walls.

Lack of co-ordination was serious given the lack of Rhodesian manpower, since a prevailing assumption was that it was mainly whites who should serve. Another problem in this regard was the spectre of white emigration – the 'chicken run' – outpacing new immigration. There were no more than 4,600 regulars in 1968, with a front-line BSAP strength of 6,400. As the war progressed, however, so the national service net was widened for whites, Asians and coloureds. The initial term of service was increased to 12 months in 1972, with the upper age of eligibility increasing from 25 in 1972 to 50 in 1977 and to 59 in January 1979. Perhaps 2,000 foreigners also served in the Rhodesian forces, and there were 3,000 South African military and police in support between 1967 and 1975. In practice, however, the needs of the economy precluded full mobilisation, and it was rare for the Rhodesians to have more than 25,000 men in the field: the greatest effort was the 60,000 men briefly deployed for the internal elections in April 1979.

In fact, the majority of the security forces had always been black volun-teers, and the Rhodesian African Rifles (RAR) was expanded from one to four battalions. The BSAP also increasingly depended upon black recruits. Moreover, after the internal settlement in 1978, pressure arose for black conscription, which commenced in January 1979. There is little evidence of any widespread disciplinary difficulties among black regulars or police, but conscription was resented and it was never fully implemented.

Consideration was also given to arming loyal Africans, and a pilot scheme was launched in the Msana Tribal Trust Land (TTL) in 1978. The internal settlement then offered the opportunity of recruiting blacks loyal to Muzorewa or Sithole, the so-called Security Force Auxiliaries (SFA) being raised to take over responsibility for the TTLs. Known in Shona as *Pfumo reVanhu* (Spear of the People), the SFAs were effectively private armies attached to Muzorewa's and Sithole's political parties, and often little more than the unemployed given a makeshift military training. About 10,000 were deployed to protect the TTLs in Operation Favour, with responsibility for security over 15 per cent of the country.

Large numbers of men were needed for static guards on important installations, railways and farms. Additional units such as the Guard Force, raised in 1976, and the black and coloured Defence Regiment, raised in 1978, could assist, but the lack of manpower brought severe restraints and governed strategy and tactics. It was felt vital, for example, to contain infiltration in frontier areas, hence the frequency with which the Rhodesians undertook spoiling raids into Zambia and Mozambique. Walls had served in Malaya, and the Rhodesians also studied Israeli techniques and the methods of the *flechas* in Angola. Unfortunately, however, the lack of co-ordination in command and control prevented the development of a coherent British-style strategy, and COMOPS's adoption of a mobile counter-offensive strategy was little more than a means of inflicting high kill ratios, since no attempt could be made to hold any cleared areas until the SFAs became available. Only in 1979 was so-called 'Vital Asset Ground' identified, equating to the white areas of the interior.

Another reflection of strained resources was the development of the 'Fire Force' concept to offset lack of men through a concentration of firepower and mobility. If guerrillas were located, a Cessna Lynx would attack with fragmentation bombs or napalm to fix the guerrillas in position. Four of five Alouette helicopters, each carrying a 'stick' of four of five men, would then deploy to drive the guerrillas back on to about fifteen paratroopers dropped at low level from a C-47 Dakota transport aircraft. Four such Fire Forces were available, but as the war escalated so their reaction time became slower amid competing demands for their services. By mid-1979, they were said to be accounting for 75 per cent of all guerrilla casualties inside Rhodesia, although the Selous Scouts also claimed that they were responsible for 68 per cent of kills. Other specialised units emerged, such as the Police Anti-Terrorist Units (Pates) and the mounted Grey's Scouts and new techniques, the latter including development of heavily armoured vehicles such as the Hyena, Rhino and Pookie intended to survive mine blasts.

While the guerrillas adjusted to Rhodesian techniques, the kill ratio remained highly favourable to the security forces. It never dropped below 6:1 and at times was as high as 14:1, with some individual operations attaining 60:1. But infiltration could not be closed off, although various additional methods were used. A physical barrier – the *cordon sanitaire* – of border minefields eventually covered 537 miles of the frontiers with Zambia and Mozambique at a cost of R$2,298 million. Rains, however, washed away the mines, animals blundered into unfenced areas, and there were always too few men to maintain adequate patrols. Resettlement was also unsuccessful. A pilot scheme began in the Zambezi valley in December 1973, but it only began in earnest with the removal of 46,000 Africans from the Chiweshe TTL into 21 'protected villages' (PVs) in Operation Overload in July 1974. In all, 234 PVs were constructed by January 1978 with an estimated population of anything between 350,000 and 750,000. Too frequently, however, the Rhodesians did not use resettlement as a basis for winning hearts and minds. Many PVs lacked facilities, while others were not sufficiently protected by the Guard Force or the African District Security Assistants (DSAs) deployed by the Ministry of Internal Affairs. Enforced urbanisation struck at tribal values and, in September 1978, as many as 70 PVs were abandoned.

Generally, the Rhodesian approach to winning hearts and minds fell short of what was required. An early attempt by the 'Sheppard Group' failed in 1974 to develop a coherent socio-economic strategy, and psychological warfare methods only emerged in 1977, although there was some success in a contest with the guerrillas over control of traditional *mhondoro* spirit mediums among the Shona. As outsiders coming into even Shona districts, ZANLA sought to win support through the mediums conferring 'ancestral' legitimacy on them. However, the emphasis in Rhodesian efforts was too much on increasing African representation in government and too little on improving the lot of the rural African. Punitive measures went hand in hand with positive inducements, so that rewards for information and full-scale amnesties were balanced by collective fines, strict food control from 1977 under Operation Turkey, constantly amended regulations and the progressive extension of the death penalty. The preference for control rather than concession was also illustrated by the extension of martial law over 90 per cent of Rhodesia by September 1979.

The new Portuguese methods and the influence of popular commanders like Spinola, Costa Gomes and Arriaga was sufficient to produce stalemate in Guinea, low-intensity stalemate in Angola and the possibility of outright victory in Mozambique. It must also be said, however, that the Beira railway was coming under increasing attack in Mozambique after 1972 as the formidable defences of the Cabora Bassa dam forced the insurgents elsewhere, including the Zambezia region, which they reached for the first time in July 1974. However, the price of that relative success was international criticism damaging to Portugal's prestige, ever-increasing expenditure damaging to the domestic economy and expansion damaging to the army's cohesion.

In terms of the international position, the proclamation of an 'independent' state by PAIGC in September 1973 was recognised by 70 countries and welcomed in the UN General Assembly, which had proved a constant and vociferous critic of Portuguese policy. Portugal argued that it was fighting the

West's battle against communism and, as a member of NATO, was particularly safeguarding the strategic importance of the Cape Verde Islands on the Atlantic sea route. In practical terms, it derived support only from South Africa and Rhodesia. In terms of the economic impact, defence expenditure as a proportion of the national budget rose from 25 per cent in 1960 to 42 per cent in 1968, although this was offset by the contributions made by the colonies themselves, which reduced it by 16 per cent over the period as a whole. The military cost of the overall counter-insurgency effort in real terms increased from 170.8 million escudos in 1967 to 4,438.8 million escudos in 1973. In terms of casualties, the cost to the Portuguese was not great. They suffered 8,290 dead by 1974, 5,797 of whom were metropolitan Portuguese as opposed to colonists or blacks, a substantially smaller loss than that of the French in Algeria or the United States in South Vietnam. In addition, there were perhaps 30,000 wounded or disabled. Yet the cost in money and lives was still a considerable burden for Portugal in terms of its economy and population. There were probably an additional 80,000 civilian casualties and between 100,000 and 150,000 insurgent casualties in the three colonies.

It was the impact of the African campaigns upon the army that was most serious. Already by 1970 it was apparent that Portuguese ground patrols were either entirely black in composition or comprised only two or three white Portuguese with 20–30 Africans. Professional soldiers such as those serving in the elite units of paratroopers, commandos, marines and naval fusiliers were serving alongside increasingly unenthusiastic conscripts confined to garrison duties and social programmes. It is estimated that 110,000 conscripts failed to report for service between 1961 and 1974 at a time when the manpower pool was decreasing anyway as a result of emigration, which had always been a marked feature of Portuguese society. There was growing indifference within Portugal itself and increasing hostility from white colonists, with whom the army had little sympathy.

There is no particular evidence of a morale problem as such among Portuguese forces in the colonies. Heavy drinking was reported, but no widespread drug abuse and little desertion. Indeed, as most white Portuguese troops were of peasant origin and used to deprivation, army conditions were often better than those they had experienced at home. There was a growing sense of isolation, however, with little domestic interest in the war and the increasing opposition to it. In many respects, it was the reaction of the officer corps rather than the rank and file that was significant.

The regular officer corps, which had a tradition of intervention in politics, was increasingly disillusioned with the politicians and especially resented the dilution involved in the conscription of large numbers of university graduates or *milicianos* (militia) as officers, the officer corps becoming more lower middle class, more provincial and more democratic in attitudes. Pay was poor and promotion slow, while the Portuguese also retained a separate staff corps. Some younger regular officers were moonlighting to make ends meet, even though white settlers tended to suggest that Portuguese officers were fighting an 'air-conditioned war' of some comfort.

More often than not, *milicianos* commanded the static garrisons while regulars conducted the actual fighting. Thus, when the so-called Rebelo decrees of July 1973 gave the *milicianos* accelerated promotion through counting reserve service towards seniority, younger professional officers founded the Movimento das Forças Armadas (Armed Forces Movement, MFA). Beyond its professional grievances, however, the MFA had a wider political, economic and social programme, since industrialisation and modernisation in Portugal had resulted in pressures on housing and high inflation, amounting to 72 per cent by 1974. There was a general feeling that Portugal was suffering from economic backwardness, social inequalities and political rigidity. Foreign-dominated commercial cartels were also opposed to the war.

When Spinola, who had returned from Guinea to be deputy chief of staff, was dismissed in March 1974 for criticising government colonial policy in his polemic *Portugal e o Futuro* (Portugal and the Future), the MFA started to plot a coup. This overthrew Caetano's government in April, and Spinola was installed as the new president in May but was ousted by more radical elements in September. They changed his favoured option of federation with the colonies to complete withdrawal. As indicated earlier, Guinea passed to the control of PAIGC and Mozambique to Frelimo, but there was a bitter civil war in Angola, in which the limited assistance received by FNLA and UNITA from South Africa and the United States was substantially outweighed by that of the Soviet Union and Cuba for MPLA. MPLA, therefore, had won the civil war by March 1976 and FNLA disappeared, but UNITA continued to fight on.

The Portuguese had growing problems in Mozambique by 1974, but not serious enough to suggest that they were in any sense losing the war. Throughout their colonies they retained control of all major routes and all urban areas. In military terms neither side had won or lost, but, as in so many other counter-insurgency campaigns, the ultimate outcome was decided elsewhere. In this case, it was a military coup in Portugal itself that destroyed the fabric of the Salazarist state and its 'historic' mission in Africa.

As indicated previously, the Portuguese withdrawal immediately impacted upon Rhodesia but, in any case, there had always been an external dimension. Some Rhodesian operations were undertaken to put direct pressure on the guerrillas or their African hosts. Thus, in October and November 1976 Rhodesian operations inside Mozambique (Operation Mardon) were intended to frustrate attempts to launch a guerrilla offensive to coincide with negotiations brokered by the United States in Geneva. There were similar raids on economic targets inside Mozambique and Zambia in the autumn of 1979 to persuade the presidents of these states to adopt a more compliant attitude in the forthcoming London talks. That on the heavily armed and protected ZANLA base at New Chimoio (Operation Diago) on 27

September resulted in over 2,000 guerrilla dead for the loss of just two Rhodesians. In fact, the Rhodesians had operated in Mozambique since 1969, although the first large-scale raid did not occur until August 1976. The first major incursion into Zambia was in October 1978 after ZIPRA shot down a civilian airliner and massacred the survivors. There were also raids into Botswana and a bombing raid on Angolan targets in February 1979. Rhodesia's neighbours were also partly dependent upon the Rhodesian railways. However, Rhodesia, in turn, depended upon South Africa, and South African personnel were withdrawn in 1975 since the prime minister, John Vorster, feared escalation would jeopardise his own relations with black African states. Vorster's successor did put some South African forces back into Rhodesia to guard vital areas such as the Beit Bridge, but increasingly the South Africans pressed Smith to concede majority rule.

By the end of 1979, rural administration had broken down in many TTLs, large numbers of schools and hospitals had closed and native agriculture was seriously affected by loss of cattle and the spread of diseases formerly under control. There were parallel strains for the white population in the form of increasing taxes, declining output, inflation and social tension. Officially, the war cost the lives of 468 white civilians and 1,361 members of the security forces. An official total of 7,790 black civilians and 10,450 guerrillas were recorded as being killed inside Rhodesia, but civilian and guerrilla losses may have exceeded 30,000. At the end, the Rhodesians had surrendered no city or major communications route and the guerrillas had not succeeded in establishing 'liberated zones', although many areas were contested. Remarkably inefficient in a military sense, the guerrillas were effective at political subversion, and whether the Rhodesians could have contained the insurgency indefinitely is a moot point. Manpower had always been the problem for the Rhodesians, who had attempted for too long to exert control everywhere rather than concentrating on key areas. In a military sense, the war was not lost, but Rhodesia's resources were stretched dangerously thin, even without the constant interplay of dominating political considerations. In the end, those political considerations determined the war's outcome.

As suggested, the South African role was a significant one. South Africa itself enjoyed considerable success in its counter-insurgency operations from 1966 to 1984. The initial internal nationalist challenge to white rule from the South African version of the African National Congress (ANC), its military wing, Umkhonto we Sizwe (Spear of the Nation) and the more militant Pan-Africanist Congress (PAC), with its military wing, Poqo (Pure), between 1961 and 1964 was easily contained by the South African Police (SAP), especially its Security Police branch. The nationalists were forced to regroup outside South Africa and to try to infiltrate back through neighbouring Rhodesia, Angola and Mozambique, a near impossible task while Rhodesia and the Portuguese held firm. As previously indicated, in 1967, SAP units were deployed in Rhodesia, and an average of about 3,000 South Africans remained there until August 1975. South African Defence Force (SADF) personnel were also seconded to Rhodesia from the 1970s until 1980. The principal army effort, however, was in South West Africa or Namibia against the guerrillas of the South West African People's Organisation (SWAPO) and its military wing, the People's Liberation Army of Namibia (PLAN).

SWAPO was originally formed in 1957 as the Ovamboland People's Congress, being renamed in April 1960. Its support was among the Ovambo tribe, which represented about 46 per cent of the African population of the territory. Led by Sam Nujoma, SWAPO set up headquarters in Tanzania and bases in Zambia so that it could attempt to infiltrate into Namibia through the Caprivi Strip, a 250-mile corridor linking Zambia to Namibia but bordered by both Angola and Botswana. The first SWAPO group infiltrated through the strip in late 1965, and the first clash with South African forces occurred in August 1966.

The South Africans were able to close off the Caprivi Strip through continuous patrols backed by air power, but Ovamboland remained strongly pro-SWAPO so that martial law was introduced there in February 1972. The Portuguese withdrawal from Angola in 1974–75 provided SWAPO with new bases along the 1,000-mile frontier between Angola and Namibia. By 1978, SWAPO had increased its strength to about 10,000 men trained and equipped by the Soviet, Cuban and other Eastern bloc personnel in Angola. SWAPO also received the backing of the UN General Assembly in December 1976, the UN deeming South Africa's occupation of Namibia to be illegal. The former German South West Africa had been granted to South Africa as a mandate by the League of Nations in 1920, but the UN had refused to permit its permanent incorporation into South Africa in 1946 and revoked the mandate in October 1966, subsequently renaming it Namibia and demanding its independence in June 1968. SWAPO's tactics were characterised by the South Africans as 'shoot and scoot', being largely dependent upon long-range bombardment by mortars and rockets, supplemented by mine laying.

Technically, the SADF was initially acting only in support of the SAP, and it was not until 1974 that it assumed responsibility for operations. The new factor was the Portuguese withdrawal from Angola, which gave SWAPO direct access to Namibia. SWAPO was to claim that the South Africans had 100,000 men in Namibia by 1980 but, in reality, the number never exceeded 40,000. Increasingly these included white commando units raised in Namibia itself and African units raised from the San, Ovambo, Okavango and East Caprivi peoples in what was eventually called the South West Africa Territory Force. San trackers proved especially useful. The South Africans also held a constitutional conference at Turnhalle with representatives of South West Africa's various ethnic groups in 1975, which recommended the territory become an independent unitary state. While not formally accepted by the South Africans, who came under pressure from the West not to endorse the recommendation, Pretoria did encourage the emergence of the multi-racial Democratic Turnhalle Alliance (DTA) as a viable alternative to SWAPO.

SADF units were also committed to the Angolan civil war in support of UNITA between August 1975 and March 1976. The border with Angola was then sealed with a 1,000-mile *cordon sanitaire* of fences, minefields and free-fire zones. There was also an attempt to introduce a hearts and minds programme in Namibia itself, with troops used to assist with agricultural and irrigation projects as well as to act in medical and educational roles. Resettlement was introduced in the Caprivi and Okavango areas. Learning from Rhodesia, the SADF used Reconnaissance Commandos (Recondos) modelled on the Selous Scouts and Mobile Reaction or Quick Reaction Forces, using helicopters and mine-proofed combat vehicles such as the Ratel. In emulation of both the Rhodesians and the Israelis, the South Africans also mounted both hot pursuit operations and pre-emptive strike operations against guerrilla concentrations in Zambia, Botswana and Angola. Operation Protea, for example, was a successful thirteen-day strike 100 miles into Angola in August 1981, which may have killed around 1,000 Cuban, SWAPO and Angolan troops. A pseudo force known as the Buffalo Battalion using former FNLA guerrillas also operated inside Angola, while the South Africans continued to assist UNITA. At the same time, the Frelimo government in Mozambique was undermined by South African support for Resistançia Naçional Moçambicana (Mozambique National Resistance, Renamo), also known on occasions as Movimento Naçional da Resistència de Mocambique (MNR). Originally established by Rhodesia's Central Intelligence Organisation to undermine Frelimo's support for ZANU, Renamo was led after 1983 by Alfonso Dhlakama. It controlled an estimated 85 per cent of Mozambique by 1986, benefiting from Frelimo's narrow tribal base and from the resistance of the other tribes to Frelimo's Marxist ideology and attempted suppression of traditional cultural and religious practices.

South African military success was rewarded in 1984 by the Lusaka and Nkomati accords. In February 1984, under the Lusaka agreement, the Angolans dropped support for SWAPO in return for the cessation of South African raids, while, in March 1984, the Nkomati agreement saw Mozambique drop its support of the ANC in return for South Africa ending support for Renamo. This facilitated negotiations between South Africa and SWAPO, and agreement was reached on independence in November 1988, linked, in turn, to the withdrawal of Cuban troops from Angola. The UN supervised a cease-fire in April 1989 and also elections, which SWAPO won, in November 1989. Namibia became independent on 21 March 1990 with Nujoma as its first president. It was international pressure, therefore, and not military action by SWAPO or its allies, that led to wider agreements on independence for Namibia in 1990 and the emergence of a new South Africa in 1994. Fighting has continued, however, in Mozambique and Angola.

Further reading

On African campaigns generally, see Anthony Clayton, *Frontiersmen: Warfare in Africa since 1950* (London, 1999) and, from the perspective of an uncritical sympathiser with the guerrillas, Basil Davidson, *The People's Cause* (London, 1981).

On Kenya, see Anthony Clayton, *Counter-insurgency in Kenya* (Manhattan, 1984); Randall Heather, 'Intelligence and Counter-insurgency in Kenya, 1952–56' *Intelligence and National Security* 5 (1990), pp. 57–83; David A. Percox, 'British Counter-insurgency (COIN) Policy in Kenya, 1952–56: Extension of Internal Security (IS) Policy or Prelude to Decolonisation?' *Small Wars and Insurgencies* 9 (1998), pp. 46–101; David Throup, 'Crime, Politics and the Police in Colonial Kenya, 1939–63' in Anderson and Killingray, *Policing and Decolonisation*, pp. 127–57; Frank Kitson, *Gangs and Counter-gangs* (London, 1960); Fred Majdalany, *State of Emergency* (London, 1962); Robert Edgerton, *Mau Mau: An African Crucible* (London, 1990); W.O. Maloba, *Mau Mau and Kenya: Analysis of a Peasant Revolt* (Bloomington, 1993); Frank Furedi, *The Mau Mau War in Perspective* (London, 1989); and Furedi, 'Kenya: Decolonisation through Counter-insurgency' in A. Gorst, L. Johnman and W. Scott Lucas (eds), *Contemporary British History, 1931–61: Politics and the Limits of Policy* (London, 1991), pp. 141–68. For a debate on the extent to which minimum force was or was not applied in Kenya, see John Newsinger, 'Minimum Force, British Counter-insurgency and the Mau Mau Rebellion' and Tom Mockaitis, 'Minimum Force, British Counter-insurgency and the Mau Mau Rebellion: A Reply' both in *Small Wars and Insurgencies* 3 (1992), pp. 47–57, 87–89.

On Borneo, see Raffi Gregorian, 'Claret Operations and Confrontation, 1964–66' *Conflict Quarterly* 11 (1991), pp. 46–72; H.D. James and D. Sheil-Small, *The Undeclared War: The Story of the Indonesian Confrontation, 1962–66* (London, 1971); and J. Mackie, *Konfrontasi: The Indonesia–Malaysia Dispute, 1963–66* (Oxford, 1974). Mockaitis, *British Counterinsurgency, op. cit.*, covers Kenya, while his *British Counterinsurgency in the Post-imperial Era* (Manchester, 1995) covers Borneo.

On Portugal, see John Cann, *Counterinsurgency in Africa: The Portuguese Way of War, 1961–74* (Westport, 1997); Cann, 'Operation Mar Verde: The Raid on Conakry' *Small Wars and Insurgencies* 8 (1997), pp. 64–81; Cann (ed.), *Memories of Portugal's African Wars, 1961–74* (Quantico, 1998); T.H. Henriksen, 'Lessons from Portugal's Counter-insurgency Operations in Africa' *Journal of the Royal United Services Institute for Defence Studies* 123 (1978), pp. 31–35; Henriksen, 'Portugal in Africa: Comparative Notes on Counterinsurgency' *Orbis* (1977), pp. 395–412; Henriksen, 'Some Notes on the National Liberation Wars in Angola, Mozambique and Guinea-Bissau' *Military Affairs* 41 (1977), pp. 30–36; Henriksen, 'People's War in Angola, Mozambique and Guinea-Bissau' *Journal of Modern African Studies* 14 (1976), pp. 377–99; Henriksen, *Mozambique: A History* (London, 1978); Henriksen, *Revolution and Counterrevolution:*

Mozambique's War for Independence, 1964–74 (London, 1978); Marlyn Newitt, *Portugal in Africa* (London, 1981); Newitt, *A History of Mozambique* (London, 1995); W.S. Van der Waals, *Portugal's War in Angola, 1961–74* (Rivonia, 1993); Douglas Wheeler, 'African Elements in Portugal's Armies in Africa, 1961–74' *Armed Forces and Society* 2 (1976), pp. 233–50; Wheeler, 'The Portuguese Army in Angola' *Journal of Modern African Studies* 7 (1969), pp. 425–39; Douglas Porch, *The Portuguese Armed Forces and the Revolution* (London, 1977); A.J. Venter, 'Why Portugal Lost Its African Wars' in A.J. Venter (ed.), *Challenge: Southern Africa within the African Revolutionary Context* (Gibraltar, 1989), pp. 224–72; and Ian Beckett, 'The Portuguese Army: The Campaign in Mozambique, 1964–74' in Beckett and Pimlott, *Armed Forces and Modern Counter-insurgency*, pp. 136–62.

On Rhodesia, see J.K. Cilliers, *Counter-insurgency in Rhodesia* (London, 1985); Paul Moorcraft and Peter McLaughlin, *Chimurenga: The War in Rhodesia, 1965–80* (Marshalltown, 1982); Peter Godwin and Ian Hancock, *Rhodesians Never Die: The Impact of War and Political Change on White Rhodesia, 1970–80* (Oxford, 1993); L.H. Gann and T.H. Henriksen, *The Struggle for Zimbabwe: Battle in the Bush* (New York, 1981); Peter McLaughlin, 'Victims as Defenders: African Troops in the Rhodesian Defence System, 1890–1980' *Small Wars and Insurgencies* 2 (1991), pp. 240–75; Richard Wood, 'Counter-punching on the Mudzi: D Company, 1st Rhodesian African Rifles, on Operation Mardon, 1 November 1976' in *ibid.*, 9 (1998), pp. 64–82; J. Bowyer Bell, 'The Frustration of Insurgency: The Rhodesian Example in the Sixties' *Military Affairs* 35 (1971), pp. 1–5; A.R. Wilkinson, *Insurgency in Rhodesia, 1957–73* (London, 1973); R. Reid-Daly and Peter Stiff, *Selous Scouts: Top Secret War* (Alberton, 1982); T. Arbuckle, 'Rhodesian Bush War Strategies and Tactics: An Assessment' *Journal of the Royal United Services Institute for Defence Studies* 124 (1979), pp. 27–32; G. St J. Barclay, 'Slotting the Floppies: The Rhodesian Response to Sanctions and Insurgency, 1974–77' *Australian Journal of Defence Studies* 1 (1977), pp. 110–20; T. Ranger, 'The Death of Chaminuka: Spirit Mediums, Nationalism and the Guerrilla War in Zimbabwe' *African Affairs* 81 (1982), pp. 349–69; Ranger, *Soldiers in Zimbabwe's Liberation War* (London, 1995); D. Lan, *Guns and Rain: Guerrillas and Spirit Mediums in Zimbabwe* (London, 1983); and Ian Beckett, 'The Rhodesian Army: Counter-insurgency, 1972–75' in Beckett and Pimlott, *Armed Forces and Modern Counter-insurgency*, pp. 163–89.

On South Africa, see Francis Toase, 'The South African Army: The Campaign in South West Africa/Namibia since 1966' in Beckett and Pimlott, *Armed Forces and Modern Counter-insurgency*, pp. 190–221; Paul Moorcraft, *African Nemesis: War and Revolution in Southern Africa, 1945–2010* (London, 1990); H.R. Heitman, *War in Angola: The Final South African Phase* (Gibraltar, 1990); and W. Steenkamp, *South Africa's Border War* (Gibraltar, 1989). On southern Africa generally, see David Burns, 'Insurgency as a Struggle for Legitimation: The Case of Southern Africa' *Small Wars and Insurgencies* 5

(1994), pp. 29–62. On Renamo, see Tom Young, 'Renamo and Counter Revolutionary Insurgency' in Paul Rich and Richard Stubbs (eds), *The Counter-insurgent State* (London, 1997), pp. 149–69; and A. Vines, *Renamo: Terrorism in Mozambique* (York, 1991).

7

THE TRANSITION TO URBAN
INSURGENCY

Marxists had long regarded an urban proletariat as the true basis for insurrection, but the success of Mao Tse-tung's principles of rural revolutionary war in China proved immensely seductive after 1945. However, there had been some recourse to urban terror by the Irgun and LEHI against the British in Palestine between 1945 and 1947. The trend continued with EOKA's campaign against the British on Cyprus between 1955 and 1959; with that by the Front de Libération Nationale (National Liberation Front, FLN), against the French in Algeria between 1954 and 1962; with that by the Fuerzas Armadas de Liberación Nacional (Armed Forces of National Liberation, FALN), in Venezuela between 1963 and 1965; and that against the British in Aden from December 1963 to November 1967. Indeed, the leader of EOKA, George Grivas, wrote an account of his campaign in 1964, *Guerrilla Warfare and EOKA's Struggle*, which offered significant pointers to future urban guerrillas, although he had intended it as a kind of primer for Western governments faced with communist insurgency.

Although the disastrous outcome of urban action for the FLN in Algiers in 1957 and for FALN in Venezuela should have served warning of its inherent dangers for the guerrilla, urban guerrilla warfare was increasingly attractive. This was particularly so in Latin America, where the failure of the *foco* theory of rural revolutionary warfare associated with Che Guevara, and emanating primarily from Fidel Castro's success on Cuba between 1956 and 1959, played a significant role in shifting revolutionary action to the cities. In view of the failure, in turn, of urban guerrilla warfare in Latin America, Castro was to argue that the city was 'the graveyard' of the revolutionary.

While there was much substance in Castro's dictum, however, urban guerrilla warfare still proved a difficult challenge for security forces, particularly in liberal democracies. Total repression was not generally a practicable option for liberal democracies, which had to find other more politically acceptable responses to the threat posed by urban insurgency. Begin in Palestine had calculated that the British would not be willing to resort to total repression and, in many respects, Cyprus and Aden posed similar difficulties. Indeed, while it tends to be said that the British have been the most successful exponents of counter-insurgency since 1945, both Cyprus and Aden were among the comparative failures, although primarily for reasons beyond the control of the security forces. Similarly, Algeria was ultimately a failure for the French army, whose new doctrine of *guerre révolutionnaire* resulted in an institutional politicisation threatening the stability of the French state itself. In less democratic states, urban guerrilla warfare did not prove as potent and was more easily suppressed, since there was not the same self-imposed restraint on the part of the security forces.

Turning first to the British experience of urban action, Cyprus was a part of the Ottoman Empire when occupied in 1878 as a base for British operations against any Russian invasion of Turkey. It was then formally annexed by Britain in 1914 when Turkey entered the First World War as an ally of Germany, becoming a British Crown colony in 1923. The majority of the population was of Greek origin, amounting to 78 per cent in 1955, but with a substantial minority of Turkish origin, amounting to 18 per cent in 1955. The aim of the Greek Cypriots was not independence but *enosis*, or union with Greece, despite the fact that Cyprus had never been regarded as part of modern Greece. *Enosis* was not a new phenomenon and, as previously related, had sparked troubles on the island in 1931. But it acquired new significance with the election to the leadership of the island's Greek Orthodox Church in 1950 of Michael Mouskos as Archbishop Makarios III. Having left Palestine and being forced to contemplate withdrawal from Egypt, Britain had transferred its Middle Eastern Command to Cyprus in June 1954 and believed it essential to retain its last remaining base in the eastern Mediterranean. It was announced in July 1954, therefore, that there could be no question of any change in sovereignty, although limited self-government was offered.

While using the Greek government to continue to pressure Britain through action at the UN, the Greek Cypriots decided to try to raise the cost of the British presence through a military campaign on Cyprus itself, establishing EOKA in 1953. A retired colonel in the Greek army, although Cyprus-born, George Grivas returned to Cyprus in November 1954 to assume military command under the pseudonym of 'Dighenis', a heroic figure from Greek history. When in December 1954 the UN General Assembly declined to discuss the Cyprus question, demonstrations occurred in Nicosia, followed by the first bomb attack on 1 April 1955. Talks between the British, Greek and Turkish governments failed to reach agreement in London in August, and Field Marshal Sir John Harding was then appointed as Governor to take a strong line against EOKA. A state of emergency was declared on 26 November 1955 and endured until Grivas ordered a cease-fire on 31 December 1958, by which time all parties had accepted the compromise of independence. This was negotiated in London in February 1959 and came into effect with Makarios as first president on 14 December 1959.

In the case of Aden, this had been occupied in 1839 as an important coaling and bunkering station on the route to India and, from 1954, a major oil-refining port. Aden itself became a Crown colony in 1937, while sixteen of the twenty separate emirates, sheikhdoms and sultanates within the surrounding Aden Protectorate became the Federation of South Arabia in 1958, Aden joining the federation in January 1963. Aden was increasingly important as a military base for Britain, and it was intended to retain it even as the federation moved to independence, the headquarters of Middle East Command moving there from Cyprus in 1960. The 1964 Defence White Paper indicated that independence would proceed by 1968. There was a growing nationalist movement among Adenis, however, who wanted independence on their own terms separate from the semi-feudal protectorate states. This coincided with the rise of Arab nationalism generally, not least as represented by the republican regime that came to power in neighbouring Yemen in 1962.

With some territorial claims to Aden, and backed by Nasser's Egypt, the Yemen encouraged revolt among the tribesmen of the Radfan region of the federation. This brought a series of British military operations in early 1964, mounted against the advice of the British commander of the federal army, Brigadier James Lunt, who believed it would only create more difficulties in the area. At the same time, there was also backing for the two principal nationalist groups in Aden, the National Liberation Front (NLF), a Marxist group emerging in June 1963, and the Front for the Liberation of Occupied South Yemen (FLOSY), which emerged in May 1965. Indeed, of the 220,000 inhabitants of Aden, at least 80,000 were of Yemeni birth or descent. The first overt sign of opposition was a grenade attack, which injured the British High Commissioner, Sir Kennedy Trevaskis, on 10 December 1963, after which terrorist incidents escalated steadily. Then, on 22 February 1966, the Wilson government's Defence White Paper indicated that, as part of the general reduction in British defence expenditure, the base at Aden would not be retained after South Arabian independence. This undermined at a stroke not only the federal authorities but also the whole counter-insurgency effort. Amid an increasingly violent struggle for power between FLOSY and the NLF, ultimately won by the latter, British forces finally withdrew on 28 November 1967 with power transferred to the NLF.

There were strikingly similar tactics on the part of the insurgents in both Cyprus and Aden, although it should be noted that, as well as operating in urban areas like Nicosia, EOKA also operated in the Troödos mountains. Grivas had no pretensions to achieving a military victory, and the aim was always to make continued control of Cyprus politically unacceptable to the British government, winning 'a moral victory through a process of attrition, by harassing, confusing and finally exasperating the enemy forces, with the objective of achieving our main aim'. Like Guevara later, Grivas believed that independent military action by small groups of insurgents could succeed without the necessity of forging a Maoist-style conventional army, but, unlike

Guevara, Grivas did not neglect either careful preparation before opening his campaign or the cultivation of popular support. While a natural conservative, as befitted a former career soldier, Grivas had an extraordinary grasp of the needs of an insurgent campaign, establishing tight internal security through a cellular structure, which would prove resistant to counter-intelligence work. Initially, no more than 80 activists were involved, organised into squads of five or six. At the height of the campaign in 1956, there were no more than 350 guerrillas operating in seven mountain groups of between five and fifteen activists, and 50 urban groups of between four and five individuals. A network of 750 members of EOKA's passive wing were organised in village groups, while, in the towns, women, youths from the 'Young Stalwarts' and children were commonly used to carry weapons or to shadow targets for the active operatives.

The latter's chosen methods of attack included arson, sabotage, raids on police armouries, street murder, mining and especially bombing. Indeed, while 2,976 bombs were neutralised, 1,782 EOKA bombs exploded during the campaign, causing £10 million worth of damage. Members of the security forces were assassinated, Ledra Street in Nicosia becoming known as 'murder mile'. Especially targeted were Greek Cypriot police and the Special Branch, two of the latter's first three officers being killed almost at once. One Greek Cypriot Special Branch officer was murdered at a political rally in plain view of hundreds of witnesses, none of whom could apparently remember anything. At least twenty Greek Cypriot policemen co-operated with EOKA as informants, while others helped EOKA activists to escape and even sheltered them. One bomb was even discovered under Harding's bed. EOKA propaganda was also skilful, with a particular emphasis on alleged British atrocities, and followed up with orchestrated demonstrations, riots, boycotts and strikes. Like later urban guerrillas, Grivas intended to provoke a repressive reaction from the British, which would increase international pressure on them, but it would appear from his subsequent justifications for EOKA's terrorism that, to quote Susan Carruthers, he 'craved respect rather than ignominy'.

In Aden, terrorism was also the chosen method of both FLOSY and the NLF in trying to force the British to leave and, like EOKA, NLF had a cellular structure. The first attacks were frequently amateurish in the extreme, with terrorists often blowing themselves up – in one early attack the terrorist threw the pin instead of the grenade – but they became more effective and more numerous. Grenades were favoured over the revolvers mainly used for assassination in Cyprus, but roads were mined and sniping took many lives, as on another infamous 'murder mile', a single sniper killing fourteen Europeans near Steamer Point in the last month of British occupation. Carefully staged riots were often also designed to lure troops into the range of snipers. From 286 incidents in 1965, the total rose to 540 in 1966 and to 2,900 in 1967. The various local police forces were thoroughly infiltrated by the terrorists, who eliminated the Arab members of Special Branch. Moreover, in a particularly notorious incident, the South Arabian Police and the Aden Armed Police both mutinied on 20 June 1967, killing 22 British servicemen and taking over the Crater district of the town for fifteen days until control was regained by Lieutenant-Colonel Colin Mitchell and the 1st Battalion of the Argyll and Sutherland Highlanders on 4 July. The outbreak appears to have been due in part to the perception of British support for Israel, which had just destroyed its Arab enemies in the Six Day War. Once it became obvious that the British would not stay, intelligence all but dried up as even committed supporters of the British presence feared the reprisals that might follow withdrawal.

It is clear that British troops operated under difficult circumstances in both Cyprus and Aden. In the case of Cyprus, the capability of EOKA was seriously underestimated, and there was a tendency to believe that only a minority of Greek Cypriots actively supported *enosis*. In a sense this was right, but EOKA targeted those like the Greek Cypriots in the police force who might not subscribe to its cause so ruthlessly that passive support was converted into active assistance. EOKA killed more Greek Cypriots than the British and Turks together. No one ever collected the £10,000 reward on Grivas's head, and the British even resorted to collective fines, as in the case of the £35,000 levied on Limassol in September 1956 and the £40,000 on Famagusta in the same month. Lengthy curfews were also tried as well as corporal punishment inflicted on delinquent youths. However, both collective fines and corporal punishment were suspended in December 1956. Nor was there much co-ordination of army and police until the arrival of Harding as both Governor and director of operations in October 1955.

In fact, Harding did not have as much political authority as Templer had had in Malaya and, in practice, he delegated operational control to his chief of staff. There was also an additional civilian under-secretary for internal security to assist liaison as well as a director of intelligence. As in Malaya and Kenya, an integrated command and intelligence committee structure down to district level was established. Greek police were replaced with seconded British personnel and increasing numbers of Turks so that, by 1958, only 30 per cent were Greeks, compared with 62 per cent in 1954. The rank and file of the newly raised Auxiliary Police was also largely recruited from Turks in August 1955, and the Mobile Reserve Unit, established a month later, was wholly Turkish. Dependence upon Turks, however, naturally alienated the Greeks further, and the campaign was conducted in a climate of allegation and counter-allegation. Substantial reinforcements were brought to the island to bring British strength up to 20,000 troops and 4,500 police. As a result, Harding was able to create a mobile reserve, which he committed in May 1956 to hunting down the guerrilla groups in the Troödos in Operation Pepperpot. This was reasonably successful in reducing EOKA guerrilla activity in the mountains, despite the uneven quality of the national servicemen employed and the sheer size of the area encircled. It did result in the capture of Grivas's illuminating diaries, which assisted in filling the intelligence gap to some extent. Operation Sparrowhawk in October 1956 effectively cleared the Kyrenia range. Grivas thereafter concentrated EOKA's efforts in the towns.

Somewhat heavy-handed in his approach to the press, Harding also tried, not entirely successfully, to beef up the British propaganda effort. The attempt to equate EOKA with communism was unconvincing, but there was some success in demonstrating the link between EOKA and Makarios, who was deported from the island to the Seychelles by Harding in March 1956. EOKA atrocities, such as the murder of Mrs Margaret Cutliffe while shopping in Famagusta for her daughter's wedding dress in October 1958, helped to reinforce the government's message for British audiences. But the Labour opposition was highly ambivalent towards a continuing British presence and, in the end, a deal had to be done with Makarios, who was released from detention in March 1957 and returned to Cyprus in late 1958. The involvement of the Greek government was also a constant trial, and the British resorted to jamming Athens Radio in January 1956.

The Suez operation in November 1956 hindered Harding's campaign, as did the later deployment of British troops to Jordan in 1958. Between December 1956 and March 1957, however, EOKA suffered what Grivas admitted were 'hard blows' as attention switched to the towns with large-scale arrests and detentions and the successful infiltration of some EOKA groups through so-called Q patrols of defectors or pro-British Cypriots. Sixteen EOKA personnel were killed and 60 others captured in this phase of the campaign. Harding's civilian successor as Governor from October 1957, Sir Hugh Foot, was more liberal in approach but was prepared to sanction the mass arrest of 2,000 suspects in July 1958 and, later that year, to dismiss thousands of Greek civilian workers from employment at the British bases in order to prevent further sabotage. Foot's military commander, Major-General Sir Kenneth Darling, also increased covert patrolling, while decoy forces were used to lure the unwary among remaining guerrillas in the mountains into ambushes.

The increasing pressure was certainly a major factor in the decision by EOKA to call a cease-fire in December 1958, but, at most, the security forces had only been able to restrict insurgent activity to what might be deemed an acceptable level. In a way, therefore, a kind of impasse had been reached at a cost of the lives of at least 90 insurgents, 104 servicemen, 50 policemen and 238 civilians. It might be argued that both sides could claim a partial victory in that, while EOKA did not secure *enosis*, it remained able to carry out attacks to the end of the emergency. Similarly, while the British had not destroyed EOKA, they were able to retain sovereign base areas at Akrotiri and Dhekelia under the compromise solution of an independent Cyprus under a power-sharing constitution.

Despite the experience of the past, the British were slow to find any solution to the insurgency in Aden. Partly, this was due to the reluctance of the federal authorities to take strong action. Increasingly, indeed, federal officials and even local governments in the emirates, sultanates and sheikhdoms either left the country altogether or threw in their lot with NLF as it became clearer that it rather than FLOSY would prevail in the internecine struggle for power after British withdrawal. The British did not enjoy the kind of colonial arrangement that had pertained in Malaya and, therefore, it was not possible to appoint a single individual with complete civil and military power. Indeed, all too many agencies were involved in determining security policy, with the British government, the British High Commissioner, the Aden state government and the South Arabian federal authorities all involved. Similarly, ten different agencies were initially involved in intelligence work. Indeed, it was only in 1965 that a Security Policy Committee was established and only in June that same year that the GOC Middle East Land Forces was designated security commander and the intelligence agencies brought under a single army officer, Brigadier Tony Cowper. Even then it was not until February 1967 that the security commander actually assumed complete responsibility for internal security, with the committees previously established actually replaced by the normal chain of command.

Moreover, as in Cyprus, intelligence was never forthcoming freely from the population: the only claimant of one large reward was murdered two days after collecting it. Thus, there was no opportunity in Aden to 'turn' insurgents for pseudo work, the SAS being confined to covert surveillance operations. Trial by jury had to be suspended at an early stage through intimidation by the terrorists and recourse had to detention and the deep interrogation techniques of disorientation later used in Northern Ireland. These were criticised by the UN in November 1965, and there was further UN condemnation of Britain's presence in Aden in June and December 1966. At home, some of the Labour government's own supporters in the House of Commons were equally vociferous in opposition to continuing British occupation, and the government was uncomfortable with the colonial role generally.

British forces were also under immense pressure, with restrictions placed on their ability to open fire first or to use heavy weapons with, for example, troops not permitted to use the 76 mm guns on armoured cars even when ambushed in Crater in June 1967. Nonetheless, covert observation, road blocks, aggressive patrolling and cordon and search did have some effect until the Labour government pulled the rug from under their own troops by announcing withdrawal so far in advance. In 1964, just two British servicemen had been killed, six in 1965 and five in 1966, but the total was 44 in 1967. To this total of 57 dead was added 651 British military personnel wounded. In all, 382 individuals were killed in terrorist incidents between 1964 and 1967 and 1,714 wounded. Troops greatly resented the way in which they had been exposed to greater attack by government action, and Colin

'Mad Mitch' Mitchell in particular criticised the perceived softly-softly approach, as well as quarrelling with his superior, Major-General Philip Towle. Subsequently, the government's announcement of the disbandment of the Argylls as part of the defence cuts was regarded as petty revenge, although it was one of the more junior regiments in the Army List. In the event, a vigorous press campaign led to the regiment's reprieve.

In both Cyprus and Aden, the security forces were opposed by insurgents enjoying active support from other states, and who were able to mobilise international opinion in their favour in the UN and other forums. In neither case was winning hearts and minds practicable when the insurgents enjoyed considerable support among the local population. Even if co-ordination of intelligence was achieved, that local support made it all but impossible to obtain worthwhile intelligence anyway and certainly made separating insurgent from population similarly impossible. Nor did the British government have any clear political aim in either case, policy shifting decisively during both campaigns. The existence of competing Greek and Turkish communities with external constituencies in the form of the Greek and Turkish governments in the case of Cyprus, and the confused political composition of the South Arabian Federation, made clear policy options difficult to shape. There was increasing communal violence between Greek and Turkish Cypriots, not least in 1958, while there was also the internecine conflict of NLF and FLOSY in Aden. In the case of Aden, the complexity in local administration bedevilled co-ordination of civil and military agencies, although this was achieved on Cyprus.

With few political options available, the security forces were left with only military options in both campaigns. In addition, in the case of Aden, that led to arguably the greatest problem of all, which was increasing media coverage of such campaigns. Previously, campaigns like Malaya and Borneo had been little reported and, indeed, it is inconceivable that the Claret operations of the Confrontation could have been as well hidden from media attention later in the 1960s. By 1962, it was estimated that four out of every five British families had television, and the escalation of violence in Aden in 1967 undoubtedly had a media impact. Indeed, press coverage of the Radfan operations in 1964 had already resulted in a poor reception internationally for what seemed like a colonial power using heavy weapons against tribesmen. That had its effect in terms of the restrictions placed on British troops in Aden. Moreover, while there were far fewer British dead in Aden than in Malaya, Kenya or Borneo, the increased media coverage gave far greater significance to those deaths. Certainly, this had some influence on the Labour government's desire to quit Aden as soon as possible, and the relatively small losses were used as a justification for withdrawal.

The wider lessons of Cyprus and Aden and the British army's experience of urban insurgency were somewhat muted through the kind of collective amnesia about counter-insurgency lessons noted already with respect to other

British campaigns. This effect was enhanced by the obsession with the success in Malaya, which was marked in new manuals of counter-insurgency that were produced, namely the revision of the 1957 manual *Keeping the Peace* in 1963 and the appearance of *Land Operations: Counter-Revolutionary Operations* in 1969. These effectively ignored Palestine, Cyprus and Aden and, indeed, urban insurgency generally in ways that would not be helpful when the army was deployed on the streets of Ulster in 1969.

Turning to Algeria, one legacy of the war in Indo-China so far as the French army was concerned was that it was determined that it should not suffer another such defeat as a result of what it regarded as a lack of political and national will within France itself to meet the challenge of modern insurgency. Certainly, Indo-China had been a formative experience for the army, and many younger officers absorbed all they could of the Maoist insurgency they had faced in order to formulate a new counter-insurgency doctrine to replace that of *tache d'huile*. That doctrine was *guerre révolutionnaire* and was to be applied to the next major insurgency, that of the FLN in Algeria between November 1954 and July 1962.

In some respects, it was a natural development of *tache d'huile*, building into the French response the recognition that the Viet Minh had established a highly integrated and structured organisation and had employed a new mixture of political, military and psychological means to infiltrate the population and effect an alternative system of authority to that of the French colonial government. As expressed by one of the new French theorists, Georges Bonnet, the revolutionary warfare of the Viet Minh had simply been a matter of 'partisan (guerrilla) warfare + psychological warfare'. The weaknesses of the Maoist method appeared to be the vulnerability of the insurgents during the initial phase of conflict, before Maoist preparation had established any deep-rooted support among the population and when the insurgents were highly likely to be dependent upon a logistic base conceivably in a neighbouring state. Indeed, there was an assumption that any discontent or unrest would stem from agitation on the part of the insurgents rather than from any underlying grievances.

Consequently, the aim of the security forces must be to effect an early separation of population from insurgents through extensive resettlement and the construction of physical barriers along international frontiers. Once under French control, the population would be subjected to suitably reforming policies but, if necessary, also to military coercion in order to contain or prevent support for the insurgents. In fact, many French officers interpreted *guerre révolutionnaire* as a genuine social revolution to win the support of the population, and some critics were even to accuse advocates of the new doctrine such as Yves Godard and Jacques Massu of practising rural socialism. As far as the insurgents were concerned, however, the military campaign would be waged by both military and psychological means without restraint. Thus, what was termed 'construction' would be closely linked to 'destruction'.

French officers were inculcated in the new doctrine at the Centre d'Instruction de Pacification et de Contre-Guerilla (Centre for the Teaching of Pacification and Counter-Guerrilla) established at Arzew in Algeria's Oran province in March 1956. It was articulated in print primarily in articles in military journals such as *Revue Militaire d'Information* and *Revue de Défense Nationale*, although both Bonnet and Roger Trinquier published books, the latter's *La Guerre moderne*, originally published in 1961, being translated in 1964 as *Modern Warfare: A French View of Counterinsurgency*. At the time, probably the most widely read exposition of *guerre révolutionnaire* was an anonymous pamphlet, *Contre-révolution, stratégie et tactique* (Counter-revolution, Strategy and Tactics), published in 1957 and distributed to officers throughout the army.

Just as *tache d'huile* had had political implications, with Lyautey suggesting the army might be required to regenerate French society itself, *guerre révolutionnaire* also carried an implicit political message through the army's involvement in the political sphere of any future insurgency through a psychological response. It was the belief of the practitioners of the new doctrine such as Bonnet, Charles Lacheroy, Godard, Jacques Hogard and Trinquier that it was the absolute duty of the French government and people to support the army, so that revolutionary insurgency would be opposed by equal ideological strength and purpose on the part of the authorities. There was certainly an element of a 'stab in the back' myth within the army after the withdrawal from Indo-China, and the disillusionment was increased by the belief that politicians had once more robbed the army of victory during the Suez affair in 1956. In many respects, the young zealots within the army were equally suspicious of some of their seniors, while the latter often regarded the former as excessively arrogant.

Absolutely implicit in the understanding of the new insurgency was that it would always serve communist interests and, therefore, that any avowedly nationalist leaders would be mere dupes for communists. In reality, while socialist and anti-imperialist, the FLN was not a communist group, even if it received assistance from the Soviet bloc. Algeria had been seized by France in 1830, but since 1848 it had been regarded as part of metropolitan France itself, sending elected senators and deputies to Paris. By 1954, the Muslim population was about 8.4 million, but the dominant group were French settlers and their descendants, the so-called *colons* (colonists) or *pieds noirs* (black feet: deriving either from the black boots of the French troops or the idea that colonists had feet burned black in the sun). The *colons* numbered about a million in 1954, and 25,000 of them owned more land than was owned by half a million Muslims. Whereas only 14,000 *colons* were unemployed, the figure for the Muslim population reached 900,000 amid considerable economic difficulties affecting both agriculture and industry. In theory, all Muslims could gain French citizenship, but only provided that they renounced their legal rights and obligations under Muslim law. Similarly, while half the deputies in the Algerian assembly were Muslim, the *colons* had an effective veto on legislation, which required a two-thirds majority, and elections were gerrymandered to favour the moderate Muslim Union Démocratique du Manifeste Algérien (Democratic Union of Algerian Manifest, UDMA).

Growing Muslim frustration was vividly illustrated by the Sétif uprising in May 1945, following the arrest of the nationalist Messali Haj of the Parti du Peuple Algérien (Algerian People's Party, PPA), in which 103 Europeans were killed. French retaliation may have accounted for as many as 5,000 Muslims. Significantly, many of the first leaders of the FLN were to be drawn from Muslims returning to Algeria in 1945 from wartime service with the French army, who were horrified at the scale of the French reprisals. Ultimately, a new uprising aimed at securing independence by war was planned for 1 November 1954 by the FLN, a clandestine faction of the militant Mouvement pour le Triomphe des Libertés Démocratiques (Movement for the Triumph of Democratic Liberties, MTLD), itself created in 1946 as successor to the outlawed PPA. The faction underwent a number of changes in nomenclature before emerging in April 1954 as the Comité Révolutionnaire d'Unité et d'Action (Revolutionary Committee for Unity and Action, CRUA). In turn, CRUA became the FLN with its military arm, the Armée de Libération Nationale (National Liberation Army, ALN), in May 1955, although the organisation appears to have been settled in October 1954.

The FLN's organisation was based on what its leaders knew of the Viet Minh, with Algeria divided into six regional commands or *wilayas*. The basic political organisation was cellular, while military organisation of the 'regular' *moudjahidin* (combatants) in the ALN into squads, platoons and companies reflected the French practice, with which ex-servicemen in the FLN were familiar. Irregulars or *mousseblin* (militiamen) largely remained in their own communities, while there were also specialists in terrorism known as *fida'iyin* (combatants of the faith). The collective leadership, however, was divided between Arabs and Berbers, and divisions occurred both among the main leadership, based first in Egypt and later in Tunisia, and among the *wilayas*. In December 1957, for example, Ramdane Abane, a prominent member of the Algiers *wilaya*, was murdered by three other *wilaya* chiefs, while four ALN commanders were executed in 1958 for plotting to overthrow the new provisional government established by the FLN in September 1958. There were to be other executions following attempts by some internal leaders to negotiate with the French in July 1960. Hardliners generally emerged to control the provisional government, notably Houari Boumedienne, who was to overthrow independent Algeria's first president, Ahmed Ben Bella, in 1965.

The FLN was strongest in Algiers itself and in the mountainous Berber areas of the Aurès and Kabylia. Initially, the FLN's bomb attacks, based on as few as 400 activists, were poorly co-ordinated and the movement easily broken up, leading to the dispersal of its leadership. Its campaign was only revived by the independence of Morocco and, especially, Tunisia in 1956, since it finally gave the FLN safe havens across international frontiers. The government of Pierre Mendès-France had conceded autonomy to Tunisia after limited military action in July 1954, the Mollet government then granting full independence in March 1956 when faced with the need to call out the reserves to sustain the campaign in Algeria. At the same time, Mollet also extracted France from its protectorate over Morocco, where there had also been limited fighting.

A new more militant FLN leadership, in which Abane was prominent, opened a campaign of urban terrorism in Algiers, operating from the rabbit warren of streets in the Casbah quarter. With its defeat in the 'Battle of Algiers' between January and September 1957, however, the FLN found it increasingly difficult to supply its forces inside Algeria, with an estimated 20,000 men of the ALN confined to Tunisia. Attention then switched to the FLN strongholds in the mountains, with the insurgents driven from the Kabylia by the end of 1959 and active only in the Aurès. At its height, FLN strength inside Algeria was perhaps 8,000 activists and 21,000 active supporters.

In considering the French response, it is important initially to note the influence of the *colons* on policy. They had bitterly opposed the limited Muslim representation in the Assembly, and even the radically minded Governor-General, Jacques Soustelle, changed his mind with regard to attempted political reforms following a massacre of Europeans and moderate Muslims by the FLN at Philippeville and Constantine on 20 August 1955 to mark its announcement of a 'people's revolt'. The socialist government of Guy Mollet similarly dropped more planned reforms in February 1956 in the face of settler demonstrations in Algiers, while extremists attempted the assassination of the new French commander-in-chief, Raoul Salan, in December 1956 in the belief that it would provoke a political crisis in France itself. *Colon* elements attempted a general strike in January 1958 to protest against a plan to develop cantonal autonomy, and a mob seized control of the main government buildings in Algiers on 13 May 1958 and, through a so-called Committee of Public Safety headed by Massu, demanded the establishment of a government of public safety in France, although Massu insisted he had become involved to avoid bloodshed. Amid speculation that the army would march on Paris and an actual military coup on Corsica by Massu's paratroopers, Charles de Gaulle was asked to form a government on 1 June 1958, bringing to an end the Fourth Republic. Salan, who had been intimately involved in the events in Algiers and Paris but was not a Gaullist, was eased out of the Algeria command in December 1958 and replaced by an air force officer, Maurice Challe.

Clearly, army and *colons* expected de Gaulle to stand by the concept of a French Algeria, and de Gaulle did nothing to contradict this when visiting

Algiers on 4 June 1958, during which he uttered the *colon* slogan, 'Vive l'Algérie Française!'. De Gaulle, however, did not have quite the same attachment to the French empire as some other soldiers, never having served in the colonies. Moreover, De Gaulle disliked the *colons*, who had largely backed the Vichy government during the war. De Gaulle was also more concerned with France's international status than with retaining empire if its continued possession weakened the state, although he undoubtedly believed initially that Algeria could be retained in some kind of quasi-colonial relationship with France and that moderate Muslim opinion could be mobilised to enable him to negotiate with some group other than the FLN. However, de Gaulle's growing ambivalence towards Algeria became apparent when he offered self-determination in September 1959, resulting in another attempted general strike in Algiers in January 1960 marked by the emergence of a new political expression of *colon* anger, the Front National Française (French National Front, FNF). In the event *colon* resolve wavered during 'Barricades Week' as the army seemed uncertain of its response. In November 1960, de Gaulle announced a national referendum on self-determination to embrace voters in both France and Algeria, which, while recording an overwhelming no vote among *colons* in January 1961, saw a massive vote for self-determination by French voters.

From the beginning, the French enjoyed military success, forcing the FLN on to the defensive in 1954–56, hence the FLN opting for an urban terror campaign in Algiers. This brought a swift French response, the 10th Colonial Parachute Division, commanded by Massu and fresh from participation in the Suez operation, itself partly a response to the French belief that Nasser's Egypt was the main backer of the FLN, being committed to the city on 7 January 1957. Marcel Bigeard's 3rd Colonial Parachute Regiment was sent to the Casbah to undertake a *nettoyage* (cleansing) operation. Massu immediately broke an eight-day general strike called by the FLN by forcing Muslims to go to work and breaking shops open. Total military control was imposed with constant patrolling, house to house searches and checkpoints. Using the Special Powers Law of March 1956, which set aside normal legal limitations on detention, Massu seized the police files and instituted large-scale arrests, which enabled Godard to build up a detailed intelligence picture of the FLN's order of battle in the so-called *organigramme*. Informers known as *bleus* (blues) also assisted in the process, while Trinquier's Dispositif de Protection Urbaine (Urban Security Service, DPU), divided the city into sectors, sub-sectors, blocks and buildings, with each allotted a senior inhabitant – often a Muslim ex-servicemen – to report on suspicious behaviour. A similar system of collective responsibility also pertained in rural areas. A careful census and the issue of identity cards further exerted French control in the city, and, by September 1957, the FLN had been broken in Algiers. Its leader there, Ben M'hidi, had been picked up as early as February; its leader in the Casbah, Yacef Saadi, was taken on 24 September; and its most significant terrorist, Ali la Pointe, was killed on 8 October 1957.

In rural areas, too, the French enjoyed considerable military success, despite the sheer size of Algeria, five times that of France itself. The whole of the Tunisian frontier was closed off by the physical barrier of the Morice line by September 1957, an eight-foot, 5,000-volt electrified fence backed with minefields and constantly patrolled. By April 1958, the kill ratio of those trying to infiltrate into Algeria from Tunisia was reportedly 85 per cent, after which few attempts were made to do so. This was also the case with the similar Pedron line along the Moroccan frontier. The cost in manpower was significant, however, 40,000 French troops being deployed on the Morice line.

The insurgents inside Algeria were then further isolated by large-scale *regroupement* (resettlement), involving possibly over three million people being moved into 1,840 *auto-défense* (self-defence) villages by 1960. However, too many were poorly prepared and lacked the means to become self-sufficient. At the same time, the establishment of so-called forbidden zones created an internal refugee problem, causing acute housing shortages in areas such as Algiers, Oran and Constantine. Accordingly, it was unlikely that the French would win the unqualified adherence of the Muslim population, and they consistently underestimated the nationalist appeal of the FLN.

Resettlement was allied to food control and to a psychological campaign from September 1955 onwards by the Sections Administratives Spécialisées (Special Administrative Sections, SAS) and the Sections Administratives Urbaines (Urban Administrative Sections, SAU) of the Section d'Action Psychologique (Psychological Action and Information Service), better known as the Cinquième Bureau (Fifth Bureau), headed by Lacheroy. The 660 SAS and SAU teams existing by 1959, each consisting usually of four men and each protected by 30–50 Muslim *makhzan* (guards), aimed to persuade Muslims that French administration was the more attractive long-term proposition. They were also responsible for preparing French troops for the psychological challenges of fighting insurgents. Eventually, 5,000 personnel were running over 800 rural development projects. They were spread thinly, however, with the 73 SAS teams deployed in the Kabylia covering 4,000 square kilometres and 900,000 people.

Appropriate military tactics were also employed, particularly against the FLN mountain strongholds by Challe in 1959–60, based on a refined version of traditional *quadrillage*, revived by André Beaufre in 1955, with a chequerboard of French outposts backed by mobile operations in the form of large-scale sweeps or *ratissage*. Three differing kinds of zone were identified within the *quadrillage* system: *zones interdits* (forbidden zones), which equated to free-fire zones; *zones de pacification* (pacification zones), where strict controls were applied to the rural population; and *zones d'opérations* (operational zones), equating to urban centres, liable to cordon and search operations. The mobile operations often involved French-led Muslim units or *harkis* to locate insurgents for elimination by the so-called *commandos de chasse*, groups of 60 to 80 men intended to operate in the same environment as the ALN. Some 300,000 men were deployed to the outposts, while there were 60,000 *harkis* and a further 30,000 elite French troops drawn from the Foreign Legion or the troops of *La Coloniale* used in the elite active units of the *Reserve Générale* (General Reserve). While much of the publicity went to the paratroops, they comprised no more than 5 per cent of the army in Algeria. The mobility of Challe's forces was also assisted by the arrival of new, larger Boeing Vertol H-21 helicopters, known to the troops as *bananes* (bananas), while the French air force deployed a wide range of attack aircraft to which the FLN had no answer since they possessed no anti-aircraft guns or missiles.

Other locally raised units included 'Force K', led by the FLN dissident Belhadj Djillali (aka Kobus), and the Armée Nationale Populaire Algérien (National Army of the Algerian People), led by Mohammed Bellounis. In the event, however, Benhadj was murdered by some of his own men in April 1958 and the group had to be broken up, while Bellounis had to be eliminated by the French themselves in July 1957. In all, at least a quarter of the 250,000 men the French deployed in Algeria by 1956 were Muslim. Assisted by 600 helicopters, the French had arguably all but won the war in military terms by the end of 1959.

While *guerre révolutionnaire* had its military successes, however, it did not bring equal political success. Thus, while Massu destroyed the FLN in Algiers, the sheer brutality of the French paratroops brought down international opprobrium on France. At least 3,000 Muslims from 24,000 arrested during the 'Battle of Algiers', including Ben M'hidi, disappeared while in detention. Moreover, the intelligence required to win the battle was gained primarily by systematic torture, euphemistically referred to as 'special measures', involving electric shocks to the nipples and genitals, the crushing of limbs and organs in vices and pumping air or liquid into bodies. The existence of at least ten internment camps, intended to assist in the reindoctrination of suspects, with a permanent population of at least 8,000 detainees, also attracted orchestrated international criticism, although the International Red Cross pronounced conditions largely humane in the autumn of 1959. Further damage was also done by the French forcing down inside Algeria a Moroccan aircraft carrying FLN leaders including Ben Bella in October 1956, and by the bombing of the Tunisian village of Sidi Sakiet Youssef in February 1958 as a warning to the Tunisian government in retaliation for FLN raids into Algeria: over 60 Tunisian civilians died. The FLN was especially successful in internationalising the war, gaining recognition from the Non-aligned Movement in 1955 and from the UN in 1960. In the United States, the Eisenhower administration wanted the conflict resolved before it weakened NATO, while John F. Kennedy was particularly sympathetic to the FLN as a senator and spoke of the need for French withdrawal during the 1960 presidential election.

In France itself, the reports of torture resulted in considerable intellectual, press and church protest and swung public opinion towards acceptance of

Algerian independence. In Algeria, it robbed the French of any real hopes of mobilising moderate Muslim support, especially after the leader of the UDMA, Ferhat Abbas, threw in his lot with the FLN in April 1956. The SAS and SAU undoubtedly did much for the Muslim population under their control through civic action projects, for example handling an estimated 940,000 medical visits every month. Yet they were still representatives of an imposed alien culture, and the tendency was to equate acquiescence with acceptance of French values. Moreover, resettlement broke traditional links with the land, and many sought refuge in Morocco. Furthermore, in some cases, those winning hearts and minds in the countryside were the same individuals torturing in the cities. The army was supposedly restoring order so as to create a situation in which long-term reform could be implemented, but, in reality, it had become, in the words of Martin Thomas, a case of pursuing order 'as a means to impose reform', separating the army further and further from the Muslim population in whose interests reform was supposedly to be effected. Above all, the necessarily political aspects of civic action drew the army increasingly into the political arena. Significantly, the Fifth Bureau was disbanded in February 1960. Not surprisingly, many former Fifth Bureau officers were to be prominent in the growing army opposition to de Gaulle.

Divisions between younger and older officers, as well as the suspicions of politicians entertained by many soldiers, had resulted in the issue of orders in 1957 that officers must explain the political background to the war to all ranks. Many French officers disliked the *colons* as unduly privileged, but paratroopers and others serving in Algiers in 1957 increasingly discovered that the majority of *colons* were working class like themselves. Thus, an identity of interest began to be established, especially as younger *colons* opted to join the elite units for their national service. This widened the gap between the regular and overseas army on the one hand and metropolitan French conscripts on the other. Unlike Indo-China, where there had been a French army but not one composed of Frenchmen, in Algeria there was clearly both a French army and an army of Frenchmen. Conscripts were first sent to Algeria in February 1955, some reservists were recalled in August 1955 and all reservists in April 1956, with the basic term of military service extended from 18 to 27 months. Fewer and fewer metropolitan conscripts were willing to serve in Algeria, however, and, if they did, they were primarily concerned to return home safe.

Conscripts appear to have received only a rudimentary training in counter-insurgency techniques before despatch to Algeria, and, overwhelmingly, they made up the 90 per cent of French troops undertaking static guard duties in the *quadrillage* system. By contrast, the paratroops formed almost a separate sect within the army, distinguished by *esprit para* (para spirit) and by the distinctive 'leopard' print battledress and the 'lizard' cap, also known after its designer as the *casquette de Bigeard*. The model for the character 'Colonel Raspegny' in two novels by Jean Lartéguy, *The Centurions* and *The Praetorians* and one of the models for 'Colonel Mathieu' in Pontecorvo's celebrated film *The Battle of Algiers* (1966), Bigeard summed up the para spirit, being famous for arriving to visit units by parachute, his hand to the salute as he landed. The elite units and their officers found the conscripts less willing to follow them in any precipitate political action. In threatening to march on Paris in 1958 to subordinate the government to military requirements, the army's more radical leaders simply assumed that conscripts would obey them. It should have become clear during Barricades Week in January 1960 that neither conscripts nor the metropolitan army supported the *colon* cause in the way those like Massu did. In fact, Massu's dismissal from his command precipitated the crisis in Algiers in January 1960.

It was an attempted military coup against de Gaulle in Algiers in April 1961 that fully exposed the politicisation of the army and its divisions. Four generals – the arch-imperialist Salan; the Alsatian-born André Zeller; the Algerian-born *colon* Edmond Jouhard; and Challe, who was motivated by his concern that France should not abandon its Muslim troops as it had its Indo-Chinese troops – arrived in Algiers without any particularly precise plans as to what they wished to achieve. They assumed that the army in Algeria would follow them, but in the event, only 14,000 did so on 21/22 April, principally the First Parachute Regiment of the Foreign Legion. De Gaulle then broadcast directly to the conscripts over the heads of his officers on television on the following day, while, in what became known as the war of the transistors, his prime minister did so on the radio, urging them not to support the coup. The whole affair collapsed on 25 April with Zeller and Challe surrendering and over 200 officers being arrested.

Meanwhile, Salan and Jouhard went into hiding to lead a new underground Organisation d'Armée Secrète (Secret Army Organisation, OAS), modelled partly on the FLN and partly on the DPUs. The OAS launched a terror campaign against Muslims in Algeria in the hope of provoking a violent reaction that would force the army to reassert French control. The campaign, in which Godard, Lacheroy and Massu's former chief of staff, Antoine Argoud, were heavily involved, then spread to France itself, trying to assassinate de Gaulle, notably in September 1961. The death of a number of French conscripts in OAS bomb attacks in March 1962, however, lost it the support of even those officers who regarded an independent Algeria as a sell out, and Salan was arrested shortly afterwards.

De Gaulle had begun negotiations with the FLN in April 1961 and reached agreement in March 1962. By then, there was open fighting between *colons* and troops in Algiers amid increasing violence, the majority of *colons* choosing to leave Algeria in June 1962, abandoning or burning businesses and possessions since they were permitted only two suitcases per person. Formal independence came on 3 July 1962, the war having cost France 17,456 military dead, with a further 3,663 Europeans and 30,034 indigenous inhabitants killed by the FLN to April 1961. The French estimated that the FLN had lost at least 158,000, while Algerians themselves have variously claimed between 300,000 and a million dead. In the aftermath, too, anything between 30,000 and 150,000 former *harkis* were slaughtered by the victors.

While guerrillas in Cyprus, Aden and Algeria had some success operating in urban areas in the mid-1950s to mid-1960s, the pattern of insurgency in Latin America had remained essentially rural. Just as Mao's success in China had inspired emulation in South-east Asia and Africa, so it was that of Castro on Cuba which inspired its own distinct theory of rural revolutionary warfare in the form of *foco*.

Fulgencio Batista y Zaldivar, a former sergeant in the Cuban army, had helped to overthrow Cuba's government in 1933 and had been implicated in the overthrow of two more administrations before becoming president himself between 1940 and 1944. Batista had stepped down but then again seized power in a bloodless coup in 1952, his regime becoming increasingly tainted by corruption: he was said to make $1.2 million a month from protection rackets alone. Having become involved in student politics, the young Castro participated in an unsuccessful attempt to assassinate the dictator of the Dominican Republic, Rafael Leonidas Trujillo, in 1947. He was intending to run for the Cuban Congress when Batista returned to power in 1952 but turned instead to attempts to overthrow Batista. Castro's first attempt, by leading an attack on the Moncada army barracks in Santiago de Cuba on 26 July 1953, failed. Castro was imprisoned, but he was released in an amnesty in May 1955. Moving to Mexico, he founded the 26 July Movement to continue opposition to Batista. Castro intended to land back on Cuba on 25 November 1956 with 81 followers, including his brother Raúl and Che Guevera, to coincide with an urban uprising by the 26 July Movement. For varying reasons, including bad weather, the landing from the motor yacht known as the *Gramna*, at Playa de los Colorados near Belic in the Oriente province rather than at Santiago de Cuba as intended, was delayed until 2 December 1956, by which time the urban uprising had already been suppressed. Three days later, Batista's troops decisively routed Castro's band, of whom less than two dozen, including Castro and Guevara, escaped into the Sierra Maestra mountains.

Despite this unpromising situation, Castro resolved to fight on, and his small band was reinforced and supplied by the surviving underground organisation of the 26 July Movement. The urban movement may have tied down half the Cuban army, even if individual actions such as a rising at the Cienfuegos naval base in September 1957 and the general strike in Havana in April 1958 were failures. Batista had alienated most sectors of Cuban society, in which there were great extremes of poverty and wealth, although, overall, the standard of living was higher than in most of Latin America. The economy was stagnant, however, and much of the employment seasonal. Batista's poor record on human rights also resulted in the withdrawal of US aid in 1958 despite the considerable US investment on the island. Batista's army was also poorly trained and poorly motivated, its officer corps having become highly politicised with promotions made on the basis of political reliability rather than military competence. Its unenthusiastic troops often fled rather than fight, although, as Robert Taber observed, the deployment of 5,000 men at one point to cover an area of 1,500 square miles of heavily forested terrain defied 'simple arithmetic'. Indeed, the army had all but abandoned the Sierra Maestra to Castro in August 1957 and then failed to reassert control over the mountains in May 1958 despite deploying over 11,000 men against Castro's 300 guerrillas, a total perhaps boosted to about 1,500 only in the last five months of the insurgency. One calculation is that only about 200 government troops were killed between December 1956 and January 1959, suggesting their lack of commitment to Batista. Significantly, Guevara was to describe an action at Ubero, involving only 133 men in total and resulting in all in 38 deaths as 'one of the bloodiest of the revolutionary war'. Invariably, captured soldiers were simply released by Castro's men, whereas the army's excesses alienated the population even more from the government, although Colonel Barrera Perez at least grasped the need for civic action and planned a programme in 1957, which included opening a free kitchen to serve 300 people a day. However, Perez fell foul of the chief of staff, General Tabernilla, and soon was replaced by the notoriously brutal Major Casillas. Seizing the initiative, Castro went on to the offensive himself in August 1958, and Batista's administration quickly collapsed. Batista fled to the Dominican Republic on 1 January 1959, and Castro entered Havana on 8 January.

It was a remarkable victory, but those who attempted to emulate Castro tended to ignore the special circumstances in which he had succeeded, not least Che Guevara and his collaborator, Régis Debray, who constructed *foco* in the belief that revolution on the Cuban model could be reproduced as a matter of course throughout Latin America, if not the third world as a whole.

Guevara, of course, has become a revolutionary icon of the twentieth century despite his revolutionary career being a failure and *foco* being entirely discredited when he was killed in Bolivia in October 1967.

Born in Argentina in 1928, and beginning training as a doctor at the University of Buenos Aires in 1947, Ernesto Guevara spent his vacations working as a male nurse on merchant ships and, in 1950, unsuccessfully tried his hand at marketing an insecticide. In 1954, Guevara was in Guatemala at the time the CIA engineered the overthrow of the left-wing government of Jacobo Arbenz Guzmán. The American involvement appears to have confirmed Guevara's revolutionary instincts and, moving to Mexico, he came into contact with Castro. At this time, he gained the nickname 'Ché' (Spanish for 'Buddy' or 'Chum') from the frequency with which he used the phrase in conversation. He legally adopted 'Che' (without an accent) as an additional Christian name in 1959. Joining Castro's band and surviving the initial contact with Batista's army, Guevara led one of the guerrilla columns in Castro's final advance on Havana and entered the capital six days before

Castro himself. Guevara became minister of industry and remained in the Cuban government until 1965. His principal work of military theory, the largely tactical *Guerrilla Warfare*, appeared in 1960, with subsequent brief amplification of his ideas appearing in an essay, 'Guerrilla Warfare: A Method' in 1963 and a call to arms, 'Message to the Tricontinental'. The latter was a conference of Latin American, African and Asian communist parties convened in Havana in January 1966, which largely turned its face against Cuban attempts to renew guerrilla struggle. Guevara's missive to the conference was published in English in April 1967.

Debray was a French Marxist philosopher who visited Cuba in 1961 and became professor of the history of philosophy at the University of Havana in 1966. He accompanied Guevara's group to Bolivia as a journalist. Captured in April 1967, Debray was sentenced to 30 years imprisonment but was released after three years and returned to France. His theoretical publications, *Revolution in the Revolution* (1967), *Strategy for Revolution* (1973) and *The Revolution on Trial* (1978), as well as his account of Bolivia, *Ché's Guerrilla War* (1975), suggested that he had learned little from the abject failure of *foco*. Debray re-emerged in France as a somewhat unlikely foreign policy adviser to President François Mitterand between 1981 and 1986. Subsequently, he returned to the study of philosophy, expounding a new theory he called 'mediology'.

In contrast to the classic rural guerrilla warfare theory of Mao Tse-tung, who stressed the importance of parallel but separate military and political organisation, Guevara and Debray argued that the guerrillas themselves could be a revolutionary fusion of political and military authority, with the guerrillas acting as a revolutionary 'vanguard' party in embryo. Indeed, they believed that an urban-based leadership would lead only to divisions between it and the guerrillas in the field, since, to quote Debray, 'the two worlds do not breathe the same air'. Instead of a prolonged period of careful political preparation of a population as advocated by Mao, they also assumed that a minimum level of discontent with a government would be sufficient to create objective conditions favourable to revolution. By military action alone, a small group of dedicated revolutionaries would provide the *foco* (focus) for revolution. The decisive action of the guerrillas as 'vanguard of the people' would in itself expose the corrupt and brutal nature of the authorities, who would be forced into over-reaction against the population when it proved impossible to eliminate the highly mobile guerrillas. The *foco* would thus be a catalyst for a wider popular insurrection or, to use Guevara's own words, the 'small motor of revolutionary dissolution'.

Guevara did recognise that guerrilla warfare was merely a first phase of revolution and, ultimately, a 'popular army' would be required to complete the process. There was an assumption, however, that the creation of such a popular army would be almost a matter of course, since peasants and workers would be bound to support the guerrillas. Indeed, Guevara and Debray made a virtue out of keeping the *foco* distinct from the population, although appropriate 'civil organisations' would be created to administer liberated zones and to handle the dissemination of propaganda.

The problem with the theory, however, was that it failed to take into account that Batista's regime had been corrupt, inefficient and unpopular, his army ineffective and that Batista had also lost the support of the United States. Guevara and Debray also ignored the considerable assistance that Castro's guerrillas had received from the urban-based 26 July Movement, without which Castro could not have survived. They believed that urban operations could support those in the countryside, but that the revolution would be essentially a rural one.

Since the special circumstances of Cuba did not exist automatically elsewhere, those *focos* attempted in the 1960s in Argentina, Brazil, Bolivia, Colombia, the Dominican Republic, Ecuador, Guatemala, Paraguay, Peru and Venezuela all failed. In the case of Colombia, there had been a period of civil war between liberal and conservative factions between 1948 and 1957 known as *La Violencia* (The Violence), during which communists had established so-called independent republics in some rural areas, providing a nucleus for future insurgency. At least eleven different communist insurgent groups were active in 1962 with a combined strength of perhaps 2,000 men at most. The pro-Cuban Ejército de Liberación Nacional (National Liberation Army, ELN) emerged in January 1965 under the leadership of Fabio Vásquez Castaño at a time when the Colombian army's Plan Lazo was already making serious inroads into insurgency, combining civic action, such as road building and provision of health centres, and military operations by *grupos móviles de inteligencia* (mobile intelligence groups) and platoon-sized hunter-killer teams known as *comando localizador* (unconventional warfare shock groups). Technically, ELN, which at least attempted to establish some kind of urban support along the lines of Castro's 26 July Movement, was one of 30 different guerrilla bands, mustering a combined strength of only 800 men at most, which had merged in the Fuerzas Armadas Revolucionarias de Colombia (Colombian Revolutionary Armed Forces, FARC) under the overall leadership of Manuel Marulanda Vélez (aka 'Tiro Fijo', or 'Sure Shot'). It is conceivable that FARC was actually intended as a counterweight to ELN. By 1966, however, the Colombian army had effectively brought the insurgency under control, although it was to be revived by a new generation of revolutionaries in the mid-1970s.

In Guatemala, the *foco* originated among dissident army officers who had failed to overthrow the government of General Ydígoras Fuentes on 13 November 1960. Fleeing to the mountains, the survivors formed what came to be known as Movimiento Revolucionario 13 de Noviembre (13 November Revolutionary Movement), or MR-13, under the leadership of Marco Antonio Yon Sosa and Luís Augusto Turcios Lima. Even when MR-13 joined communists and other dissidents to form Fuerzas Armadas

Rebeldes (Rebel Armed Forces, FAR) in December 1962, they were unsuccessful. Partly, this was a result of continuing fragmentation within the movement. Turcios Lima, who was killed in a car crash in October 1966, differed from Yon Sosa on the political strategy to pursue and, in 1968, FAR split entirely from the Guatemalan Communist Party. Partly, it was also through operating in the Guatemalan lowlands, where they enjoyed little support, since the most disaffected group within the population – indigenous Mayan Indians – lived mostly in the mountains. With US assistance, the Guatemalan army was also able to mount a creditable civic action programme, Colonel Carlos Araña Osorio in particular launching a model scheme – Plan Piloto – in Zacapa province, in which the army built schools, hospitals and roads. Araña was also linked with right-wing death squads, however, and it is possible that as many as 10,000 people died at the hands of the security forces in 1967–68. New insurgent groups that emerged in the 1970s, notably Ricardo Ramirez de Leon's Guerrilla Army of the Poor, therefore rejected *foco* and made sure that they operated in the mountains and that they cultivated the support of the Maya. Ultimately, the Guatemalan army struck at the guerrillas, achieving a series of successes in 1980–81 and forcing the insurgent groups to unite in the Guatemalan National Revolutionary Unity (URNG). Ramirez (aka Commandante Moran), who had assumed overall leadership of the insurgents, came to realise that negotiations were necessary and the UN brokered a deal by which the conflict was declared at an end in December 1996 after 36 years of intermittent insurgency and perhaps at a cost of 100,000 lives.

In Ecuador, a *foco* of students lasted just two days in March 1962, and in Argentina the Ejército Guerrillero del Pueblo (EGP) was destroyed in 1963–64 before it could even go into action. In Peru, Luís de la Puente Uceda's Movimiento de Izquierda Revolucionaria (Movement of the Revolutionary Left, MIR) lasted less than a month once the Peruvian army reached the area of its activity on the Mesa Pelada plateau in August 1965, de la Puente being killed. Other groups in Peru lasted scarcely longer, all being destroyed within six months.

A significant factor in the failure of the *focos* was that Castro's conversion to communism had brought renewed United States involvement. The Eisenhower administration had already responded to the Cold War in 1954 by adopting what later came to be called, in 1957, the Overseas Internal Security Program (OISP) to offer assistance to governments at risk from communism. As already indicated, the CIA had also been involved in the overthrow of Arbenz in Guatemala. The Kennedy administration's response to the Soviet Union's declared support for 'wars of national liberation' was to extend even more considerable military and economic support to governments in 'its own backyard' in Latin America thought to be at particular risk. The 'Alliance for Progress' announced in January 1961 extended $20 billion worth of aid for social and economic programmes over a ten-year period, often dispensed through the US Agency for International Development (USAID). Military training was also provided under the Mutual Security Act of 1959, Congress authorising provision of assistance for civic action programmes in September 1961. Apart from the failed attempt to topple Castro in the 'Bay of Pigs' affair in April 1961 and the successful US intervention in the Dominican Republic in April 1965, 22,000 Latin American army and police officers were trained in Panama between 1962 and 1970. In 1966, 1,323 military personnel were trained in the United States. Many thousands more were given American instruction in their own countries, amounting to at least 100,000 policemen in the case of Brazil.

In the case of Colombia, a CIA survey team including two veterans of the campaign against the Huks, Charles Bohannan and Magsaysay's former aide Napoleon Valeriano, had already advised the government on internal security in 1959–60. Some $1.5 million worth of military equipment was supplied in 1961–62, and a US army special warfare team under Brigadier-General William Yarborough also arrived in February 1962, assisting the Colombian army to draw up Plan Lazo. An estimated 1,000 US Green Berets served in Guatemala between 1966 and 1968, suffering 28 dead, while the 8th Special Forces Group based at Fort Gulick in Panama undertook over 400 separate missions in Latin America between 1962 and 1968, 52 of them in 1965 alone.

The greatest failure of all, however, was that of Guevara himself in Bolivia. Having travelled to Zaire and possibly North Vietnam after leaving the Cuban government, Guevara arrived in Bolivia in disguise in November 1966 to prove that his theory could succeed, the intention being a wider continental strategy of *foquismo* embracing Argentina, Brazil and Peru as well as Bolivia. It was a poor choice. Bolivia had enjoyed a measure of land reform in the 1950s and a nationalisation of the tin mines sufficient to deprive any *foco* of even that minimal level of discontent required by Guevara and Debray. Moreover, the Bolivian president, René Barrientos, was himself of peasant origin and fluent in the Quechua language of the Andean Indians. The Bolivian communist party of Mario Monje did not find Guevara's emphasis upon military control of the revolution congenial and did not believe that the 'same concrete historical conditions' that had pertained in Cuba could be expected in Bolivia. Consequently, it gave him no support. Generally, indeed, the ideological divide in Latin America between pro-Moscow and pro-Peking communist factions was unhelpful to the insurgents.

Since it was to be a rural campaign, Guevara ignored the radical tin-mining community. The local Indians of the remote Ñancahuazú region, in which he chose to begin his campaign, also regarded his small band of assorted followers – Cubans, Peruvians, a few Bolivians and one East German woman – as aliens, especially as none of them spoke either the Quechua or Aymara language. In fact, it could be argued that the Bolivian army was more of a 'people's army' than the *foco*. Unlike the Sierra Maestra, which provided cover but was not too difficult for movement, the jungle terrain was not conducive to mobility and Guevara's group spent much of its time lost in the jungle. Indeed, it was not really until 23 March 1967 that the Bolivian authorities were able to confirm a guerrilla presence, and this prompted an immediate request for assistance to the United States. A small US Special Forces Mobile Training Team of fifteen Green Berets under Major Robert 'Pappy' Shelton began training a new ranger battalion for the Bolivian army in June 1967, which was deployed by September. Guevara's band was broken up and, on 8 October 1967, Guevara's remaining group of seventeen guerrillas was surrounded at the village of La Higuera. Wounded and captured, Guevara was executed and his body displayed publicly in the nearby town of Vallegrande. It was once thought that the body had been thrown from a helicopter into the jungle, but in July 1997 it was identified in a grave underneath an airstrip in Vallegrande and taken to Cuba for reburial.

With the final failure of *foco*, a new generation of Latin American revolutionaries shifted the emphasis from the countryside to the towns in recognition that rural insurgency was inappropriate when the bulk of the population was increasingly urbanised. The Venezuelan guerrilla leader Moisés Moleiro remarked that a peasant revolt was no longer possible when society was no longer peasant-based. By 1967, at last 50 per cent of the population of every state in Latin America with the exception of Peru was urbanised. In some states, like Argentina and Uruguay, more than 70 per cent of the population lived in urban areas, with 40 and 46 per cent in their capital cities of Buenos Aires and Montevideo, respectively, alone. Indeed, with high unemployment, high inflation and the concentration of a large proportion of a relatively youthful population in urban slums and shanties, the widespread sense of urban deprivation appeared ripe for exploitation.

Youth itself was becoming more politicised and radicalised in the Western world through disillusionment with US involvement in Vietnam, the spread of a drugs culture and the rise of the so-called New Left and, in the United States, the phenomenon of Black Power. Indeed, of 150 urban guerrillas apprehended in Brazil in 1969, 38 per cent were students; students also accounted for 50 per cent of those arrested in 1970. Other alternatives to violence also appeared unlikely to succeed in view of US intervention in the Dominican Republic in 1965 and, subsequently, the American involvement in the overthrow of Salvador Allende's extremist left-wing government in Chile in September 1973. The kind of idealised, ennobling and morally cleansing form of revolutionary violence preached by popular radical philosophers like the Frenchman Herbert Marcuse and the Martinique-born Algerian Franz Fanon in *The Wretched of the Earth* (1963) also contributed greatly to the blinkered psyche of many emerging urban guerrillas and terrorists.

The theory of urban guerrilla warfare itself found its most developed expression in the writings of the Brazilian Carlos Marighela, whose *Minimanual*, also known as the *Handbook of Urban Guerrilla Warfare*, was published in June 1969, the year of his death in a gun battle with police. A communist activist for over 40 years, Marighela had risen to lead the party's committee in the major city of São Paulo. In December 1966, however, Marighela resigned from the party's executive committee and in July 1967 he attended a conference of the Cuban-sponsored Organisation for Latin American Solidarity (OLAS) in Havana against the wishes of the party leadership. It was now his belief that the kind of armed revolutionary activism being called for by Castro and Guevara offered better possibilities for overthrowing Brazil's military government than the party's existing electoral strategy. Joining with another disaffected communist, Mario Alves, who founded the Partido Communista Brasileiro Revolucionario (Revolutionary Brazilian Communist Party, PCBR), Marighela organised Acçâo Libertadora Nacional (Action for National Liberation, ALN) in February 1968.

While favouring armed struggle, Marighela was well aware of the difficulties of Guevara's *foco* theory of rural guerrilla warfare, that attempted in Brazil in March 1967 by the Movimento Nacionalista Revolucionario (National Revolutionary Movement, MNR), being an abject failure. Like Guevara, he rejected Mao Tse-tung's emphasis upon the need for a lengthy period of political preparation of a population for revolution. He also followed Guevara in envisaging his activists as a small elite group of dedicated and self-sacrificing revolutionaries, whose cellular organisation would assist security. Their attributes according to *Minimanual* would be absurdly multi-faceted to an extent that recalled comic book super-heroes, although apparently about the only thing they were not required to do was to wear their underpants outside their trousers. Their 'armed propaganda' – a phrase also used by Debray – would establish a revolutionary situation by undermining the government and security forces and alienating the population from the authorities by forcing government over-reaction. Unlike Guevara, however, the arena for Marighela's campaign would be the city and not the countryside. Rural action was not ruled out by Marighela and, indeed, he regarded the city as a tactical arena and the countryside as a strategic arena with revolutionary success likely to result from a combination of both urban and rural action, since, ultimately, the rural peasantry must be brought into the struggle. However, the urban campaign was the necessary starting point for subsequent extension of the revolutionary struggle to the countryside, where the critical confrontation between the authorities and the 'people's army' would ultimately take place.

The city offered soft targets and safe havens among a teeming population already likely to be politicised by social and economic deprivation. Moreover, action in cities such as Rio de Janeiro, São Paulo and Belo Horizonte guaranteed an immediate and disproportionate reaction to the actual scale of activity through the attention of the media. This represented the single most vital component for the successful promotion of the insurgent cause. Thus, actions would be designed to be spectacular and targeted not just at the Brazilian authorities but also at foreign multi-national companies in the further expectation of weakening the economy by driving out foreign (principally American) capital. In emphasising American capital, *Minimanual* and his other writings revealed Marighela's pathological hatred of the United States. The principal techniques would be the use of urban terror such as letter and parcel bombs and assassination, politically motivated kidnapping, manipulation of riots and strikes, and so on. To give one example, in September 1969 ALN kidnapped the US ambassador, Burke Elbrick, demanding the release of fifteen captured guerrillas. Bank raids were potentially problematic, however, since a careful distinction had to be made between those of the urban guerrilla and those that might be carried out by 'bandits and right-wing counter-revolutionaries'.

The expectation was that the authorities would find it difficult to combat such action while walking the thin line between craven capitulation to insurgent demands and over-reaction and repression. To quote Marighela:

> [it would be] necessary to turn political crises into armed conflicts by performing violent actions that will force those in power to transform the political situation of the country into a military situation. That will alienate the masses who, from then on, will revolt against the army and the police and thus blame them for this state of things.

In the event, Latin American authorities opted for the latter and resorted to institutionalised counter-terror without restraint. Indeed, where the security forces were unleashed without restraint, the city became, as Castro had predicted, a graveyard of the revolutionary, for the security forces were better able to exploit the more sophisticated transport systems available in urban areas and invariably had the monopoly of firepower over the insurgents. The latter were often reduced to indiscriminate bombing campaigns, which robbed the insurgents of any legitimacy among the urban population. The result was that a degree of popular welcome was afforded at least to the initial stages of the counter-terrorist policies introduced by governments. Democracy was generally sacrificed, but the guerrillas did not benefit from its disappearance. In the case of ALN, Marighela was killed in São Paulo on 4 November 1969 amid the intense police activity following Elbrick's kidnapping. Alves was arrested in January 1970 and died under torture, with the last significant figure in ALN, Carlos Lamarca, being killed in September 1971.

Numerous other urban guerrilla groups that emerged, such as the Montoneros and Ejército Revolucionario del Pueblo (ERP) in Argentina and the Tupamaros in Uruguay, suffered the same fate as ALN. In fact, the example of Venezuela between 1963 and 1965 should already have made the dangers apparent to the urban guerrilla theorists. FALN miscalculated by overstepping the line between public sympathy and public opposition in attacking innocent civilians. FALN originated in February 1963 from a fusion of dissident military officers and an earlier revolutionary group, Movimiento de Izquierda Revolucionaria (Movement of the Revolutionary Left, MIR). Led by Moleiro and formed in May 1960, MIR had failed in its attempt to emulate Castro by creating a rural *foco* group along the lines recommended by Guevara and was crushed in November and December 1960. As a result, FALN turned to urban guerrilla warfare in the capital, Caracas, where 70 per cent of the population lived. FALN's most prominent leader, Douglas Bravo, identified the city as offering insurgents 'its greatest potential in political and organisational resources, fighting traditions, mass influence, etc.', although he also recognised that it offered political, military and economic strengths to the security forces.

President Rómulo Betancourt proved equal to the challenge by keeping his armed forces in check and demonstrating an exaggerated respect for normal legal processes. Thus, he could preserve democracy and resist the attempts by FALN to provoke an extreme reaction, which would alienate the population. Betancourt believed in the use of minimum force, but within the context of maximum display of force, troops dominating the rooftops and crossroads of Caracas. When FALN attacked an excursion train in September 1963, Betancourt felt able to introduce emergency legislation with public support. He also held the scheduled elections in December 1963, and over 90 per cent of those eligible voted despite FALN's attempts to encourage a boycott. FALN fragmented soon afterwards, and Betancourt oversaw an orderly transfer of power to his successor in 1964.

In Uruguay, the Movimiento de Liberación Nacional (National Liberation Movement, Tupamaros, MLN), which operated between 1963 and 1973, was inspired in part by another theorist of urban guerrilla warfare, Abraham Guillén, a Spaniard who had fought in the Spanish Civil War and was influenced by both Marxism and anarchism. Guillén had settled in Uruguay after some years in Argentina. He understood the revolutionary potential of cities such as Montevideo, in which the social, economic and political grievances of the urban underclass could be readily exploited. He also recognised the contribution that youth, especially radical students, might make to a revolution. Like Marighela, however, Guillén did not resolve the contradiction of how a small revolutionary elite, cloaked in the anonymity of the city and operating mostly at night, would be able to build mass popular support. Guillén welcomed the advent of the Tupamaros but increasingly believed that they had developed an over-elaborate infrastructure. He also felt that their use of 'people's prisons' sent out the wrong kind of message to the population as a whole in replicating the repressive institutions of the state. Indeed, Guillén abhorred unnecessary violence.

The name 'Tupamaros' derived from Tupac Amarú, an Indian leader executed by the Spanish and, as previously related, was later adopted by the MRTA in Peru. Uruguay was unusual in Latin America in the mid-1960s in remaining a democracy. The prosperity that had underpinned democracy came to an end, however, when world demand for the country's main product

– wool – declined in the late 1950s. Prices fell and Uruguay began to suffer from both unemployment and inflation. Labour unrest increased in the capital and only large population centre, Montevideo, as living standards declined and bureaucratic corruption increased. MLN was founded by young middle-class radicals led by Raúl Sendic Antonaccio in 1963. Initially, it cultivated a 'Robin Hood' image by conducting series of bank raids and seizures of food to be distributed to the poor in the shanties surrounding Montevideo. The first armed clashes with the police did not occur until December 1966, but violence escalated steadily thereafter. There was an attempt to open a supporting rural front, and the Tupamaros also cultivated relations with other revolutionary groups in Bolivia, Chile and Argentina.

A state of emergency was declared in June 1968, with MLN adding kidnappings and seizure of radio stations to its repertoire. Often those kidnapped were businessmen employed by US-owned companies. MLN also kidnapped and murdered Dan Mitrione, a USAID expert attached to the Uruguayan police, in August 1970. The British ambassador, Geoffrey Jackson, was also kidnapped but was released in September 1971 after being held for nine months. Briefly, MLN also occupied the town of Pando, 20 miles from the capital, in October 1969 to commemorate Guevara's death. They took heavy losses in withdrawing, but it had been an undoubted propaganda coup. Responding to the MLN's challenge, President Juan María Bordaberry declared a state of internal war in April 1972, which allowed him to bring the armed forces fully into the conflict. Some 800 arrests followed large-scale cordon and search operations, most detainees being transferred to military compounds when MLN managed to organise some escapes. Within six months, a ruthless campaign of counter-terror had broken MLN, albeit at the price of jettisoning democracy when the army overthrew the government in February 1973. At the same time, the military's share of the national budget had risen from as little as 1 per cent in 1963 to 26.2 per cent by 1973. MLN had not survived to exploit the situation it had engineered, however, and the degree of military control was such that no insurrection was possible even if MLN had enjoyed wide support.

Argentina also experienced considerable political instability in the 1970s. A combination of high inflation, mass unemployment and a relatively youthful age structure created conditions for dissatisfaction in the slums and shanties that often surrounded the larger cities such as Buenos Aires. A number of groups emerged, including the Trotskyist ERP and the Peronist *Montoneros*, the latter fighting to restore former president Juan Perón to power. Perón, who followed his own unique brand of state socialism, had been overthrown by the army in 1955, and a number of earlier groups had attempted *focos* in his name in the mid-1960s. However, their failure again pointed the way to urban insurgency, and three of the earlier rural groups, Fuerzas Armadas Revolucionarias (Revolutionary Armed Forces, FAR); Fuerzas Armadas Peronistas (Peronist Armed Forces, FAP); and Fuerzas Armadas de Liberación (Liberation Armed

Forces, FAL), converted to urban action. The Montoneros emerged in 1968 and ERP, which was hostile to Peronism, in June 1970.

ERP began attacking police posts and also netted $300,000 in one bank raid at Cordoba in February 1971. A favoured tactic was temporarily taking over factories and haranguing the workforce, while, emulating the 'Robin Hood' approach of the Tupamaros, an executive of Swift Inc. kidnapped in Rosario in 1971 was ransomed in return for the re-employment of sacked workers and the distribution of $50,000 worth of food and other goods to the poor. Kidnapping and intimidation led US-owned businesses like Otis and Ford to leave, and the general manager for Fiat was murdered in April 1972, causing the firm to invest in Brazil instead. The 78-year-old Perón did return to power in September 1973, but ERP did not lay down its arms. After his death in July 1974, he was succeeded by his widow Isabel, but the army took over in March 1976. As elsewhere in South America, the army's reaction was so severe that it quickly destroyed the guerrillas and rendered them incapable of exploiting any popular unrest. Government-sponsored counter-terror in Argentina's *guerra sucia* (dirty war) destroyed both ERP and the Montoneros. The armed forces were assisted by right-wing death squads such as Alianza Anticommunista Argentine (Argentine Anti-communist Alliance, AAA), which often included off-duty police and functioned from January 1974 to July 1975. Subsequently, a variety of paramilitary groups also operated clandestinely from October 1975 until 1983. Little pretence was made at legality, with units such as GT33, attached to the Navy Engineering School, alone being responsible for an estimated 3,000 deaths. By the end of 1977, perhaps 15,000 individuals had 'disappeared'. The military only surrendered power in 1984 following the disastrous attempt to seize the Falkland Islands from Britain two years earlier.

It will be apparent that urban insurgency in the late 1960s and 1970s had much in common with international terrorism. Indeed, the motivation, methods, ideology and international links of the Tupamaros, for example, were approximately the same as West Germany's Rote Armee Faktion (Red Army Faction, RAF), popularly known after its founders, Andreas Baader and Ulrike Meinhof, as the Baader–Meinhof Gang. Just as some insurgent groups were motivated by nationalism or separatism, so were some terrorist groups such as the Basque Euskadi Ta Askatasun (ETA) and the Front de Libération du Québec (Front for the Liberation of Quebec, FLQ), whose kidnapping of British trade commissioner James Cross and murder of Quebec's minister of labour, Pierre Laporte, in October 1970 resulted in the Canadian government invoking the old War Measures Act, which remained in force until January 1971. Other terrorist groups, such as the Italian Brigate Rosse (Red Brigades) and the American group known as the Weathermen, presumed responsible for many of the 4,330 bomb incidents in the United States in 1970–71, had the same kind of revolutionary ideology as many insurgent groups. The philosophy of the Weathermen, who took their name from a lyric by Bob

Dylan, was summed up by one of their members, John Jacobs, as 'We're against everything that's good and decent'. Some groups, however, were effectively sponsored by states such as Cuba, Libya, Iran, Iraq, Syria and North Korea.

Initially, like urban guerrilla groups, recruits for terrorism came from the same social milieu infected by the radicalism of the 1960s. RAF was linked with a psychology seminar at the University of Heidelberg; the Red Brigades with the sociology department at the University of Trentino; Britain's short-lived Angry Brigade with the University of Essex; and the American Symbionese Liberation Army (SLA), best known for the kidnapping of the newspaper heiress Patty Hearst, with Berkeley. Turkey's urban terrorists, the Turkish People's Liberation Army (TPLA) and the Turkish People's Liberation Party-Front (TPLP-F) were similarly offshoots of student radicalism. The membership of such groups widened and, by the 1980s, terrorists were generally less well educated, often merely criminals or street gang thugs with noticeably less political awareness. Moreover, while terrorism had always been a tactical tool of the guerrilla, terrorist groups were increasingly characterised by their deliberate use of indiscriminate violence against the innocent, exercised without restraint almost for its own sake.

Urban insurgency had not proved very successful where governments were prepared to abandon restraint. For liberal democracies, on the other hand, urban guerrilla warfare, like international terrorism, posed an altogether more difficult proposition. Even here, however, violence could often be reduced to a sufficiently acceptable level as to amount to a kind of normality. However, it was clear by the late 1960s that modern media were becoming a significant factor for both security forces and insurgents. That significance was to be enhanced where the superpowers became directly involved in insurgency and counter-insurgency.

Further reading

On Guevara and *foco*, see Jon Lee Anderson, *Che Guevara: A Revolutionary Life* (New York, 1997); Richard Gott, *Guerrilla Movements in Latin America* (London, 1970); Che Guevara, *Guerrilla Warfare: With an Introduction and Case Studies by Brian Loveman and Thomas Davies* (Lincoln, 1985); John Gerassi (ed.), *Venceremos!: The Speeches and Writings of Che Guevara* (London, 1968); Daniel James (ed.), *The Complete Bolivian Diaries of Che Guevara and Other Captured Documents* (New York, 1968); Donald C. Hughes (ed.), *The Legacy of Che Guevara: A Documentary Study* (London, 1977); Dennis M. Rempe, 'Guerrillas, Bandits and Independent Republics: US Counter-insurgency Efforts in Colombia, 1959–65' *Small Wars and Insurgencies* 6 (1995), pp. 304–27; Rempe, 'The Origin of Internal Security in Colombia: A CIA Special Team Surveys *La Violencia, 1959–60*' in *ibid.*, 10 (1999), pp. 24–61; Rempe, 'An American Trojan Horse? Eisenhower, Latin America and the

Development of US Internal Security Policy, 1954–60' in *ibid.*, 10 (1999), pp. 34–64; John L. Churchill, 'Mayan Rebellion?: Guatemala and Chiapas' in *ibid.*, 6 (1995), pp. 357–74; Timothy Wickham-Crowley, *Guerrillas and Revolution in Latin America: A Comparative Study of Insurgents and Regimes since 1956* (Princeton, 1992); Georges Fauriol (ed.), *Latin American Insurgencies* (Georgetown, 1985); and V. Collazo-Davila, 'The Guatemalan Insurrection' in Bard O'Neill, W.R. Heaton and D.J. Alberts (eds), *Insurgency in the Modern World* (Boulder, 1980), pp. 109–36.

On Cuba, see Hugh Thomas, *The Cuban Revolution* (London, 1971); R.L. Banochea and M. San Martin, *The Cuban Insurrection, 1952–9* (New Brunswick, 1974); and Che Guevara, *Reminiscences of the Cuban Revolutionary War* (London, 1968). While wide-ranging, both Geoffrey Fairbairn, *Revolutionary Guerrilla Warfare: The Countryside Version* (Harmondsworth, 1974) and Robert Taber, *The War of the Flea* (2nd edn, London, 1968) touch on the Cuban experience.

On urban guerrilla warfare, see James Kohl and John Litt, *Urban Guerrilla Warfare in Latin America* (Cambridge, Mass., 1974); F.A. Godfrey, 'The Latin American Experience: The Tupamaros Campaign in Uruguay, 1963–73' in Beckett and Pimlott, *Armed Forces and Modern Counter-insurgency*, pp. 112–35; R. Gillespie, *Soldiers of Peron* (Oxford, 1982); Robert Moss, *Urban Guerrilla* (London, 1972); D.C. Hughes (ed.), *The Philosophy of the Urban Guerrilla: The Revolutionary Writings of Abraham Guillén* (New York, 1973); A.C. Porzecanski, *Uruguay's Tupamaros: The Urban Guerrilla* (New York, 1973); J.A. Miller, 'Urban Terrorism in Uruguay: The Tupamaros' in O'Neill, Heaton and Alberts, *Insurgency in the Modern World*, pp. 137–88; Carlos Marighela, *For the Liberation of Brazil* (Harmondsworth, 1971); and Maria Jose Moyano, *Argentina's Lost Patrol: Armed Struggle, 1969–76* (New Haven, 1995). On one aspect of the response to urban guerrilla warfare in Latin America, see the essays in Bruce Campbell and Arthur Brenner (eds), *Death Squads in Global Perspective: Murder with Deniability* (New York, 2000).

On aspects of urban and international terrorism, see John Gellner, *Bayonets in the Streets: Urban Guerrilla at Home and Abroad* (Ontario, 1974); Sabri Sayari and Bruce Hoffman, 'Urbanisation and Insurgency: The Turkish Case' *Small Wars and Insurgencies* 5 (1994), pp. 162–79; Walter Laqueur, *The Age of Terrorism* (London, 1987); Paul Wilkinson, *Terrorism and the Liberal State* (London, 1986); and David Long, *The Anatomy of Terrorism* (New York, 1990).

On Cyprus, see Nancy Crawshaw, *The Cyprus Revolt: An Account of the Struggle for Union with Greece* (London, 1978); Christopher Foley, *Island in Revolt* (London, 1962); W.I. Scobie, *The Struggle for Cyprus* (Stanford, 1975); John Reddaway, *Burdened with Cyprus: The British Connection* (London, 1986); George Grivas, *Guerrilla Warfare and EOKA's Struggle: A Politico-Military Struggle* (London, 1964); Christopher Foley (ed.), *The Memoirs of General Grivas* (London, 1964); Robert Holland, 'Never, Never Land: British Colonial Policy and the Roots of Violence in Cyprus, 1950–54' in Holland, *Emergencies and Disorder*, pp. 148–76; and David Anderson, 'Policing and Communal Conflict: The Cyprus Emergency, 1954–60' in *ibid.*, pp. 177–207 [also reproduced in Anderson and Killingray, *Policing and Decolonisation*, pp. 187–217].

On Aden, see Stephen Harper, *Last Sunset: What Happened in Aden* (London, 1978); David Ledger, *Shifting Sands: The British in South Arabia* (London, 1983); Colin Mitchell, *Having Been a Soldier* (London, 1969); and Julian Paget, *Last Post: Aden, 1964–7* (London, 1969). Paget covers both Cyprus and Aden, as well as other British experience, in *Counter-insurgency Campaigning* (London, 1967). Mockaitis covers Cyprus in *British Counterinsurgency*, *op. cit.*, and Aden in *British Counterinsurgency in the Post-imperial Era*, *op. cit.*

On Algeria, see Alistair Horne, *A Savage War of Peace: Algeria, 1954–62* (2nd edn, Harmondsworth, 1987); Horne, 'The French Army and the Algerian War, 1954–62' in Haycock, *Regular Armies and Insurgency*, pp. 69–83; Michel L. Martin, *Warriors to Managers: The French Military Establishment since 1945* (Chapel Hill, 1981); Martin, 'From Algiers to N'Djamena: France's Adaptation to Low-intensity Wars, 1830–1987' in Charters and Tugwell, *Armies in Low-intensity Conflict*, pp. 77–138; John Pimlott, 'The French Army: From Indochina to Chad, 1946–84' in Beckett and Pimlott, *Armed Forces and Modern Counter-insurgency*, pp. 46–76; John S. Ambler, *Soldiers against the State: The French Army in Politics, 1945–62* (New York, 1968); Anthony Clayton, 'The Sétif Rising of May 1945' *Small Wars and Insurgencies* 3 (1992), pp. 1–21; Clayton, *Wars of French Decolonisation*, *op. cit.*; Philip Dine, *Images of the Algerian War* (Oxford, 1984); Paul Henissart, *Wolves in the City: The Death of French Algeria* (London, 1970); G.A. Kelly, *Lost Soldiers: The French Army and Empire in Crisis, 1947–62* (Cambridge, Mass., 1965); Peter Paret, *French Revolutionary Warfare from Indochina to Algeria: The Analysis of a Political and Military Doctrine* (New York, 1964); Alf Andrew Heggoy, *Insurgency and Counterinsurgency in Algeria* (Bloomington, 1972); John Talbott, *The War Without a Name: France in Algeria, 1954–62* (New York, 1980); Talbott, 'The Myth and Reality of the Paratrooper in the Algerian War' *Armed Forces and Society* 3 (1976), pp. 69–86; Martin Alexander and Philip Bankwitz, 'From *Politiques en Képi* to Military Technocrats: De Gaulle and the Recovery of the French Army after Indochina and Algeria' in George Andreopoulos and Harold Selesky (eds), *The Aftermath of Defeat: Societies, Armed Forces, and the Challenge of Recovery* (New Haven, 1994), pp. 79–102; Martin Thomas, 'Policing Algeria's Borders, 1956–60: Arms Supplies, Frontier Defence and the Sakiet Affair' *War and Society* 13 (1995), pp. 81–100; Thomas, 'Order before Reform: The Spread of French Military Operations in Algeria, 1954–58' in Killingray and Omissi, *Guardians of Empire*, pp. 198–220; Jean-Charles Jauffret, 'The Origins of the Algerian War: The Reaction of France and its Army to the Emergencies of 8 May 1945 and 1 November 1954' in Holland, *Emergencies and Disorder*, pp. 17–29; and Benjamin Stora, 'Algeria: The War without a Name' in *ibid.*, pp. 208–16.

8

INSURGENCY AND THE
SUPERPOWERS

As already indicated, many of the 'wars of liberation' waged during the Cold War era were effectively 'proxy wars' with the Soviet Union and its satellites backing insurgent groups and the United States giving some degree of support to its allies or, in the case of Latin America, more direct support to its hemispheric neighbours. However, both superpowers became themselves directly embroiled in insurgency campaigns in the sense that, rather than simply advisers, American and Soviet ground forces were ultimately committed on a large scale. Both South Vietnam between 1965 and 1973 and Afghanistan between 1979 and 1989 indicated once more that armed forces tend to operate within almost a preordained tradition with respect to counter-insurgency. In each case, however, what might be termed a strategic culture proved unhelpful and led to ignominious withdrawal.

It will already be apparent that the United States was no stranger either to the projection of its military power overseas or to the waging of counter-insurgency. However, predominant cultural attitudes made it difficult for Americans to comprehend the nature of many of their irregular opponents. The fact that Americans themselves had once fought for their own independence led many in the United States to cast any opponent in an almost heroic light. In 1870, Wendell Philipps had referred to three leading Indian-fighting officers – George Custer, Phil Sheridan and Eugene Baker – as the 'true savages' on the great plains. Certain elements of the press had given great prominence to allegations of atrocities in the Philippines in 1901–2 in the same way that another journalist, Carleton Beals, gave considerable publicity to Sandino in the 1920s and Robert Taber to Castro in the 1950s. On the other hand, US servicemen had clearly often reflected a contempt for the others' cultures that had been counter-productive, which complicated the undoubted emphasis upon civic action in American counter-insurgency practice and tended towards the assumption that the indigenous inhabitants would be willing to assimilate American cultural values.

Though undertaken from the best of motives, American insistence on fiscal and political integrity had sometimes proved the greatest cultural shock of all, while the desire to effect stability through guaranteeing honest elections and establishing efficient gendarmerie was often seen as a 'quick fix' since there was no desire on the part of the United States for a protracted presence. Americans, indeed, might be characterised as inherently impatient in the face of protracted conflict, reinforcing the desire to minimise American casualties through the application of technology and firepower. In turn, the belief in firepower also seemingly went hand in hand with growing institutional resistance in the US army and, to a lesser extent, among US marines to unconventional warfare. As already suggested, the army had drawn few lessons from its experiences on the great plains or in the Philippines and had tired of pacification by 1909, not least through civil–military disputes that had arisen both in the Philippines and on Cuba. It was professionally far more rewarding to turn to the fields of St Mihiel and the Argonne in the First World War and, later, to the European theatre in the Second World War and to Korea.

Presidential identification of insurgency as a predominant threat to American interests during the Kennedy administration, therefore, was not shared by an army, as Larry Cable puts it, 'configured, equipped and trained according to a doctrine suitable for conventional warfare, or for warfare in the nuclear battlefield of Europe'. Moreover, as Andrew Krepinevich has argued, that doctrine – what he characterises as the 'army concept' – was that of Omar Bradley's 12th Army Group and the road from the Normandy beaches to the Elbe. So-called 'pentomic' divisions were developed in the mid-1950s to give greater flexibility on the nuclear and conventional battlefield through the deployment of self-sufficient battle groups, with considerable firepower available to them and with mobility based on greater use of helicopters. It was assumed to some extent that greater flexibility would automatically aid operations against guerrillas, and, therefore, that the same methods used in conventional warfare would equally serve for counter-guerrilla warfare. It was only in 1962, however, that the basic Field Manual (FM) 100–5 *Field Service Regulations: Operations* included two brief chapters on unconventional and irregular warfare. There was a distinct emphasis in them on what would more properly be defined as partisan warfare, which was to be dealt with by offensive action such as 'cordon and search' and what came to be known as 'search and destroy'. Little consideration was given to psychological warfare or civic action. Although there was some reference to the significance of intelligence, it was Greece and Korea rather than the Philippines or Malaya that had informed the doctrinal concepts.

FM 31–20 *Operations against Guerrilla Forces*, first issued in 1951, and FM 31–15 *Operations against Airborne Attack, Guerrilla Action and Infiltration* in 1953, continued the emphasis on partisan warfare. Subsequently, FM 31–15 was renamed *Operations against Irregular Forces* and then, in 1964, *Special Warfare Operations*. Various editions of FM 31–21 *Guerrilla Warfare* continued to regard counter-insurgency operations as a continuum of conventional operations, while FM 31–22 *US Army Counterinsurgency Forces*, issued in 1963, was actually intended only for US Special Forces and not the army as a whole. FM

31–16 *Counterguerrilla Operations*, issued in 1967, continued the emphasis upon the offensive and maintaining continuous pressure on the guerrillas and stressed the importance of firepower, mobility and aggressive leadership. There were certainly a number of American theorists of 'counter-revolution' attempting to outline measures for the successful defeat of Maoist-style insurgency, including John Pushtay, whose *Counterinsurgency* was published in 1965, and Colonel John J. McCuen, whose *The Art of Counter-revolutionary Warfare* was published in 1966. US professional military journals, however, gave little coverage to the analysis of insurgency and counter-insurgency.

Air mobility was seen as particularly useful, since it could fix the guerrillas in place and render them vulnerable to heavy ground- and air-delivered firepower. Indeed, the recommendations of the Howze Board in January 1962 would result in the creation of the 11th Air Assault Division (Test) in February 1964. Married to assessments by the Army Concept Team in Vietnam, the process ended with the activation of the 1st Air Cavalry Division (Mobile) in June 1965 for service in South Vietnam, the formation seeing its first major action in the Ia Drang valley in October and November 1965. Ia Drang, however, proved a false dawn. Having stood and fought conventionally, and suffered heavily as a result, the North Vietnamese reverted to guerrilla warfare. At peak, the Americans had 5,000 helicopters in South Vietnam, including the ubiquitous Bell AH-1 Huey Cobra gunship. Sooner or later, however, troops had to land and fight, but they proved reluctant to move beyond the 'umbilical cord' of the landing zone and were usually content to dig in and await fire support while their opponents slipped away.

The value of fire support from artillery against guerrillas was also stressed in a number of manuals pertaining to artillery doctrine in the belief that, whatever the actual experience of counter-guerrilla operations thus far, it would at least have a psychological impact. Firepower generally would be brought to bear because continuous operational pressure – 'harassment' – would force the guerrillas into revealing their location and enable their encirclement. Another general assumption was that all guerrillas would need to be supplied across an international frontier, but that infiltration could be prevented by establishing free-fire zones or a 'friendly population buffer'.

Similarly, although the marines had devoted considerable attention to small wars in the 1920s and early 1930s, the creation of the Fleet Marine Force in 1933 led inexorably to the experience of the beaches of the Pacific in the Second World War. Amphibious warfare, therefore, proved more seductive as a subject for study after 1945, with no time now allocated to small wars at Quantico until 1960. In 1957, the Hogaboom Board identified a likely deployment of the marines in proxy wars rather than on NATO's Central Front and, indeed, such an interventionary role was performed in the Lebanon in 1958. However, it was recognised that counter-guerrilla operations were a possibility, and, in 1962, Fleet Marine Force Manual (FMFM) 21

Operations against Guerrilla Forces built largely on the *Small Wars Manual* of 1940, with some revisions echoing what have been characterised as the more 'muscular' aspects of British experience in Malaya, such as population and food control. There was an emphasis upon psychological and civic action as well as small-unit operations, but also a paler reflection of the army's reliance upon firepower. Moreover, when retitled and renumbered as FMFM 8–2 *Counterinsurgency Operations* in 1963, the manual displayed even more acceptance of the army's approach. Generally, marines were to prove far more flexible towards counter-insurgency in Vietnam than the army, but it should be noted that there were still at least 60 amphibious beach assaults, primarily mounted, in the words of Paddy Griffith, 'in the hope that the enemy would oblige by opposing them'.

The net result of these trends in the armed forces was that the thrust behind the emergence of a new emphasis upon counter-insurgency in the early 1960s came not from the military, but from Kennedy. He established the Special Group, Counterinsurgency (SGCI) in January 1961 and also aimed for some kind of national training school in counter-insurgency. Although Walt Rostow, the special assistant for national security, had served in the wartime OSS, however, the SGCI's knowledge of insurgency and counter-insurgency was not large. Indeed, the chairman, General Maxwell Taylor, was more interested in limited war than counter-insurgency, while Rostow himself subscribed largely to economic solutions, believing communist-inspired revolution 'a disease of the transition to modernisation'. Roger Hilsman, Director of the State Department's Bureau of Intelligence and Research and, later, Assistant Secretary of State for Far Eastern Affairs, who had served with Merrill's Marauders in wartime Burma, saw the solution in efficient administration, believing that political activity should take precedence over military activity and that only limited military deployment might be necessary. In many respects, the civilian approach, which was heavily influenced by social scientists, as incorporated in the US Overseas Internal Defense Policy (USOIDP) statement of August 1962 and evident in the Inter-departmental Seminar on Counter-insurgency (IDS) taught at the State Department from June 1962 onwards, was postulated on insurgency being a product of communist subversion and intimidation. The remedy, therefore, lay in socio-economic development and appropriate nation-building measures based on concepts of security, good government and progress.

In some measure, this approach was inspired by Malaya. Hilsman, Rostow and other civilians were reasonably favourably disposed towards the kind of measures advocated by the head of the British Advisory Mission to South Vietnam (BRIAM), none other than Robert Thompson. This approach, however, lost impetus following Kennedy's assassination, the army having largely dismissed it as a passing 'fad' of the 'New Frontier crowd'. Consequently, although Kennedy's interest had compelled some increase in the army's attention to counter-insurgency, the desire to wage a 'real war' played a major role in the defeat of American efforts to save South Vietnam from communist insurgency.

Following the Geneva agreement of July 1954, which had partitioned North and South Vietnam on the seventeenth parallel and established a Demilitarised Zone (DMZ), elections were due to be held to reunite the country in 1956. In the event, the elections were never held, amid mutual recriminations on the likelihood of a 'free and fair' outcome. The new Republic of South Vietnam under President Diem was supported by the USA as a bulwark against communism. Diem, however, ruled a fragmented society divided by religious and ethnic differences. He himself was a Catholic in a largely Buddhist society, and, in addition, private armies were maintained by the Binh Xuyen bandits and by sects such as the Hoa Hoa and Cao Dai. Diem also faced escalating insurgency by communists backed by Ho Chi Minh's government in Hanoi. Military and political subversion of South Vietnam began as early as August 1957, but at a relatively low level. The North Vietnamese leadership only resolved to escalate the level of conflict in January 1959 as a result of the growing unpopularity of Diem in the South, but also of the damage that Diem was doing to party cadres through an enhanced anti-communist campaign in the South.

Ostensibly, the Mat Tran Dan Toc Giai Phong Mien Nam Viet Nam (National Front for the Liberation of South Vietnam, NLF), was founded on 20 December 1960 as a coalition of opposition groups dedicated to the overthrow of Diem. Its president, Nguyen Huo Tho, was a non-communist, and the religious sects as well as ethnic minorities were all represented. In reality, the NLF was a front for the communists, and the effective nucleus of the People's Liberation Armed Forces (PLAF) was the 10,000 or so former members of the Viet Minh who had remained in the South upon partition of Vietnam in 1954. Soon popularly known as the Viet Cong (VC) from the derogatory term used by Saigon to describe the communists, the PLAF was swelled both by further infiltration from North Vietnam and by local recruitment. In Long An province, for example, such local recruits were most often youths trying to avoid conscription. The conflict was never one of northern Vietnamese against southern Vietnamese, and VC membership is estimated to have doubled between 1960 and mid-1961, doubled again by late 1961, and doubled once more by early 1962, to reach a strength of about 300,000. Similarly, the overall communist leadership in Hanoi was national rather than regional, with a preponderance of those from the central provinces of North and South.

The VC was organised according to the Vietnamese version of Mao's revolutionary guerrilla warfare principles as espoused by Giap and Truong Chinh. Headed by Le Duan and Le Duc Tho, the Trung Uong Cuc Mien Nam (Central Office for South Vietnam, COSVN), a revival of the old southern committee in existence during the war against the French, usually operated from Laos or, occasionally, from the Tay Ninh province in South

Vietnam. The VC's aim was to undermine Diem by both political and military means. Thus, a whole network of three inter-zonal and seven zonal headquarters, 30 provincial committees and numerous district, town and village committees strove to promote other communist front organisations, to spread propaganda and to establish 'liberated zones'. Over 11,000 South Vietnamese were abducted or murdered in 1964 alone as the VC struck at the rural administration in the South. The eventual estimated total of communist assassinations and abductions between 1957 and 1972 amounted to over 95,000. The regular North Vietnamese Army (NVA) – also referred to as the People's Army of North Vietnam (PAVN) – was involved in the South from the beginning but, at this stage, primarily as technical experts, such as those in Group 559, which began organising the supplies for the VC along the so-called Ho Chi Minh Trail through Laos in May 1959.

The trail remained only a single track until as late as 1964. Between 1965 and 1971, however, it was increasingly expanded until it embraced over 8,000 miles of roads driven through mountain and jungle, with its own labour force of 50,000 men and its own 25,000-strong garrison. It was defended against the threat from American air power by over 1,000 anti-aircraft guns. The trail complex included pipelines, barracks, and underground storage and repair facilities. Between 20 and 35 per cent of supplies sent down the trail were lost, the greater proportion due to American air strikes assisted by electronic monitoring devices. But this rate of loss was from an average tonnage transported of 10,000 tons a week by 1970. On just one day in December 1970, the Americans estimated that there were 15,000 vehicles on the trail. Consequently, the momentum of communist operations was easily sustained. In addition, the infiltration rate of troops into South Vietnam from the trail increased from about 5,000 a year in 1960 to an estimated 90,000 in 1966.

Whereas it had taken up to three months to traverse the trail in the early 1960s, the journey time to the South from the port of Haiphong, where Soviet supplies were landed in North Vietnam, had been cut to just ten days by 1975. Since both Laos and Cambodia were theoretically neutral states, the United States was constrained from throwing ground troops across the trail in a way that would have seriously disrupted it. The Americans were able to close the coastal route into the South by 1968, and the so-called Sihanouk Trail into the Mekong delta from Cambodia was also closed to the communists by the advent of General Lon Nol's government in Cambodia in March 1970, but this did not seriously affect communist operations.

The VC's military organisation comprised the regular Quan Doi Chu Luc (main force units), who were trained and equipped to meet the South Vietnamese army, or Army of the Republic of Vietnam (ARVN), albeit on terms of its own choosing; full-time guerrillas, who could co-operate with the main force units if necessary; and part-time militia, who largely remained at village level. The primary VC strategy was to consolidate control of rural areas and to encourage urban unrest. VC tactics and, indeed, those of the NVA, included ambush, mine laying and booby-trapped man-traps such as pits filled with the sharpened bamboo stakes smeared in excrement known as *punji-sticks*. As is well known, extensive tunnel systems were used to conceal units.

Diem came under increasing pressure and, worried by the communist success in the countryside, the Kennedy administration increased the number of American advisers in South Vietnam. The US Special Forces had been training the ARVN since June 1957, but they began organising the Civilian Irregular Defense Groups (CIDG) in December 1961. In February 1962, Military Assistance Command, Vietnam (MACV) was established in succession to the former Military Assistance Advisory Group (MAAG). In 1963, Buddhist hostility to Diem resulted in widespread rioting, and the US administration gave some encouragement to the coup by the ARVN, in which Diem was murdered, in November 1963. Military governments succeeded each other rapidly until the end of 1964, when Air Vice-Marshal Nguyen Cao Ky and General Nguyen Van Thieu brought a degree of political stability. It became increasingly clear to the North Vietnamese leadership, therefore, that, despite the fall of Diem, US support for South Vietnam would necessitate the commitment of the NVA. In December 1963, therefore, it was resolved to escalate the level of conflict once more. Increasing communist pressure in the South, however, triggered the involvement of US ground forces. As famously summed up in November 1964 by the Assistant Secretary of Defense, John McNaughton, the US objective was now 70 per cent to avoid a humiliating defeat, 20 per cent to keep South Vietnam out of communist hands and 10 per cent to enable its people to enjoy a better way of life.

On 2 August 1964, the *USS Maddox* was apparently attacked by North Vietnamese patrol boats, and President Lyndon Johnson ordered bombing attacks against North Vietnam. Five days later, the Gulf of Tonkin Resolution by the US Congress empowered Johnson to conduct the war without further congressional approval. Immediate US reaction was confined to air raids, which were stepped up in February 1965 in response to a VC attack on US barracks at Pleiku. Operation Rolling Thunder was launched on 2 March 1965 and continued until 31 October 1968. On 8 March 1965, US marines landed at Da Nang ostensibly to guard US airfields. Initially, an 'enclave' strategy was mooted, in which US troops would protect only their own bases. However, the commander of MACV (COMUSMACV), General William C. Westmoreland, believed that only US forces could take on the VC main force units and those NVA units increasingly being infiltrated down the Ho Chi Minh Trail in the 'main force war'. It was left to the ARVN to continue to wage the 'other war' of pacification in the villages. Accordingly, US troop strength reached 184,000 by the end of 1965, with the overarching definition of victory being the ending of Hanoi's direct control of and support for insurgency in the South. Initially, and for some time to come, therefore, to quote Larry Cable, 'it didn't really matter to very many at the time if the US won or lost the "other war"'.

It was assumed that bombing North Vietnam would force Hanoi into negotiations, but, in reality, it gifted the North Vietnamese a propaganda victory in projecting the image of a small country assailed by a superpower's war machine. In any case, the effectiveness of the bombing was limited by self-imposed restrictions on the part of the Americans to avoid targeting the Red River dikes, Haiphong harbour and the centre of Hanoi for political reasons, such as not hitting Soviet supply ships in Haiphong and thus risking escalation. Nor did bombing stop the flow of men and supplies down the Ho Chi Minh Trail, and in any case, NVA and VC units required few supplies since they were not engaged in continuous combat operations. Thus, the 643,000 tons of bombs dropped on North Vietnam and 2.2 million tons of bombs dropped over South Vietnam between 1965 and 1968 made little contribution to stopping the communists. Similarly, the US army believed that it could dictate the ground war and could inflict such heavy casualties on the NVA and VC that Hanoi would give up the struggle. In reality, a strategy of attrition could not work when the communists were prepared to accept any price until the Americans lost their own resolve.

The failure to translate an undoubted degree of military success into a political victory placed increasing pressure on the Johnson administration. In April 1967, Westmoreland was told that he could not have more than the 'minimum' 550,000 men he demanded to secure victory. In any case, the army was ill prepared for the guerrilla tactics used even by the regular NVA. US commanders favoured inappropriate large-scale 'search and destroy' operations using large numbers of helicopters and relied on firepower to substitute for permanent occupation of the ground. As previously indicated, the 'air mobile' concept became a noted feature of the 'main force war'. Yet, as one official study reported in 1967, 88 per cent of all engagements were actually initiated by the NVA and VC, who retained the ability to accept or refuse contact on their own terms.

Ironically, it was the massive military defeat of the VC during the Tet offensive in January 1968 that proved the turning point in American resolve. In launching largely conventional assaults on the major urban centres of South Vietnam, the VC lost most of the estimated 45,000 communist casualties. It is reasoned that, while Hanoi intended to provoke a popular uprising in the South, it had also taken the opportunity to neutralise any possible future rival to its own leadership in the South. In fact, a significant proportion of communist strength in the South remained locally recruited as late as the eventual cease-fire in 1973, although varying considerably from region to region. Giap had repeated his error against the French in 1951 by launching a premature conventional offensive, which exposed the communists to the full weight of their opponent's firepower. Images of the VC breaking into the US embassy in Saigon, however, made a profound impact on American audiences, which had believed the war was being won.

The media did have an impact upon the British remaining in Aden, and in

South Vietnam, it is said, the media asserted the public's right to know in the pursuit of freedom of the press rather than seeing its duty as supporting national interests. The press in a liberal democracy would be expected to act as a watchdog to expose incompetence, inadequacy and cover-ups of various kinds. However, it was also important to get a good story, as summed up by one Vietnam reporter remarking, 'I don't care if I get it right; I only care if I get it first.' Naturally enough, the military had a different priority and tended to separate the public's desire to know from the public's right to know in the interests of operational security, and in an effort to maintain the morale of its own forces and of their families at home, and undermining and discrediting the insurgents. Journalists' rights are often effectively abrogated in major wars, since the greater the perceived threat, the greater the willingness to tolerate imposed restrictions on freedom. Vietnam, however, was a conflict of limited intensity, and in the view of many Americans, not one vital to the interests of the United States. Thus, it was likely that, in the absence of any real censorship, elements of the media would oppose American involvement.

Yet there is some debate as to whether the popular perception of the impact of the media is correct, irrespective of the particular example of Tet. Indeed, it is now accepted that the American media tended to follow public moods rather than the other way about, and media coverage seems merely to have reinforced views already held. Not that much coverage of combat in close-up was shown, although the media coverage did tend to show fairly faithfully the way in which the war seemed to lack any coherent pattern. What did affect public opinion and, of course, this was also a point made about Aden, was the casualty rate. Support for the war in the United States fell by 15 per cent each time casualties increased by a factor of ten, i.e., when casualties rose from 1,000 to 10,000, 15 per cent was lost in the public opinion polls. Johnson decided not to run for re-election and announced a pause in the bombing campaign on 31 October 1968 to allow peace talks to begin in Paris.

Richard Nixon was elected US president in November 1968 on the promise of finding 'peace with honour'. Nixon also wanted a 'Vietnamisation' of the war, with the ARVN gradually assuming responsibility for all operations. It involved a dual strategy of negotiation coupled with maintaining military effort, and Nixon sought to put additional pressure on Hanoi by a major incursion into Cambodia to cut the Ho Chi Minh Trail in April 1970. As a result, Congress reasserted its authority and repealed the Gulf of Tonkin Resolution. There was a similar incursion by ARVN forces into Laos in February 1971, when the absence of direct American involvement brought near catastrophe.

US troop strength declined to 239,000 by 1971, with a damaging fall in both morale and effectiveness. There were certainly problems of bifurcation with respect to the collapse of American military morale. The exact opposite pertained to the situation in Algeria and Portuguese Africa, however, for it was apparent that conscripts – draftees – did most of the fighting and the regulars – lifers – enjoyed less exposure to combat. In 1969, for example, draftees represented 39 per cent of army personnel in South Vietnam but suffered 62 per cent of casualties. Moreover, through draft dodging, those compelled to serve were often the more underprivileged within US society, a problem compounded by Project 100,000 scheme, conceived by the Secretary of Defense in the Kennedy and Johnson administrations, Robert McNamara, which had used the army as a dumping ground for those of low intelligence and social problems with inevitable repercussions for military efficiency. All this contributed to the range of other internally generated factors that damaged morale such as the rotation policy, by which enlisted men served for longer periods than officers; and the resulting 'turbulence' in units and 'ticket punching' by regular officers determined to achieve demonstrable results while they were with units. It was also alleged that draftees arrived imbued with the latest developments in social attitudes, ideas and customs, which included hostility to the war, the drug culture and Black Power. While US servicemen were influenced to some degree by domestic pressures, however, these were not as significant as the internally generated policies within the army in attacking self-belief as to the mission in South Vietnam. The effect of force deterioration generally was seen in such areas as the inflation of the notorious body count, drug taking, 'fragging' of overzealous officers and NCOs, 'combat refusal', and increasing military crime.

Another conventional offensive launched by Giap across the DMZ in March 1972 was destroyed by American air power. Reduced to perhaps 200,000 by 1971 through the greater co-ordination of American and South Vietnamese counter-insurgency efforts, the VC took little part in the offensive. A southern-based Provisional Revolutionary Government (PRG) had been formed in 1969, but it was only nominally in the forefront of the continuing negotiations in Paris. In April 1972, Nixon resumed bombing North Vietnam in Operation Linebacker I. Each time the negotiations in Paris became bogged down, Nixon increased the pressure. Operation Linebacker II between 19 and 30 December 1972, with previous restrictions on targets removed, persuaded the North Vietnamese to sign a cease-fire agreement on 9 January 1973. As Hanoi well knew, however, Nixon's only real aim was to withdraw US troops, and little was done to ensure the future security of South Vietnam. Although Nixon promised to use air power again if the North Vietnamese attacked, he fell from office over the Watergate affair in August 1974. In South Vietnam, Thieu's government was becoming more unpopular. There had never been a real cease-fire in many areas, and the NVA had continued to consolidate its strength. In early 1975, a new communist offensive took the ARVN by surprise and it rapidly crumbled. Saigon fell on 30 April 1975. The cost of the Vietnam War was an estimated three million lives, including 46,397 American servicemen killed in action and 10,340 who died from other causes.

It needs to be emphasised that the insurgency environment that existed when American ground forces were committed to South Vietnam in 1965 was exceptionally difficult. South Vietnam was an artificial creation of the Geneva agreements and not a nation-state. There were substantial racial minorities and divisions both of religion and between urban and rural populations. In a state lacking any unifying commitment to a national identity, the kind of political factionalism experienced since 1954 could only add to its vulnerability. Moreover, in guarding against possible coups, Diem had constructed an administrative system of competing agencies and internal friction and rivalries, which promoted bureaucratic inefficiency. The supposed land reform programmes instituted by Diem between 1955 and 1960 had also only resulted in increasing the power of landlords. The overthrow of Diem resulted in two years of even greater political instability in Saigon, while the situation in the countryside deteriorated markedly. Even President Thieu admitted in early 1965 that the communists exercised some degree of control over 75 per cent of the country, compared with perhaps 60 per cent four years earlier. At the same time, the widespread and enduring corruption at the highest levels of government and society robbed all South Vietnamese administrations of legitimacy. Yet, while ritually denounced by Hanoi as American puppets, successive administrations in Saigon resisted US attempts to enforce reforms. Indeed, since for much of the war the South Vietnamese knew the USA could hardly threaten to withdraw, there was little realistic American leverage over Saigon.

Unlike Malaya or the Philippines, South Vietnam was also extremely vulnerable to infiltration through Laos and Cambodia. An estimated 28,000 North Vietnamese military personnel had already infiltrated the South by 1964. Moreover, while the NVA and VC are estimated to have lost 330,000 casualties between 1965 and 1967, their strength in the South grew by an estimated 180,000, the majority from infiltration rather than from local recruitment. Any decision on the part of the United States to occupy the DMZ, as was considered in 1965 and 1966, or any part of either North Vietnam or neutral Laos would have had immense political consequences. Indeed, the limited incursions into Cambodia in 1970 and into Laos in 1971 both attracted much controversy. Creating a permanent static defensive line would also have required enormous logistic effort and subjected American forces to constant artillery bombardment from North Vietnam. The construction of the 'McNamara line' along the DMZ between April and September 1967 was a compromise solution in substituting a system of minefields, sensors and designated 'free-fire' zones for a permanent garrison. The line was principally conceived by Robert Fisher of the so-called 'Jasons', a group of systems analysts in the Pentagon's Advanced Research Projects Agency, who advised McNamara on technical issues relating to the war. In the event, it was not possible to prevent continued infiltration through Laos, and the concept was discredited by the ability of the North Vietnamese to concentrate large forces around Khe Sanh prior to the opening of the Tet offensive in January 1968. By default, therefore, much strategic initiative was surrendered to the communists.

The sheer determination of the leadership in Hanoi to accept any sacrifice necessary to achieve subjugation of the South was also a major factor. It is difficult, indeed, to envisage any advantages enjoyed by the USA in South Vietnam in any way comparable to those enjoyed by the authorities in either Malaya or the Philippines at the outset of insurgency. Indeed, coupled together, the unpopularity and incompetence of the Saigon government, the vulnerability of South Vietnam to infiltration and the ruthless determination of Hanoi posed a formidable challenge to any strategy that might have been adopted, let alone an approach to counter-insurgency that would not only display those disadvantages inherent in American practice generally but also lacked the support of the American military.

In terms of major requirements for success, giving sufficient priority to political action to prevent the communists gaining popular support over military action would have necessitated not only an entirely different perspective on the part of the US army but also, more crucially, a dramatic transformation in the nature of the Saigon government. Similarly, establishing complete civil–military co-operation would have been difficult given the reluctance of Westmoreland to consider exercising operational control over allied and South Vietnamese forces in the belief, with particular reference to the ARVN, that this would smack of 'colonialism' and stifle leadership and initiative. In any case, however, there was considerable division of authority within the US command structure itself. Westmoreland was simultaneously responsible to both the Commander-in-Chief, Pacific (CINCPAC) and the Commander-in-Chief, US Army, Pacific, but in reality, communications went direct to the Joint Chiefs of Staff in Washington. Within the theatre, Westmoreland had no direct control over the marines, no control over naval operations and no control over air operations outside South Vietnam or Laos. Civilian agencies were only nominally under MACV and reported to their superiors in Washington or the US ambassador, who was actually the senior US representative in South Vietnam.

Equally, there was little co-ordination between intelligence agencies. The Australians, who sent a Task Force to South Vietnam, found fourteen agencies besides themselves gathering intelligence in Phuoc Tuy province. Moreover, in many respects, there was information overload. The MACV Intelligence Centre in Saigon alone was receiving three million pages of captured enemy documents every month by 1968. Computers, automatic data processing and systems analysis were used to try to make sense of all this, but the appropriate technology existed only in Washington, with further delays in assessment and dissemination, which in any case tended to produce rather vague 'trends' analysis. Increasingly, technology played an important part, including satellite information, remotely piloted vehicles (RPVs), electronic and signals intelligence (ELINT and SIGINT), high-flying aircraft such as the U-2, tactical aircraft taking photographs, radar and sensors. The latter included those air-dropped (ADSIDS) along the Ho Chi Minh Trail, disguised, for example, as buffalo droppings or TURDSIDS.

Given that the role of the US military essentially became that of fighting the 'main force war' and that an ARVN, equally trained for a conventional role, was given the responsibility for the 'other war' against the VC, the appropriate use of military force to support pacification was also difficult to achieve. Clearly, too, lasting political reform to prevent the recurrence of insurgency was somewhat redundant in the South Vietnamese context. Diem's 'personalism' offered little. Under Thieu's Central Pacification and Development Council, some limited local democracy was introduced in 1969, and the Land to the Tiller programme, introduced in March 1970, redistributed 2.5 million acres over the next three years. There was even an anti-corruption drive in response to the campaign by the People's Front against Corruption in 1974, but such measures came too late and drew a largely cynical response. The land issue, for example, had long been exploited by the communists, and the NLF had itself redistributed land in those areas under its control, conditional upon assistance to the cause. Thieu was effectively forced to legitimise the land redistribution that had already taken place without conditions, while the communists were able to discredit Land to the Tiller by arguing both that they had forced it upon Saigon and that it was merely returning land to its rightful owners.

In many ways, therefore, the only requirement of successful counter-insurgency actually pursued in any meaningful sense was that of separating insurgents from the population and winning hearts and minds. Unfortunately, however, the one aspect of true counter-insurgency consciously attempted was a failure. One problem was that, effectively, only two components of US forces in South Vietnam were actually trained, or had the inclination, for winning hearts and minds: the Special Forces and the marines.

The Special Forces had been revived in June 1952 but had enjoyed little favour until they received the personal backing of Kennedy, who officially authorised the wearing of the green beret, although it had been worn since 1956. The 1st Special Forces Group (SFG) was deployed to South Vietnam in 1957 and teams from the 7th SFG in May 1960. The 5th SFG was then deployed to South Vietnam in October 1964 to assume control of all special forces operations. FM 31–21 *Guerrilla Warfare and Special Forces Operations*, first issued in 1955, had originally seen the Special Forces as operating as partisans in any European conflict between NATO and the Warsaw Pact. By 1961, however, as a result of the work of 1st SFG in training ARVN commandos, it was recognised that they could also train indigenous forces for counter-guerrilla operations. Moreover, enabling legislation for USAID in 1961 permitted the use of army forces for civic action. Consequently, a new mission undertaken by the Green Berets from December 1961 onwards was the attempt to win for Saigon the support of the Montagnard tribesmen of the Central Highlands, and other minority groups such as the ethnic Khmers and ethnic Chinese Nungs. The primary means of doing so was the establishment of the CIDG.

Conceived by David Nuttle and Gilbert Layton, the first CIDG was established by Captain Ron Shackleton among Rhade tribesmen around Buon Enao in Darlac province. By October 1965, there were 30,400 'cidgees' and eventually 80,000 in 80 major units. Dilution resulted, however, when control of the programme passed from the CIA to MACV in July 1963, since the latter was only interested in the contribution that the CIDG could make to the main force war and expanded the force rapidly. Thus, 11,250 CIDG were involved in the Border Surveillance Programme by July 1964, but spread so thinly as to be largely ineffective in preventing infiltration. Similarly, the Special Forces themselves were increasingly diverted to other roles, such as the provision, with the CIDG, of 'Apache' teams of scouts and the joint reconnaissance and hunter-killer teams of Project Delta. Initially codenamed 'Leaping Lena' and producing long-range reconnaissance patrols (LRRPs, or 'Lerps'), Delta evolved into the so-called 'Greek alphabet' teams codenamed Delta, Omega, Sigma and Gamma in May 1964 and the quick-reaction 'Mike Force' in October 1964, the latter under the control of the Studies and Observation Group (SOG). Special Forces A-Teams were increasingly placed on the Laotian frontier as a 'trip wire', but they suffered from the introduction of NVA units, with a number of camps being overrun in 1964–65. Subsequently, mobile guerrilla forces of A-Teams and Mike Force companies were established to maintain a presence in VC-controlled areas in 1966–67. Meanwhile, control of the CIDG was handed over to the South Vietnamese Special Forces or Luc Luong Dac Biet (LLDB), nicknamed both 'Look Long Duck Backs' and 'Lousy Little Dink Bastards' by the Americans. As a result, there was a series of mutinies in the CIDG in 1964–65, and the CIDG programme was closed down at the end of 1970.

As for the marines, within their own tactical areas of responsibility in Corps Tactical Zone (CTZ) I, General Lewis Walt of III Marine Amphibious Force, with the approval of the USMC Commandant, General Wallace Greene, and the Commanding General of Fleet Marine Force Pacific, Lieutenant-General Victor Krulak, a former Special Assistant for Counterinsurgency and Special Activities to the Joint Chiefs of Staff, attempted to pursue his own strategy distinct from that of Westmoreland at MACV. So-called 'Country Fair' operations began experimentally in late 1965, with a full programme launched in February 1966. This allowed for the screening of the local population in cordon and search operations combined with entertainment and medical treatment in a 'country fair' atmosphere. Over 46,000 people were screened in 1966, and 20,000 received some form of medical treatment. 'Golden Fleece' operations were also conducted to safeguard the annual harvest.

Combined Action Platoons (CAPs) were instituted in 1965, initially by Captain Jim Cooper at Thanh My Trung and comprising fifteen marines and 34 members of the Popular Forces (PF), or 'Ruff Puffs', formerly known as the Dan Ve (Self-Defence Corps). Some 75 CAPs had been created by 1967 and 115 by 1969 tasked with attacking the infrastructure of the VC, protecting the government's infrastructure and the population, collecting intelligence, and training militia. In reality, CAPs were not the unlimited tactical success often portrayed by their champions and could only survive in the presence of conventionally deployed marine forces. But, in any case, MACV was unimpressed with marine 'oil spot' techniques, which remained limited to CTZ I, and the marines also had a wider commitment to the defence of the DMZ. Indeed, in July 1966 only 15 per cent of marine activities were devoted purely to what could be characterised as counter-guerrilla operations, and their tactical areas of responsibility within CTZ I included only one-fifth of its villages. Moreover, Hanoi's deployment of the NVA along the DMZ was deliberately designed to draw the marines away from pacification, the threat to the major base at Khe Sanh becoming a reality with the attacks upon it in January 1968, which preceded the main Tet offensive and continued until April 1968. Through increasing commitments elsewhere, only 38 CAPs remained operational by the end of 1970 and even fewer in 1971.

Not unexpectedly, US army commitment to pacification was less impressive. The architect of 'search and destroy', General William Depuy, significantly criticised the marines, arguing that they 'came in and just sat down and didn't do anything. They were involved in counterinsurgency of the deliberate, mild sort.' By contrast, the army's Operations Thayer II and Pershing in CTZ II between February and April 1967 were characterised by the 1st Cavalry Division (Airmobile) as 'short-duration, high-impact pacification'. Pacification consisted primarily of band concerts and daily visits to the already large number of refugee camps created by earlier operations. Over 12,000 people were forcibly moved from their homes during the two operations, few of whom could be found alternative accommodation. Indeed, for a variety of reasons, an estimated 1.2 million internal refugees were generated between December 1965 and June 1967, and there is a possibility that 3.5 million South Vietnamese were internal refugees at one time or another between 1964 and 1969.

Pacification was largely left to the ARVN, but, as already suggested, the ARVN was trained for conventional operations and had as little interest in pacification as the US army, although it did agree to commit 60 per cent of its battalions to revolutionary development in October 1966. Little use was made of the Regional Forces (RF) or PF, formerly the Bao An (Civil Guard), who were poorly armed and treated with disdain by the ARVN, who rarely went to their assistance. Yet the RF and PF accounted for between 12 and 30 per cent of VC/NVA combat deaths annually while consuming only between 2 and 4 per cent of the annual costs of waging the war. Indeed, the success of the RF and PF was marked by their becoming a major target for communist attack: with the exception of the period of the Tet offensive, indeed, they consistently took a higher proportion of casualties than the ARVN.

The efforts of the South Vietnamese civilian agencies were no better directed or conceived. The Chieu Hoi (Open Arms) programme instituted in 1963 was said to have resulted in 75,000 communists defecting to the government by 1967. However, there is some suspicion that many *hoi chahn* (ralliers) were merely seeking temporary respite from the conflict before slipping back into the jungle, while others with little connection to the communists were seeking monetary gain. In 1969–70, perhaps only 17,000 of the 79,000 defectors were genuine. Once again, it was only the marines who made use of genuine defectors by forming them into the Kit Carson Scouts in October 1966.

An even greater failure was the resettlement programme. It was developed from the fortified *agrovilles* (rural towns) sited along strategic highways in April 1959 with 300 to 500 families grouped around rural community development centres. In the event, the *agrovilles* were constructed with forced labour and were resisted by the rural population to the extent that the programme was abandoned in 1961. Partly modelled on Israeli *kibbutzim* and partly sold to Diem by Robert Thompson and BRIAM, a new 'strategic hamlets' programme emerged in 1962. Thompson had been invited to visit Saigon by Diem in April 1960 and was then appointed to head BRIAM in September 1961. Britain saw it as a cheap means of demonstrating solidarity with the United States, which took on more significance when Britain needed US support during the Malaysian/Indonesian Confrontation. The problem was that, as co-chairman of the Geneva conference, Britain could not be seen to be involved in any military activity, and BRIAM consisted of Thompson and four others drawn from the Malayan civil service or police who could be portrayed as a purely civilian mission. In addition, South Vietnamese police had received training in Malaya for some time prior to BRIAM's establishment and continued to attend courses in Malaya.

It emerged that Kennedy thought highly of Thompson, and they were to meet in April 1963. Thompson's views were also welcomed by the civilian counter-insurgency experts around Kennedy such as Hilsman. However, American officials in South Vietnam and the American military establishment did not believe that the lessons of Malaya could be applied to Vietnam and resented Thompson's access to Diem. At Diem's request, Thompson produced an outline plan for pacification in November 1961, which targeted the Mekong delta region as the first priority for a resettlement programme since this was where the communist Viet Cong (VC) was weakest. Thompson envisaged 'strategic hamlets' of approximately 300 houses in areas of low risk and larger 'defended hamlets' in areas of greater risk. Protection, curfews and food control measures would be the responsibility of the Dan Ve, with the Bao An as the 'permanent static framework' at provincial level backed by mobile ARVN forces. As in Malaya, joint intelligence committees down to district level would ensure civil–military co-ordination. A paper by Hilsman in February 1962, 'A Strategic Concept for South Vietnam', which saw the need for a political solution to insurgency and emphasised civic action to win hearts and minds, embodied many of Thompson's ideas. However, Thompson's proposals conflicted with those of MAAG, which under its own 'Geographically Phased National Level Operation Plan for Counter-insurgency' of September 1961 wanted to give the priority to the so-called War Zone D to the north-east of Saigon, where the VC infrastructure was strongest.

The compromise was Operation Sunrise in March 1962, which began resettlement in Binh Duong province north of Saigon, which Diem regarded as important, to be followed by Operation Sea Swallow in the Phu Yen coastal province, of which Diem remarked to Thompson, 'It makes the Americans happy and it does not worry either me or the Viet Cong'. At the same time, however, these operations were coupled with Diem's adoption of a Delta Pacification Plan, establishing the Inter-ministerial Committee on Strategic Hamlets in February 1962 under the chairmanship of his brother, Ngo Dinh Nhu. However, it became clear that Diem and Nhu had a different interpretation of resettlement to that of Thompson, since they saw it merely as a means of extending physical control and their political influence over the rural population.

As a result, 3,225 strategic hamlets with a population of 4.3 million had been established by September 1962 alone out of a planned total of 11,316, but without adequate preparation or protection. In theory, there was nothing wrong with a programme that aimed to have government cadres prepare the population for resettlement, move with them to reorient them, and to provide basic services, with younger peasants trained to defend the new settlements in co-operation with the police and ARVN. In practice, however, the population was wedded to its traditional land in ways that made it unsuitable for resettle-ment. The supposed benefits did not appear commensurate with the sacrifice imposed on the population, and few of the strategic hamlets were economi-cally viable. In any case, the programme had become an end in itself, hence the apocryphal, 'If you stand long enough down there, they'll throw a piece of barbed wire round you and call you a strategic hamlet'. By July 1963, there were supposedly 7,200 strategic hamlets with a population of 8.7 million. Even if exaggerated, it was still a gross perversion of the original concept. So many settlements could not possibly be defended adequately, and the govern-ment's showpiece first hamlet at Ben Truong was itself burned to the ground by the VC in August 1963.

Thompson's influence with the South Vietnamese all but disappeared with the overthrow and murder of Diem and Nhu in November 1963. He had also been involved in the establishment of the Chieu Hoi programme and, subse-quently, was able to persuade McNamara of the benefits of appointing a single individual to co-ordinate American efforts in Vietnam, much as Templer had played a proconsular role in Malaya. When Maxwell Taylor was given such an appointment in 1964, however, he did not have the same powers enjoyed by Templer and chose not to exercise those he did have. With its usefulness clearly expended, BRIAM was wound down in March 1965. Subsequently, like Kennedy, Nixon was impressed by Thompson, who counselled against escalation of the war in 1969 and thereby reinforced Nixon's decision to begin Vietnamisation.

It says much for the South Vietnamese approach generally that when the USA insisted on the more dynamic name of 'revolutionary development' for the existing *xay dung nong thon* (rural construction) programme in February 1966, Saigon merely announced that the title would now be translated into English as 'revolutionary development'. Originating with the Hop Tac (Co-operation) Programme in September 1964, rural construction had been based on civic action or revolutionary development cadres known as people's action teams (PATs), whose function embraced 98 separate tasks including undertaking censuses, training militias, organising hamlet administration and defence, and improving the social, economic and educational environment. However, the teams were often drawn from urban youths and outsiders to the villages and strategic hamlets – the latter renamed 'new rural life hamlets' from January 1964 onwards – to which they were allocated. Moreover, the programme fell far short of the original aims of one of its 'intellectual fathers', Colonel Nguyen Be, a former Viet Minh commander, who had envisaged an integration of military and civilian efforts through a People's Self-Defense Force (PSDF) and a comprehensive reform programme including the provision of local autonomy, land redistribution and decentralised education policy. By 1967, however, it was claimed that 67 per cent of the population was 'secure' or 'relatively secure', compared with 42 per cent three years earlier.

All these various initiatives also suffered from a lack of overall co-ordination, the US Information Agency, the CIA and USAID all conducting their programmes independently, although nominally all reported to the US ambassador in Saigon. The missing ingredient was finally supplied in May 1967 by combining the revolutionary development programme with the US Office of Civil Operations, itself established in November 1966, in a new organisation known as Civil Operations and Revolutionary Development Support (CORDS), renamed Civil Operations and Rural Development Support in 1970. It was headed by Robert 'Blowtorch' Komer, initially appointed Special Assistant for Pacification to President Johnson in March 1966, who now ranked as a deputy to Westmoreland and as an ambassador. Only CIA covert operations and USAID's land reform programme remained outside his control. Initially, however, it still took time to agree a common approach among the agencies and personalities brought together and to persuade the South Vietnamese to co-operate, by which time the political struggle for the economic and physical security of the population had already been lost.

Komer had frequently urged a much greater emphasis upon pacification, regarded the ARVN as unsuited for pacification and favoured finding a means of tying the US army to a clear and hold approach to operations rather than search and destroy. This was highly unlikely given the views of Westmoreland and the Chairman of the Joint Chiefs of Staff, General Earle Wheeler, that pacification was a distinctly secondary consideration. Moreover, Komer's suggestions have been likened to a shotgun approach rather than a proper evaluation of pacification priorities. He also appears not to have balked at creating more internal refugees, not perceiving the way in which this aspect of US military operations damaged genuine pacification and nation building. Again, it could be argued that the kind of strategy evolved by Komer within the so-called Rostow Group at the end of 1966 was less relevant than it might have been two years previously. Nonetheless, CORDS gave a new impetus to pacification, although still being allocated only 4 per cent of the budget in the fiscal year 1969.

Primarily, CORDS sought greater results through the Hamlet Evaluation System (HES), introduced alongside the similar Pacification Evaluation System (PACES) and the Phung Hoang (Phoenix) Programme. Resettlement had continued apace, and the HES embraced 12,750 hamlets and 200 villages spread across 244 districts in 44 provinces. Unfortunately, the desire for statistical scorecards resulted in HES becoming to pacification what the body count came to represent for the army. Subjective ratings to indicate progress on an A–E scale and the way the questionnaire was actually constructed, using 37 multiple-choice questions per hamlet per month, meant that hamlets rated as satisfactory without being secure. In 1970, the rating system was made more objective through the application of a mathematical technique known as Bayesian probability analysis, based on 21 monthly and 56 quarterly questionnaires and four monthly and 58 quarterly village questionnaires. It was more sophisticated, but without noticeable differences in the interpretation of results. Thus, by June 1970, 95 per cent of the population was considered secure or relatively secure with a firm government hold on 32 out of the 44 provinces. Other statistics suggested, for example, that 75 per cent of the population had access to television by 1972, but such statistics had little relevance to success. Indeed, data from sources other than HES such as public attitude surveys suggested that the residents of the hamlets felt far less secure than suggested by HES, although there were clearly improvements in 1969–70.

Phoenix was a somewhat belated recognition of the significance of the VC infrastructure in supporting the revolution. Built on the special platoons established in Quang Ngai province in 1965, Phoenix began as the Intelligence Co-ordination and Exploitation Programme (ICEX) on 16 June 1967. It utilised existing CIA and South Vietnamese resources and became officially named Phoenix on 20 December 1967. The intention was to co-ordinate all intelligence activities in the South Vietnamese countryside in such a way as to enable provincial security committees to identify and then arrest VC agents. It was estimated that the VC might have as many as 70,000 such agents. Little progress was made, however, since the South Vietnamese disliked sharing intelligence with the Americans. Nor did the South Vietnamese government wish to involve its national police, whose task was seen more as preventing coups. Moreover, commitment to Phoenix was uneven, with some districts releasing as many as 60 per cent of suspects, some from bribery or fears of communist retaliation.

The shocks of the Tet offensive revived Phoenix in the same way that it led generally to the Accelerated Pacification Campaign (APC) in November 1968, with Saigon tailoring RF, PF, the police, the CIA-run Provincial Reconnaissance Units (PRU), the Nhan Dan Tu Ve (People's Self-Defense Force, PSDF) and even the ARVN to the task in hand. American units were also allocated to the APC. The PSDF, which was established on the back of the rural construction programme in early 1968, reached a strength of 1.3 million by 1970 and, with the application of compulsion, 4 million by 1972, while the PRU numbered about 4,000 by 1970. Americans attached to the programme were to be phased out by January 1969, but, in practice, about 650 Americans remained closely involved. However, abuses and corruption plagued Phoenix, and the quota for the number of VC to be eliminated each month, introduced by Saigon in August 1969, gave it the reputation of an assassination programme. Komer's successor as director of CORDS, William Colby, ordered American advisers to report any indiscriminate killing, but it is clear that some abuses occurred.

It was also the case that the intelligence was often unreliable and that too many of those eliminated were lower-level cadres rather than the higher VC leadership intended. Supposedly, by August 1972, Phoenix had neutralised over 81,000 VC, over 26,000 of whom had been killed. However, it was estimated that only 40 per cent were members of the Communist Party, and only 3 per cent were members of regional, provincial or national status. Yet, while Phoenix has been criticised, the North Vietnamese have generally agreed that it caused them heavy grass-roots efforts by the time it ended in March 1973. Similarly, they also disliked the impact of the PSDF. Like much else, however, these developments came too late in the war.

There are those who argued that only the main force war could have brought American success and that, if anything, it was waged too defensively. Thus, Hanoi's material and psychological links with the South could have been severed by a series of defended works along defensible frontiers, including inside Laos. This would have left, as Harry Summers has argued, 'the internal problem to the South Vietnamese themselves', since insurgency was merely a symptom of Hanoi's aggression. Others at the time criticised American strategy, including Komer and the 'Young Turks' of the Program for the Pacification and Long-term Development of South Vietnam (PROVN), an Army Staff study that, in March 1966, recommended giving pacification the main priority, albeit mostly by the ARVN. Although effectively suppressed, PROVN was eventually echoed in the endorsement by Westmoreland's successor, Creighton Abrams, of a greater emphasis on pacification in March 1969, although, in practice, Abrams's 'one war' approach did little to change military attitudes. Another critic was John Paul Vann, whose stock answer during the war to what immediate steps could be taken to strengthen the war effort was to recommend removing an American division. Vann, who was killed during the ARVN operations in Laos in 1971, argued that the Saigon government was structurally incapable of generating the social revolution required to win the war and wanted much greater American involvement in the 'other war'.

Westmoreland argued that there were simply not sufficient Americans to put in every village, but occupying every village was not essential. Indeed, it might have been possible, as Krepinevich argues, to defend South Vietnam through an enclave strategy, with American forces backing up the ARVN from secure bases, particularly if those American forces had been converted to a light infantry role to support more CAPs with just a few conventional divisions to deal with major communist incursions. It needs to be said, however, that it took 20,000 marines to defend the 800 square miles of the Da Nang air base adequately, and even this force did not prevent continued communist activity in the vicinity. Indeed, it follows from both viewpoints that neither the external threat from the NVA nor the internal threat from the VC was being adequately addressed.

Of course, one strategy did not preclude the other, and the real error was an artificial compartmentalisation of the 'main force' and 'other' wars. When American forces were committed in 1965, the situation was more than purely an insurgency, and a sophisticated strategy was required appropriate to a conflict that had to be fought at a number of different levels simultaneously. Clearly, the nature of the insurgency posed particular problems, but progress was made in 1970–71, although arguably largely as a result of the losses suffered by the NVA and, especially, the VC during the Tet offensive. Indeed, Eric Bergerud's detailed study of Hau Nghia province close to Saigon, building on the earlier study by Jeffrey Race on the neighbouring Long An province, not only points to the significance of Tet but also suggests that the enhanced counter-insurgency effort failed to result in a fundamental change in political attitudes among the rural population towards Saigon. In the case of Long An, despite the increasingly optimistic HES statistics, by 1968 the number of communists surrendering and the percentage of land tax collected were decreasing, the numbers avoiding Saigon's draft and the estimated communist strength increasing. In Hau Nghia, it was the communists rather than the government who possessed most legitimacy in the eyes of the rural population. Thus, communist cadres were often seen as more honest and efficient than government officials. In such circumstances, progress was made because Tet temporarily changed the balance of forces in the province.

However, everything depended upon the shield of the US military, but, after 1969, it was clear that Vietnamisation would remove that shield and thus invalidate any slim chance of success in changing grudging preference into whole-hearted support. In that sense, the war was always unwinnable.

The US military emerged from the Vietnam experience with a determination to avoid any more Vietnams. Indeed, under what became known in the 1980s after President Reagan's Secretary of Defense as the Weinberger doctrine, various criteria had to be fulfilled before it would be appropriate to commit US ground forces to combat. These included a need for clear objectives, a clear intent to win and the clear support of Congress and people for the objectives sought. The criteria were evident in the US intervention in Grenada in 1983, Panama in 1989 and the Persian Gulf in 1990. However, the army remained split over the lessons of Vietnam and, in the wake of the Yom Kippur War between Arabs and Israelis in October 1973, the 1976 and 1982 editions of FM 100–5 *Field Service Regulations: Operations* omitted the Kennedy-era chapters on sub-limited war scenarios. Its 1986 version maintained that the new 'AirLand Battle' doctrine intended for conventional warfare in Europe or similar theatres applied equally to what was now generally referred to as low-intensity warfare, defined as embracing a rag-tag of tasks including peace keeping and military provision of humanitarian aid as well as the counter-guerrilla and counter-terrorist role.

The same assumption was made by FM 90–8 *Counterguerrilla Operations* in 1986. Similarly, FM 31–22 *Command, Control and Support of Special Forces Operations* in 1981 focused on how special forces could assist large-scale military operations. FM 100–20 *Low Intensity Operations* in the same year continued to emphasise what has been characterised as a 'quasi-conventional' approach to insurgency. Its 1990 version, *Military Operations in Low Intensity Conflict*, treated insurgency and counter-insurgency in the same chapter as merely different sides of the same phenomenon and still gave undue emphasis to the notion that most insurgency would be supported externally, almost to the exclusion of internally generated challenges to government. Other 1980s tactical manuals mentioned low-intensity warfare hardly at all and, in any case, it can be argued that the very definition of low-intensity warfare emphasised the tactics involved in this form of conflict and not the underlying causes. Indeed, it has been suggested by Michael Shafer that the high-profile conference on low-intensity warfare organised by Weinberger at the Defense Department in January 1986 showed fundamentally little change in attitudes from the 1960s, with a continuing emphasis on Soviet subversion as the root cause of insurgency in the third world. Previous military practice also went unchallenged in the Training and Doctrine (TRADOC) pamphlet PAM 525–44 *US Operational Concept for Low Intensity Conflict* in 1988 and its successor, Joint Publication (Joint Pub) 3–07 *Joint Doctrine for Military Operations Other Than War*, in 1990.

Operations other than war (OOTW) had now superseded low-intensity warfare as the preferred description of the spectrum of conflict embracing counter-insurgency, peace keeping and other non-conventional operations. Indeed, a new FM 100–20 *Military Operations Other Than War* was being prepared in 1994 to replace *Military Operations in Low Intensity Conflict*. A distaste for what was now termed 'foreign internal defense' rather than counter-insurgency remained marked in the US military in the 1990s, and one military author, Rod Paschall, argued that, since the role was so destructive of military 'norms', it should even be contracted out to commercial security organisations in future.

Another indicator of unchanged attitudes within the American military was that being assigned as a special adviser to the armed forces in states judged at risk like El Salvador was not regarded as a fast track to promotion. Moreover, the performance of the Salvadoran army was somewhat reminiscent of that of the ARVN. El Salvador was the scene of escalating violence through the 1970s, culminating in the creation of a common guerrilla front, Frente Farabundo Martí de Liberación Nacional (Farabundo Martí National Liberation Front, FMLN), in 1980, which fought against the government until a cease-fire in 1992. It was named after Farabundo Martí, the communist who had fought with Sandino in Nicaragua in the 1920s and who had then been executed following the failure of a communist revolt in El Salvador in 1932. The nucleus of the FMLN was the earlier Fuerzas Populares de Liberación – Farabundo Martí (Popular Liberation Forces – Farabundo Martí, FPL-FM), which had begun to resist the military-dominated right-wing government of El Salvador in 1970. FMLN action included attacks on economic targets such as bridges, electricity supplies and irrigation systems in addition to temporary occupation of towns, to which the foreign press was invited to see the lack of government control before the insurgents slipped away. In many respects, FMLN attacked military targets only to distract attention from their economic targets, aimed at disrupting the production of the three main export crops of coffee, sugar and cotton from the provinces of San Vicente and Usulatan. At the period of their maximum ascendancy between 1981 and 1984, the insurgents could mount attacks with as many as 600 men at a time, a considerable achievement given their relatively poor level of internal support. Externally, however, FMLN enjoyed considerable support from a wide range of states, even France granting them formal recognition.

After a succession of military governments, pressure from the United States brought the more moderate José Napoleón Duarte to the presidency in 1980. However, Duarte appeared unable to control right-wing death squads, including those drawn from the National Guard, National Police, Treasury Police and armed forces. Death squads were responsible for the murder of Archbishop Oscar Romero in March 1980 and three American nuns in the following December. Then, in new elections in March 1982, Duarte was replaced as president by Roberto D'Aubuisson of the right-wing Alianza Republicana Nacionalista (Nationalist Republican Alliance, ARENA), who was closely involved with the death squads. The United States intervened to compel D'Aubuisson to step down after only a week, but death squad murders were still running at a rate of 1,200 a week by the end of 1982. Through Congressional opposition following the Vietnam experience, however, American advisers were restricted to the city limits of the capital, San Salvador, or to undertaking training in neighbouring Honduras, a problem in view of the so-called 'Soccer War' between Honduras and El Salvador in 1969. There were only nineteen advisers in 1979, but the number increased to 55, the first being killed in May 1983. Four specialised *casador* (hunter) anti-guerrilla battalions were trained and, between 1981 and 1983 alone, US aid totalled $235 million.

Despite the advisers' best efforts at promotion of small-unit operations, the security forces appeared unable to suppress the insurgency, primarily because most of those Salvadoran officers trained in the United States had imbibed the emphasis there on conventional operations. Thus, US-supplied howitzers were used for 'harassment and interdiction' fire of possible rather than known guerrilla positions, much as in South Vietnam. Similarly, heavily equipped Salvadoran troops were moved largely by helicopter or lorry and did not represent 'feet on the ground'. They rarely operated in less than battalion strength and depended on close fire support. Measures also included population relocation to 'drain the sea to catch the fish'. Yet at least the army was aware of the need to win the wider battle for legitimacy, and some reforms were instituted.

Duarte returned to power in 1984 and began negotiations with FMLN, but these failed to halt the fighting and ARENA, now led by Alfredo Cristiani Buchard, won the 1989 elections. Cristiani, too, attempted negotiations. Fighting continued, however, with a major FMLN offensive in November 1989, which forced the government to impose a state of siege in San Salvador. By 1990, an estimated 75,000 people had been killed in El Salvador. Peace accords were finally signed between FMLN and the government in January 1992.

American efforts were also not entirely successful in sponsoring a guerrilla warfare campaign in Nicaragua, where Frente Sandinista de Liberación (Sandinista National Liberation Front, FSLN) held power between 1979 and 1990, although American objectives were ultimately realised. FSLN was named for Sandino, who had been arrested and executed in 1934 on the orders of the director of the National Guard, Anastasio Somoza García. Two years after Sandino's death, Somoza seized power in Nicaragua and, although he was assassinated in 1956, control passed to his son, Luis Somoza Debyle. When Luis died in 1967, the presidency was assumed by his younger brother, Anastasio Somoza Debyle.

The tight hold on power maintained by the Somoza dynasty alienated even the more privileged members of Nicaraguan society, and both conservative and liberal factions attempted periodic challenges to the family. FSLN was formed in July 1961 by Carlos Fonseca Amador, Silvio Mayorga and Tomás Borge, but the Sandinistas as they became known enjoyed little initial success. Indeed, it was only in the early 1970s that a deteriorating economic situation stimulated support for the Sandinistas. This was coupled with the widespread disillusionment with the government following its failure to cope with the aftermath of a major earthquake in Managua in 1972 and the rumours that Somoza had pocketed international aid funds. The Sandinistas opened a more sustained guerrilla campaign in the Matagalpa mountains in December 1974, to which Somoza's response was the imposition of martial law. Recognising the potential for exploiting the general disaffection with the government, the Sandinistas modified their Marxist ideology in 1978 to extend their own popular appeal. Riots and strikes became commonplace as more of the population vented their displeasure at Somoza and his National Guard through the course of the year. The National Guard resorted to artillery, helicopter gunships and defoliants as the Sandinistas extended their military activity from the mountains to the main towns, thus combining urban terrorism and rural guerrilla warfare. The Sandinistas began a new offensive in May 1979 and closed on Managua. On 17 July 1979, Somoza fled to the United States, finally being assassinated in Paraguay in 1980.

The United States was alarmed at the prospect of Marxist control of Nicaragua and especially feared that the Sandinistas would now supply arms to FMLN in El Salvador. An economic embargo was imposed on Nicaragua and military assistance channelled to opponents of the Sandinistas, many of whom were former National Guardsmen. Several different groups, collectively known as the Contras (short for *Contrarevolucionario*, or counter-revolutionary) and numbering about 15,000, began a guerrilla campaign against the Sandinistas from bases in both Honduras and Costa Rica in 1981. There were two principal groups of Contras. Alianza Revolucionaria Democrática (Democratic Revolutionary Alliance, ARDE) was based in Costa Rica and led first by a former Sandinista guerrilla, Eden Pastora Gomez ('Commander Zero'), and later by Fernando Chamorro Rapaccioli ('El Negro'). The larger Fuerzas Democráticas Nicaragüenses (Nicaraguan Democratic Forces, FDN) was based in Honduras and led by Enrique Bermúdez. However, the Contras were swelled by anti-Sandinista bands recruited by wealthier peasantry from among the landless. Indeed, one analysis suggested that only 25 per cent of the Contras owned property, 60 per cent were under 25, and 90 per cent were illiterate or only semi-literate. The Indian population on the Atlantic coast also opposed Sandinista attempts to change their traditional way of life, forcing the government into maintaining a strong military presence and resorting to resettlement.

The US Senate voted to suspend American military aid to the Contras in 1984, but non-military aid was resumed in June 1985. The deputy director for political and military affairs on Reagan's National Security Council, Lieutenant-Colonel Oliver North, sought to continue supporting the Contras by diverting funds received from illegal arms sales to Iran. The Iran–Contra affair became known in November 1986, with North subsequently tried and convicted on three charges in February 1989. In Nicaragua itself, where the Sandinistas claimed the Contras had killed 10,000 people, peace negotiations were undertaken from 1983 onwards by the so-called Contadora group of Colombia, Mexico, Panama and Venezuela, but it proved a tortuous process frequently interrupted by the resumption of fighting. Eventually, agreement was reached in 1989 for the demobilisation of the 8,000 remaining Contras under UN supervision and the holding of new elections. Held in February 1990, these resulted in a sweeping electoral defeat for the Sandinistas at the hands of a fourteen-party coalition known as the Union Nacional de la Oposición (National Opposition Union).

The course of events in El Salvador and Nicaragua has understandably made the United States wary of direct involvement in Latin America and, in the case of Colombia, it has kept more at arms length. The surviving guerrilla groups enjoyed little success after the 1960s, but the continued existence of the Marxist FARC, the pro-Cuban ELN and the Maoist Ejército Popular de Liberación (Popular Liberation Army, EPL) required the Colombian armed forces to sustain the counter-insurgency effort. Moreover, a new pro-Cuban group, Movimiento 19 de Abril (19 April Movement, M-19), entered the field in 1976, following a split in the radical nationalist National Popular Alliance (ANAPO) party, which had failed to secure the presidency in the elections held in April 1970. Faced with the growing power of the drugs cartels, the government sought a series of cease-fires with the guerrilla groups in 1984, but those with M-19 and EPL broke down in 1985, while ELN remained distant from the process. M-19 gained considerable publicity from its seizure of diplomats in the Dominican Republic's embassy in Bogota in 1980, leading to a 61-day siege. Similarly, it seized the Supreme Court building in the capital in November 1985, with eleven judges and over 100 others dying in the subsequent gun battle. As the revived level of insurgency and the escalating drugs conflict prompted reaction from right-wing *sicarios* (death squads), the guerrilla movements forged a new organisation in 1987 known as the Co-ordinatora Guerrillera Simón Bolivár (Simon Bolivar Guerrilla Co-ordinating Board, CGSB), taking its name from the liberator of Bolivia, Colombia, Ecuador, Panama, Peru and Venezuela from the Spanish.

M-19, however, led by Carlos Pizzaro Leongomez, signed a new cease-fire in March 1989. Following a peace agreement in March 1990, M-19 participated in the national, provincial and local elections. FARC, which is thought to make $500 million a year from its links with the drugs cartels, remains the largest guerrilla movement in the field. ELN, which has about 5,000 guerrillas, still operates in the north-eastern foothills of the Andes and, with fewer links to the drugs cartels, has concentrated on attacking the multi-national oil companies operating in the Casanare region. In February 1998, the excommunicated Catholic priest Manuel Perez Martinez, who had led ELN since

1973, reached an accord paving the way for negotiations with the government. However, Perez died in April 1998, and it would appear that his successor, Nicolas Rodriguez Bautista, was not committed to the negotiations.

In 1999, therefore, the United States began training the Colombian army once more to meet the twin challenge of the remaining insurgents and the drugs cartels, in order to reduce the flow of drugs to the American mainland, 'Plan Colombia', to which the US Congress committed $1.6 billion in 1999, included provision for training three Colombian battalions, which would also be equipped with Black Hawk helicopters and Huey-2 helicopter gunships. It remains to be seen whether the United States will be drawn further into the conflict.

As South Vietnam fell, the communist Khmer Rouge (Red Khmers) were also beginning to consolidate their control over neighbouring Cambodia, Phnom Penh having fallen on 8 April 1975. Similarly, Vientiane, the capital of Laos, fell to the Pathet Lao in June 1975. As previously indicated, the 'dominoes' did not fall further, since communist insurgency was defeated in Thailand. The communist victories in South-east Asia, however, particularly when coupled with the weakness of the United States in the wake of Watergate, encouraged the Soviet Union to greater adventurism in its own foreign policy. Thus, Soviet aircraft were made available to transport Cuban troops to intervene successfully in the civil war in Angola in November 1975 and in the Ogaden War between Ethiopia and Somalia in November 1978. US interests were further weakened by the fall of the Shah of Iran to internal revolution in January 1979. The Soviet Union then intervened directly in Afghanistan in December 1979, the first time Soviet forces had been used outside the Soviet bloc. However, the war in Afghanistan was to prove as great a burden for the Soviets as South Vietnam had for the United States.

Soviet forces went to the assistance of a Marxist government that had come to power in Kabul through a military coup in April 1978. The hostility of the revolutionary government towards Islam and tribal culture led to increasing opposition, while the ruling People's Democratic Party itself was increasingly split into rival factions known as the *Khalq* (Masses) and the *Parcham* (Flag). After repeated requests by the government in Kabul, the Soviets intervened on 24–27 December 1979 under the terms of the Soviet–Afghan Treaty of Friendship and Co-operation of December 1978. They installed Babrak Karmal of the *Parcham* in power, but the Soviet presence quickly led to the emergence of Islamic fundamentalist guerrillas known as the *Mujahidin* (Warriors of God), an alliance of at least seven different Sunni Muslim resistance groups that came together more formally in 1985 as the 'Islamic Unity of Afghan Mujahidin'. Largely based in Pakistan, the 90,000 or so *Mujahidin* became increasingly effective and, even if their unity was often fragmented with a struggle between moderate and radical factions, they still had the unifying ideology of Islam and the appeal of the *jihad* (holy war) against the infidel.

One of the most prominent military commanders was Ahmad Shah Massoud, the 'Lion of the Panjshir' valley, who endeavoured to establish his own administration and even briefly concluded a truce with the Soviets. He successfully resisted at least nine separate Soviet attempts to control the valley, which lay close to the strategic Salang route between Kabul and Termez on the Soviet–Afghan border. In April and May 1984, for example, Massoud evaded between 15,000 and 26,000 Soviet and Afghan troops committed against him. Soviet forces remained in Afghanistan until 14 February 1989, by which time the conflict with the guerrillas had officially cost the Red Army just over 13,000 dead or missing, with over 35,000 wounded in action, over 50,000 injured on active service, and over 415,000 men having suffered from disease. The Afghan army apparently suffered about 26,000 dead, while the conflict as a whole may have resulted in the deaths of at least 200,000 Afghans and possibly as many as a million. With Soviet withdrawal, Kabul fell to the *Mujahidin* in April 1992, being occupied initially by Massoud on behalf of Burhanuddin Rabbani's Jam'iat-i Islami-yi Afghanistan (Islamic Society of Afghanistan). Fighting then continued between rival groups, with an extremist Islamic faction known as Taleban (Religious Students Movement) taking Kabul in September 1996. Najibullah Admazi, who had replaced Babrak Karmal in 1986, was seized and executed.

The swift military suppression of East Berlin in 1953, Hungary in 1956 and Czechoslovakia in 1968 did not require the Soviets to display the full range of the techniques learned in the 1920s. However, it was noticeable that Soviet military journals soon began to re-examine the techniques of Frunze in Central Asia and, eventually, new mountain warfare training centres were established in Azerbaijan and Tajikistan, although seemingly this did not improve Soviet performance. The Soviets also discovered that counter-insurgency offered a welcome training experience in the absence of conventional active service since 1945 and were able to test out new equipment such as the AK-74 rifle, the AGS-17 automatic grenade launcher and the Su-25 attack aircraft. Initially, however, the Soviets were clearly surprised by the failure of the insurgents to conform to the tactical doctrine expected of them and there was a distinct lack of flexibility in their response to guerrilla tactics. Air power certainly remained an integral component in the Soviet response in Afghanistan, especially the use of Mi-24 Hind helicopters both as gunships and as a means of deploying troops to high ground or to cut off guerrilla groups. At least 500 helicopters were deployed to Afghanistan by 1982, perhaps 200 of which were Hinds: over 300 were lost during the course of the war, together with a large amount of other equipment, including over 1,300 armoured personnel carriers. Chemical weapons were also used extensively, including Sarin and Soman nerve agents and the tricothecene toxin known as 'yellow rain'. The Soviets also encouraged their infantry to take the fight to the guerrillas rather than remain in their armoured personnel carriers when under attack. However, the problem was that the mechanised infantry were not trained to fight separated from their vehicles and were too heavily equipped to pursue guerrillas on foot. Increasing use was therefore made of helicopter-borne air assault brigades to take the offensive, since the mountain valleys did not permit the deployment of large ground formations. Blocking movements by such forces were often successful, but there were not enough such units and not enough helicopters. Tanks proved less than ineffective in escorting convoys through the poor elevation of their guns in mountainous terrain, and 2SU-23-4 self-propelled anti-aircraft guns were pressed into service instead.

The Soviets did not have the monopoly of firepower, for the *Mujahidin* were far better armed than previous guerrilla opponents, not least after their receipt of Stinger anti-aircraft missiles from the United States in 1986, which forced the Soviets into less effective high-altitude bombing. Clearly, however, they had a superiority of firepower based on a strategy characterised as a mixture of scorched earth and migratory genocide. An estimated 4 million refugees had already been generated by 1982. Soviet strategy was intended to hold the major centres of Kabul, Kandahar and Herat, to keep open the Salang road from Kabul to the Soviet Union, and to isolate main areas of opposition at minimum cost. Indeed, they did not lose control of the major urban centres or strategic routes, the largest Soviet concentration being around Kabul, with other significant deployments at Mazar-i-Sharif, Herat, Kandahar and Jelalabad. However, it was estimated that perhaps between 75 and 90 per cent of the country was not under their control or that of their largely ineffective and demoralised Afghan allies. Moreover, Soviet forces were vulnerable even on main routes, as suggested by the reported death of 700 Soviet troops in a bomb attack on the key Salang tunnel in October 1982.

The Soviets had about 120,000 men in Afghanistan by 1986, primarily allocated to 40th Army, also referred to as the 'Limited Contingent of Soviet Forces in Afghanistan'. They were supported by 30,000 men operating from Soviet territory. In all, 642,000 men were rotated through Afghanistan at some stage or other. Like American forces in South Vietnam, however, it appeared that the Soviets increasingly suffered from morale problems with drug taking, black marketeering, and internal ethnic and sectarian conflicts. Rations appear to have been poor and disease rife. Little realistic psychological training had been given to prepare troops for the strain of guerrilla warfare, and official explanations for their role in Afghanistan were increasingly hardly credible. As in Vietnam, there were distinct differences between those regarded essentially as garrison troops – about 80 per cent of the total – and the elite counter-insurgency units such as the air assault brigades and the *Spetsnaz* (Special Forces). The problems were compounded by the *dedovshchina* (rule of the grandfathers) system of 'hazing', by which newly arrived conscripts were subjected to considerable intimidation. With the

Soviet economy already suffering gravely from the ill-conceived attempt to match US defence spending, war costs of perhaps $3 billion annually added to the overall burden, which brought the entire Soviet system to collapse in 1991.

The collapse of the communist system exposed further internal weaknesses in the Red Army, or Russian army as it became once more in 1991. Thus, its handling of Chechen unrest between 1994 and 1996 was again largely ineffective, with lessons from Afghanistan such as the need for better tactical groupings, infantry trained in fire and manoeuvre, and better understanding of how to direct fire support neglected. The second Chechen war since 1999 has again revealed similar difficulties despite efforts at military reform. Inhabiting an area of the northern Caucasus on the frontier between the Russian Federation, of which Chechnya is part, and Georgia, the Chechen (or Nokhchi) are an Islamic people. They periodically fought against the occupying Russian army from the late eighteenth century onwards and for the neighbouring Daghestani leader, Shamil, during his revolt against Russia between 1834 and 1859. Chechens also supported the unsuccessful attempt to create an independent Republic of the North Caucasus during the Russian Civil War. Chechen unrest continued after the consolidation of Soviet control, and the Soviets resorted to mass deportations to Siberia in both 1937 and 1944. The Chechens were not allowed to return until 1957.

When the Soviet Union began to disintegrate in 1991, power was assumed by the Pan-national Congress of the Chechen People (OKCHN) under the leadership of Dzhokhar Dudayev. Independence was declared on 2 November 1991, but this was never recognised by the Russian Federation as successor to the Soviet Union. Opposition to Dudayev within Chechnya resulted in sporadic violence, and the Russian Federation took the opportunity to intervene in December 1994. Russian forces took the Chechen capital, Grozny, on 8 February 1995, but at great cost. Indeed, in the initial assault on 31 December 1994, one motor rifle brigade with an additional attached motor rifle battalion lost 20 out of its 26 tanks and 102 out of its 120 armoured personnel carriers. Moreover, the Chechens continued to wage guerrilla warfare. Dudayev was killed in a Soviet rocket attack in April 1996 and was succeeded by Zelimkhan Yandarbiyer. A cease-fire and peace agreement were eventually brokered in August 1996 on the basis of postponing any decision on Chechnya's independence until 2001. Elections then resulted in the victory of a moderate, Aslan Maskhadov, in January 1997, but the question of Chechnya's status within the Russian Federation remained unresolved.

Some Chechen warlords subsequently tried to export an Islamic revolution to neighbouring Daghestan, and Chechens were also blamed for bomb explosions in Moscow and elsewhere. Consequently, Russian forces undertook operations to drive 'illegal bandit formations' from Daghestan in August 1999 and intervened once more in Chechnya in October 1999. Vladimir Putin successfully campaigned for the Russian presidency in succession to Boris

Yeltsin in March 2000 almost entirely on his stand against Chechen 'terrorism'. Grozny was bombarded by artillery, and aircraft struck not only at the capital but also at economic assets such as dams and oil installations, while airborne assault units sealed the frontier with Georgia. After being bogged down for a while on its outskirts, the Russians took Grozny on 8 February 2000. The Chechens, however, withdrew to the south and have continued to resist in a conflict that has already generated at least 213,000 refugees.

Both Chechen wars have seen some confusion of command and control among Russian federal forces and divisions between the army under the control of the Defence Ministry and troops of the Interior Ministry, leading to the institution of joint force groupings for the second intervention. Units in the first war were often undermanned and poorly trained, and there was some combing out of conscripts of little experience before the second intervention. While Russian public support was greater for the second than the first war, reflecting much improved Russian control of information policy, it did not necessarily follow that conscripts were better motivated. Some 40 per cent of all Russian casualties in the first war were caused by accidents due to poor training or carelessness, and since the renewal of the conflict there appears to have been a tendency to rely upon so-called *contratniki* (contract servicemen), who are not regulars in the accepted sense of the word but more akin to mercenaries. As a result of the changes, however, 90,000 troops were deployed in the second war, as opposed to 30,000 in the first.

It was clearly intended to minimise casualties by fighting at maximum range, relying as so often in the past on concentrated firepower, including so-called fuel–air or thermobaric weapons, which create fireballs, such as the Buratino multiple-rocket launcher system. Above all, the Russians seem to have wished to keep the Chechens from closing with their units. Overall, however, despite the fall of Grozny, the Russian army seems little better prepared than in either Afghanistan or the first Chechen war to wage a prolonged guerrilla conflict, in which it seems to be losing between 20 and 50 men a week.

The experiences of the remaining superpower of the United States and the former superpower of the Soviet Union and its Russian federal successor state in combating insurgency have not been positive. As General John Galvin has suggested, insurgencies are 'uncomfortable wars' for soldiers at the best of times. In the case of particularly large conventional war machines, insurgencies are seemingly especially baffling and, as a 'poor man's war', clearly retain their potential to embarrass those for whom military hardware and resources are plentiful.

Further reading

The literature on the American involvement in South Vietnam is vast. Among many general histories, see George C. Herring, *America's Longest War:*

The United States and Vietnam, 1950–75 (New York, 1979); Stanley Karnow, *Vietnam: A History* (2nd edn, New York, 1984); Philip Davidson, *Vietnam at War: The History, 1946–75* (2nd edn, New York, 1988); Gabriel Kolko, *Anatomy of a War: Vietnam, the United States and the Modern Historical Experience* (New York, 1985); Guenther Lewy, *America in Vietnam* (New York, 1978); Gerard De Groot, *A Noble Cause? America and the War in Vietnam* (London, 2000); and Spencer Tucker, *Vietnam* (London, 1999).

On the US army generally, see Bruce Palmer, *The Twenty-Five Year War: America's Military Role in Vietnam* (Lexington, 1984); Shelby Stanton, *The Rise and Fall of an American Army: US Ground Forces in Vietnam, 1965–73* (Novato, 1985); Harry Summers, *On Strategy: A Critical Analysis of the Vietnam War* (2nd edn, New York, 1984); Cincinnatus [Cecil B. Currey], *Self-Destruction: The Disintegration and Decay of the US Army during the Vietnam Era* (New York, 1981).

On American counter-insurgency practice, see Larry Cable, *Unholy Grail: The US and the Wars in Vietnam, 1965–68* (London, 1991); Cable, *Conflict of Myths, op. cit.*; Shafer, *Deadly Paradigms, op. cit.*; Blaufarb, *Counterinsurgency Era, op cit.*; Andrew Krepinevich, *The Army and Vietnam* (Baltimore, 1986); Krepinevich, 'Recovery from Defeat: The US Army and Vietnam' in Andreopoulos and Selesky, *Aftermath of Defeat*, pp. 124–42; A.H. Paddock, *US Army Special Warfare: Its Origins* (Washington, 1982); Ronald Spector, *Advice and Support: The Early Years of the US Army in Vietnam, 1941–60* (New York, 1985); Jeffrey Clarke, *Advice and Support: The Final Years, 1965–73* (Washington, 1988); Peter Dunn, 'The American Army: The Vietnam War, 1965–73' in Beckett and Pimlott, *Armed Forces and Modern Counter-insurgency*, pp. 77–111; Donald Hamilton, *The Art of Insurgency: American Military Policy and the Future of Strategy in Southeast Asia* (Westport, 1998).

Specific aspects are covered by Jeffrey Race, *War Comes to Long An: Revolutionary Conflict in a Vietnamese Province* (Berkeley, 1972); Eric Bergerud, *The Dynamics of Defeat: The Vietnam War in Hau Nghia Province* (Boulder, 1991); Richard A. Hunt, *Pacification: The American Struggle for Vietnam's Hearts and Minds* (Boulder, 1995); Michael A. Hennessy, *Strategy in Vietnam: The Marines and Revolutionary Warfare in I Corps, 1965–72* (Westport, 1997); Ian Beckett, 'Robert Thompson and the British Advisory Mission to South Vietnam, 1961–65' *Small Wars and Insurgencies* 8 (1997), pp. 41–63; Carnes Lord, 'American Strategic Culture in Small Wars' in *ibid.*, 3 (1992), pp. 205–16; L. Sorley, 'To Change a War: General Harold K Johnson and the PROVN Study' *Parameters* 28 (1998), pp. 93–109; Douglas Valentine, *The Phoenix Program* (New York, 1990); Dale Andrade, *Ashes to Ashes: The Phoenix Program and the Vietnam War* (Lexington, 1990); Mark Moyar, *Phoenix and the Birds of Prey* (Annapolis, 1997); Lawrence Grinter, 'South Vietnam: Pacification Denied' *Southeast Asian Spectrum* 3 (1975), pp. 49–78; J.T. Wirtz, *The Tet Offensive* (New York, 1991); and Peter Braestrup, *Big Story* (New Haven, 1983).

Comparisons between Malaya and Vietnam can be found in Sam Sarkesian, *Unconventional Conflicts in a New Security Era: Lessons from Malaya and Vietnam* (Westport, 1993); Deborah Avant, *Political Institutional and Military Change: Lessons from Peripheral Wars* (Ithaca, 1994); and Tim Lomperis, *From People's War to People's Rule: Insurgency, Intervention and the Lessons of Vietnam* (Chapel Hill, 1996).

Among important memoirs, or biographies, see Robert Komer, *Bureaucracy at War: US Performance in the Vietnam Conflict* (Boulder, 1986); Roger Hilsman, *To Move a Nation: The Politics and Foreign Policy in the Administration of John F. Kennedy* (New York, 1967); and Neil Sheehan, *A Bright Shining Lie: John Paul Vann and America in Vietnam* (New York, 1988).

On the North Vietnamese and Viet Cong, see Duiker, *Communist Road to Power in Vietnam, op. cit.*; J.M. Gates, 'People's War in Vietnam' *Journal of Military History* 54 (1990), pp. 325–44; Douglas Pike, *PAVN: People's Army of North Vietnam* (Novato, 1986); Pike, *A History of Vietnamese Communism* (Stanford, 1978); Pike, *War, Peace and the Viet Cong* (Cambridge, Mass., 1969); Pike, *Viet Cong* (Cambridge, Mass., 1966); and George Tanham, *Communist Revolutionary Warfare: From the Viet Minh to the Viet Cong* (2nd edn, New York, 1967).

On El Salvador, see J. Dunkerley, *The Long War: Dictatorship and Revolution in El Salvador* (London, 1982); Hugh Byrne, *El Salvador's Civil War: A Study of Revolution* (Boulder, 1996); Philip Williams and Knut Walter, *Militarisation and Demilitarisation in El Salvador's Transition to Democracy* (Pittsburgh, 1997); Max Manwaring and Court Prisk, 'A Strategic View of Insurgencies: Insights from El Salvador' *Small Wars and Insurgencies* 4 (1993), pp. 53–72; and John Waghelstein, 'Ruminations of a Pachyderm or What I Learned in the Counter-insurgency Business' in *ibid.*, 5 (1994), pp. 360–78. On Nicaragua, see William Robinson and Kent Norsworthy, *David and Goliath: Washington's War against Nicaragua* (London, 1987); and R. Pardo-Maurer, *The Contras, 1980–89: A Special Kind of Politics* (New York, 1990). For death squads, see Michael Schroeder, 'To Induce a Sense of Terror: Caudilo Politics and Political Violence in Northern Nicaragua, 1926–34 and 1981–95' and Cynthia Arnson, 'Window on the Past: A Declassified History of Death Squads in El Salvador', both in Campbell and Brenner, *Death Squads in Global Perspective*, pp. 27–56, 85–124. On Colombia, see Paul Oquist, *Violence, Conflict and Politics in Colombia* (Berkeley, 1978); Paul Eddy, Hugo Sabogal and Sara Walden, *The Cocaine Wars* (London, 1988); and Jorge Osterling, *Democracy in Colombia: Clientist Politics and Guerrilla Warfare* (New Brunswick, 1989).

For the continuing debate on counter-insurgency in the US military, see Larry Cable, 'Re-inventing the Round Wheel: Insurgency, Counter-insurgency and Peacekeeping post Cold War' *Small Wars and Insurgencies* 4 (1993), pp. 228–62; Rod Paschall, *LIC 2010* (New York, 1990); Paschall, 'Low-Intensity Conflict Doctrine: Who Needs It?' *Parameters* 15 (1985), pp. 33–45; M.T. Klare and P. Kornbluh (eds), *Low Intensity Warfare* (New York,

1988); Max Manwaring (ed.), *Uncomfortable Wars* (Boulder, 1991); Steven Metz, 'An American Strategy for Low-Intensity Conflict' *Strategic Review* 17 (1989), pp. 9–17; Metz, 'AirLand Battle and Counterinsurgency' *Military Review* 70 (1990), pp. 32–41; Metz, 'A Flame Kept Burning: Counterinsurgency Support after the Cold War' *Parameters* 25 (1995), pp. 31–41; J.M. Gates, '"Low Intensity Conflict" and "Military Operations Short of War": The Humpty Dumpty Approach to the Development of Doctrine' *Military Affairs* 68 (1988), pp. 59–63; Loren Thompson (ed.), *Low-Intensity Conflict: The Pattern of Warfare in the Modern World* (Lexington, 1989); Richard Schultz, Robert Pfaltzgraff, Uri Ra'anan, William Olson and Igor Lukes (eds), *Guerrilla Warfare and Counterinsurgency: US–Soviet Policy in the Third World* (Lexington, 1989); Jennifer Morrison Taw and John Peters, 'Operations Other Than War: Implications for the US Army' *Small Wars and Insurgencies* 6 (1995), pp. 375–409; David Keithly and Paul Melshen, 'Past as Prologue: USMC Small Wars Doctrine' in *ibid.*, 8 (1997), pp. 87–108; and Kimbra Krueger, 'US Military Intervention in Third World Conflict: The Need for Integration of Total War and LIC Doctrine' *Low Intensity Conflict and Law Enforcement* 4 (1995), pp. 399–428.

On the Soviet experience in Afghanistan, see David Isby, *War in a Distant Country, Afghanistan: Invasion and Resistance* (London, 1989); Isby, *The War in Afghanistan, 1979–88: The Soviet Empire at High Tide* (Hong Kong, 1990); Oleg Sarin and L. Dvoretsky, *The Afghan Syndrome: The Soviet Union's Vietnam* (Novato, 1993); Scott McMichael, *The Stumbling Bear: Soviet Military Performance* (London, 1991); Mark Galeotti, *Afghanistan: The Soviet Union's Last War* (London, 1995); Milan Hauner, *The Soviet War in Afghanistan: Patterns of Russian Imperialism* (Lanham, 1991); Roy Oliver, *Islam and Resistance in Afghanistan* (Cambridge, 1990); Oliver, *Afghanistan: From Holy War to Civil War* (Princeton, 1994); Lester Grau, *The Bear Went over the Mountain: Soviet Combat Tactics in Afghanistan* (London, 1998); Roger Reese, *The Soviet Military Experience: A History of the Soviet Army, 1917–91* (London, 2000). On Chechnya, see Carlotta Gall and Thomas de Waal, *Chechnya: Calamity in the Caucasus* (New York, 1998); Anne Aldis (ed.), *The Second Chechen War* (Shrivenham, 2000); and Carl Van Dyke, 'Kabul to Grozny: A Critique of Soviet (Russian) Counter-insurgency Doctrine' *Journal of Slavic Military Studies* 9 (1996), pp. 689–705

9

FORWARD TO THE PAST

With the end of the Cold War and its concomitant ideological competition, it is clear that the pattern of military activity has changed. Moreover, increasing globalisation and the economic and political links that bind major states have made inter-state conflict much more difficult to sustain unilaterally. In Western societies, too, the growing unwillingness to risk large-scale casualties in warfare has coincided with the so-called 'revolution in military affairs' resulting from technological development to produce the kind of 'virtual war' practised in the Gulf and to a much greater extent in Kosovo. However, sanitised 'cyber-war' and the supposed 'New World Order' ushered in by the collapse of communism have not prevented intra-state conflict. Indeed, insurgency is just as prevalent, especially where the state system has remained underdeveloped in many parts of Africa, Asia and Latin America. Moreover, new imperatives have also encouraged insurgencies, which in some cases have increasingly blurred the distinctions between war and organised crime. Insurgency, therefore, remains a crucial challenge in the contemporary world.

The most recent examples of British counter-insurgency – that in the Dhofar province of Oman between June 1965 and December 1975, with particular reference to the period after July 1970, and that in Northern Ireland since August 1969 – illustrate how far lessons have been genuinely learned over the last 60 years, and also serve to establish contemporary patterns of insurgency and urban terrorism. Dhofar was only a small-scale conflict, although one in which failure would have had enormous repercussions for the West's strategic interests, for Oman overlooked the strategically vital oil route of the Strait of Hormuz, through which oil tankers carried 30 per cent of the United States' oil requirements, 70 per cent of Europe's and 90 per cent of Japan's. To quote Tony Jeapes, it was 'a classic of its type, in which every principle of counter-insurgency operations built up over the last fifty years in campaigns around the world by the British and other armies ... was employed'. However, Dhofar was an almost traditional rural campaign, whereas Northern Ireland has witnessed the mix of urban terrorism and rural insurgency that is likely to predominate in the future. That it has occurred in a democratic state has posed particular problems, and the British army has at least succeeded in reducing violence to what might be deemed an 'acceptable' level.

The flexibility of the British army has not been the model followed elsewhere, and both the Indian army and the Israeli Defence Forces (IDF), which have also faced long-running insurgencies, have persisted with largely conventional responses to similar models of rural insurgency and urban terrorism. The challenge of insurgency, however, is one being faced primarily by post-independence governments in developing countries. More often than not, the conditions relating to contemporary insurgency in the post-Cold War world have made insurgency a particularly potent threat.

Turning first to the more recent British experience, the relatively isolated and mountainous Dhofar province of Oman had been even more neglected than the rest of the country by its sultan, Said bin Taimur, who had little interest in using his growing oil revenues for the well-being of his people. Desperate for education and money, many Omanis illegally left this effectively feudal state, from which all symbols of modernity from medical drugs to bicycles, trousers and cigarettes were banned. There had been a brief insurgency in 1957, which had ended with the commitment of the SAS and the defeat of the rebels on the Jebel Akhdar (Green Mountain) in January 1959. Fuelled by both Arab nationalism and socialism, however, exiles founded the Dhofar Liberation Front (DLF) in the early 1960s, launching an insurrection on 9 June 1965 in the mountainous hinterland of Dhofar known as the *jebel*.

Neither the DLF nor the Sultan's Armed Forces (SAF) were sufficiently strong to prevail in this opening phase, and the insurgency drew renewed vigour from the emergence of a Marxist government in the People's Democratic Republic of Yemen (PDRY) when the British withdrew from the former Aden Protectorate in November 1967. The DLF was taken over by Marxist hardliners led by Muhammad Ahmad al-Ghassani and renamed the Popular Front for the Liberation of the Occupied Arabian Gulf (PFLOAG) in 1968, the title being slightly amended to the Popular Front for the Liberation of Oman and the Arabian Gulf in 1971 after the absorption of another small insurgent group. With Said firmly ruling out any concessions to the mountain tribes or *jebalis* backing the insurgents, little progress could be made until, with British support, he was overthrown by his son, Qaboos bin Said, on 23 July 1970. Under Qaboos, a more familiar pattern of counter-insurgency then began, guided by a British Army Training Team (BATT) drawn from the SAS and by various seconded or contract British officers attached to the SAF. Assisted also by both Imperial Iranian and Jordanian forces arriving in 1973 and 1974, respectively, the insurgency was brought to an end with Qaboos' formal declaration that the war was over on 11 December 1975. At peak, the British had perhaps 500 men in Oman in one capacity or another, while the SAF deployed about 10,000 troops in the Dhofar by 1974. PFLOAG probably had about 2,000 active fighters and 3,000 part-time militia at its peak in 1968–69.

In the case of Northern Ireland, British troops were committed to the streets following the formal request of the Northern Ireland government for military assistance on 14 August 1969 amid increasing communal and sectarian violence. Deployment was intended to safeguard Catholic areas in the light of the virtual collapse of the Royal Ulster Constabulary (RUC) under the pressures arising from the escalating civil rights campaign by the Northern Ireland Civil Rights Association (NICRA) over the previous two years. Living standards had improved in the 1950s and had stimulated the growth of a Catholic middle class, Catholics forming 38 per cent of the population by 1969. The prime minister of Northern Ireland, Captain Terence O'Neill, had hoped to draw these Catholics into public life but merely raised greater expectations than could be satisfied by the limited concessions on offer amid continuing discrimination against Catholics in housing and employment. In the event, it was to be the Catholic working-class community who were to be drawn into confrontation with the RUC. Formed in February 1967, NICRA demanded reform of the local government franchise and legislation against discrimination. Supposedly non-sectarian, NICRA embraced nationalist groups such as the Derry Citizens Action Committee and the radical People's Democracy. The latter rejected a reform package put forward by O'Neill in November 1968, and one of their marches from Belfast to Londonderry in January 169 met a violent Protestant reaction at Burntollet Bridge. O'Neill resigned in May, and his successor, Major James Chichester-Clark, announced further concessions. These were resented in turn by the Protestants, who sought to reassert their own perceived rights during the annual 'marching season' in July and August. Catholics erected barriers around 'Free Derry' in response, and the RUC rapidly became exhausted and demoralised in the disturbances that ensued.

Troops were initially welcomed by the Catholics. However, the army was not directed to establish a permanently strong presence in the Catholic areas, which became effective 'no-go' areas shielded not only from Protestants but also from normal policing. Moreover, at this stage, the army was increasingly seen to be acting in the interests of an institution discredited in nationalist eyes, namely the Stormont government. The old-style Marxist IRA, which had continued to exist since the division of Ireland in 1921 and had conducted unsuccessful campaigns in Britain and Northern Ireland both in 1939 and between 1956 and 1962, was caught somewhat by surprise by the course of events. Its hesitancy resulted in a breakaway by mostly northern militants, who formed the Provisional IRA (PIRA) in December 1969, determined to provoke and exploit confrontations between troops and the Catholics. Street violence increased throughout the spring of 1970 and reached its peak in 1971–72, the first soldier being killed on 6 February 1971.

Internment had worked well during the limited IRA campaign of 1956–62 and, against the army's advice, was introduced on 9 August 1971 under the provisions of the 1922 Civil Authorities (Special Powers) Act

(Northern Ireland). A total of 1,576 individuals were arrested in four months, 934 of whom were detained. Internment, however, was marked by poor and defective police intelligence, with many of the new younger emerging militants missed, while the fact that only Catholics were arrested exacerbated the situation on the streets. Many officers believed that, while it gave reassurance to the Protestants, it should have been coupled with the imposition of direct rule as a sop to the Catholics. In the event, direct rule of the province was assumed by Westminster on 24 March 1972. It was welcomed by the army as likely to lead to clear political direction without the intervention of the Stormont government, but the army was directed not to enter the no-go areas and to scale down overt patrolling and surveillance. Together with the disastrous error by the Heath government in negotiating a 'pause' with PIRA, this enabled PIRA to regroup within the no-go areas and led to the so-called 'Bloody Friday' on 21 July, when a series of 22 bombs were detonated in Belfast city centre. Operation Motorman was mounted with 27 battalions to repossess the no-go areas on 31 July 1972. Internment ceased in December 1975, but direct rule has continued, although an assembly and power-sharing executive was restored to the province in 1998. By February 1997, the 'Troubles' had cost 3,211 lives.

The Official IRA, as the original group became known after December 1969, announced a cease-fire in May 1972. As already indicated, PIRA announced a brief cease-fire between 26 June and 9 July 1972, followed by others from 22 December 1974 to 22 November 1975, from 31 August 1994 to February 1996 and since July 1997. PIRA has perhaps 600 activists, but several thousand active supporters and conceivably 80,000–90,000 political sympathisers. The Trotskyist Irish Republican Socialist Party (IRSL) and its military wing, the National Liberation Army (INLA), broke away from the PIRA in December 1974 but was a small organisation and one much disrupted by internal blood-letting in 1987. It declared a cease-fire in August 1998. With the cease-fire of PIRA in July 1997 and the entry of its political representatives, Sinn Féin, into all-party talks in September 1997, there were further splits in the Republican movement. Continuity IRA and its political wing, Republican Sinn Féin, had already emerged in 1986 after Sinn Féin recognised the parliament in the Irish Republic. The Real IRA and its political wing, the 32 County Sovereignty Movement, emerged in late 1997 with an estimated 400 members and was responsible for the Omagh bomb attack in August 1998. It, too, then issued a cease-fire statement, although incidents have continued, not least in London with bombs on railway lines and a rocket attack on the headquarters of MI6 on the Thames Embankment.

On the other side of the sectarian divide, various Protestant paramilitaries have emerged, including the Ulster Defence Association (UDA), which has links with the Ulster Freedom Fighters (UFF) and has perhaps between 1,500 and 2,000 members; and the Ulster Volunteer Force (UVF), which has perhaps between 750 and 1,000 members. Ironically, the first policeman to be killed in the 'Troubles' was a victim of the loyalist paramilitaries in October 1969. Increasingly active through the late 1980s and 1990s, the Protestant paramilitaries declared a cease-fire on 13 October 1994.

At peak, there were 22,000 troops in Ulster in 1971–72, but there has been a policy of 'Ulsterisation' since the announcement of the 'Way Ahead' policy on 12 January 1977 and the number had fallen to 11,000 prior to the present cease-fire. In addition, the RUC has about 13,000 men and women, while the Ulster Defence Regiment, formed in December 1969 in succession to the discredited and disbanded RUC Reserve or 'B Specials', had a strength of about 7,700 by 1975: it became a part-time element of the regular Royal Irish Regiment in July 1992.

Turning to insurgent methods in Dhofar, PFLOAG was able after 1967 to operate from a safe haven at Hauf inside the PDRY, raiding into Dhofar and maintaining camel-borne supply routes to so-called 'liberated areas'. Known to the SAF as *adoo* (enemy), the insurgents were highly mobile and well armed with Soviet and Chinese weapons, preferring either ambush at short range or, by choice, a longer range bombardment enabling them to withdraw quickly. They disliked fighting at night, which they used for movement or mine laying, and were not capable of holding ground permanently except in the vicinity of Hauf, where they were covered by PDRY artillery.

By comparison, the terrorist campaign in Northern Ireland has been rather more sophisticated and, in common with other contemporary insurgencies and terrorist campaigns has been conducted both in rural and urban areas and on an international stage. Indeed, there has been a dual military and political strategy, expressed by Danny Morrison as one of the 'bullet and the ballot box', pursued by a collective leadership. In Northern Ireland itself, the Provisionals have constantly changed the nature of the military threat but, generally, have favoured bombing, sniping and murder, with occasional attempted longer-range bombardment of isolated strongpoints. Indeed, J. Bowyer Bell has argued that, like other revolutionary movements in the middle of an armed struggle, PIRA is tactically conservative and 'has little time to allot to any sort of internal analysis'. It is, therefore, something of a prisoner of its own history, and its 'tomorrow tends to be like its yesterday'. The organisation has been strengthened by adoption of a cell structure in 1977 and, despite security force successes, the deeper political divisions in Northern Ireland have meant that there has been no shortage of recruits to make good its losses.

There has also been a mainland bombing campaign on occasions such as the attack on a ceremonial escort of the Life Guards in Hyde Park and the Royal Green Jackets Band in Regents Park on 20 July 1982, the mortar attack on Downing Street on 7 February 1991 and the Warrington bomb on 20 March 1993. As in the case of the INLA bomb attack at Warrenpoint and the murder of Lord Mountbatten at Mullaghmore in County Sligo, both on 27 August 1979, or the PIRA attack on the Grand Hotel, Brighton on 12

October 1984 during the Conservative Party conference, the emphasis has been on the spectacular because the terrorists have understood the importance of media coverage. They recognise that one successful attack on the mainland is worth far more than any in Ulster. There have also been PIRA and INLA operations against British troops in Europe, as, for example, with the attempted bombing of the Royal Anglian Regiment Band at Gibraltar in March 1988. They have maintained links with other terrorist groups overseas, and PIRA has successfully operated as a semi-criminal oligarchy in extorting funds in Northern Ireland to the tune of possibly £500,000 to £750,000 per annum in addition to drawing upon financial assistance from groups overseas such as NORAID in the United States.

Like PFLOAG, it can also be argued that the Provisionals, INLA and the other republican groups have also enjoyed sanctuary across an international frontier, in this case that with the Irish Republic. This has been described as a 'leaking sieve', although the republic has stronger anti-terrorist legislation than Britain and much of the problem related to the 123-mile length of the border. In south Armagh alone, for example, there were 169 officially recognised crossing points and a larger number of unofficial ones. Indeed, there was one well-publicised case of SAS men crossing the border in error in May 1976 and being arrested by the Irish police, or Gardai. Bowyer Bell has argued, however, that PIRA embarked on a protracted campaign with few viable political options, grave difficulties in obtaining any degree of military escalation and dependent upon 'maintaining an intensity level high enough to attract London's attention' in the hope that, in the long term, Britain would tire of the problem. It is what he calls a 'slogan strategy'.

In their differing ways, therefore, the threats posed by PFLOAG and the Provisionals were equally challenging, and it is instructive to compare the response in terms of those six elements of a successful counter-insurgency strategy identified earlier in this volume: namely, the recognition of the need for a political rather than a purely military solution; the necessity for complete civil–military co-operation; the equal necessity for a co-ordinated intelligence effort; the need to split active insurgents from their supporters; the use of appropriate military measures; and the need for long-term political reforms to prevent a resurgence of trouble.

In terms of the recognition of the need for a political response, this certainly came to Dhofar with Qaboos' assumption of power. Within 24 hours of his coup, Qaboos began to establish a modern centralised administration, lifting all restrictions on movement within and outside the state, releasing political prisoners and announcing a development plan for the whole of Oman to provide education, housing, communications and medical facilities based on the increasing oil revenues. In the Dhofar itself, a Dhofar Development Committee supervised the expenditure of £218 million on roads, schools, clinics, mosques and wells between 1971 and 1975.

In Northern Ireland, there has been a recognition from the beginning on the part of successive British governments that a political solution is required. Initially, the expectation was that once the army had separated the communities, a dual process of effecting reform and establishing normal policing would soon solve the problem. Indeed, the view of Harold Wilson's Home Secretary, James Callaghan, that 'the border is not an issue' became something of a policy mantra all too evident in the Hunt Committee report on policing in 1969, the Cameron Commission report on the original disturbances and, later, the Scarman Tribunal report on the causes of the violence. This assessment proved all too optimistic, and political initiatives have come in bewildering succession: the imposition of direct rule; the short-lived power-sharing executive of January to May 1974, brought down by a province-wide Protestant general strike; the devolution proposals of 1977; the establishment of the Northern Ireland assembly from 1982 to 1986; the Anglo-Irish or Hillsborough agreement of November 1985; and talks on new devolution proposals between 1990 and 1992. In 1996, elections were announced for a consultative body to proceed to all-party talks on the basis of conditions suggested by the US-sponsored Mitchell Commission of December 1995. A peace forum was elected in May 1996 and negotiations eventually led to an agreement in April 1998, allowing for recognition of the principle of consent, by which Ulster would remain part of the United Kingdom so long as the majority willed it so, an assembly and a power-sharing executive, a North–South ministerial council, a so-called Council of the Isles, and a commitment to paramilitary disarmament. The new executive began work in 1999, but the peace process remains a tentative one, not least from the failure of PIRA to commit itself to decommissioning its weapons.

The difficulty has been that there is no real political life or tradition in the sense that, in most democratic systems, political debate takes place inside a generally accepted framework. By contrast, in Northern Ireland, a large minority does not support the existence of the constitution and the state, while significant elements within the majority will not accept any compromise suggestive of the surrender of sovereignty to the Irish Republic, which claimed Ulster under articles II and III of its own constitution until 1998. Moreover, religion has become the basis for murderous tribalism, and there are vested interests on all sides militating against a solution satisfactory to all parties.

As far as civil–military co-operation is concerned, this was secured in Oman with the establishment of the National Defence Council, meeting for the first time in May 1973, while the Dhofar Development Committee, which met weekly under the chairmanship of Sheikh Braik bin Hamoud, acted as the co-ordinating body at provincial level with representatives of the army, police, and civil and intelligence agencies. The greatest difficulty remained co-ordinating operations with the Imperial Iranian Battle Group (IIBG), since virtually all decisions affecting the Iranians had to be cleared personally with the Shah of Iran. In Northern Ireland, a series of co-ordinating committees have also evolved with security policy meetings, the security co-ordinating meeting and the Operations Co-ordinating Group at the top of the structure and, beneath them, regional, divisional and subdivisional action committees. Significantly, however, unlike the committee structure established in other British campaigns, civil representatives in Northern Ireland have not been included at regional, divisional and subdivisional level, thus failing to provide political input and direction at lower levels.

Moreover, the structure evolved only gradually, and there has been frequent friction between army and RUC. Initially, the army took primacy and had the main responsibility for public order, and it was not answerable to the Stormont government, which continued to exist until direct rule was imposed in March 1972. As brigade commander in Belfast in 1970, the veteran of the counter-gangs in Kenya, Frank Kitson, attempted better civil–military co-operation through initiating the divisional action committees. A single civil affairs representative was appointed in September 1971 to help the army to liaise with the police, government departments and the local community in Belfast, and this was extended to the province as a whole in the following year. 'Ulsterisation', announced in January 1977, re-established police primacy, with first-line support to the RUC to be provided by the UDR and the army very much in support. In effect, it substituted internal security for counter-insurgency. The then GOC in Northern Ireland, Lieutenant-General Sir Timothy Creasey, who significantly had been commander of the SAF in Oman from September 1972 to March 1975 and, as such, enjoyed direct access to Qaboos, had serious reservations about police primacy. In particular, the death of eighteen members of the 2nd Battalion, Parachute Regiment and Queen's Own Highlanders at Warrenpoint in August 1979 suggested to Creasey that police primacy was premature.

Indeed, relationships deteriorated to such an extent that, in October 1979. both Creasey and the RUC Chief Constable, Sir Kenneth Newman, who had apparently joked about Creasey's 'Malayan views', were removed. Sir Maurice Oldfield, former head of MI6, was established as security co-ordinator, with Lieutenant-General Sir Richard Lawson as the new GOC and Jack, later Sir John, Hermon as the new Chief Constable. Oldfield, who was suffering from cancer, was succeeded briefly by Sir Brooks Richards, but the post lapsed in 1981. It did not amount to a director of operations, as was the case with Templer in Malaya, primarily through the reluctance to suggest anything other than an air of normalcy but also through the complex political infrastructure in Northern Ireland.

Intelligence co-ordination was actually one of the poorest aspects of the campaign in the Dhofar, and it was fortunate that PFLOAG did not pose a threat of subversion outside the province. Indeed, there was no police force in Dhofar until November 1971, and it was limited to traffic duties and minor crime in the main town of Salalah. Military intelligence was obtained from air and ground reconnaissance and direct ground contact, and most derived from captured insurgents. Initially, the Oman Intelligence Service (OIS) proved reluctant to share information derived from interrogation with the SAF until Creasey demanded improvements in 1972.

Co-ordination was difficult in Northern Ireland when the army had to build an intelligence network from scratch in 1969, not least in view of the suspicion of the RUC among Catholics and the neglect of intelligence by the RUC through financial constraints and lack of foresight. It was a difficult challenge in a relatively small province, in which society was characterised by membership of narrow kinship groups of one kind or another. Outsiders might speak with a convincing local accent but would have no past in common with those in the groups they sought to infiltrate. It was a situation not perhaps envisaged by Frank Kitson, whose *Low Intensity Operations*, published in 1971, attracted much controversy by challenging more traditional British approaches to counter-insurgency.

Following his service in Kenya, Kitson had moved to Malaya during the latter stages of the emergency and then to Oman, where he participated in the defeat of insurgents on the Jebel Akhdar. Kitson then served in Cyprus from 1962 to 1964, experiencing UN peace-keeping operations, and wrote *Low Intensity Operations* while a Ministry of Defence-sponsored defence fellow at the University of Oxford from 1969 to 1970. When it was published, Kitson was commanding 39 Infantry Brigade in Belfast.

Kitson's starting point was that, like other major armies, the British trained mostly for conventional warfare when the majority of its operations since 1945 had been in some form of low-intensity conflict. Kitson therefore believed it as important to train and educate the army for counter-insurgency as for conventional war. Kitson's analysis of the nature of insurgency itself differed little from that of other theorists of counter-insurgency such as Thompson and merely reflected evolving British practice. However, Kitson's suggested response to insurgency differed considerably from Thompson's in terms of the relationship between army and police. Kitson argued that the police were usually the first target for insurgent attack and, in effect, the army frequently had to rebuild the intelligence organisation anyway. It would be better, therefore, to train army officers in advance to take early control of intelligence operations, since the army was the primary user of intelligence. Coupled with Kitson's call for a radical overhaul of the army's training with regard to counter-insurgency – he also wanted a permanent corps of indigenous 'trackers' – the issue of military primacy aroused particular controversy primarily because the book's publication coincided with the escalation of the 'Troubles'. Thus, in some quarters, Kitson found himself depicted quite unjustly almost as a potential military dictator, particularly by one left-wing French journalist, who claimed that Kitson had been sent to Belfast as a 'testing ground' for his theories. In reality, Kitson had little opportunity to implement his idea outside his own brigade area.

In the longer term Kitson was more successful. The manual *Land*

Operations Volume III Counter-Revolutionary Operations, which replaced the 1963 edition of *Keeping the Peace* in 1969, stressed much of the accumulated experience though focusing heavily on Malaya and markedly skating over urban situations such as Palestine, Cyprus and Aden, although it did stress the importance of intelligence and that it should be centrally controlled. The 1977 edition reflected more of Kitson's approach, especially his flexibility, which freed the army from its fixation on Malaya.

In Northern Ireland, a variety of methods were used to fill the manifold intelligence gaps, including local censuses, confidential telephone numbers, constant patrolling, snap searches and vehicle checks: possibly four million vehicles were stopped between 1 April 1973 and 1 April 1974 alone. Deep interrogation, based on sensory deprivation, was also used on some suspects following internment. However, deep interrogation was ended following Lord Gardiner's minority report condemning the practice in March 1972. It was subsequently alleged that new RUC specialist interrogation centres resorted to abuses in 1977–78, and further safeguards were introduced in March 1979. Covert operations attracted similar controversy, especially when connected to the deployment to south Armagh of the SAS, whose presence was officially announced in January 1976. As Tom Mockaitis has suggested, special forces may attract undue political attention, especially if operating in plain clothes in an urban environment unless solely confined to intelligence work, since operating out of uniform and conducting ambushes of known terrorists risks the suspicion that they are exceeding the law. Incidents such as that in May 1987 at Loughall RUC Station, when eight terrorists walked into an SAS ambush in which a passing motorist was also killed, and in March 1988 when three terrorist bombers were killed in Gibraltar, led to such attention amid wider allegations of a 'shoot to kill policy' – investigated by the Stalker Inquiry in 1984. The Field Research Unit (FRU), established in 1980 to deal with informers, has also been a subject of controversy in recent years. In 1989, in investigating allegations of collusion between the UDR and Protestant paramilitaries, the Stevens Inquiry exposed the use of informers by FRU, one of whom was to be convicted of a number of terrorist offences. Subsequently, there have been other allegations that some murders had been permitted to occur in order to preserve the cover of an agent placed in the UDA.

Earlier covert operations were also often problematic. The plain-clothes Mobile Reconnaissance Force (MRF), initiated by Kitson, which included former terrorists known as 'Freds', established the 'Four Square Laundry', which examined washing from West Belfast for traces of explosives. However, its cover was blown in October 1972. With the disbanding of the MRF, covert surveillance passed to 14 Intelligence Company, later 14 Intelligence and Security Company and then made part of the Intelligence and Security Group with an attached SAS troop. Its efforts were supplemented by Close Observation Platoons from 1976 onwards, but there was clearly a lack of co-ordination between army and Special Branch, the RUC also maintaining its own surveillance units. In May 1977, PIRA murdered Captain Robert Nairac while he was on undercover duties, although apparently they were not clear whether he was a soldier or a member of the Official IRA. Rivalries between MI5 and MI6 also exacerbated co-ordination problems.

The difficulties of intimidation of witnesses also forced such measures as the introduction of 'Diplock' courts sitting without juries from 1973 onwards, extended detention under the Prevention of Terrorism Act and Northern Ireland (Emergency Provisions) Acts and the assumption that a refusal to answer questions implied guilt under the Criminal Evidence (Northern Ireland) Order. The 'super-grass' informer system was also employed between 1982 and 1986, but 50 of the 120 individuals convicted on such evidence had the verdicts overturned when the trials were suspended. Consequently, in later years, much depended on permanent battalion tactical areas of responsibility (TAORs), which assisted continuity, and the accumulation of local knowledge. Surveillance has also become increasingly sophisticated, including the computerised Vengeful system for vehicle identification, aerial infrared and thermal imaging equipment, and so-called heli-telly flights by helicopters.

Splitting insurgents from supporters was again easier in Dhofar than it has proved in Northern Ireland. The effort in Dhofar was spearheaded by the British Army Training Team (BATT) drawn from the SAS, deployed to Oman following Qaboos' appeal for assistance. The BATT plan for victory, as outlined by Lieutenant-Colonel John Watts in 1970, included not only the need to acquire intelligence on the threat posed by PFLOAG but also an information service to disseminate government policies, medical assistance to the *jebalis*, veterinary facilities for the improvement of their prized cattle and directly involving the people in the fight for their province. Spearheading the plan were the civil action teams (CATs), a phrase originated by Watts's assistant, Major Peter de la Billiere. CATs established centres by laying down a track; dug wells, which became a focus for population and cattle in an arid country; and then introduced education and medical facilities and longer-term improvement in cattle stocks and market opportunities for local goods. In many respects, the CATs took the place of the kind of lower-level committees that had established co-ordination in earlier campaigns.

What assisted the process was PFLOAG's mistake in attempting to impose an ideological Marxism, which was anathema to the two fundamental principles of *jebali* life, namely Islam and the tribal system. Indeed, it led directly to the defection from PFLOAG of 24 of the most experienced of the former DLF guerrillas in September 1970, who became the nucleus of the first pseudo unit or *firqat* (force). The SAS were at the heart of the *firqats*, an SAS officer Captain Mike Kealy directing a notable defence of Mirbat by a *firqat* in July 1972, which marked the real turning of the tide against PFLOAG on the *jebel*. However, there were always some difficulties in handling the 1,600 members of the 21 different *firqats* that existed by the end of the campaign. Moving to a tribal basis, however, and making each *firqat* responsible for the selection of its own centres, increased reliability and, although always volatile, they became an effective territorial home guard, driving a real wedge between insurgents and people. The government centres were also successful, with the establishment of the first permanent presence on the *jebel* in October 1971 at 'White City', later renamed Medinat Al Haq (City of the Truth) in the Wadi Darbat. It was quickly followed by the organisation of the first cattle drive in November 1971 to bring livestock to market. A Civil Aid Department (CAD) was established in 1973 by a former SAS man, Martin Robb, and, as areas of the *jebel* were cleared, so Robb's department would fly in prefabricated buildings for schools, clinics and shops. By June 1975, a total of 35 wells had been dug and 150 miles of motorable track laid. An efficient propaganda campaign was also waged through leaflets, which highlighted the Marxist threat to Islam. Radio Dhofar was also significant, with transistor radios being first given and later sold cheaply to *jebalis*, the subtle distinction being that when PFLOAG guerrillas smashed a radio someone had purchased, it resulted in a rather different reaction than when a radio that had been given freely and could be replaced freely was smashed. SAS information specialists devised a highly effective campaign around the slogan, 'Islam is our Way, Freedom is our Aim', which thoroughly discredited the appeal of the insurgents' Radio Aden.

Further separation of insurgent from population occurred with the establishment of physical barriers to cut across PFLOAG infiltration routes from the PDRY. The so-called Leopard line established west of Salalah in December 1971 was not entirely successful. Moreover, Operation Simba in April 1972 to establish a permanent base at Sarfait close to the Yemeni border at Hauf ran into difficulties when it was found to be too difficult to move down to the lower plateau and the sea, and that the caravan route to be intercepted was not visible from the position. As a result, the air-supplied base was maintained under something like siege conditions. Much more successful were the Hornbeam and Damavand lines in 1973–74 and 1975, respectively. Constructed from December 1973 to June 1974, the Hornbeam line effectively replaced the Leopard line with 15,000 coils of wire and over 4,000 mines backed by five main patrol bases and artillery positions. The Damavand line, named after Iran's highest peak, was constructed by the IIBG once they had cleared Rakhuyt in January 1975. Insurgent camel trains were also increasingly attacked from the air, air power also generally being of great significance in supplying the SAF in the field and enabling the construction of the fortified lines.

In Northern Ireland, such a separation of population from insurgent has not proved possible given the intransigent nature of the respective communities. Indeed, symptomatic of the problem was the Ulster version of the Berlin Wall, constructed in 1969 to separate Catholic and Protestant areas. The army's civil representatives were intended to try to deal with problems arising in relations between army and civilian population, while the army also responded to the new conditions of media exposure by training its officers in media relations and establishing an information policy office in September 1971. The army also built a number of youth centres, but this was not part of any wider co-ordinated campaign. Indeed, it was still the case in 1975 that the real points of contact between government as a whole and the 250,000-strong Catholic community in West Belfast amounted to no more than six sub-post offices, two police stations, four civil affairs advisers, a 'public cleansing yard', a welfare office and a housing executive repair yard. This failure to win hearts and minds has also been despite the substantial progress towards correcting the discrimination that affected Catholics prior to 1969 through largely economic measures such as the expenditure of £130 million on housing renovation schemes in Belfast alone since 1971, and legislation such as the Fair Employment (Northern Ireland) Act in 1976.

Similarly, Sir Arthur Young, who had remodelled the Malayan police and had also attempted unsuccessfully to do the same in Kenya, was brought to Northern Ireland to remodel the RUC in 1969. Young, however, failed to remodel the RUC in the image of the Metropolitan Police largely through not recognising the extent of the threat from the Provisionals. His successors, especially Newman, were more successful in modernising the police, and the RUC has emerged with improved quality and morale, although this is not to say that it is necessarily any more acceptable in hardline nationalist areas. Moreover, while the standard of living of Catholics has increased markedly and the province is awash with money, the unemployment rate among Catholics remains higher than among Protestants, and they are still under-represented in skilled trades and the professions. Similarly, while Sinn Féin enjoys fluctuating support at the ballot box, core support for the nationalist cause has not been eroded.

Turning to the appropriate use of force, the obvious difference is that the war in the Dhofar remained a secret war, in which the activities of the seconded and contract officers and the SAS were largely unattributable to the British government. Indeed, there was a subtle difference of emphasis between Whitehall's desire to win the war safely and Oman's desire to win quickly, so that the British ambassador and the British government were not informed in advance of the air strikes against Yemeni artillery positions inside the PDRY in October and November 1975 that finally sealed the isolation of the remnants of PFLOAG inside Dhofar in the following month. The series of operations that concluded the war were to all intents and purposes conventional, with artillery and air support considered vital to success.

In Northern Ireland, British forces have from the beginning had to conduct themselves in the full glare of the media and in circumstances in which any alleged excesses have been liable to maximum exploitation by the terrorists. Moreover, the kind of measures used in colonial situations were hardly appropriate for part of the United Kingdom. Initially, the army was poorly prepared and equipped for riot control, and it has been said that some banners initially unfurled to warn crowds to move back were in Arabic! One old-style cordon and search operation was carried out in the Lower Falls district of Belfast in July 1970 with a curfew and a systematic 36-hour search, which turned up over 100 weapons and 21,000 rounds of ammunition, but at the price of further alienating Catholic opinion and gifting a propaganda success to PIRA. Similarly, a major search of Catholic areas by 700 troops in January 1971 resulted in rioting. Over 250,000 house searches between 1972 and 1976 turned up a further 5,800 weapons and over 661,000 rounds, but the political costs remained high. Of course, internment brought particular pressures, the period of maximum troop deployment in 1971–72 including the 'Bloody Sunday' incident on 30 January 1972 in Londonderry when thirteen died in a confrontation with the 1st Battalion, Parachute Regiment. Generally, however, the army has avoided the use of excessive force, the yellow card first being issued in 1972 to govern the conditions under which soldiers could use their weapons.

Subsequently, with the scaling down of the military presence after 1977, there have been two differing kinds of duty tour, with six-month 'roulement' tours for areas subject to most risk and two and a half year tours for quieter areas, with continuity enabling the build-up of local knowledge. 'Tin City' training facilities were also provided in Britain to enable units to familiarise themselves with the tactical skills required for duties in Northern Ireland. Nine battalions were involved in all after 1977, with 'framework operations' being conducted mostly in the border areas to deter terrorism by routine patrolling and vehicle check points. Indeed, the border area in south Armagh is the only area in which the army now has delegated primacy. Specialist support is offered to the RUC in terms of such areas as bomb disposal, and covert operations continue. Prior to the cease-fire, it could be argued that through its tactical flexibility and decentralised command to patrol level, the army had succeeded in establishing what the then Home Secretary, Reginald Maudling, defined in 1971 as an 'acceptable level of violence'.

There remains consideration of the need to put into place reforms sufficient to prevent resurgence of insurgency. In Oman, the reforms begun in 1970 have been extended to produce the infrastructure of a modern state with improved communications, industry, and medical and educational facilities. In Dhofar, modernisation has also proceeded apace, and the *jebalis* have a significant measure of autonomy, increasing their vested interest in the *status quo*. In short, the Dhofar experience represents a model campaign in every way. In Northern Ireland, however, the jury is still out and much rests on the current 'peace process', which may or may not prove successful in the long term. Clearly, however, for reasons largely beyond the control of the security forces, the campaign against terrorism in Northern Ireland has not fulfilled a number of those requirements identified as keys to successful counter-insurgency.

The British has not been the only army to confront the increasing combination of traditional rural guerrilla tactics with urban terrorism. Others to do so are the Israeli Defence Forces (IDF), whose approach has been very different, and the Indian army. Although trained in the British tradition, the Indian army has also followed its own path in counter-insurgency. Neither the IDF nor the Indian army, however, has shown the kind of flexibility that has enabled the British to cope with the evolving pattern of insurgency.

Apart from its long-running confrontation with Pakistan, which has resulted in wars in both 1965 and 1971, the Indian army has also faced considerable internal insurgency. Indeed, it has been calculated that 75 per cent of Indian casualties between 1947 and 1984 have occurred in internal conflicts. There has been sporadic guerrilla opposition to India's control of Assam on the eastern frontier, with an on-going campaign against the Naga since 1956 and against the Mizo between 1966 and 1988, with additional challenges in Manipur and Tripura in the 1970s. The disputed territory of Kashmir, seized by India in 1947, has remained a source of tension between India and Pakistan. In addition, Kashmiri separatists have been increasingly active since 1988, frequently publicising their cause by the detention of Western tourists while significantly escalating attacks on Indian troops in both rural and urban areas. Apart from Pakistani support, the Islamic militants have also drawn active support from Afghans, Tajiks and groups from the Middle East.

Division of the Punjab between India and Pakistan in 1947 has similarly resulted in conflict, and Sikh separatists supporting the establishment of 'Khalistan' emerged in the early 1980s. Indian troops forcibly expelled Sikh extremists from the sacred Sikh Golden Temple in Amritsar in June 1984, killing over 600 and, amid escalating communal violence, the Indian prime minister, Mrs Indira Gandhi, was assassinated by a Sikh member of her bodyguard in October 1984. Sikh militants were again expelled from the Golden Temple in 1988. Mrs Gandhi was succeeded as prime minister by her son, Rajiv Gandhi. Having subsequently lost office, he, too, was later assassinated by a suicide bomber while electioneering in May 1991. In this case, his assassin was a member of the Liberation Tigers of Tamil Eelam (LTTE), popularly known as the Tamil Tigers, who opposed India's intervention in Sri Lanka, to which an Indian Peace-keeping Force (IPKF) was deployed between August 1987 and March 1990 and soon drawn into military operations against the LTTE.

Like other armies, the Indian army has regarded 'real war' as its most significant role. The fact that the Nagas fought a largely positional war from behind fixed defences in the first phase of their insurgency between 1956 and 1964 reinforced this tendency, but the Nehru government was concerned that the Nagas should not be regarded as enemies as such but, to quote Rajesh Rajagpolan, 'as misguided citizens who had to be politically won over rather than militarily defeated'. Consequently, there was at least in theory a new emphasis upon avoiding excessive force, with close study of both British counter-insurgency in Malaya and Maoist insurgency in China. Indeed, in many respects, minimum force had been imposed upon the army by its political leaders, although some abuses undoubtedly still occurred. A recognition of the need to separate guerrilla from population was derived from Malaya, and resettlement was applied in Nagaland in 1957–58 before being suspended as a result of opposition from moderate Naga elements. However, it was revived on a very limited scale in 1963. While adopting resettlement, the Indians did not follow the British example of small-unit operations. Methods therefore remained traditional and reflected the army's conventional bias. Thus, cordon and search operations were conducted against the Naga and troops deployed both in a large number of small jungle outposts supplied by air and in all main centres.

The outbreak of Mizo insurgency in 1966 forced the army into establishing a counter-insurgency and jungle warfare training centre and into compiling a suitable counter-insurgency manual for the first time. Yet large-scale operations remained the norm. Experimental 'lighter insurgency battalions' between 1968 and 1970 were deployed on largely conventional tasks such as sealing the borders, and even the use of helicopter-borne units did not fundamentally alter doctrine. A resettlement scheme for protected and progressive villages (PPVs) was established in northern Mizoram in 1967 but was legally opposed and hence not subsequently extended to central and southern areas. By the 1980s, the Indian army no longer believed that insurgencies could be defeated militarily in the absence of radical changes to its conventional doctrine. That, however, was regarded as too high a price to pay and, consequently, the army now believed that only political solutions to insurgency should be pursued.

In the case of Kashmir, the Indians did establish the Rashtriya Rifles as a specialised counter-insurgency force and also raised units from surrendered insurgents. Moreover, it also adopted another British measure in ensuring close co-operation between the civil and military authorities in its continuing operations in Assam and Kashmir. However, it has been suggested that the Indian state used death squads against Sikh militants in the Punjab and also in Assam in the 1980s and 1990s, albeit mostly plain-clothes police in the Punjab or, in the case of Kashmir and Assam, pseudo forces recruited from former insurgents and paramilitary militias. It is further suggested that the former emphasis upon minimum force has been lost, with the army directing an increasingly brutal campaign waged by the militias and Hindu 'village defence committees'.

The army's overall view, however, has not been changed either by its experiences in Kashmir or by that in Sri Lanka, where large-scale operations were undertaken against the Tamil insurgents with little success. A Dravidian people inhabiting southern India and northern and eastern Sri Lanka, the Hindu Tamils form about 18 per cent of the population of Sri Lanka, whereas the Buddhist Sinhalese represent about 74 per cent. Tamils were introduced as plantation labour by the British and enjoyed a degree of advantage, which ceased with Ceylon's independence in 1948. Indeed, Tamils of Indian origin were technically rendered stateless by being denied citizenship by both Ceylon and India. Sinhalese governments progressively sought to raise the status of the Sinhalese majority through such means as Sinhalese replacing English as the official language in 1956. As a result, ethnic violence steadily increased and Tamil demands for autonomy grew. These demands were manifested in the emergence in the 1970s of several groups calling for the establishment of a separate state of 'Eelam'. The most militant group was the LTTE, founded by a radical student, Vellupillai Prabhakaran, in 1972 in response to the adoption of a republican constitution for the new Sri Lanka, which institutionalised Sinhalese domination. Ironically, encouragement was given to the separatists both by the Indian government and by that of the Indian state of Tamil Nadu despite the Marxist orientation of most of the Tamil separatist groups in Sri Lanka and the potential dangers of encouraging similar Tamil separatism in India itself.

There was an abortive cease-fire in Sri Lanka between June 1985 and January 1986, but, with violence escalating rapidly, India intervened in August 1987. The LTTE refused to disarm, and the Indians were forced to undertake military operations against them. The LTTE was confined to the Jaffna peninsula but not destroyed, and the IPKF was withdrawn in March 1990, leading to a deterioration in the security situation. The conflict, which has cost at least 18,000 lives since 1983, continues.

Despite military successes that have often provided buffer zones between the Israeli heartland and neighbouring Arab states, Israel has remained vulnerable to infiltration. Indeed, occupation of Arab territory as a more defendable perimeter has presented its own security problems, since it has invariably meant extending control over the Arab population. IDF battlefield prowess also stimulated the growth of the Palestine Liberation Organisation (PLO) in June 1964, increasing the terrorist threat. Founded at a meeting in Cairo of a Palestinian National Council, which was itself a 'government in exile', the PLO was effectively an umbrella organisation. Among its member groups was al-Fatah (Conquest), whose leader, Yasser Arafat, became chairman of the PLO as a whole in 1969. Other groups associated with the PLO have included the Popular Front for the Liberation of Palestine (PFLP), the Arab Liberation Front (ALF) and Black September, which carried out the terrorist attack on Israeli athletes during the Olympic Games in Munich in 1972.

After the defeat of the Arab states in the 'Six Day War' in June 1967, terrorism and guerrilla action, largely in emulation of the Vietnamese model of a national liberation struggle, became the principal means by which the Arabs struck back at Israel, initially from Jordan. However, the PLO's destabilising presence led to its expulsion from Jordan in September 1970. It then shifted its bases to Lebanon, prompting major interventions by the IDF in 1978 and 1982, forcing its headquarters to move to Tunisia. In July 1988,

King Hussein of Jordan ceded to the PLO his claims to the West Bank, which had been occupied by Israel since 1967. In November 1988, the PLO declared the independence of a Palestinian state based on the occupied West Bank but, at the same time, it also recognised Israel's right to exist in the expectation that this would facilitate negotiations. The PLO lost its remaining bases in southern Lebanon in July 1991 when expelled by the Lebanese army. Nonetheless, as part of the wider Middle East peace process sponsored by the United States, the PLO was able to take over the administration of some parts of the Gaza Strip and the West Bank in September 1993.

In response to the PLO threat, the Israelis always took a robust attitude, regarding terrorism as a genocidal assault on the Jewish people in view of the Arab states' declared intent to destroy the state of Israel. The IDF has not in the past regarded internal security as representing as significant a role as major conventional threats to its borders. Moreover, in keeping with its offensive military doctrine, the IDF's response has taken the form of instant retaliation by hot pursuit operations, air strikes, artillery bombardment or reprisal commando raids, with the intention both of responding immediately to any insurgent action as a means of destroying those responsible and of longer-term attrition of the insurgent threat. Unit 101, for example, was formed under Ariel Sharon in August 1953 specifically to undertake retaliatory commando raids and carried out its first attack on the Jordanian village of Qibya in October, dynamiting 45 houses and killing over 60 civilians. Nor has Israel shrunk from accepting the risks of targeting host states, the response to the murder of three Israelis on Cyprus being an air attack on the PLO's head-quarters in Tunis in October 1985. The Israelis also targeted specific individuals, such as the spiritual head of the Islamic fundamentalist Hezbollah (Party of God), Hussein Abbas Musawi, who was assassinated in February 1992, while others have been abducted. The belief is that the removal of key members of the opposing infrastructure will both paralyse opponents and give full rein to internal rivalries among those seeking to succeed to the leadership. The Israeli incursions into Lebanon in 1978 and 1982 might also be regarded as very large-scale retaliatory operations following Arab terrorist incidents, that in 1982 being intended to destroy the PLO's infrastructure in the country.

In the occupied territories of the West Bank, Gaza Strip, Sinai and Golan Heights after 1967, which contained a population of 980,000 Arabs, the Israelis installed fixed defences against infiltration, employing electrified fences, minefields, sand treated with phosphorescence to aid tracking, infrared devices to trigger fixed machine guns, dusting of roads for footprints, and sensors. The system was backed by roving patrols drawn from *sayaret* (special forces) and *sayaret tsanhanim* (paratroop special forces). Until the PLO was forced out of Jordan in 1970, it attempted hit and run raids across the river but, in what was characterised as the 'battle of the paratroopers', the IDF largely intercepted them in the mountainous Judaean and Samarean Deserts before they could get into Israel itself. Indeed, between 1968 and 1970 the IDF claimed to have killed or captured 1,151 PLO guerrillas for the loss of 138 IDF personnel, with fewer than one in five guerrillas escaping. Guerrilla camps were also hit in Jordan itself, such as that at Karameh in March 1968. The IDF also undertook a census of the Arab population and imposed such 'preventive detentions', curfews, deportations and collective fines as they felt necessary. To some extent, there was a carrot attached to the stick, with the Jordanian administration left in place on the West Bank and movement allowed across the Jordan River under the 'open bridge' policy.

In the case of the urban terrorism encountered in the West Bank and Gaza Strip, the Israeli approach has also tended to be heavy-handed, as during the large-scale Palestinian disturbances known as the *Intifada* (Shuddering) between December 1987 and the establishment of a Palestinian authority under peace accords with the PLO in September 1993. The *Intifada* itself was partly a response to Israel's role in Lebanon, but it also reflected continued alienation among the predominantly youthful Palestinian refugee population, 80 per cent of whom were under 34 years of age. Many involved in the disturbances were employed in Israel proper and spoke Hebrew but felt themselves poorly treated and subject to frequent harassment at work and in transit to places of work. However, a large exchange in May 1985 of 1,150 Palestinians in detention for three IDF soldiers captured in Lebanon had released known agitators back into the community. The disturbances also marked the emergence of hardline Islamic groups such as Hamas (Zeal), which have continued to challenge Arafat's leadership of the Palestinian cause, and which contributed to the revival of the *Intifada* in 2000 and drew a familiar Israeli response.

Initially, indeed, the IDF did not regard the *Intifada* as much more than sporadic rioting representing only a low-level threat to law and order. With the incorporation of more co-ordinated mass demonstrations, boycott of Israeli goods, other forms of passive resistance and terrorism, it had been transformed by 1991 into something more serious that required a substantial change in doctrine and outlook. Indeed, the Israelis themselves admitted that 250,000 IDF personnel had undertaken service in the West Bank and Gaza at one time or another between 1987 and 1993, requiring an enhancement of the number of conscripts called up annually and disrupting conventional training programmes. Moreover, like the involvement in the Lebanon between 1982 and 1985, the *Intifada* generated some evasion of conscription, and claims of conscientious objection increased. For different reasons, the IDF also found itself assailed by critics on both political left and political right amid the wider politicisation evident in Israeli society over the question of the extension or otherwise of Jewish settlements in the occupied territories.

Troops had not been trained or equipped for a constabulary role and curfews, detention and physical force were the usual form of response. In 1988, however, a specialised crowd control unit known as Alpha emerged to design new non-lethal weapons such as water and gravel dischargers and new types of plastic bullet. Containment and surveillance operations were also stepped up by new covert squads known as *Henza*, taking their name from the initial letters of the title in Hebrew. Selective deportations of known Hamas agitators were used, with known terrorists also being hunted down by plain-clothes *mista' arvim* (masqueraders). Generally, however, the situation appears to have stifled initiative to some extent in ordinary IDF units because of the greater need to take cognisance of the rules of engagement. Indeed, some feared that the *Intifada* would have a detrimental effect on the army's ability to undertake 'real operations by forcing too many accommodations to meet its special circumstances'.

Much the same pattern of a heavy-handed IDF approach was evident in the security zone established in south Lebanon in 1985, from which the Israelis finally withdrew in May 2000. There was often little concept of a hearts and minds approach to the indigenous Lebanese Shi'a, who often suffered from retaliatory IDF bombardments against Hezbollah. Some 40,000, for example, fled from the large-scale strikes of the IDF Operation Grapes of Wrath in April 1996, which followed increased violence in the security zone. The Israelis, however, did attempt to win the support of the Christian Maronite community in Lebanon with a civic aid programme and equipped the Maronite militia known as the South Lebanon Army (SLA). The Maronite militia or *Ketaeb* was itself of long standing and had been deeply involved in the civil war that had erupted in Lebanon in 1975 as a result of the pressures of the Palestinian influx after 1967. Hezbollah and its military wing, the Islamic Resistance Movement, tended to specialise initially in suicide car bomb attacks but became more sophisticated over time, resulting in higher Israeli and SLA losses. Between May 1993 and May 1997, for example, the IDF suffered 105 dead in south Lebanon and the SLA suffered 76 dead. Moreover, there was evidence on occasions of poor morale among the IDF compared with its previous high commitment to sacrifice, possibly related to over-reliance upon defended locations and long-range bombard-ment. In any case, the IDF has become increasingly anxious to avoid casualties, which might lead to political fallout in Israel itself, something evident at the time of the loss of 73 soldiers in a helicopter collision in February 1997. At the same time, defections from the SLA increased after 1995. Consequently, the IDF formed a new special unit, Egoz (Almond) in July 1995 to take aggressive ground action against Hezbollah supply routes and reportedly established a new guerrilla warfare school in September 1997.

The long-running commitment of the British, Indian and Israeli armies to counter-insurgency reflects both the prevalence and the persistence of insur-gency in the modern world. Indeed, as previously suggested, the passing of the process of European decolonisation and the end of the ideological conflicts that were essentially by-products of the Cold War have not diminished the proliferation of insurgency. In fact, the proliferation in the developing world of readily available weapons from former Eastern bloc sources has had a significant impact. Indeed, insurgents in the developing world can now frequently equal the firepower of government forces, with the outcome of insurgencies determined more by the military capabilities of the insurgents than by that of government forces weakened by the incompetence, corruption and lack of legitimacy on the part of many of those who rule such states. The problems inherent in modernisation, against which the popularity of contemporary radical ideologies such as Islamic fundamentalism have been one response, and the materialism of relative deprivation have equally robbed governments of legitimacy. Moreover, social, economic and political problems have been exacerbated by rapid urbanisation and demographic growth throughout the developing world. Those countries with the greatest rate of population growth are also often those with the weakest economies, so that the developing world has both the largest share and the largest urban share of the world's population. Moreover, urbanisation and population growth have developed independently of the mitigating industrialisation common to urbanisation and population growth in the developed world during the eighteenth and nineteenth centuries. The predominance of an alienated population that is largely youthful has also provided ready recruits for insurgencies in developing countries, child soldiers being all too common in a number of contemporary African insurgencies.

Some insurgencies have the appearance of what Steven Metz has called 'spiritual insurgency' in response to modernisation and globalisation, embracing elements of natavism, while it has been argued by Christopher Clapham that others are essentially 'reform insurgencies', in which the theoretical intention is to seek radical reform of the state. There are equally what Metz has characterised as 'commercial insurgencies' and W.G. Thom as 'economic insurgencies', in which mineral resources or drugs have been the real prize of a cynical quest for power. Indeed, although weapons have become widely available, the absence of Cold War sponsors has forced insurgents to purchase them, raising the economic cost of insurgency and reinforcing the significance of drugs trading or mineral commodities in sustaining an insurgent challenge. Thus, insurgency appears little more than warlordism or organised crime. Commercial rewards have also seen the involvement in some insurgencies or counter-insurgencies of private security firms supplying 'corporate armies'. Of course, more traditional causes have contributed equally to contemporary insurgencies, not least ethnicity and separatism. Indeed, Metz argues that spiritual insurgencies are more likely to occur in states with a heterogeneous identity of ethnicity, race, tribe or religion such as those of the Middle East, where Islam confronts Western-style liberalism, or much of Africa and Asia. Commercial insurgency, he argues, is defined by geography in terms of the existence of mineral deposits, as in some African states, or suitable soils for the cultivation of drugs, as in parts of Asia and Latin America.

The challenge has forced states that, in some cases, were themselves created as a result of successful insurgency against colonial powers to become 'counter-insurgent states' themselves. Clearly, not all insurgencies have succeeded, and much has still depended upon the skills of individual insurgent leaders. Moreover, Eric Young has suggested that, in the contemporary world, the key to insurgent success is no longer the ability to wage protracted warfare but the ability to establish a base rapidly and move on the capital, which is the only focus of power in so many states in the developing world. Compared with earlier periods, when protracted rural insurgency was difficult to contain but urban insurgency generally easily contained, the sheer growth of population has diminished the former advantages of the security forces in urban areas and, without the monopoly of firepower once enjoyed, the security forces of developing states have been increasingly vulnerable to a combination of rural and urban action.

Turning to examples of contemporary insurgencies, Islamic fundamentalism certainly figured in the opposition to the Soviet intervention in Afghanistan and, as already indicated in this and previous chapters, has also been a factor in Kashmir, Israel's occupied territories and the Philippines. It has been a factor, too, in Eritrea, Chad, Sudan and Algeria.

In Eritrea, Islam was one of the formative influences on the Eritrean Liberation Front (ELF), while one of the factors that led to the emergence of the Eritrean People's Liberation Front (EPLF) as a rival insurgent group was its desire to promote a less sectarian and more revolutionary message in a society divided equally between Sunni Muslims and Coptic Christians.

The former Italian colony of Eritrea was passed to Ethiopian control in September 1952 since, without it, Ethiopia would have no access to the sea. Accordingly, despite previous assurances given about autonomy, Ethiopia annexed Eritrea in November 1962. The ELF had already been formed by exiled Eritreans in 1961, but its guerrilla operations against Ethiopian forces were largely unsuccessful. In 1970, Marxist elements of the ELF broke away to form the EPLF and effectively eclipsed it by the late 1970s. For a time there was hope that the group of Marxist army officers known as the Derg (Committee), who overthrew Emperor Haile Selassie in September 1974, might grant real autonomy to their fellow Marxists in Eritrea. Indeed, General Aman Andom, who became head of state, was an Eritrean. However, autonomy was not forthcoming, and when Andom was killed in February 1977, Mengistu Haile Mariam seized power.

Mengistu and the Derg had no intention of relinquishing control of Eritrea, but EPLF strength had grown from about 2,500 in 1974 to 43,000 by 1977. Even with an attempted mass mobilisation in a so-called 'peasant's march', and with assistance after 1977 from the Soviets and Cubans, the Ethiopian army could not destroy the EPLF. Nonetheless, the war was increasingly bitter, and the Eritreans claimed that nerve gas was used against them. Certainly, Mengistu exploited the large-scale drought, which left over a million dead in the region between 1983 and 1985, by trying to ensure that humanitarian supplies did not reach Eritrea. A massive population relocation programme was also instituted in the guise of moving people to more fertile areas. Soviet support for Mengistu lessened after 1985, and the EPLF steadily increased its control in Eritrea. In 1988, the EPLF, now shorn of much of its earlier Marxist ideology, which inhibited winning Muslim support, and led by Issayas Afeworki, seized the main Ethiopian base at Afabet and joined forces with the Ethiopian Peoples' Revolutionary Democracy Front (EPRDF). Three years later, the EPLF finally succeeded in clearing Eritrea of Ethiopian troops, while the EPRDF's successes led to Mengistu fleeing the country in May 1991. Following a UN-sponsored referendum in April 1993, Eritrea received its independence on 24 May 1993.

In Sudan, conflict was essentially one between the Muslim north and the Christian south, in which the Muslim north has largely prevailed. In Chad, it was the Africanised and Christian southern government that was toppled. The original revolt against the southern-dominated government was initiated in 1968 by Front de Libération Nationale (National Liberation Front, Frolinat). The French supported the government, while Libya gave support to Frolinat. Libyan intervention caused factionalism in Frolinat, and a cease-fire was negotiated in 1976. Elements within Frolinat, however, refused to accept it and continued the struggle, resulting in a large-scale French intervention in March 1978.

A former member of Frolinat, Hissèni Habré, who led the Forces Armées du Nord (Northern Armed Forces, FAN), accepted the office of prime minister in February 1979 but then moved against the government himself. The French brokered a deal by which a government of national unity was forged in March 1979 with another former Frolinat figure, Goukouni Oueddai, as president. This soon fell apart, with Habré's exclusion from the government in March 1980 leading to the resumption of an increasingly complex civil war and further Libyan and French intervention, the latter sending forces in both 1983 and 1986. Followers of Oueddai and Habré, who eventually personally gave up the struggle, have continued to contest control of the state. However, Chad fell under the control of yet another faction in March 1990, Idriss Déby's Mouvement Patriotique du Salut (Patriotic Salvation Movement, MPS), which had trained in Sudan with possible assistance from Libya.

In Sudan itself, the Anya-Nya (Viper's Poison), including many mutineers from the former British-trained Sudan Defence Force and largely Dinka people, took up arms against the Islamic military government between 1958 and 1972, a conflict that cost at least 500,000 lives and that also generated over a million refugees. Despite the peace accords signed in Addis Ababa, which gave the Christian south a degree of autonomy, fighting never entirely stopped. With the introduction of Islamic *sharia* law in 1983, fighting increased dramatically. The Marxist Sudan People's Liberation Army (SPLA), also largely Dinka in composition, emerged in July 1983 with Ethiopian backing. However, the Derg's support for the SPLA's leader, John Garang, resulted in factionalism and, in any case, its support was lost with the collapse of the Mengistu regime in 1991. The SPLA, therefore, suffered some setbacks in the early 1990s but survived through forging new alliances with the EPRDF, the EPLF, the government of Uganda and other dissidents in the north. It had also been successful in establishing its own local administration in the south. From 1987 onwards, the SPLA also received support from the Nuer militia, who now referred to themselves as Anya-Nya II. Previously, it had fought for Khartoum but was alienated by the increasing Islamic influence over the government. A cease-fire was brokered by former US president Jimmy Carter in 1995 but soon broke down. Some SPLA elements and other groups signed a peace agreement in April 1997, but Garang remains in the field in a conflict has cost at least 1.2 million lives since 1983.

In Algeria, exploitation of oil and natural gas deposits in the Sahara initially brought independent Algeria considerable prosperity, but falling oil prices resulted in increasing economic and social difficulties in the 1980s, with unemployment running generally at 33 per cent and possibly as much as 75 per cent among urban youths. It could be argued that the post-independence FLN governments had never succeeded in establishing their legitimacy through a relentless drive for modernisation, an Arabisation that had imposed Arabic on the Berbers, and the dominance of a single-party government. Thus, the new liberalisation introduced into the political process after the death of Boumèdienne in 1978, which saw over 50 parties formed, raised expectations of an end to authoritarianism. In December 1991, the first round of elections to the National People's Assembly under a new constitution resulted in the majority of seats contested being won by the coalition of fundamentalists known as Front Islamique du Salut (Islamic Salvation Front, FIS). This had been formed in 1989 by Abbasi al Madani, Ahmed Belhadj and Imam Abdelbakr Sahraoui in the belief that Algeria should become a fully Islamic republic ruled by strict adherence to Muslim law. The FLN secured just fifteen out of the 430 seats, with the FIS winning 231 and the socialists 25.

The Algerian army then cancelled the second round in January 1992, which would have distributed the remaining seats, resulting in a continuing terrorist campaign by the FIS against the authorities. The army detained at least 10,000 people in the first few months and closed opposition newspapers, while so-called *ninjas* in the security forces carried out summary executions. There have been an estimated 75,000 deaths since 1992 in a conflict that has been marked by the brutality of the FIS, which has routinely tortured, castrated and disembowelled its victims. It has also targeted foreigners, with over 50 journalists and 100 others being murdered by 1996 alone, including the French Archbishop of Oran. The campaign was also exported to France itself by Madani Mezerag's even more radical Armed Islamic Group (GIA).

Including so-called 'Afghans' with experience of fighting against the Soviets in Afghanistan, the GIA hijacked an aircraft in December 1994, probably with Iranian assistance, and set off bombs in Paris over the summer and autumn of 1995.

Separatism and ethnicity have also fuelled insurgency in Africa, the Middle East and Asia. Clear elements of ethnicity were involved in the conflicts in Eritrea and Sudan and in the original resistance of Frolinat in Chad. Shorn of the additional Islamic aspect, however, further examples of separatism are the conflicts in Western Sahara, Kurdistan, East Timor and Tigray.

In Western Sahara, Frente Popular para la Liberación de Saguira el Hamra y Rio de Oro (Popular Front for the Liberation of Saguiet el Hamra and Rio de Oro, Polisario) has been fighting against Morocco in the former Spanish territory of Western Sahara since 1976, Saguiet el Hamra being the northern and Rio de Oro the southern part of a territory originally designated separately but then united as Spanish Sahara in 1958. Western Sahara was claimed by both Morocco and Mauritania, but Polisario, which had emerged in 1973, was supported by Algeria and, subsequently, by Libya in its demand for independence. In December 1974, the UN referred the matter to the International Court of Justice, which reported in October 1975 that the Western Saharan population should be given the right of self-determination. The Moroccan response to the announcement of the Court's decision was the so-called 'Green March' of unarmed civilians to occupy Western Sahara, still then under Spanish control. In November 1975, Spain agreed to withdraw, and Morocco and Mauritania duly partitioned the territory. Polisario formally declared the existence of a Sahrawi Arab Democratic Republic on 27 February 1976 under the presidency of Mohammed Abd al-Aziz.

An economic crisis led to a military coup in Mauritania, and it renounced all claim to Western Sahara in July 1979. Morocco, however, occupied the vacated Mauritanian territory and continued to fight Polisario, whose government in exile was recognised by the Organisation of African Unity (OAU) in February 1982. Polisario had heavy weapons at its disposal and an estimated 10,000 men at the height of the fighting between 1979 and 1981. Faced with the sheer size of the territory, the Moroccans were largely forced on the defensive, between 1981 and 1987 constructing a 'wall of sand' 1,440 kilometres long in two separate two-metre berms filled with mines and sensors to try to cut off Polisario's infiltration routes from Algeria in the east. The annual cost of the war to Morocco has been calculated at $400 million, approximating to 3 per cent of GDP. Polisario, however, found Algeria and Libya increasingly unwilling to back its campaign to the same extent as at the beginning, and it experienced logistic difficulties in maintaining the 10,000–15,000 men of the Sahrawi People's Liberation Army. Indeed, there were some well-publicised defections from Polisario to the Moroccans. There was a UN sponsored cease-fire in 1989, but it broke down after ten months over the interpretation of who would be entitled to vote in any referendum on self-determination. The cease-fire was revived in September 1991, pending a referendum on self-determination. It has yet to be held, and both sides appear prepared to continue the struggle.

The Kurds form a distinct cultural and linguistic group totalling 20 million people, representing the largest nation in the world without its own state. A tribal people, the Kurds inhabit 625,000 square kilometres of Kurdistan, embracing parts of Armenia, Iran, Iraq, Syria and Turkey. A Kurdish rising failed in Iraq in 1945, but a Soviet-sponsored Mahabad Republic was established briefly in Iran in 1946 before Soviet withdrawal led to its collapse in June 1947. With the resulting exile of Mustafa Barzani, leadership of the Kurdish Democratic Party (KDP) inside Iraq devolved on the urbanised left-wing intellectuals Jelal Talabani and Ibrahim Ahmed in the 1950s.

With the establishment of an Iraqi republic by Abd al-Karim Qasim in 1958, the KDP was legitimised and Barzani returned but, increasingly hostile to Kurdish aspirations, Qasim responded to Barzani's demand for autonomy by a full-scale onslaught on the Kurds in September 1961. Autonomy rather than independence remained the Kurdish goal, but this was unacceptable to successive Iraqi governments. Moreover, the Iraqis attempted to exploit internal tribal divisions, recruiting their own Kurdish militia. Nor was Barzani in full control of all those in revolt, Ahmed and Talabani initially establishing the standing military force known as the Peshmarga (Those Who Face Death). Despite eventually mustering 50,000 men, the Kurds were unable to export their campaign from the mountains, although, equally, the Iraqis were unable to operate beyond the plains and resorted to indiscriminate aerial bombing. Negotiations brought temporary cease-fires, and an armistice in March 1970 offered autonomy within four years. Amid mutual recriminations on whether its terms were being fulfilled, fighting erupted again in April 1974. The revolt collapsed in April 1975, when the Shah of Iran withdrew his previous support for the Kurdish cause. Barzani moved to the United States, and his followers split between a KDP led by his sons and Talabani's Patriotic Union of Kurdistan (PUK). The Shah's overthrow in 1979 brought new demands by Iranian Kurds, with which Talabani made common cause. The fighting that broke out inside Iran was then complicated by the onset of the Iran–Iraq War (1980–88), in which both sides attempted to exploit Kurdish grievances.

Kurdish unrest also spread to Turkey in 1984, led by the Kurdistan Workers' Party (PKK), where it continues. Renewed hostility towards the Kurds in Iraq by Saddam Hussein's government in the aftermath of the Gulf War brought the establishment of a UN-protected Kurdish zone around Arbil in northern Iraq in April 1991. American-supervised elections in this protected zone in 1992 were designed to end the rivalry between the KDP and the PUK, but the elections were inconclusive, and fighting broke out between them in January 1994. In September 1996, Iraqi forces intervened in support of the KDP, enabling it to secure control of the protected zone, although the United States then retaliated against this violation of the UN zone with missile strikes against Iraq. In May 1997, the Turkish army also entered the protected zone, with the co-operation of the KDP, to attack PKK groups.

The former Portuguese colony of East Timor in the East Indies saw fighting between rival groups once the Portuguese began to withdraw in April 1974. When the Portuguese finally withdrew in August 1975, the power struggle had been won by Frente Revolucionária Timorense de Libertação e Independência (Revolutionary Front for the Liberation and Independence of Timor, Fretilin). Fretilin declared East Timor's independence on 28 November 1975, but this was not recognised either by Portugal or Indonesia, West Timor having become part of Indonesia when the Dutch had quit the Dutch East Indies in 1949. On 7 December 1975, Indonesian 'volunteers' invaded East Timor and on 14 August 1976 it was announced that East Timor was to be absorbed into Indonesia. The ensuing guerrilla conflict had cost the lives of an estimated 60,000 people by the end of 1979 alone. As Fretilin was dominated by communists, Australia recognised Indonesian sovereignty in 1978 as preferable to an independent communist state. However, most members of the UN condemned continued Indonesian occupation, and Indonesian forces were frequently accused of violating human rights.

In the event, Australia was compelled to intervene at the head of an international peace-keeping force in 1999, driving the Indonesian army and pro-Indonesian militias back into West Timor, from whence they, in turn, have waged a guerrilla campaign against the peace-keepers.

The Tigray People's Liberation Front (TPLF), which emerged to fight against the Marxist regime in Ethiopia, was one of a number of ethnically based groups in opposition, and it eventually led the EPRDF coalition in Ethiopia. Formed in February 1975, the TPLF benefited from oppression by the Derg, which embraced new taxation, requisition, conscription, attacks on the Ethiopian Orthodox Church and a land reform programme. In fact, the TPLF shared the Derg's Marxist orientation, albeit with a Maoist tinge, but in practice took a much more pragmatic line towards what it regarded as the necessary transition from neo-feudalism to socialism. Deriving some support from the EPLF in Eritrea, the TPLF succeeded in driving Mengistu's forces out of Tigray in 1989, assuming leadership of the new EPRDF in 1990.

There is perhaps a rather thin dividing line between separatism and ethnicity, but it might be argued that the latter is more a question of sub-groups rather than distinctly national groups. Examples are the insurgencies in Burma, Laos, and Rwanda.

The government of the new state of Burma after its independence in January 1948 proved extremely nationalistic when only 65 per cent of its 42 million inhabitants were actually ethnic Burmese. As already indicated, hill tribes such as the Karen and Kachin had little wish to be incorporated into the Burmese state, and there was a series of insurgencies, including the Karen Revolt in 1949, which were not overcome until 1955. The Karens had been granted autonomy in 1951, and this was accepted by most former insurgents in 1964, although one militant from the former Karen National Defence Organisation (KNDO), Mahn Ba Zan, continued the struggle until government amnesty terms were finally accepted in May 1980. Burma, however, remained unstable throughout the period after independence, experiencing frequent periods of military rule, a situation worsened both by the 'golden triangle' of heroin production in the north-east and the resulting activities of warlords engaged in the drugs trade, and by the political weakness of the communists, who exacerbated conflict by allying themselves with the various ethnic opponents of government. By 1988–89, at least 25 different groups were actively resisting the military government of what was now called Myanmar, principally the Karen National Union, the Kachin Independence Organisation and Shan groups.

Hill tribes have also figured in the continued opposition to communist rule in Laos. During the Pathet Lao's struggle against the Laotian government, the leader of the 40,000 anti-communist 'Secret Army' supported by funding from the CIA between 1961 and 1967 was Vang Pao, a H'mong officer in the Laotian Royal Army. Meo and Kha tribesmen also fought against the communists. Following the fall of Vientiane to the communists in 1975, Vang Pao and his leading followers reached an agreement with the Pathet Lao that, in return for their departure from Laos, the H'mong would be left alone. However, the communists began to arrest former 'Secret Army' members. As a result, the H'mong rose in revolt under the leadership of Pa Kao Her. The H'mong guerrillas regard themselves as *Chao Fa* (God's disciples), reflecting a traditional H'mong belief in the periodic appearance of a *chaofa* (messiah). Arms were received from the Chinese in the late 1970s and also some assistance from Thailand, although the Thais were wary of jeopardising trading links with Laos. It remains a bitter struggle, in which the communists have used chemical agents against the H'mong.

In the case of the former Belgian colony of Rwanda, society was divided between the majority Hutu, comprising about 84 per cent of the population, and the minority Tutsi tribal groups. Towards the end of Belgian rule in 1959, the Hutus were favoured more than the Tutsi, who had previously enjoyed Belgian support, and the Hutus consolidated their power in the new state. Consequently, Tutsi *inyenzi* (cockroach) raids were mounted into Rwanda from neighbouring Burundi in the early 1960s. In the 1980s, Tutsi refugees supported Yoweri Museveni's National Resistance Army (NRA) fighting the government of Milton Obote in Uganda, which had increasingly oppressed them. Originally known as the Rwandan Alliance for National Unity (RANU), the main organisation of Tutsi refugees transformed itself into the Front Patriotique Rwandais (Rwandan Patriotic Front, FPR) when Museveni secured power in Uganda in January 1986.

In Rwanda itself, the Hutu-dominated government of President Juvenal Habyarimana responded to growing opposition by rhetorically embracing democracy, but this failed to prevent widespread Tutsi support for the FPR when it invaded Rwanda in October 1990 under the leadership of Fred Rwigyema, Museveni's former chief of staff. Initially, however, a conventional strategy proved an error and the FPR was thrown back and Rwigyema killed. As a result, FPR resorted to guerrilla tactics, but its continued operations resulted in a sustained campaign of genocide against the Tutsi in Rwanda by the Hutu. This followed Habyarimana's death when his plane was mysteriously shot down, probably by Hutu extremists, in April 1994 when he was returning from peace negotiations in Tanzania. The genocide may have resulted in a million Tutsi deaths at the hands of the army and the Hutu militia known as the *interahamwe* (one together). With Ugandan support, the FPR succeeded in overthrowing the Hutu government, despite the support of France and Zaire for it. The defeated government, together with 1.2 million Hutu refugees, fled into Zaire in July 1994 and as the Former Government of Rwanda (FGOR) waged guerrilla war in turn against the FPR.

A further complication was the emergence of the so-called Alliance des Forces Démocratiques pour la Libération du Congo-Zaire (Alliance of Democratic Forces for the Liberation of Congo-Zaire, ADFL) in October 1996. Associated with Laurent Kabila, a long-term opponent of Zaire's President Mobutu Sese Seko, it attacked FGOR forces. Kabila had led the People's Revolutionary Party (PRP) for over 30 years but had had little success until the civil war in Rwanda spilled into Zaire. Kabila became the unexpected beneficiary of the ailing Mobutu's unpopularity, creating the ADFL in alliance with the Tutsi and other opposition groups. Assisted by Rwanda's new rulers, Kabila entered Kinshasa as Mobutu fled in May 1997, and Zaire was renamed the Democratic Republic of Congo. In turn, however, Kabila found himself opposed by new guerrilla forces after he demanded the withdrawal of Rwandan forces in July 1998. The rebels are backed by Uganda, Rwanda and UNITA, while Kabila has received backing from Zimbabwe, Angola, Chad and Namibia. A cease-fire broke down in 1999, and Kabila was assassinated by a bodyguard in January 2001. It remains to be seen how the situation will develop.

If the conflict in Laos is one example of what might be termed unfinished business from earlier struggles, this is also true of some continuing power struggles whose origins lie in past guerrilla conflicts. Reference has already been made to the struggle by UNITA against the MPLA in Angola after 1975 and to that by Renamo against Frelimo in Mozambique. In the case of Angola, the international agreement on the independence of Namibia in December 1988 paved the way for negotiations between MPLA and UNITA and a cease-fire and new elections in September 1992, which were won by MPLA. UNITA then resumed its guerrilla campaign, but pressure from the United States brought new negotiations in October 1993. Progress towards peace continued under the supervision of the UN and, in theory, UNITA joined a government of national unity and reconciliation in April 1997. Jonas Savimbi, however, distanced himself from the process and continues to lead UNITA guerrillas.

Similar unfinished business continues in Cambodia. As is well known, the Khmer Rouge instituted a terror campaign after seizing control of Cambodia in April 1975. The number who died in the excesses of 'Year Zero' is unknown but may well have exceeded 1.4 million. The terror in what was known, after December 1975, as Democratic Kampuchea also resulted in hundreds of thousands of refugees fleeing into Thailand and Vietnam. Many were ethnic Vietnamese, exacerbating the tensions that had arisen between the Khmer Rouge and the North Vietnamese communists. Clashes had occurred between North Vietnamese and Khmer Rouge forces as early as 1974, but the real crisis in relations between the two new states came when Khmer Rouge forces advanced into Vietnamese territory in both April and September 1977. In retaliation, the Vietnamese briefly invaded Kampuchea in December 1977 and, in December 1978, named a former Khmer Rouge officer, Heng Samrin, as head of a Kampuchean National United Front for National Salvation (KUFNS), invading Kampuchea once more. Phnom Penh fell on 7 January 1979, with Heng Samrin installed as head of state of a new People's Republic of Kampuchea. The Khmer Rouge, however, continued to wage guerrilla warfare against the Vietnamese-backed government from bases close to the Thai frontier.

The situation was further complicated by the emergence of non-communist forces opposed to Vietnamese control. A former Cambodian prime minister, Son Sann, founded a Khmer People's National Liberation Front (KPNLF). Prince Norodom Sihanouk, who had ruled Cambodia as prime minister from 1955 to 1960 and as head of state from 1960 to 1970, and had also been its elected king from 1941 to 1955, re-emerged as head of the National United Front for an Independent, Neutral, Peaceful and Co-operative Cambodia (FUNCINPEC). In June 1983, both groups joined the Khmer Rouge in a somewhat fragile Coalition Government of Democratic Kampuchea (CGDK), with Sihanouk at its head. Vietnamese troops began to withdraw from Kampuchea in February 1989, and UN-sponsored peace negotiations resulted in all parties joining a Supreme National Council chaired by Sihanouk in September 1990. A peace agreement was then reached in October 1991 and a UN force moved in to supervise demobilisation of the rival factions. Led by Sihanouk's son, Prince Norodom Ranariddh, FUNCINPEC won new elections in May 1993 and the prince became joint prime minister with Heng Samrin's successor, Hun Sen. In September 1993, Sihanouk was once more elected king of what was again called Cambodia.

The elections had been boycotted by the Khmer Rouge, who resumed their guerrilla campaign but became increasingly fragmented, with large-scale defections to the government in August 1996. This fragmentation culminated with the notorious leader of the Khmer Rouge, Pol Pot, executing his own defence minister in June 1997. Pol Pot was then captured by his rival, Ta Mok, and apparently sentenced to life imprisonment, subsequently dying of a reported heart attack while being carried towards the Thai frontier in April 1998. At the same time, the governing coalition also fell apart, with Hun Sen staging a military coup against Ranariddh in July 1997. Under a Japanese-sponsored initiative, Ranariddh returned to Cambodia in April 1998, pending new elections to be held in July 1998.

Turning to those insurgencies essentially intended to seize power or resources, an example of a 'reform insurgency' was that of Museveni's NRA, which seized power in Uganda in January 1986. The EPRDF might also qualify as a reform insurgency movement. On the other hand, commercial or economic insurgency is reflected in Charles Taylor's National Patriotic Front of Liberia (NPFL), which seized power in Liberia in September 1990, or the many warlord groups in Somalia.

Museveni first formed the Front for National Salvation (Fronasa) in opposition to Idi Amin's dictatorship in 1971. Disillusioned by the government under the former president, Milton Obote, which was imposed by Tanzania when it overthrew Idi Amin in 1978–79, Museveni took up arms again in 1981. Having been influenced both by Frelimo's campaign in Mozambique and the writings of Franz Fanon, Museveni cultivated popular support while striving to reduce ethnic tensions within the NRA. In many respects, it could be argued that the NRA's success was something of an advertisement for Guevara's *foco* theory, since Museveni began with just 35 men in 1981 and enjoyed no external support, but he did not make the mistake of omitting political mobilisation of the people. As in some other modern African insurgencies, Museveni's army was predominantly young, perhaps as many as a fifth being under 14 years of age. He was also assisted by the brutality of Obote's army, which overthrew its own government in July 1985, leading to further instability. Subsequently, Museveni influenced the emergence of the FPR and provided initial backing for the ADFL in Zaire as well as for the SPLA in Sudan. In turn, however, Museveni's government was opposed by the curious quasi-religious Holy Spirit Movement (HSM), which emerged among the Acholi tribal supporters of the short-lived military government under the leadership of a spirit medium, Alice Auma (aka Alice Lakwena), in 1986. Her forces were defeated in 1987, but the movement's leadership was assumed by her father, Severino Lukoya, and, in 1989, by her cousin, Joseph Kony, who changed the name to the Lord's Resistance Army.

While essentially intending to control commodities, warlord groups involved in economic or commercial insurgency such as the NPLF in Liberia and Ali Mahdi Mahamed's Somalia Salvation Alliance (SSA) and Mahamad Faarah Haasan Aididi's Somali National Alliance (SNA) in Somalia also display elements of ethnicity. Charles Taylor's NPLF emerged victorious in July 1997 after an eight-year struggle, first against the government of the former sergeant, Samuel Doe, who seized power in 1980 and was murdered in September 1990, and second against rival factions. Control of Liberia's diamonds and gold was the main prize. Doe, however, had massacred Gio and Mano people and, in turn, the NPLF massacred the Krahn and Mandingo deemed to have supported Doe, who was himself a Krahn. However, the NPFL was but one of at least seven factions, including other Krahn groups, vying for power, and it was a splinter group of the NPLF, Prince Yormie Johnson's Independent National Patriotic Front of Liberia (INPFL), that actually took the presidential palace and killed Doe. Taylor's eventual victory owed much to Nigerian support, Nigeria being the principal partner in the Economic Community of West African States (ECOMOG) peace-keeping force introduced into Liberia in August 1990. Initially, Taylor had opposed Nigerian intervention but came to the realisation that he could not succeed without their support. By 1997, perhaps 200,000 had died in Liberia, including child soldiers, who were recruited by all factions.

Incipient warlordism emerged in Somalia following the fall of President Mahamad Siyaad Barré's Marxist regime in January 1991 and the disintegration of former opposition groups, which had themselves been fighting Barré. Partly, the Somali groups reflected clan affiliations, the SSA being of the Habr Gedir sub-clan of the Hawiye and the SNA of another Hawiye sub-clan and the Daarood clan. What has been characterised as 'political entrepreneurship' was more significant in the chaotic situation that emerged in attempts to control what little trade Somalia possessed. It prompted unsuccessful international peace-keeping or rather peace-enforcing intervention between December 1992 and March 1995, marked by the withdrawal of US troops in March 1994 following a disastrous attempt in the previous October to capture Aididi, in which eighteen Americans died. Aididi himself was killed in August 1996, but the factional fighting continues, with possibly 250,000 deaths between 1991 and 1997.

Economic insurgency has also marked the situation in Sierra Leone, where the distinction between insurgency and criminality has been fine indeed. Led by Alfred Foday Saybana Sankoh, a former army corporal, the Revolutionary United Front (RUF) emerged from the alienated youth culture of Freetown. Trained in Libya and linked to Taylor's NPLF, Sankoh launched his campaign from Liberia in March 1991. In many cases, the RUF simply abducted young recruits from the urbanised ghettos known as *pote*, where drug taking was already rife and crime and unemployment high. The army, which seized power itself under Captain Valentine Strasser in 1992, responded by recruiting its own young irregulars, with the result that the hapless population was caught between equally unattractive options. Assisted by a South African-based commercial security firm, Executive Outcomes, the army improved its performance from 1995 onwards and raised *kamajo* (militia) civil defence units. They often had a better knowledge of their locality than the insurgents and began to enjoy significant success. Indeed, the RUF negotiated a peace agreement in November 1996 with the newly elected government of President Ahmad Tejan Kabbah, Strasser having been ousted in turn in January 1996.

However, the general uncertainty at the apparent end of the conflict saw a new alliance between the RUF and dissident soldiers, which resulted in Kabbah's overthrow in May 1997. Kabbah hired another commercial security company, the British-based Sandline International, to help him to win back power. In the event, however, an ECOMOG force, again led by Nigeria, restored Kabbah in January 1999 and a new deal was brokered by which Sankoh joined the government. However, fighting broke out again in April 2000 as UN forces replaced those of ECOMOG, the UN in turn being bolstered by British forces, which moved in to retrain the army. A new cease-fire was brokered in November 2000, but it remains to be seen how the situation will develop. Indeed, when a British patrol was held hostage by a faction known as the West Side Boys, British paratroopers and SAS were committed to rescue them in September 2000.

Amid these continuing insurgencies around the world, it is clear that insurgents have access not only to ever more sophisticated weapons but also to the information revolution and information technology that is widely available commercially. Indeed, in Mexico, the otherwise obscure Zapatista Army for National Liberation (EZLN, Zapatistas), who take their name from the Mexican revolutionary killed in 1917, Emiliano Zapata, successfully hacked into the Mexican government's website in the mid-1990s to use the internet for their own message. Led by 'Marcos' and claiming to represent the rights of indigenous Mayan Indians in the southern state of Chiapas, the EZLN emerged in January 1994, but there has been a tenuous cease-fire since negotiations began in October 1995. Similarly, during its holding of the Japanese embassy in Lima in December 1996, a stand-off that continued until April 1997, the MRTA's 'Solidarity Website' was 'hit' over 88,000 times and continued to generate considerable interest, with 172,000 hits having been recorded by May 1998. The average was 100 hits a day, but at peak interest it reached over 700 hits a day. The MRTA thus used on-line technology to explain, justify and rationalise its violence to an international audience. In southern Lebanon, Hezbollah has also relayed pictures of its ambushes of IDF units on the internet, while, as already indicated, rival websites promoted the Russian and Chechen version of events during the Chechen war. Another sign of the times was that, when the US peace-keeping force was in Somalia, it found that it could not easily break the cellphone communications being used by warlord groups.

Clearly, the technology has changed, but in other respects, much remains the same in terms of insurgency. Indeed, as a master of deception, if suddenly transported forward 2,500 years, Sun Tzu would surely appreciate such use of the internet. In terms of guerrilla warfare and insurgency, the past is not another country. Indeed, to use another literary allusion, the past of guerrilla warfare and insurgency represents the shadow both of things that have been and of those that will be.

Further reading

On Dhofar, see John Akehurst, *We Won A War: The Campaign in Oman, 1965–75* (Salisbury, 1982); Tony Jeapes, *SAS Secret War* (London, 1996); Peter Thwaites, *Muscat Command* (London, 1995); D.C. Arkless, *The Secret War: Dhofar, 1971–72* (London, 1988); Pimlott, 'British Army' in Beckett and Pimlott, *Armed Forces and Modern Counter-insurgency*, *op. cit.*; Mockaitis, *British Counterinsurgency in the Post-imperial Era*, *op. cit.*, who also covers Northern Ireland; Bard O'Neill, 'Revolutionary War in Oman' in O'Neill, Heaton and Alberts, *Insurgency in the Modern World*, pp. 213–34; Major-General Kenneth Perkins, 'Oman, 1975: The Year of Decision' *Journal of the Royal United Services Institute for Defence Studies* 124 (1979), pp. 38–45; and Perkins, *A Fortunate Soldier* (London, 1988).

On Northern Ireland, see Desmond Hamill, *Pig in the Middle: The Army in Northern Ireland, 1969–85* (2nd edn, London, 1986); Michael Dewar, *The British Army in Northern Ireland* (London, 1985); Robin Evelegh, *Peace-keeping in a Democratic Society* (London, 1978); Mark Urban, *Big Boys' Rules: The SAS and the Secret Struggle against the IRA* (London, 1992); Caroline Kennedy-Pipe and Colin McInnes, 'The British Army in Northern Ireland, 1969–72: From Policing to Counter-Terror' *Journal of Strategic Studies* 20 (1997), pp. 1–24; McInnes, *Hot War Cold War*, *op. cit.*; John Newsinger, 'From Counterinsurgency to Internal Security: Northern Ireland, 1969–92' *Small Wars and Insurgencies* 6 (1995), pp. 88–111; Stephen Deakin, 'Security Policy and the Use of the Military: Military Aid to the Civil Power, Northern Ireland 1969' in *ibid.*, 4 (1993), pp. 211–27; J. Bowyer Bell, 'An Irish War: The IRA's Armed Struggle, 1969–90: Strategy as History Rules OK' in *ibid.*, 1 (1990), pp. 241–65; Bowyer Bell, *The Irish Troubles: A Generation of Violence, 1969–92* (New York, 1993); Tim Pat Coogan, *The IRA: A History* (11th edn, London, 1998); and Michael McKinley, 'Northern Ireland' in Peter Young (ed.), *Defence and the Media in Time of Limited War* (London, 1991), pp. 116–41.

On Asia, see Martin Smith, *Burma: Insurgency and the Politics of Ethnicity* (London, 1991); S. Mahmud Ali, *The Fearful State: Power, People and Internal War in South Asia* (London, 1993); C. Budiarjo and L.S. Liong, *The War against East Timor* (London, 1984); Ram Mohan, *Sri Lanka: The Fractured Island* (Harmondsworth, 1989); Rajesh Rajagopalan, '"Restoring Normalcy": The Evolution of the Indian Army's Counterinsurgency Doctrine' *Small Wars and Insurgencies* 11 (2000), pp. 44–68; Alexander Evans, 'The Kashmir Insurgency: As Bad as it Gets' in *ibid.*, pp. 69–81; Patricia Gossman, 'India's Secret Armies' in Campbell and Brenner, *Death Squads in Global Perspective*, pp. 261–86; Alexander Evans, 'Subverting the State: Intervention, Insurgency and Terror in

South Asia' *War Studies Journal* 2 (1996), pp. 17–29; Hugo Toye, *Laos: Buffer State or Battleground?* (Oxford, 1968); and M. Brown and J. Zasloff, *Apprentice Revolutionaries* (Stanford, 1986).

On Africa, see Christopher Clapham (ed.), *African Guerrillas* (Oxford, 1998), which has essays on Eritrea, Tigray, Sudan, Somalia, Uganda, Rwanda, Liberia, Zaire and Sierra Leone. Rich and Stubbs, *The Counter-insurgent State*, has essays on Algeria, as well as Sri Lanka and Afghanistan. See also Clayton, *Frontiersmen, op. cit.*; H. Erlich, *The Struggle over Eritrea, 1962–78: War and Revolution in the Horn of Africa* (Stanford, 1983); Ruth Iyob, *The Eritrean Struggle for Independence: Domination, Resistance, Nationalism* (Cambridge, 1995); John Young, *Peasant Revolution in Ethiopia: The Tigray People's Liberation Front, 1975–91* (Cambridge, 1997); D. Pool, *Eritrea: Africa's Longest War* (London, 1982); Richard Sherman, *Eritrea: The Unfinished Revolution* (New York, 1980); Tony Hodges, *Western Sahara: The Roots of a Desert War* (Westport, 1983); Gregg Bauer, 'The Moroccan–Polisario Conflict: Prospects for Western Saharan Stability in the 1990s' *Small Wars and Insurgencies* 5 (1994), pp. 111–29; Paul Richards, *Fighting for the Rain Forest: War, Youth and Resources in Sierra Leone* (Oxford, 1996); Crawford Young and Thomas Turner, *The Rise and Decline of the Zairean State* (Madison, 1986); Mark Huband, *The Liberian Civil War* (London, 1998); Roger Glickson, 'Counterinsurgency in Southern Sudan: The Means to Win' *Journal of Conflict Studies* 15 (1995), pp. 45–59; W.G. Thom, 'Congo-Zaire's 1996–97 Civil War in the Context of Evolving Patterns of Military Conflict in Africa in the Era of Independence' *Small Wars and Insurgencies* 19 (1999), pp. 93–123; O. Peter St John, 'Algeria: A Case Study of Insurgency in the New World Order' in *ibid.*, pp. 196–219; and Lawrence Cline, 'Egyptian and Algerian Insurgencies: A Comparison' in *ibid.*, 9 (1998), pp. 114–33.

On the Middle East, see Stuart Cohen, 'How Did the Intifada Affect the IDF?' *Conflict Quarterly* 14 (1994), pp. 7–22; Stuart Cohen and Efraim Inbar, 'Varieties of Counter-insurgency Activities: Israel's Military Operations against the Palestinians, 1948–90' *Small Wars and Insurgencies* 2 (1991), pp. 41–60; Raphael Cohen-Almagor, 'The Intifada: Causes, Consequences and Future Trends' in *ibid.*, pp. 12–40; Clive Jones, 'Israeli Counter-insurgency Strategy and the War in Southern Lebanon, 1985–97' in *ibid.*, 8 (1997), pp. 82–108; Mordechai Nisan, 'The PLO and Vietnam: National Liberation Models for Palestinian Struggle' in *ibid.*, 4 (1993), pp. 181–210; S.M. Katz, *Israeli Special Forces* (Osceola, 1993); Bard O'Neill, *Armed Struggle in Palestine* (Boulder, 1978); Gunther Rothenberg, 'Israeli Defence Forces and Low-intensity Operations' in Charters and Tugwell, *Armies in Low-Intensity Conflict*, pp. 49–76; and Z. Schiff and R. Rothstein, *Fedayeen* (New York, 1972).

For contemporary developments, see Steven Metz, 'Insurgency after the Cold War' *Small Wars and Insurgencies* 5 (1994), pp. 63–82; Michael Dartnell, 'Insurgency On-line: Elements for a Theory of Anti-government Internal Communications' in *ibid.*, 10 (1999), pp. 116–35; Jennifer Morrison Taw and

Bruce Hoffman, 'The Urbanisation of Insurgency: The Potential Challenge to US Army Operations' in *ibid.*, 6 (1995), pp. 68–87; and Eric Young, 'The Victors and the Vanquished: The Role of Military Factors in the Outcome of Modern African Insurgencies' in *ibid.*, 7 (1996), pp. 178–95.

INDEX

Abane, Ramdane 161–2
Abbas, Ferhat 166
Abd al-Aziz, Mohammed 241
Abd el-Kader 12, 28
Abd el-Krim, Mohammed ben 13, 33, 41
Abrams, Creighton 203
Abu Klea, Battle of (1885) 33
Abyssinia *see* Ethiopia
Acçâo Libertadora Nacional (ALN)
   175–6
Accelerated Pacification Campaign
   (APC) 202
Aden 129, 151–5, 157–9, 168, 190–1, 226
Admazi, Najibullah 210
Adowa, Battle of (1896) 33
Afeworki, Issayas 239
Afghanistan 12, 35, 183, 209–12, 238, 241
Afghan War: First (1839–42) 12; Second
   (1878–80) 12, 35
African National Congress (ANC):
   Rhodesian 132; South African 145
Aguinaldo, Emilio 1
Aididi, Mahamad Faarah Haasan 247–8
Airpower 43, 126, 138, 189–90, 210, 213,
   228–9
al Madani, Abbasi 240
Albania 58, 67, 90
Alexander, Harold 59
al-Fatah 233
al-Ghassani, Muhammad Ahmad 218
Algeria 12, 28, 40–1, 238, 240–1
Algerian War (1954–62) 79, 115, 117,
   143, 151–2, 159–68, 191
Algiers, Battle of (1957) 162–3, 165, 167
Ali la Pointe 163
Ali Pasha 9
Alianza Anticommunista Argentine
   (AAA) 179

Alianza Popular Revolucionaria
   Americana (APRA) 83–4
Alianza Republicana Nacionalista
   (ARENA) 205–6
Alianza Revolucionaria Democrática
   (ARDE) 207
Allen, Ethan 3
Allende, Salvador 174
Alliance des Forces Démocratiques pour
   la Libération du Congo-Zaire
   (ADFL) 245, 247
Alves, Mario 175–6
American Civil War (1861–5) 9–12,
   29–31
American Indian Wars (1866–90) 24,
   32–4, 37
American League for a Free Palestine
   (ALFP) 89
American War of Independence
   (1775–83) 3–4, 89
Amherst, Jeffrey 3
Amin, Idi 247
Amritsar (1919) 44, 46
Andom, Aman 238
Anglo-Irish War (1919–21) 16–18, 44–6
Angola 32, 79, 130–1, 133–9, 142, 144–7,
   245–6
Angolan Civil War (1974–6) 144, 147,
   209
Angry Brigade 180
Annual, Battle of (1921) 33
Antonov Revolt *see* Tambov Revolt
Anya-Nya 239–40
Appian 1
Arab Revolt (1916–17) 19–20
Arab Revolt (1936–39) 20, 45, 47, 87, 91
Araña Osorio, Carlos 172
Arbenz Guzmán, Jacobo 169, 172

Argentina 169, 171–4, 176–9
Argoud, Antoine 167
Armatulai 9
Armed Islamic Group (GIA) 240–1
Armée de Libération Nationale (ALN) 161–2
Armée Nationale Populaire Algérien (ANPA) 165
Arriaga, Kaulza de 137–8, 142
Ashanti War, Second (1873–4) 32, 35
Auma, Alice 247
Australian Army 124, 194, 243
Austro-Prussian War (1866) 12

Ba Maw 17
Baader, Andreas 179
Baader–Meinhof Gang 179–80
Bach-Zelewski, Erich von 64
Bagnold, Ralph 55
Bailén, Battle of (1808) 9
Baker, Eugene 183
Bao An see Regional Forces
Bao Dai 111–4, 117
Baratieri, Oreste 33
Barker, Evelyn 94
Barré, Mahamad Siyaad 248
Barricades Week (1960) 163, 167
Barrientos, René 173
Barry, Tom 16
Barzani, Mustafa 242
Basmachi Revolt (1918–31) 49–50
Batista y Zaldivar, Fulgencio 168–9, 171
Baylis, John ix
Bay of Pigs (1961) 173
Be, Nguyen 200
Beals, Carleton 183
Beaufre, André 164
Begin, Menachem 17, 87–8, 91, 151
Belhadj, Ahmed 240
Belhadj Djillali 165
Bell, Franklin 37
Bellounis, Mohammed 165
Bem, Józef 15
Ben Bella, Ahmed 161, 165
Ben M'hidi 163, 165
Bergerud, Eric 203
Bermúdez, Enrique 207
Betancourt, Rómulo 177
Bevin, Ernest 92
Bianco, Carlo 15
bifurcation between regulars and conscripts 143–4, 166–7, 191–2

Bigeard, Marcel 163, 166–7
Bird, C. W., 35
Bismarck, Otto von 31
Black and Tans 45
Black September 233
Blalock, Keith 11
'Bloody Sunday' (1972) 230
Boer War (1899–1902) 12–14, 16, 18, 32–3, 36, 38–40, 42, 72, 93
Bohannan, Charles 173
Bolivia 170–1, 173–4, 178, 208
Bonaparte, Joseph 6
Bonaparte, Napoleon see Napoleon I, Emperor
Bonnet, Georges 159–60
Booth, Ken ix
Bordaberry, Juan 178
Border Surveillance Programme 196
Borge, Tomás 207
Bose, Subhas Chandra 17
Botha, Louis 13–14
Boucher, Charles 95
Boumèdienne, Houari 161, 240
Bowden, Tom 47
Bowyer Bell, J. 221–2
Braddock, Edward 2
Bradley, Omar 184
Braik bin Hamoud, Sheikh 223
Braun, Otto 71
Bravo, Douglas 177
Brazil 171, 173–6, 179
Breen, Dan 16–17
Brererton, Colonel 46
Brigate Rosse 179–80
Briggs, Harold 100–2, 107
Briggs Plan 100
Bristol riots (1831) 46
British Advisory Mission to South Vietnam (BRIAM) 107, 186, 198–200
British Army 2–4, 6, 8, 13–14, 16–18, 20, 24–5, 31–6, 38–40, 42–8, 55–6, 68, 86, 88–91, 93–5, 100–1, 103, 107, 109, 111–12, 124–30 153, 155–9, 217–30, 236, 249
British Army Training Team (BATT) 218, 227
British Military Mission to Greece (BMM(G)) 93
British South Africa Police (BSAP) 135, 139–40
Brunei People's Party 123

Bryan, William 13
Bugeaud, Thomas-Robert 28–9, 40
Bulgaria 16, 90, 93
Burgoyne, John 3
Burma 12, 17, 35, 46–7, 55–6, 79, 100, 103, 109, 186, 243–4
Butler, Smedley 38
Bystrzanowski, Józef 15

Cable, Larry 108, 184, 189
Cabora Bassa Dam 134–5, 142
Cabral, Amilcar 79, 132, 139
Caetano, Marcello 130
Calabrian Revolt (1806–11) 5–7, 9, 27
Callaghan, James 223
Callwell, Charles 12, 32, 35–6, 40
Cambodia 110–13, 117, 188, 191, 193, 209, 246–7
Campbell-Bannerman, Henry 39
Cape Frontier Wars (1779–1878) 12
Carlist Wars (1833–40) 15
Carpenter, Frank 125
Carruthers, Susan 154
Carter, Jimmy 240
Casillas, Major 169
Castaneda, Mariano 104
Castaño, Fabio Vásquez 171
Castro, Fidel 151, 168–73, 175–7, 183
Castro, Raúl 168
Cathelineau, Jacques 5
Catling, Richard 129
Central Intelligence Agency (CIA) 109, 172–3, 196, 200–2, 244
Central Office for South Vietnam (COSVN) 187
Cetniks 65–6
Ceylon 39
Chad 238–9, 241, 245
Chaffee, Adna 37
Challe, Maurice 162, 164–5, 167
Chamorro Rapaccioli, Fernando 207
Chao Fa 244
Charette de la Contrie, François Athanase 5
Charters, David 25
Chechen Wars (1994–5, 1999–2000) 212–13, 249
Chiang Kai-shek 70–2, 76
Chichester-Clark, James 219
Chickerema, James 132
Chieu Hoi Programme 198–9
Chile 174, 178

Chindits 20, 55–6
Chinese Civil War (1926–49) 70–8, 114
Chin Peng 96, 98, 101, 103
Chipenda, Daniel 133
Chirau, Jeremiah 132
Choltitz, General von 59
Chouans 5
Chrzanowski, Wojciech 15
Churchill, Winston 18, 55
Chu Luc 114
Chu Teh 71–2
Civil Operations and Rural Development Support (CORDS) 200–1
Civilian Irregular Defense Groups (CIDG) 189, 196
Clapham, Christopher 237
Clark, Thomas 11
Clarke, Basil 45
Clarke, George Rogers 3
Clausewitz, Carl von 14, 73
Clinton, Henry 4
Colby, William 202
Cold War (1946–91) 121, 172, 183, 217, 236–7
Collins, Michael 16–17
Colombia 171, 173, 208–9
colonial warfare 12–14, 31–49
Combined Action Platoons (CAPs) 197, 203
Cominform 97
Comintern 76
Comité Revolucionaire de Mocambique (Coremo) 133
Comité Révolutionaire d'Unité et d'Action (CRUA) 161
Commandos 13–14, 18, 55, 72, 93–4, 138, 143, 146
Commercial Insurgency 237, 247–9
Communist Party of the Philippines (CPP) 106
Confederacy 10–12, 30–1
Confrontation, Indonesian/Malaysian (1962–6) 121–3, 127–8, 130, 158, 198
Congo, Belgian 131; Republic of 134
Contadora Group 208
Contras 207–8
Cooper, Jim 197
Co-odinatora Guerrillera Simón Bolivár (CGSB) 208
cordon sanitaire 141–2, 147
Cornwallis, William 4

Corpus, Victor 106
Corvey, Le Mière de 4
Costa Gomes, Francisco da 138, 142
Costa Rica 207
counter-gangs 127, 224
Cowper, Tony 157
Creasey, Timothy 224–5
Cristiani Buchard, Alfredo 206
Crook, George 34
Cross, James 179
Cruz, Viriato da 133
Cuba 32, 36, 83, 144, 146–7, 151,
    168–71, 173–4, 180, 184
Cunningham, Alan 95
Custer, George 30, 33–4, 183
Cutliffe, Margaret 156
Cyprus 34, 44, 46, 129, 151–9, 168,
    225–6, 234
Czechoslovakia 210

Dade, Francis 29
Dallin, Alexander 61
Dalton, Charles 44
Damavand Line 228
Dan Ve see Popular Forces
Darby, William 55
Darling, Kenneth 156
Darnand, Joseph 59
D'Aubisson, Roberto 205–6
Davidov, Denis 4
De Gaulle, Charles 58, 111, 162–3, 166–7
de Kock, M. H. 41
de la Billiere, Peter 227
de la Puente, Luís 172
De La Rey, Koos 13
de Lattre de Tassigny, Jean 115–16
d'Elbée, Maurice 5
de Paiva Couceiro, Henrique
De Wet, Christiaan 13–14, 16
De Wet, Piet 14
Debray, Régis 169–71, 173, 175
Déby, Idriss 239
Decker, Carl von 4
Dederer, John 4
Delestraint, General 58
Democratic Turnhalle Alliance (DTA)
    147
Denning, B. C. 46
Depuy, William 197
Derg 238, 240, 243
Dhlakama, Alfonso 147
Dhofar Development Committee 222–3

Dhofar Liberation Front (DLF) 218, 227
Dhofar War (1966–75) 79, 217–8, 221–5,
    227–30
Diaz, Juan Martín 7, 9
Diem, Ngo Dinh 109, 117, 187–9, 193,
    195, 198–9
Dien Bien Phu, Battle of (1954) 114–17
Dimitrov, Georgi 76
Dimokratikos Stratos Ellados (DSE)
    87–8, 90, 93, 108
Dirty War (1976–7) 179
Dispositif de Protection Urbaine (DPU)
    163, 167
Dobie Force 128
Doe, Samuel 248
Dominican Republic 49, 168, 171,
    173–4, 208
Donovan, 'Wild Bill' 56
Duarte, José Napoleón 205
Dudayev, Dzhokhar 212
Dutch Army 32, 34, 41–2, 110
Dutch East Indies 32, 35, 41–2, 86,
    109–10, 117
Dyer, Reginald 46
Dylan, Bob 179–80

Easter Rising (1916) 16
East Timor 241, 243
Ecuador 171–2, 208
Economic Community of West African
    States (ECOMOG) 248–9
Economic Development Corps
    (EDCOR) 104–5
Egypt 92, 153, 161, 163
Eire see Irish Republic
Eisenhower, Dwight 114, 165
Ejército de Liberación Nacional (ELN)
    171, 208
Ejército Guerrillero del Pueblo (EGP)
    172
Ejército Popular de Liberación (EPL)
    208
Ejército Revolucionario del Pueblo
    (ERP) 176, 178–9
El Salvador 205–8
Elbrick, Burke 176
Ellinikos Laikos Apeleftherotikos Stratos
    (ELAS) 67–8, 87–8, 90
Emmerich, Andreas 4
Engels, Friedrich 12, 14
Eritrea 238–9, 241, 243
Eritrean Liberation Front (ELF) 238

Eritrean People's Liberation Front
(EPLF) 238–40, 243
Erskine, George 124–6
Esdaile, Charles 5, 9
Ethiopia 32–4, 43, 56, 209, 238–40, 243
Ethiopian Peoples' Revolutionary
Democracy Front (EPRDF) 239–40,
243, 247
Ethniki Kai Koinoniki Apeleftherosi
(EKKA) 67
Ethniki Organosis Kyprion Agoniston
(EOKA) 18, 151–6
Ethniko Apeleftherostiko Metopo
(EAM) 67–8
Ethnikos Agrotikos Syndesmos
Antikommounistikis (EASAD) 68
Ethnikos Dimokratikos Ellinikos
Syndesmos (EDES) 67
Euskadi Ta Askatasun (ETA) 179–80
Ewald, Johann von 4
Ewing, Thomas 30
Executive Outcomes 248

Faidherbe, Louis 40
Fairn Committee (1959) 128
Falklands War (1982) 25, 179
Fang Chih-min 71
Fanon, Franz 174, 247
Farran, Roy 95
Farrow, Edward 38
Ferguson, Champ 10
Ferguson, Patrick 3–4
Fergusson, Bernard 94–5
Ferret Force 95, 98, 107, 127
Fertig, W. 56
Fifth Bureau 164, 166
Fire Force 141
Firqat 227–8
Fisher, Robert 193
Flechas 137, 141
Foco 79, 82, 151, 168–74, 177, 247
Foertsch, General 65
Fonseca Amador, Carlos 207
Force 136 50
Foot, Hugh 156
Franco, Francisco 21
Franco–Austrian War (1859) 15
Franco–Prussian War (1870–1) 12, 14,
24, 31
francs-tireurs 12, 31, 42–3, 58
Frederick, Robert 55
Freedman, Lawrence ix

Frémont, John 30
French Army viii, 5–9, 12–13, 24, 26–9,
31, 33–4, 40–1, 80, 112–17, 143, 152,
159–60, 162–7
French Foreign Legion 165, 167
French Indo-China 33, 40, 68, 80, 86,
109–17, 159–60, 166
French Revolutionary and Napoleonic
Wars (1793–1815) 4–9, 26–9
Frente de Libertação de Moçambique
(Frelimo) 133–5, 144, 147, 245, 247
Frente Farabundo Martí de Liberación
Nacional (FMLN) 205–7
Frente Nacional de Libertação de Angola
(FNLA) 133–4, 144, 147
Frente para a Libertação e Independência
de Guine (FLING) 133
Frente Revolucionária Timorense de
Libertação e Independência (Fretilin)
243
Frente Sandinista de Liberación (FSLN)
see Sandinistas
Front de Libération du Québec (FLQ)
179
Front de Libération Nationale (FLN)
151, 159–67, 240
Front de Libération Nationale (Frolinat)
239
Front for the Liberation of Occupied
South Yemen (FLOSY) 153–4, 157
Front for the Liberation of Zimbabwe
(Frolizi) 132
Front Islamique du Salut (FIS) 240
Front Patriotique Rwandais (FPR)
244–5, 247
Frontinius 1
Front National Française (FNF) 163
Frunze, M. V. 210
Fuentes, Ydígoras 171
Fuerzas Armadas de Liberación (FAL)
178–9
Fuerzas Armadas de Liberación Nacional
(FALN) 151, 176–7
Fuerzas Armadas Peronistas (FAP) 178
Fuerzas Armadas Rebeldes (FAR)
171–2, 178
Fuerzas Armadas Revolucionarias de
Colombia (FARC) 171, 208
Fuerzas Democráticas Nicaragüenses
(FDN) 207
Fuerzas Populares de Liberación-
Farabundo Martí (FPL-FM) 205

Fujimori, Alberto 84
Fuller, J. F. C. ix

Gage, Thomas 2
Galliéni, Joseph-Simon 40–1
Galvin, John 213
Gandhi, Indira 231
Gandhi, Rajiv 231
Garang, John 240
García, Alan 84
Gardiner, Lord 226
Garibaldi, Giuseppe 15
Garnett, John ix
Gates, Horatio 4
Gatewood, John 11
Geneva Agreement (1954) 114, 117, 187
German Army 12, 31–2, 34, 42–3, 50, 55, 57–68, 72, 109–10
German East Africa 32, 42–3
German South West Africa 31, 42–3
Giap, Vo Nguyen 79–81, 116–17, 187, 190, 192
Gibraltar 222, 226
Gibson, William 125
Giraldius Cambrensis 1
Godard, Yves 159–60, 163, 167
Gorham, Joseph 2
Gracey, Douglas 112
Grand, Lawrence 18
Grant, U. S. 30
Gray, Nicol 94–5, 98, 101
Greece 58, 67–8
Greek Civil War (1944–8) 67–8, 86–8, 90–1, 93–5, 107–8, 184
Greek National Army (GNA) 88, 90, 93–4, 108
Greek War of Independence (1821–7) 9–10, 29
Green Berets see United States Special Forces
Greene, Hugh 101
Greene, Nathanael 4
Greene, Wallace 196
Grenada 204
Grey's Scouts 141
Griffith, Paddy 24, 29, 186
Griffith, Samuel 76
Grivas, George 18, 151–6
Groupement de Commandos Mixtes Aéroportés (GCMA) 115
Groupement Mixte d'Intervention (GMI) 115

Grupos Especiais (GE) 138
Grupos Especiais Pára-quedistas (GEP) 138
Gualteri, Niccolo 6
Guatemala 169, 171–2
Guatemalan National Revolutionary Unity (URNG) 172
Gubbins, Colin 18
Guerre Révolutionnaire 115, 117, 136, 152, 159–60, 163–7
Guerrilla Army of the Poor 172
Guescelin, Gertrand du 2
Guevara, Ernesto 'Che' 79, 82, 151, 153–4, 168–71, 173–5, 177–8, 247
Guillén, Abraham 177
Guinea, Portuguese 32, 79, 130–4, 136–7, 139, 142, 144; Republic of 139
Gulf of Tonkin Resolution (1964) 189, 191
Gulf War (1990–1) 25, 204, 217, 242
Gurney, Henry 95, 101
Guzmán Reynoso, Abimael 83–4
Gwynn, Charles 44, 46

Habré, Hissèni 239
Habyarimana, Juvenal 245
Habsburg Army 2
Haganah 47, 87–8
Haiduks 2
Haile Selassie 56, 238
Haiti 5, 32, 38, 49
Haj, Messali 161
Halleck, Henry 30
Hamas 235–6
Hamlet Evaluation System (HES) 201
Hamley, Edward 31
Handcock, Peter 42
Harding, John 152, 154–6
Harrington, Samuel 48
Hatta, Mohammad 109
He Long 71
Healey, Denis 128
Hearst, Patty 180
Hearts and Minds 26, 28, 37–8, 40–1, 49, 101–2, 104–5, 107, 125–7, 130, 135, 137–8, 142, 147, 158–9, 164–6, 183–4, 195–7, 200–1, 203–4, 227–30
Hecht, Ben 89
helicopters 103, 115, 127, 138, 141, 147, 165, 185, 209–11
Henderson, Ian 127, 129
Heneker, W. C. G. 35

Herero Revolt (1904–7) 42–3
Hermon, John 224
Heydrich, Reinhard 57
Hezbollah 234, 236, 249
Hickman, John 139–40
Hillsborough Agreement (1985) 223
Hilsman, Roger 186, 198–9
Himmler, Heinrich 57, 63–4
Hinde, Robert 124–5
Hitler, Adolf 62–3, 87
Hittites 1
H'mong 82, 244
Ho Chi Minh 60, 79–80, 111–13
Ho Chi Minh Trail 188–91, 195
Hoche, Louis-Lazare 26–7
Hofer, Andreas 6
Hogaboom Board 185
Hogard, Jacques 160
Holland, J. C. F. 18
Holyoak, Eric 127
Holy Spirit Movement (HSM) 247
Home Guard: British 21; Kikuyu 125,
    128; Malayan 102
Honduras 206–7
Hop Tac Programme 200
Hornbeam Line 228
Hot Pursuit 139, 141, 147, 234
Howard, Michael ix
Howze Board 185
Hoxhar, Enver 67
Hoyt, George 10
Hsuchow, Battle of (1948–9) 78
Hsu Hsiang-ch'ien 71
Hukbalahap 68, 79, 96–9, 104–5, 173
Hundred Years War 2
Hungarian Uprising (1956) 210
Hunt Committee (1969) 223
Hussein, King 234
Hutu 244–5

Iban 127–8
Ibrahim Ahmed 242
Independent National Patriotic Front of
    Liberia (INPFL) 248
India 31, 34–5, 39, 44, 46–8, 91–2
Indian Army (post 1947) 135, 218,
    231–3, 236
Indian Army, British 34–5, 56, 112
Indian Mutiny (1857) 12, 34
Indonesian Army 123–4, 127–8, 243
Intelligence 16, 45, 101, 104, 107, 117,

124, 127, 129, 137, 140, 154–7, 165,
    194–5, 202, 224–7
Internal Macedonian Revolutionary
    Organisation (IMRO) 15–16
International Red Cross 165
Internment 219–20
Intifada 235–6
Iran 180, 208, 218, 223, 228, 242;
    Imperial Iranian Battlegroup (IIBG)
    223, 228
Iran-Contra Affair (1986) 208
Iran–Iraq War (1980–8) 242
Iraq 180, 242–3; Revolt (1920–1) 44
Ireland 16–18, 44–6
Irish National Liberation Army (INLA)
    220–2
Irish Republic 222–3
Irish Republican Army (IRA) 16–18,
    44–5, 219, 227; Continuity 220;
    Official 219–20, 227; Provisional
    (PIRA) 219–23 227, 230; Real 220
Irish Republican Socialist Party (IRSL)
    220
Irgun Zvai Leumi 17, 87–9, 151
Islamic Fundamentalism 209–10, 234–5,
    237–41
Islamic Resistance Movement 236
Israel 155, 233–6, 238
Israeli Defence Forces (IDF) 218, 231,
    233–6, 249
Isandlwana, Battle of (1879) 33
Italian Army 32–4, 43, 64–7
Italo–Turkish War (1911–12) 43
Itote, Waruhiu 123

Jabotinsky, Vladimir 17
Jackson, Geoffrey 178
Jacobs, John 180
Jagdkommandos 63–4
James, Frank 12
James, Jesse 12
Jam'iat-i Islami-yi Afghanistan 210
Janatha Vimukthi Peramuna (JVP) 79
Japanese Army 55–7, 68, 76–9, 96,
    109–12
Jasons Group 193
Jeapes, Tony 217
Jenkin, William 101
Jenkins, Trevor 129
Jennison, Charles 10
Jewish Agency 47, 87–8
Johnson, Lyndon B. 189–92, 200

Johnson, Yormie 248
Johnston, Milus 11
Joint US Military Advisory and Planning Group (JUSMAPG) 93–4, 107–8
Joint US Military Assistance Group (JUSMAG) 105, 107, 109
Jomini, Antoine-Henri 25
Jordan 218, 233–5
Jouhard, Edmond 167

Kabbah, Ahmad Tejan 249
Kabila, Laurent 245
Kachin Independence Organisation 244
Kachins 56, 243
Kamienski, Henryk 15
Kampuchea see Cambodia
Kampuchean National United Front for National Salvation (KUFNS) 246
Kani, Inocêncio 139
Karen National Defence Organisation (KNDO) 244
Karen National Union 244
Karen Revolt (1949–55) 56, 244
Karens 56, 243
Karmal, Babrak 209–10
Kashmir 231–2, 238
Kealy, Mike 227
Kennedy, John F. 24, 81, 165, 172, 184, 186, 189, 192, 195, 198, 200, 204
Kenya African Union (KAU) 122
Kenya police 124, 128–9
Kenyan Emergency (1952–60) 103, 121–30, 136, 155, 158, 224–5, 229
Kenyata, Jomo 122, 124
Kerdphol, Saiyud 82
Khalq 209
Khe Sanh, Siege of (1968) 197
Khmer People's National Liberation Front (KPNLF) 246
Khmer Rouge 209, 246–7
Khrushchev, Nikita 81, 121
Kikuyu 122, 124–6, 128
Kimathi, Dedan 122, 127
Kim Il Sung 77
King Philip's War (1675–6) 25
King's Mountain, Battle of (1780) 3
Kirk, George 11
Kit Carson Scouts 198
Kitchener, Herbert 39
Kitson, Frank 127, 129, 224–6
Kléber, Jean Baptiste 26
Klephts 2, 9

Komer, Robert 200–2
Kommounisitikon Komma Ellados (KKE) 87, 90
Kony, Joseph 247
Korean War (1950–3) 24, 98–100, 108, 114, 117, 184
Kosovo 217
Krepinevich, Andrew 184, 203
Kruger, Paul 13
Krulak, Victor 196
Kuomintang (KMT) 19, 55, 70–3, 76–8, 111–12
Kurdish Democratic Party (KDP) 242–3
Kurdistan Workers' Party (PKK) 242–3
Kurds 241–3
Ky, Nguyen Cao 189

Lacheroy, Charles 160, 164, 167
La Gort Dillie, P. M. 41
Lai Tek 98
Lamarca, Carlos 176
Langdon-Davies, John 21
Lang Son, Battle of (1885) 33
Lansdale, Edward 104–5, 108–9
Laos 82, 111–13, 116–17, 187–8, 191, 193, 196, 202–3, 209, 243–5
Laporte, Pierre 179
Lartéguy, Jean 166
Lathbury, Gerald 125–6
Lawrence, Thomas Edward 18–20
Lawson, Richard 224
Layton, Gilbert 196
Le Duan 187
Le Duc Tho 187
Lea, George 128
Lebanon 185, 233–6, 249
Lee, Charles 3–4
Lee, Robert E. 10–11
Lehame Herut Israel (LEHI) 17, 87–9, 95, 151
Lenin, V. I. 14–15
Leopard Line 228
Lewes, Jock 55
Liberation Tigers of Tamil Eelam (LTTE) see Tamil Tigers
Liberia 247–8
Libya 180, 239, 241, 248
Lidbury, David 125
Liddell Hart, Basil 19
Lidice 57
Lieber Code (1863) 30
Lin Piao 74

List, Field Marshal von 65
Little Big Horn, Battle of the (1876)
    33–4
Liu Po-ch'eng 71
Long March, the (1934–5) 72, 74
Lon Nol 188
Lord's Resistance Army 247
low-intensity conflict viii, 204–5
Luc Luong Dac Biet (LLDB) 196
Lukoya, Severino 247
Lunt, James 153
Lusaka Agreement (1984) 147
Lyautey, Louis-Hubert-Gonsalve 40–1,
    160

Maaten, Klaas van der 41–2
MacArthur, Arthur 36–7
MacArthur, Douglas 36
MacBride, John 16
Maccabeus, Judas 1
Macdonald, A. M. 128
Macdonald White Paper 92
Macek, Anton 65
Machardo, Gustavo 19
Machel, Samora 133
Madagascar 40
Magsaysay, Ramón 104–5, 108–9, 173
Maguire, C. Miller 35
Mahamed, Ali Mahdi 247
Mahn Ba Zan 244
Maji Maji Rising (1905–7) 32, 42–3
Majuba, Battle of (1881) 33
Makarios III, Archbishop 152, 156
Makhno, Nestor 18
Malabar Revolt see Moplah Rebellion
Malayan Communist Party (MCP) 95–8,
    101–3, 126
Malayan Emergency (1948–60) 79, 81,
    86, 95–105, 107, 121, 124–9, 136,
    139–41, 155, 157–9, 184, 186, 193–4,
    198–200, 224–6, 229, 232
Malayan People's Anti-Japanese Army
    (MPAJA) 56, 68, 96
Malayan Races Liberation Army
    (MRLA) 96, 98
Malvar, Miguel 13
Mancuso, Paolo 6
Mannès, Charles-Antoine 27
Manstein, Erich von 63
manuals and publications 4, 9, 15, 18,
    20–1, 28, 32, 34–5, 40–2, 44–6, 48, 50,
    64, 76, 79–80, 91, 103, 107, 127, 129,

136, 151, 159–60, 170, 174–6, 184–6,
    195, 204–5, 210, 225–6
Mao Tse-tung 1, 4, 20–1, 68, 70–6,
    78–84, 86, 98–9, 114, 132–3, 151,
    153, 159, 168, 170, 175, 185, 187, 208,
    232, 243
Maoris 12
Maquis 58–9, 63, 116
Marcos, Ferdinand 106–7
Marcuse, Herbert 174
Marighela, Carlos 174–7
Marion, Francis 3
martial law 44, 46, 92, 95
Martí, Farabundo 19, 205
Martin, Clifford 88, 92
Martin, Lawrence ix
Marulanda Vélez, Manuel 171
Marx, Karl 12, 14
Maskhadov, Aslan 212
Massoud, Ahmad Shah 210
Massu, Jacques 159, 162–3, 165, 167
Mau Mau 121–30
Maudling, Reginald 230
Mauritania 241
Mayorga, Silvio 207
Mazzini, Giuseppe 15
McCuen, John 185
McKinley, William 13
McNamara, Robert 192–3, 199
McNamara Line 193
McNaughton, John 189
McNeill, John 10
media 158, 190–1, 229–30, 249
Meinhof, Ulrike 179
Mendès-France, Pierre 162
Mendietta, Jean de 7, 9
Mengistu Haile Mariam 238–40, 243
Meos 116, 244
Merrill's Marauders 55, 186
Metz, Steven 237
Mexican War (1846–7) 29–30
Mexico 40, 168–9, 208, 249
Mezerag, Madani 240
MI5 227
MI6 220, 224, 227
Mihailovic, Draza 65–6
Miles, Nelson 37
Milice 59
Military Assistance Advisory Group
    (MAAG) 189, 199
Military Assistance Command, Vietnam
    (MACV) 189, 194, 196–7

Milorg 58
Min Yuen 100
Mina, Francisco Espoz y 7, 9, 27
Mitchell, Colin 155, 157–8
Mitchell Commission 223
Mitrione, Dan 178
Mitterand, François 170
Mizo 231–2
Mobutu Sese Seko 134, 245
Mockaitis, Tom 25, 47, 226
Mohammad, Seyid 43
Moleiro, Moisés 174, 177
Mollet, Guy 162
Moltke, Helmuth von 31
Mondlane, Eduardo 133, 139
Monje, Mario 173
Montagnards 200
Montgomery, Bernard 91–2, 95
Montoneros 178–9
Moplah Rebellion (1921) 44, 46
Morant, Harry 'Breaker' 42
Morgan, Daniel 4
Morgan, John Hunt 10
Morice Line 164
Morocco 40–1, 162, 164–6, 241
Moros 37–8, 106
Morrison, Danny 221
Mosby, John 10, 30
Moscoso, José 9
Most, Johannes 15
Moulin, Jean 56
Mountbatten, Lord 221
Mouvement Patriotique du Salut (MPS)
    239
Mouvement pour le Triomphe des
    Libertés Démocratiques (MTLD) 161
Mouvement Republicain Populaire
    (MRP) 113
Movimento das Forças Armadas (MFA)
    144
Movimento Nacionalista Revolucionario
    (MNR) 175
Movimento Popular de Libertação de
    Angola (MPLA) 133–4, 144, 245
Movimiento de Izquierda
    Revolucionaria (MIR): Peru 172;
    Venezuela 176–7
Movimiento de Liberación Nacional
    (MLN) see Tupamaros
Movimiento 19 de Abril (M-19) 208
Movimiento Revolucionario 13 de
    Noviembre (MR-13) 171

Movimiento Revolucionario Tupac
    Amar (MRTA) 84, 177, 249
Moyano, Maria Elena 84
Moyne, Lord 87
Mozambique 32, 130–1, 133–8, 142,
    144–5, 147, 245, 247
Mueveni, Yoweri 244–5, 247
Mugabe, Robert 79, 132
Mujahidin 209–11
Mulcahy, Richard 17
Musawi, Hussein Abbas 234
Muzorewa, Abel 132, 141

Nagas 231–2
Nairac, Robert 227
Namibia 121, 130, 146–7, 245
Napoleon I, Emperor 5–7, 9, 24, 27–8
Nasser, Gamar Abdel 153, 163
Nasution, Abdul Harris 79
National Front for the Liberation of
    South Vietnam see Viet Cong
National Liberation Front (NLF) 153–4,
    157–8
National Patriotic Front of Liberia
    (NPFL) 247–8
National Popular Alliance (ANAPO) 208
National Resistance Army (NRA) 244,
    247
Navarre, Henri-Eugène 116–7
Nedic, Milan 65
Nehru, Pandit 231
Neto, Angostinho 133
Newman, Kenneth 224
New People's Army (NPA) 106
New Zionist Organisation 87
Nhan Dan Tu Ve see People's Self-
    Defense Force
Nhu, Ngo Dinh 199
Nicaragua 18–19, 32, 43, 48–9, 205–8
Nixon, Richard 191–2, 200
Nkomati Agreement (1984) 147
Nkomo, Joshua 132
Nkrumah, Kwame 79
Non-aligned Movement 165
North Atlantic Treaty Organisation
    (NATO) 143, 165, 185, 195
North, Oliver 207–8
North Vietnamese Army (NVA) 188–90,
    192–3, 196–7, 203
North West Frontier 31, 35, 42–3, 47–8,
    56
Northern Ireland 129, 157, 159, 217,

219–23, 225–30; Civil Rights Association (NICRA) 219
Nujoma, Sam 146–7
Nunes da Silva, Artur 136
Nuttle, David 196

Oberkommando der Wehrmacht (OKW) 62–4
Oberkommando des Heeres (OKH) 63
Obote, Milton 244, 247
Office of Strategic Services (OSS) 50, 56, 109, 111
Ogaden War (1978) 209
Okamura, Yasuji 78
Oldfield, Maurice 224
Oman 217–18, 221–5, 227–30
Omdurman, Battle of (1898) 33
O'Neill, Terence 219
Operations: Agatha (1946) 91; Anvil (1954) 126; Bagration (1944) 61; Chui (1955) 126; Claret (1964–6) 128, 158; Country Fair (1966) 196; Diago (1979) 144–5; Favour (1978) 141; First Flute (1955) 126; Golden Fleece (1966) 196; Grapes of Wrath (1996) 236; Hammer (1955) 126; Linebacker I (1972) 192; Linebacker II (1972) 192; Lorraine (1952) 115–16; Mar Verde (1970) 139; Mardon (1976) 144; Motorman (1972) 220; Nó Gordio (1970) 138; Overload (1974) 142; Pepperpot (1956) 155; Pershing (1967) 197; Protea (1981) 147; Rolling Thunder (1965–8) 189; Sea Swallow (1962) 199; Shark (1946) 91; Simba (1972) 228; Sparrowhawk (1956) 156; Sunrise (1962) 199; Thayer II (1967) 197; Turkey (1977) 142; Zitadelle (1943) 61
Operations Other Than War (OOTW) viii, 204–5
Organisation d'Armée Secrète (OAS) 167
Organisation of African Unity (OAU) 241
O'Rorke, M. S. 125
Otis, Elwell 37
Oueddai, Goukouni 239

Pa Kao Her 244
Paardeburg, Battle of (1900) 13

pacification 27–8, 37–8, 42, 107, 114–15, 189, 195, 197–8, 202–3
Paice, Mervyn 88, 92
Pakistan 231
Palarea, Juan 7
Palestine 17, 43, 47, 86–95, 98, 126, 151, 159, 226
Palestine Liberation Organisation (PLO) 233–5
Palestine police 93–5, 98
Palmach 87–8
Panama 204, 208
Papagos, Alexander 93, 108
Paraguay 171
Parcham 209
Parti du Peuple Algérien (PPA) 161
Partido Africano da Independência de Guiné e Cabo Verde (PAIGC) 79, 132–6, 139, 142, 144
Partido Komunista ng Pilipinas (PKP) 97
Partisan Ranger Act (1862) 10
partisans vii, 9, 15, 55, 59–68, 108, 184
Paschal, Rod 205
Pasdora Gomez, Eden 207
Pathet Lao 82, 116, 209, 244
Patriotic Union of Kurdistan (PUK) 242
Pavelic, Ante 64
Pearce Commission (1972) 131
Peard, Roger 48
Pedron Line 164
Peninsular War (1808–14) 1, 6–9, 14, 25, 27–8
People's Democracy 219
People's Liberation Armed Forces (PLAF) 187
People's Liberation Army (PLA) 78
People's Revolutionary Party (PRP) 245
People's Self-Defense Force (PSDF) 200, 202
Percox, David 124
Perez, Barrera 169
Perez Martinez, Manuel 208–9
Perón, Isabel 179
Perón, Juan 178–9
Pershing, John 37–8
Peru 79, 81–4, 171–4, 208
Peshmarga 242
Pezza, Michele 6
Pfumo reVanhu 141
Phoenix Programme 201–2
Philippines 13, 34, 36–8, 56, 68, 79, 81, 86, 96–9, 104–9, 183–4, 193–4, 238

Philipps, Wendell 183
Pickens, Andrew 3
Pizzaro Leongomez, Carlos 208
Plutarch 1
Pol Pot 247
police 16–17, 45, 93–5, 98–9, 102, 104, 124, 128–9, 137, 139–40, 154–5, 224–6, 229
Polish Army 3
Polish Home Army 59
Polybius 1
Ponomarenko, P. K. 60
Pontecorvo, Guilo 167
Popular Forces (PF) 197–8, 202
Popular Front for the Liberation of the Occupied Arabian Gulf (PFLOAG) 218, 221–2, 224, 227–9
Popular Front for the Liberation of Palestine (PFLP) 233
Popular Front for the Liberation of Saguiet el Hamra and Rio de Oro (Polisario) 241–2
Poqo 145
Porlier, Juan Diaz 7, 9
Portuguese Army 8, 32, 34, 121, 135–9, 142–4
Prabhakaran, Vellupillai 233
Pratt, Richard 37
Prendergast, John 129
Price, Sterling 10
Program for the Pacification and Long-term Development of South Vietnam (PROVN) 202–3
Project 100,000 192
propaganda 45, 49, 61, 89, 92–4, 101, 104–5, 126, 154, 156, 183, 190, 228–30
Provincial Reconnaissance Units (PRU) 202
Prussian Army 2, 12
Psarros, Dimitrios 67
Pseudo Forces 101, 105, 127, 138, 140, 147, 156–7, 224, 227–8, 232
Puller, Lewis 'Chesty' 48
Pushtay, John 185
Putin, Vladimir 212

Qaboos bin Said 218, 222, 224, 227
Qasim, Abd el-Karim 242
Quantico 48, 185
Quantrill, William 10, 12, 30
Quirino, Elpido 99, 104

Quisling, Vidkun 59

Rabbani, Burhanuddin 210
Race, Jeffrey 203
Radfan 48, 153, 158
Rajagpolan, Rajesh 231
Rallis, Ioannis 67
Ramirez de Leon, Ricardo 172
Ramos, Alberto 99, 104
Ranariddh, Norodom 246–7
Reagan, Ronald 204, 207
Red Army 15, 43, 43, 49–50, 59–62, 66, 108, 209–13
Red River Expedition (1870) 32
Reformist Insurgency 237, 247
Regional Forces (RF) 197–8, 202
Reichenau, Walther von 62
Reid-Daly, Ron 140
Reille, Honoré 27
resettlement 36–40, 93, 100, 102, 104–5, 115, 125, 137, 142, 147, 159, 164, 198–201, 206, 227, 232
resistance 9, 55, 57–60, 67
Resistançia Naçional Moçambicana (Renamo) 147, 245
Revolutionary United Front (RUF) 248–9
Reynier, Jean 2
Rhodes, Cecil 131
Rhodesian Army 139–42, 144–5
Rhodesian War (1966–80) 79, 121, 129–32, 135, 139–42, 144–6
Rice, S. R. 39
Richards, Brooks 224
Rif Revolt (1921–6) 13, 21, 33, 41
Ritchie, Neil 95
Robb, Martin 228
Roberto, Holden 133–4
Roberts, Frederick 38–9
Rocca, Albert de 8
Rochejaquelein, Henri de la 5
Rodriguez Bautista, Nicolas 209
Rogers, Robert 2–3
Roguet, C. M. 28
Roman Army 1
Romero, Oscar 205
Roosevelt, Franklin D. 111
Ropp, Theodore ix
Rostow, Walt 186
Rostow Group 201
Rote Armee Faktion (RAF) see Baader–Meinhof Gang

Rotella, Guiseppe 6
Royal Air Force 126
Royal Irish Constabulary (RIC) 16–17, 45, 94, 129; Auxiliary Division of 17, 45
Royal Laotian Army 244
Royal Military College 48
Royal Thai Army 82
Royal Ulster Constabulary (RUC) 219, 221, 224–6, 229–30
Roxas, Manuel 97, 99, 104
Ruark, Robert 126
Ruffo, Fabrizio 6
Russian Army, Imperial 3, 9, 15, 31, 33, 36
Russian Civil War (1917–21) 18, 60, 212
Rwanda 243–5; former government of (FGOR) 245
Rwigyema, Fred 245

Saddam Hussein 242
Sahraoui, Imam Abdelbakr 240
Sahrawi People's Liberation Army 241
Said bin Taimur 218
St Clair, Arthur 4
Salan, Raoul 116, 162, 167
Salazar, António 131, 137, 144
Samrin, Heng 246
Sandinistas 206–8
Sandino, Augusto 18–19, 43, 48, 183, 205–6
Sandline International 249
Sanfedisti 6
Sankoh, Alfred Foday Saybana 248–9
Sann, Son 246
Santa Cruz y Marcenado, Don Alvaro Navia Osoric, Marqués de 26
Saratoga, Battle of (1777) 3
Sarawak United People's Party 123
Savimbi, Jonas 79, 133–4, 246
Scott, Winfield 29
Search and Destroy 190, 197
Secret Intelligence Service (SIS) 91
Sections Administratives Spécialisées (SAS) 164, 166
Sections Administratives Urbaaines (SAU) 164, 166
Seeckt, Hans von 72
Selous, Frederick 140
Selous Scouts 140–1, 147
Seminole Wars 29
Sen, Hun 246–7

Sendero Luminoso 83–4
Sendic Antonaccio, Raúl 178
Senegal 134
Senoi Pra'aq 103
Senussi 43
Sétif Uprising (1945) 161
Seven Years War (1756–63) 2–3
Shackleton, Ron 196
Shafer, Michael 204
Shamil 12–13, 36, 212
Sharon, Ariel 234
Shelton, Robert 'Pappy' 174
Sheridan, Philip 30–1, 183
Shy, John 3–4
Sierra Leone 248–9
Sihanouk, Norodom 246
Sihanouk Trail 188
Sikhs 231–2
Silvestre, Fernández 33
Simson, Hugh 44–6
Sinn Féin 16–17, 220, 229; Republican 220
Sino–Vietnamese War (1979) 82
Sithole, Ndabaningi 132, 141
Six Day War (1967) 155, 233
Skene, Andrew 48
Slater, Hugh 21
Slovak Rising (1945) 59
Smith, Ian 129, 131–2, 139, 145
Smith, Jacob 37
Smuts, Jan 13–14
Snouck, C. 41
Soccer War (1969) 206
Somali National Alliance (SNA) 247–8
Somali Salvation Alliance (SSA) 247–8
Somalia 209, 247–8
Somaliland 43
Somoza Debyle, Anastasio 206–7
Somoza Debyle, Luis 206
Somoza García, Anastasio 49, 206
Soustelle, Jacques 162
South Africa police (SAP) 145
South African Army 140, 145–7
South African War see Boer War
South Lebanon Army (SLA) 236
South Vietnamese Army (ARVN) 188, 191–2, 195, 197–9 201–3, 205
South West African People's Organisation (SWAPO) 146–7
Soviet Army see Red Army
Soviet Union viii, 57, 70
Spanish American War (1898) 36

Spanish Army 6, 8–9, 13, 20–1, 26, 32–4, 36, 41
Spanish Civil War (1936–9) 20–1, 177
Spanish Morocco 13, 21, 33
Special Air Service (SAS) 55, 93, 95, 103, 127–8, 139, 157, 218, 222, 226–9, 249
Special Branch 101, 122, 124–5, 127, 129, 140, 154–5, 226
Special Forces 55–6, 226, 234
Special Night Squads 20, 47, 87
Special Operations Executive (SOE) 18, 50, 56, 58, 67, 91, 95–6
Spetsnaz 211
Spinola, Antonio de 134, 137, 139, 142, 144
Spreckbacher, Josef 6
Sri Lanka 79, 231–3
Stalin, Joseph 60, 66, 117
Stalker Inquiry (1984) 226
Stark, John 3
Stephanus, Major 63
Stern, Avraham 87
Stern Gang see Lehame Herut Israel (LEHI)
Stevens Inquiry (1989) 226
Steyn, Marthinus 13
Stirling, David 55
Stofflet, Jean-Nicholas 5
Stolzman, Karl Bogumil 15
Strasser, Valentine 248–9
strategic hamlets 198–201
Suchet, Louis-Gabriel 27–8
Sudan 12, 33, 43, 238–41, 247
Sudan People's Liberation Army (SPLA) 239–40, 247
Suez Affair (1956) 24, 156, 160, 163
Suharto, T. N. J. 123
Sukarno, Kusno Sosro 109–10, 122–3
Sultan's Armed Forces (SAF) 218, 221, 224, 228
Summers, Harry 202
Sumter, Thomas 3–4
Sun Tzu 1, 75, 249
Sun Yat-sen 70
Swynnerton, Richard 125
Symbionese Liberation Army (SLA) 180
Syria 1, 180

Taber, Robert 169, 183
Tabernilla, General 169
Tacfarinas 1
Tache d'huile 40–1, 107, 114, 159–60

Tacitus 1
Talabani, Jelal 242
Taleban 210
Tambov Revolt (1920–1) 49–50
Tamils 79, 231–3
Tamil Tigers 231, 233
Tanzania 134, 146
Tarleton, Barnaste 3–4
Taruc, Luis 99, 104–5
Taylor, Charles 247–8
Taylor, J. R. M. 38
Taylor, Maxwell 186, 200
Taylor, Zachary 29
Tegart, Charles 47
Templer, Gerald 101–3, 124, 155, 200, 224
Tenuat Hameri 87
terrorism vii–viii, 179–80, 233–6
Tet Offensive (1968) 80, 190–1, 194, 197–8, 202–3
Thai Communist Party (CPT) 81–2
Thailand 79, 81–2, 103, 209
Tharrawaddy Revolt (1930–2) 46–7, 94, 100
Thieu, Nguyen Van 189, 192–3, 195
32 County Sovereignty Movement 220
Tho, Nguyen Huo 187
Thom, W. G. 237
Thompson, Robert 107, 109, 186, 198–200
Tigray 241, 243
Tigray People's Liberation Front (TPLF) 243
Tinsulanonda, Prem 82
Tito, Josip Broz 65–7
Touré, Samouri 13
Touré, Sékou 139
Toussaint L'Ouverture 5
Towle, Philip 158
Trevaskis, Kennedy 153
Trinquier, Roger 160, 163
Trotha, Lothar von 43
Trotsky, Leon 15, 60
Trujillo, Rafael 49, 168
Truman, Harry 111, 114
Truman Doctrine (1947) 93
Truong Chinh 79–81, 187
Tukhachevsky, Mikhail 50
Tulloch, Cromarty 'Pop' 56
Tunisia 161–2, 164–5, 233
Tunku Abdul Rahman 102
Tupamaros 176–9

Turcios Lima, Luís 171–2
Turkey 152, 158, 180, 242
Turkish Army 19–20, 243
Turkish People's Liberation Army
    (TPLA) 180
Turkish People's Liberation Party-Front
    (TPLP-F) 180
Turreau, General 26
Tutsi 244–5
26 July Movement 168, 171
Tyrolean Revolt (1809–10) 5–7, 9

Uganda 34, 240, 244–5, 247
Ukrainska Povstancha Armia (UPA) 62
Ulster see Northern Ireland
Ulster Defence Association (UDA) 220,
    226
Ulster Freedom Fighters (UFF) 220
Ulster Volunteer Force (UVF) 220
Ulundi, Battle of (1879) 33
Umkhonto we Sizwe 145
União das Populações de Angola (UPA)
    133
União Nacional para a Independência
    Total de Angola (UNITA) 79, 133–4,
    144, 147, 245–6
Union Army 30–1
Union Démocratique du Manifeste
    Algérien (UDMA) 161, 166
Union Nacional de la Oposición (UNO)
    208
United Malayan National Organisation
    (UMNO) 96, 102
United Nations (UN) 89, 92, 110, 127,
    142, 146–7, 152, 157–8, 165, 172,
    208, 225, 239, 241–3, 246, 249
United States Agency for International
    Development (USAID) 173, 178, 200
United States Army 3–4, 13, 24, 29–30,
    33–4, 36–8, 55, 93–4 107–9, 136, 143,
    173, 183–6, 189–99, 202–6
United States Marines 18–19, 43, 48–9,
    184–6, 189, 194, 196–8
United States Special Forces 173–4, 184,
    189, 195–6
urban guerrilla warfare 15, 151–68,
    174–80
Urquhart, Robert 95
Uruguay 174, 176–8
Ustase 64–5
Utley, Harold 48

Valentini, George von 4
Valeriano, Napoleon 173
Van Fleet, James 108
Van Rees, W. A. 41
Vang Pao 244
Vann, John Paul 203
Vaphiadis, Markos 87, 90
Vecingetorix 1
Velasco Alvarado, Juan 83
Vendéan Revolt (1793–6) 5, 7, 26–8
Venezuela 151, 171, 174, 176–7, 208
Vercours 58
Vermeulen Krieger, P. F. 41
Viet Cong 187–8, 190, 193, 195–9,
    201–3
Viet Minh 68, 79–80, 110–17, 159, 161,
    187, 200
Vietnam War: First (1946–54) 80,
    112–17; Second (1965–75) 24, 80,
    136–7, 143, 174, 183, , 185–204, 206;
    209, 211
Viriathus 1
Volckmann, R. 56
Vorster, John 145

Wabash, Battle of the (1791) 4
Wagner, Arthur 34
Walker, Walter 95, 103, 127–8
Walls, Peter 139–41
Walt, Lewis 196
Warner, Seth 3
Warsaw Pact 195
Warsaw Rising (1944) 59, 64
Washington, George 3–4
Watergate Affair (1974) 192, 209
Watts, John 227
Weathermen 179–80
Weinberger Doctrine 204
Westerling, Raymond 'Turk' 110
Western Sahara 241–2
Westmoreland, William C. 136, 189–90,
    194, 196, 200–1, 203
Weyler, Valeriano 36
Wheeler, Earle 201
Wickham, Charles 94
Wijeweera, Rohanna 79
Williams, Phil ix
Wilson, Harold 130–1, 153, 223
Wingate, Orde 20, 47, 55–6, 87
Wintringham, Tom 21
Wolseley, Garnet 32–3, 35

World War I (1914–18) 16, 19, 43, 48,
   135, 152, 184
World War II (1939–45) viii, 9, 17–18,
   20–1, 24, 47, 50, 55–68, 77, 81, 84, 86,
   91, 100, 109, 130, 184–6

Yacef Saadi 163
Yandarbiyer, Zelimkhan 212
Yarborough, William 173
Yeltsin, Boris 212–13
Yemen, People's Democratic Republic of
   (PDRY) 218, 221, 228–9
Yiafka 90
Yom Kippur War (1973) 204
Yon Sosa, Marco 171–2
Young, Arthur 102, 128–9, 229
Young, Eric 238
Younger Brothers 12
Younghusband, Francis 35

Yugoslavia 21, 57–8, 64–8, 90, 93

Zachariadis, Nikos 90
Zaire 133–4, 173, 245, 247
Zambia 134–5, 139, 141–2, 144–7
Zapata, Emiliano 249
Zapatista Army for National Liberation
   (EZLN) 249
Zeller, André 167
Zervas, Napoleon 67
Zimbabwe African National Union
   (ZANU) 79, 132, 135, 147
Zimbabwe African People's Union
   (ZAPU) 132, 135
Zimbabwe National Liberation Army
   (ZANLA) 135, 144
Zimbabwe People's Revolutionary Army
   (ZIPRA) 135, 145
Zulu War (1879) 12, 33

LaVergne, TN USA
09 February 2010
172571LV00002B/2/A